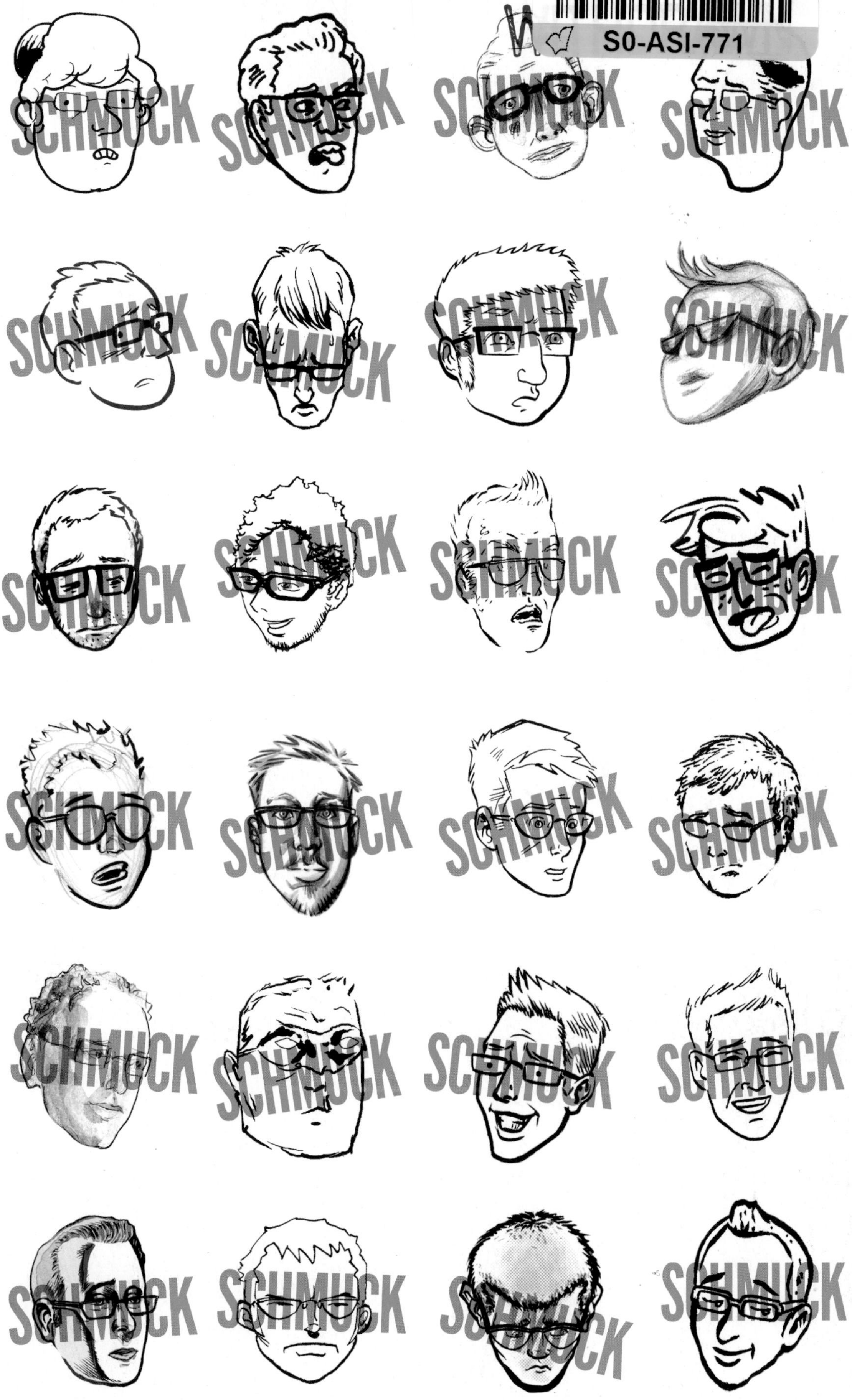
SCHMUCK
SCHMUCK
SCHMUCK
SCHMUCK
SCHMUCK
SCHMUCK
SCHMUCK
SCHMUCK
SCHMUCK
SCHMUCK
SCHMUCK
SCHMUCK
SCHMUCK
SCHMUCK
SCHMUCK
SCHMUCK
SCHMUCK
SCHMUCK
SCHMUCK
SCHMUCK
SCHMUCK
SCHMUCK
SCHMUCK
SCHMUCK

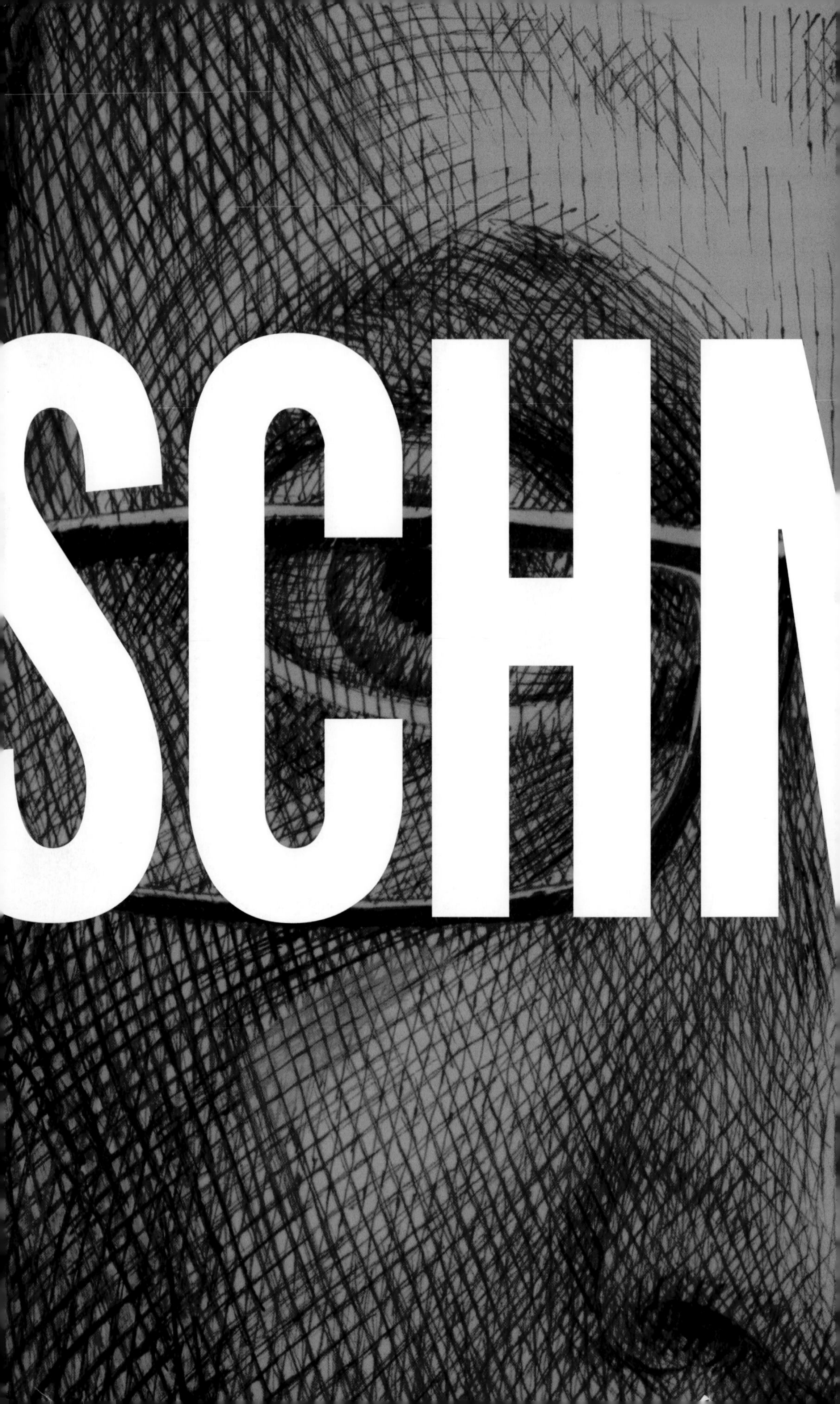
SCH

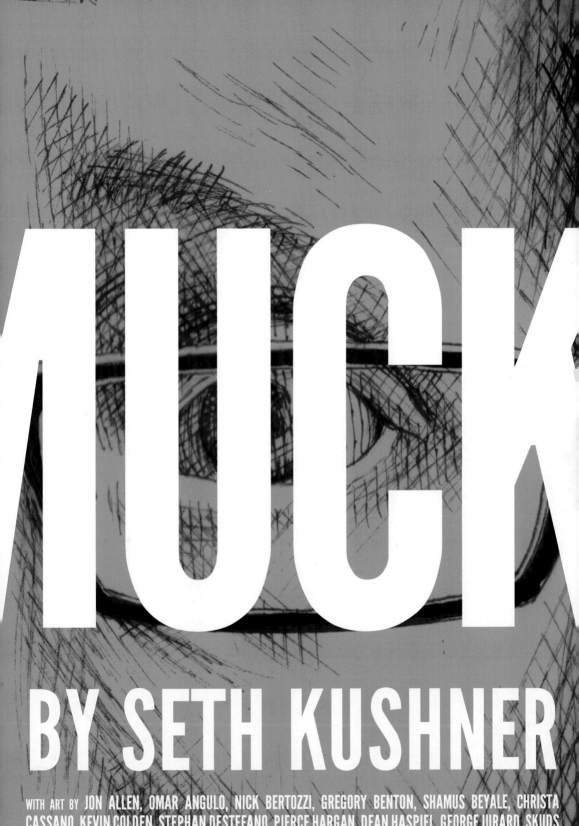

1UCK

BY SETH KUSHNER

WITH ART BY JON ALLEN, OMAR ANGULO, NICK BERTOZZI, GREGORY BENTON, SHAMUS BEYALE, CHRISTA CASSANO, KEVIN COLDEN, STEPHAN DESTEFANO, PIERCE HARGAN, DEAN HASPIEL, GEORGE JURARD, SKUDS McKINLEY, JOSH NEUFELD, TIM OGLINE, SEAN PRYOR, LELAND PURVIS, TONY SALMONS, GEORGE SCHALL, NATHAN SCHREIBER, JAMES O. SMITH, RYAN ALEXANDER-TANNER, BOBBY TIMONY, NOAH VAN SCIVER

ALL STORIES WRITTEN BY **SETH KUSHNER**

CONTRIBUTING EDITOR DEAN HASPIEL
DESIGN ERIC SKILLMAN
COVER ILLUSTRATION (KICKSTARTER EDITION) DEAN HASPIEL
COVER ILLUSTRATION (GENERAL RELEASE EDITION) JOSEPH REMNANT
AUTHOR PHOTO CARLOS MOLINA
PUBLISHED BY HANG DAI EDITIONS AND ALTERNATIVE COMICS
PRINTED IN CANADA

SCH

AN INTRODUCTION

FULL DISCLOSURE: I know Seth Kushner socially. We've met a handful of times over the years, and he has always struck me as a sweet and thoughtful person. An adult even.

So I thank the gods that *Schmuck* is a work of fiction and not a direct reflection on Seth himself, on who he is as a human being. An artist, in this case a writer, should be allowed to create what he wants. Do we judge Hitler for writing *Mein Kampf?* No. We judge him for other things. Then again, maybe we do judge him for *Mein Kampf.* After all, that is a work of non-fiction, an autobiography, and so it is a direct reflection of the man. I was simply trying to think of shocking books and for some reason *Schmuck* brought *Mein Kampf* to mind, perhaps because *Schmuck* unintentionally seems to support some of Hitler's theories of Jews as a subspecies.

Let me think of a better example. Do we judge Hitchcock for making *Psycho?* No. Even if that film reveals some of the dark corners of Hitchcock's mind, we give him a pass because it's art. And so in the same way we should give Seth Kushner a pass for the very dark corner of his mind that he has shown us in his art, in this wonderful book *Schmuck,* which you are holding at this very moment. It is telling, though, that the two works I thought of while trying to understand and introduce *Schmuck* are *Mein Kampf* and *Psycho.*

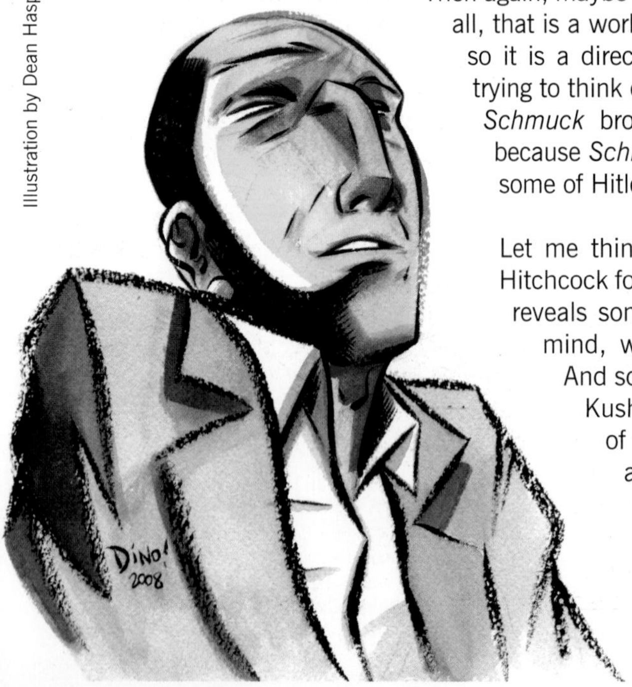
DINO!
2008

Illustration by Dean Haspiel

MUCK

BY JONATHAN AMES

For me, *Schmuck,* ultimately, is a cautionary tale, a horror story masquerading as autobiographical fiction, which I guess does explain my *Mein Kampf* and *Psycho* mash-up. Each story in this book, all of them written by Seth but illustrated by a different talented artist, is like a car accident of humiliation and stunted adolescent male behavior perpetuated years past adolescence, and you the reader are like someone passing by the accident; you can't help but to stare and gawk and wonder, even as you cringe in horror and cry out with a hash-tag attached—#toomuchinformation!

That said, *Schmuck* is also very funny and honest and brave, and I happily gobbled up each tale, often thinking of some version of, "but for the grace of God go I."

But, sadly and truthfully, since perhaps there is no God, it is where I have sometimes gone and still go. So I thank Seth Kushner for having the balls to create *Schmuck,* for sharing this dark corner of his mind and for allowing some of us out there to feel less alone as we cower in our own dark corners.

I guess that's the happy ending as it were, which is only fitting for a book called *Schmuck* and which is why, in case you

didn't notice, I also said that Seth had balls to write it, because I hope that most people are aware of the fact that the earliest definition of this Yiddish word schmuck, though it's a source of some debate, is penis, and that to call yourself a schmuck is not quite like saying that you are a cock but that you are an idiot penis.

So, from one idiot penis to another, I thank Seth for writing this book and for making me laugh and in doing so lightening my pitiful load.

(Sorry, another bad sexual pun, but I can't help it as this introduction dribbles out to a somewhat weak conclusion, so weak that I need to underscore my bad puns by italicizing them. Well, I'm a schmuck after all. Just like Seth. I mean just like Seth's fictional protagonist, and so you, the reader, especially Seth's wife, should not presume that this book is any way a reflection on Seth himself, as I averred at the start of this once strong, now flaccid intro.)

Jonathan Ames is the author of nine books, including *Wake Up, Sir* and the graphic novel *The Alcoholic,* illustrated by Dean Haspiel. He is also the creator of two television shows: HBO's "Bored to Death" and the forthcoming "Blunt Talk", which stars Patrick Stewart and will air on the Starz network.

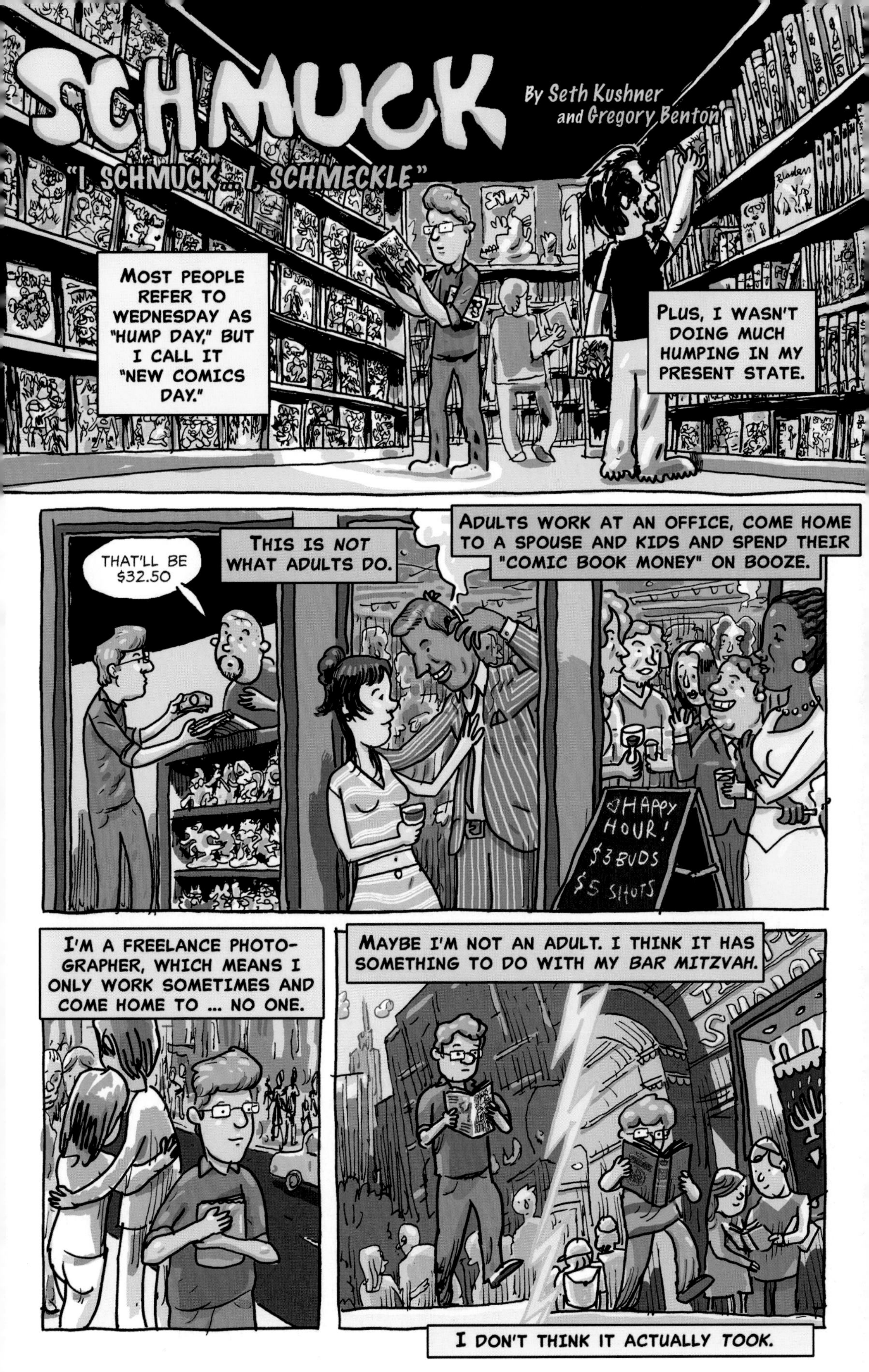

SCHMUCK
By Seth Kushner and Gregory Benton
"I, SCHMUCK ... I, SCHMECKLE"
MOST PEOPLE REFER TO WEDNESDAY AS "HUMP DAY," BUT I CALL IT "NEW COMICS DAY."
PLUS, I WASN'T DOING MUCH HUMPING IN MY PRESENT STATE.
THIS IS NOT WHAT ADULTS DO.
ADULTS WORK AT AN OFFICE, COME HOME TO A SPOUSE AND KIDS AND SPEND THEIR "COMIC BOOK MONEY" ON BOOZE.
THAT'LL BE $32.50
HAPPY HOUR! $3 BUDS $5 SHOTS
I'M A FREELANCE PHOTOGRAPHER, WHICH MEANS I ONLY WORK SOMETIMES AND COME HOME TO ... NO ONE.
MAYBE I'M NOT AN ADULT. I THINK IT HAS SOMETHING TO DO WITH MY BAR MITZVAH.
I DON'T THINK IT ACTUALLY TOOK.

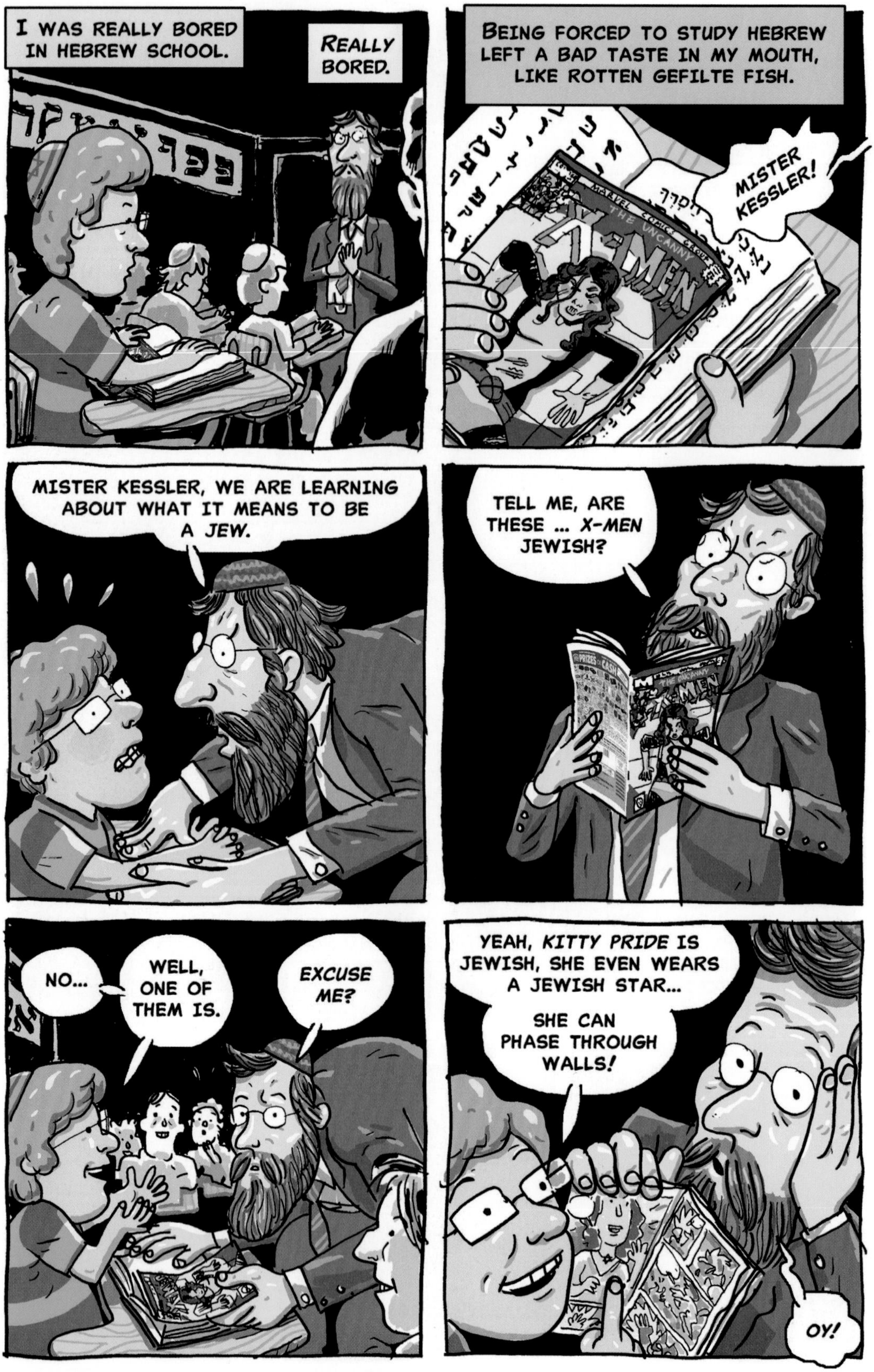
I WAS REALLY BORED IN HEBREW SCHOOL.
REALLY BORED.
BEING FORCED TO STUDY HEBREW LEFT A BAD TASTE IN MY MOUTH, LIKE ROTTEN GEFILTE FISH.
MISTER KESSLER!
MISTER KESSLER, WE ARE LEARNING ABOUT WHAT IT MEANS TO BE A JEW.
TELL ME, ARE THESE ... X-MEN JEWISH?
NO...
WELL, ONE OF THEM IS.
EXCUSE ME?
YEAH, KITTY PRIDE IS JEWISH, SHE EVEN WEARS A JEWISH STAR...
SHE CAN PHASE THROUGH WALLS!
OY!

THAT IS VERY INTERESTING MISTER KESSLER. WHEN YOU GO UP TO THE ALTAR FOR YOUR BAR MITZVAH, INSTEAD OF READING FROM THE *HAFTORAH*, BE SURE TO TELL YOUR FAMILY AND FRIENDS AND THE WHOLE CONGREGATION ALL ABOUT THE 'X-MEN.'

AND THEN, THE FATEFUL DAY ARRIVED...

I NOW PRESENT ADAM KESSLER, WHO WILL READ FROM THE TORAH FOR HIS BAR MITZVAH.

IN THE JEWISH RELIGION, A BOY BECOMES A MAN, AN ADULT, AT AGE THIRTEEN WHEN HE READS THE HAFTORAH PORTION FOR HIS BAR MITZVAH.

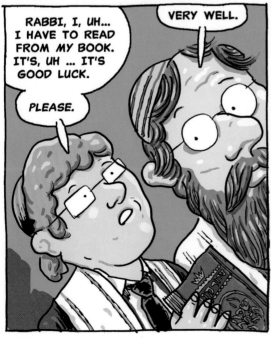

RABBI, I, UH... I HAVE TO READ FROM *MY* BOOK. IT'S, UH ... IT'S GOOD LUCK.

PLEASE.

VERY WELL.

GULP!

I NEVER ACTUALLY LEARNED TO *READ* HEBREW.

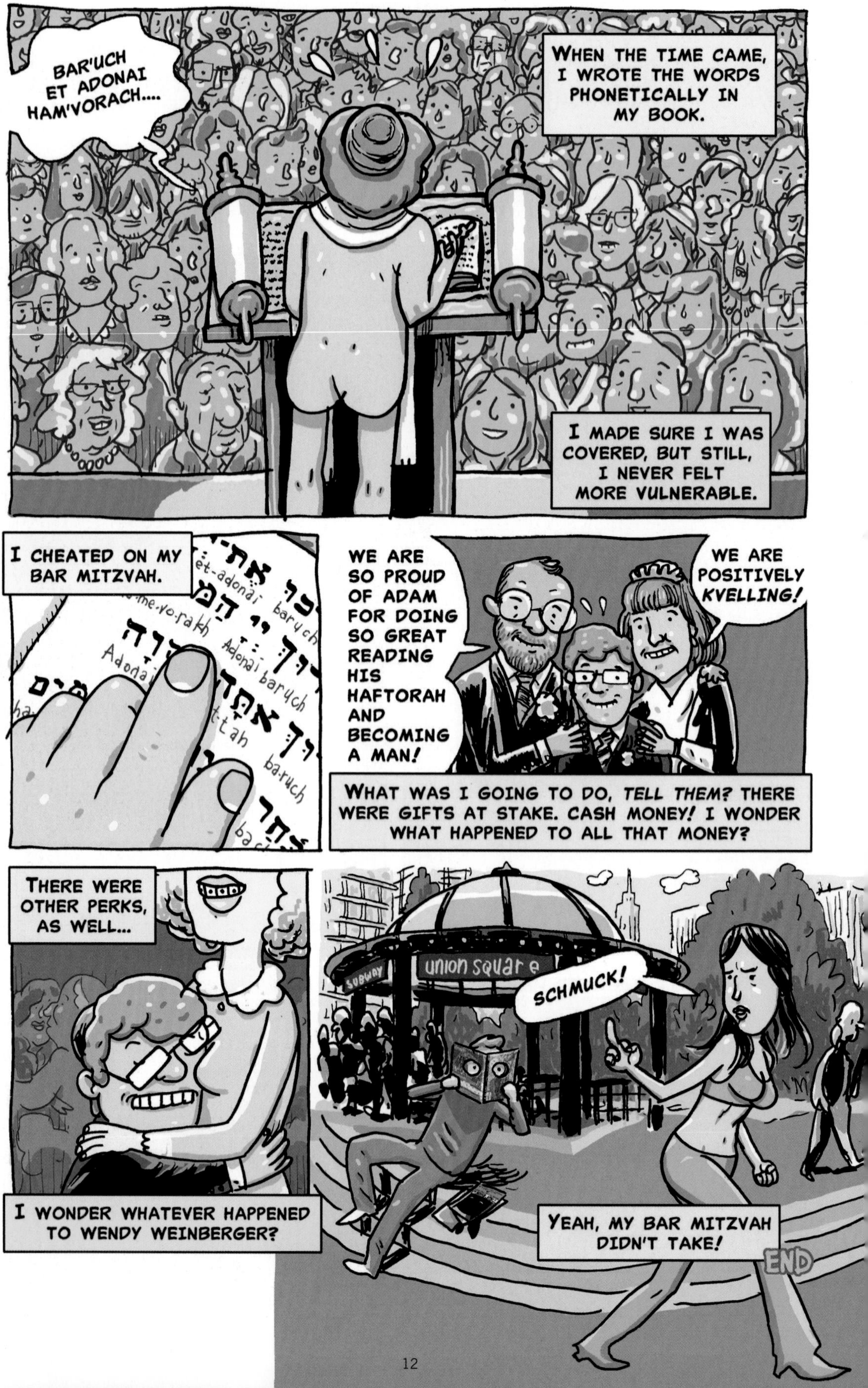
BAR'UCH ET ADONAI HAM'VORACH....
WHEN THE TIME CAME, I WROTE THE WORDS PHONETICALLY IN MY BOOK.
I MADE SURE I WAS COVERED, BUT STILL, I NEVER FELT MORE VULNERABLE.
I CHEATED ON MY BAR MITZVAH.
WE ARE SO PROUD OF ADAM FOR DOING SO GREAT READING HIS HAFTORAH AND BECOMING A MAN!
WE ARE POSITIVELY KVELLING!
WHAT WAS I GOING TO DO, TELL THEM? THERE WERE GIFTS AT STAKE. CASH MONEY! I WONDER WHAT HAPPENED TO ALL THAT MONEY?
THERE WERE OTHER PERKS, AS WELL...
I WONDER WHATEVER HAPPENED TO WENDY WEINBERGER?
SUBWAY
union square
SCHMUCK!
YEAH, MY BAR MITZVAH DIDN'T TAKE!
END

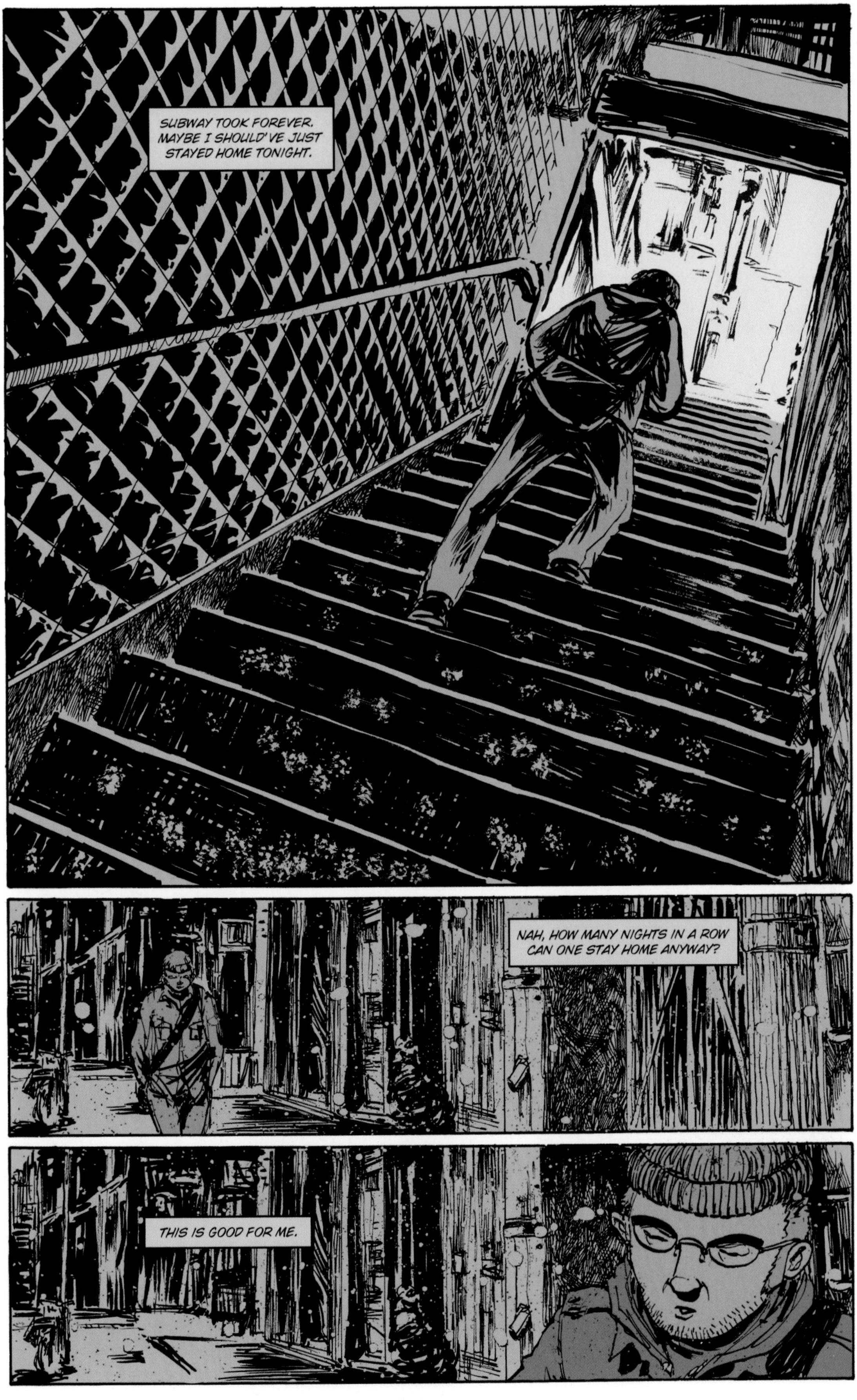
SUBWAY TOOK FOREVER. MAYBE I SHOULD'VE JUST STAYED HOME TONIGHT.
NAH, HOW MANY NIGHTS IN A ROW CAN ONE STAY HOME ANYWAY?
THIS IS GOOD FOR ME.

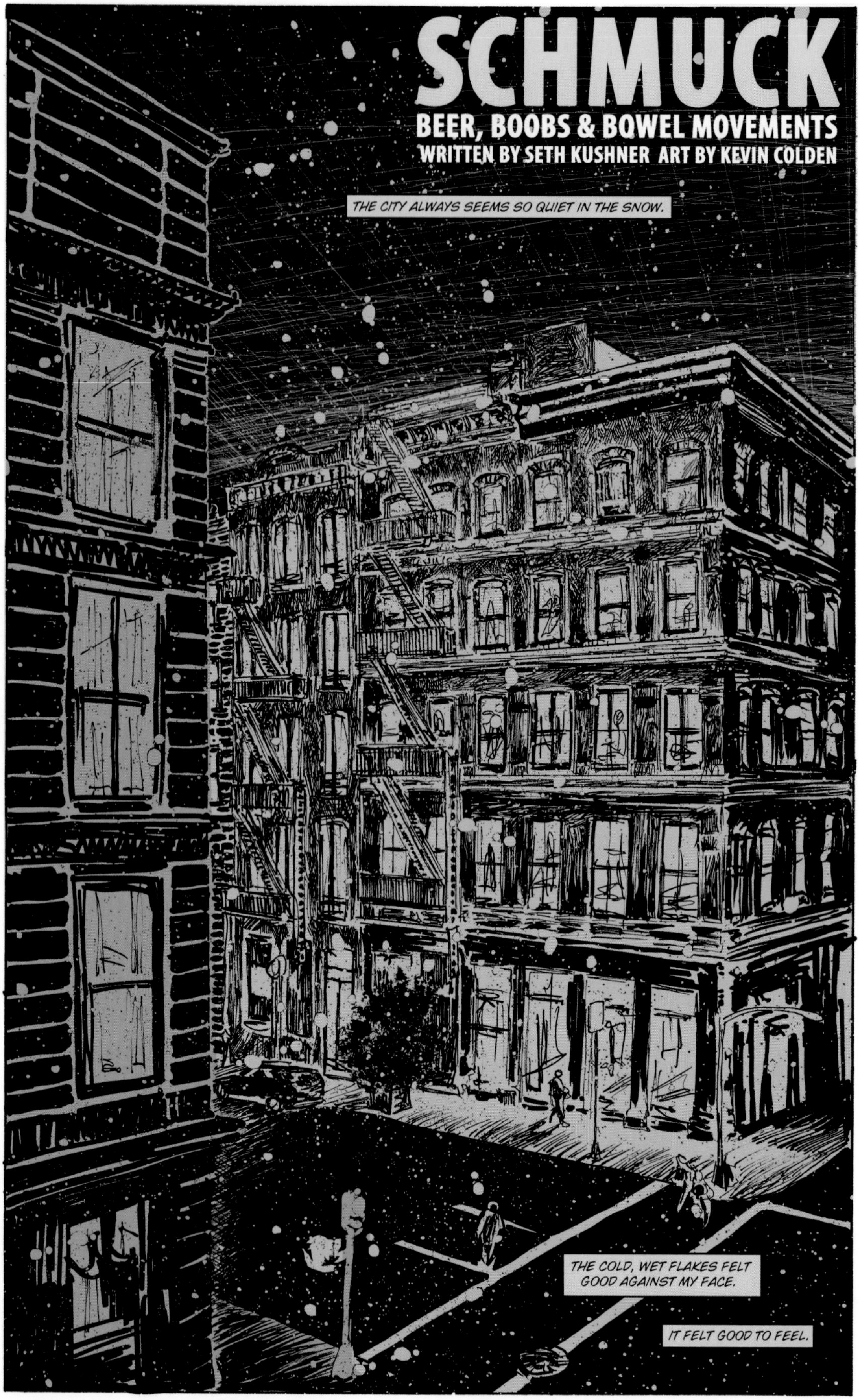
SCHMUCK
BEER, BOOBS & BOWEL MOVEMENTS
WRITTEN BY SETH KUSHNER ART BY KEVIN COLDEN
THE CITY ALWAYS SEEMS SO QUIET IN THE SNOW.
THE COLD, WET FLAKES FELT GOOD AGAINST MY FACE.
IT FELT GOOD TO FEEL.

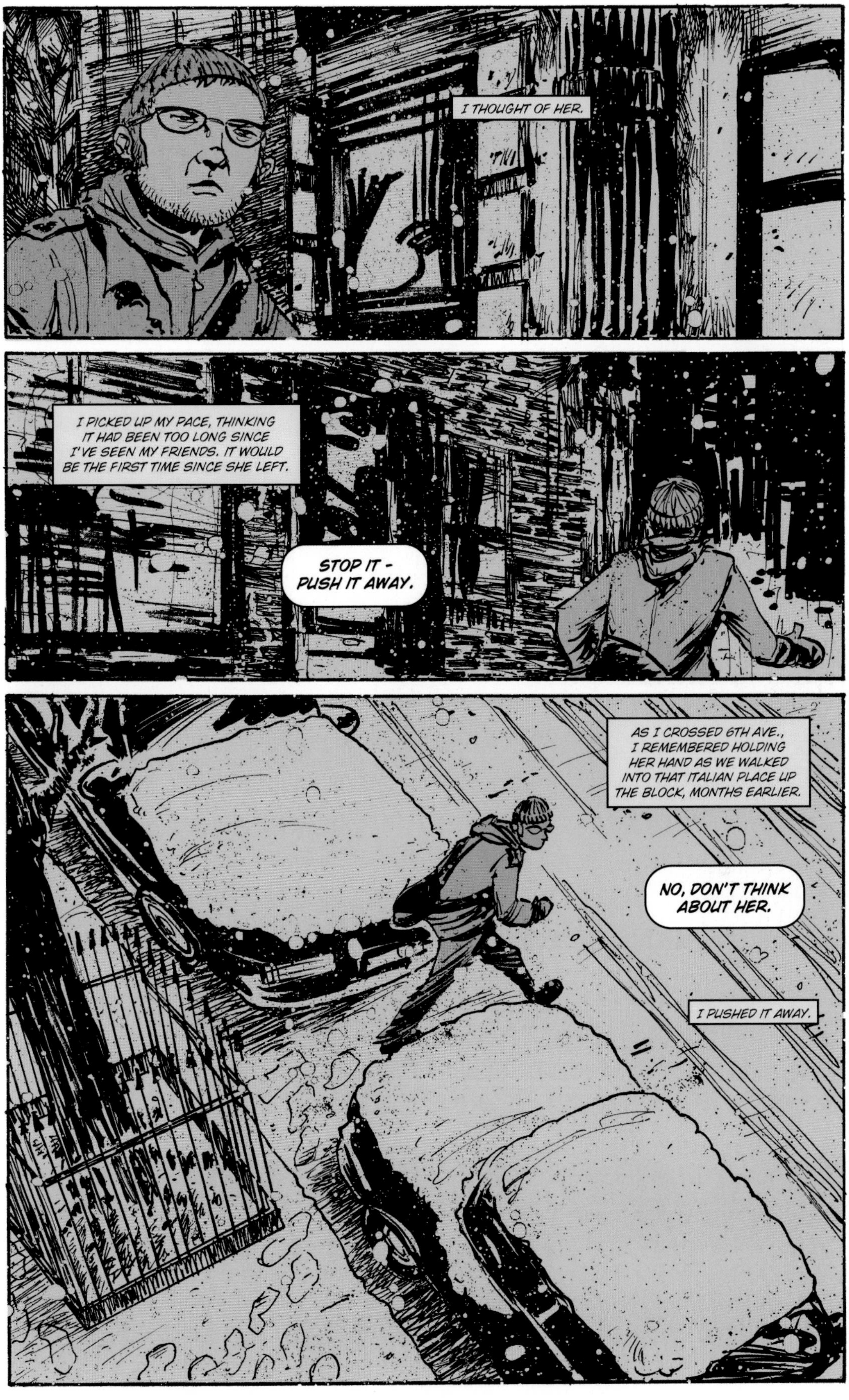
I THOUGHT OF HER.
I PICKED UP MY PACE, THINKING IT HAD BEEN TOO LONG SINCE I'VE SEEN MY FRIENDS. IT WOULD BE THE FIRST TIME SINCE SHE LEFT.
STOP IT - PUSH IT AWAY.
AS I CROSSED 6TH AVE., I REMEMBERED HOLDING HER HAND AS WE WALKED INTO THAT ITALIAN PLACE UP THE BLOCK, MONTHS EARLIER.
NO, DON'T THINK ABOUT HER.
I PUSHED IT AWAY.

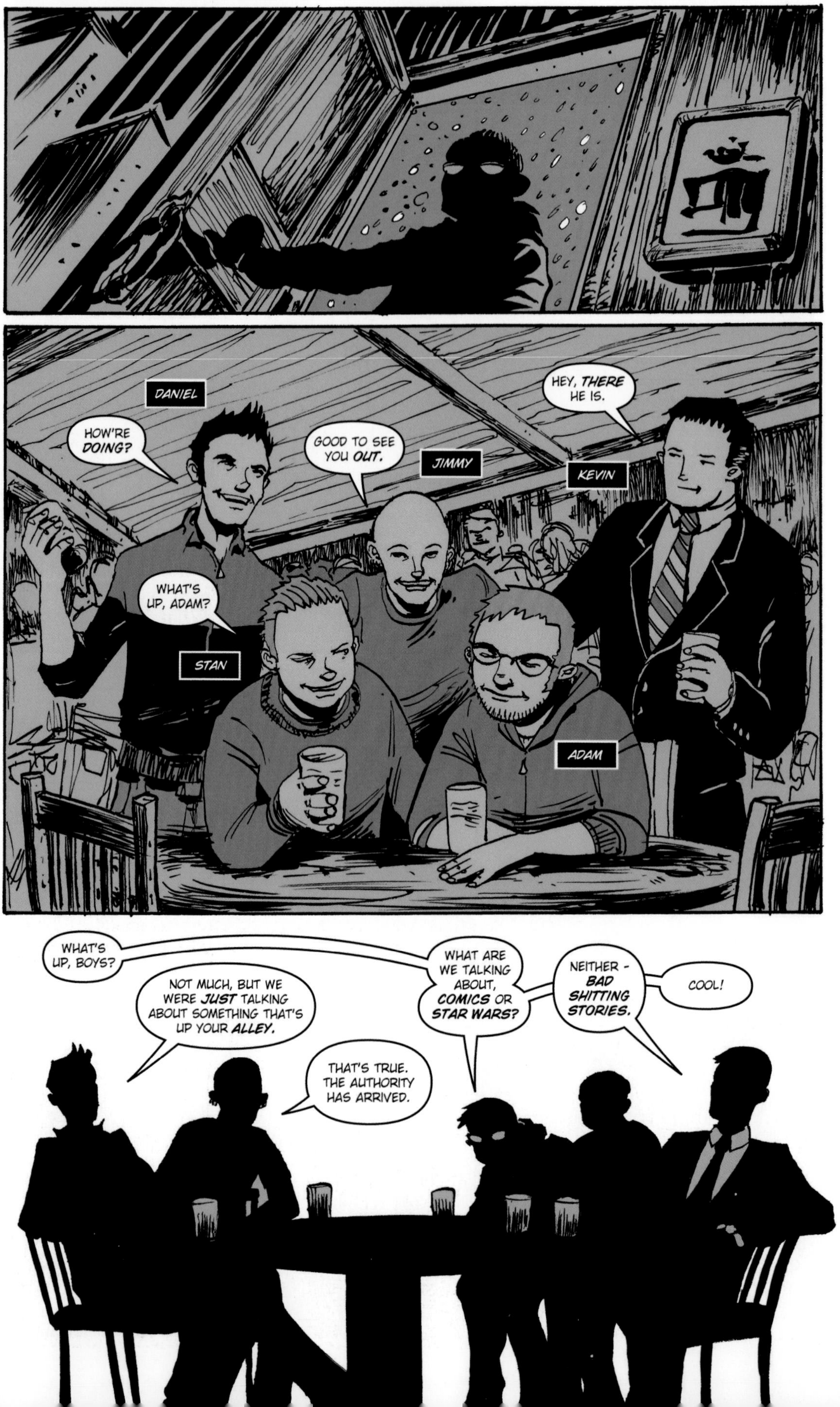
DANIEL
HOW'RE DOING?
GOOD TO SEE YOU OUT.
JIMMY
HEY, THERE HE IS.
KEVIN
WHAT'S UP, ADAM?
STAN
ADAM
WHAT'S UP, BOYS?
NOT MUCH, BUT WE WERE JUST TALKING ABOUT SOMETHING THAT'S UP YOUR ALLEY.
THAT'S TRUE. THE AUTHORITY HAS ARRIVED.
WHAT ARE WE TALKING ABOUT, COMICS OR STAR WARS?
NEITHER - BAD SHITTING STORIES.
COOL!

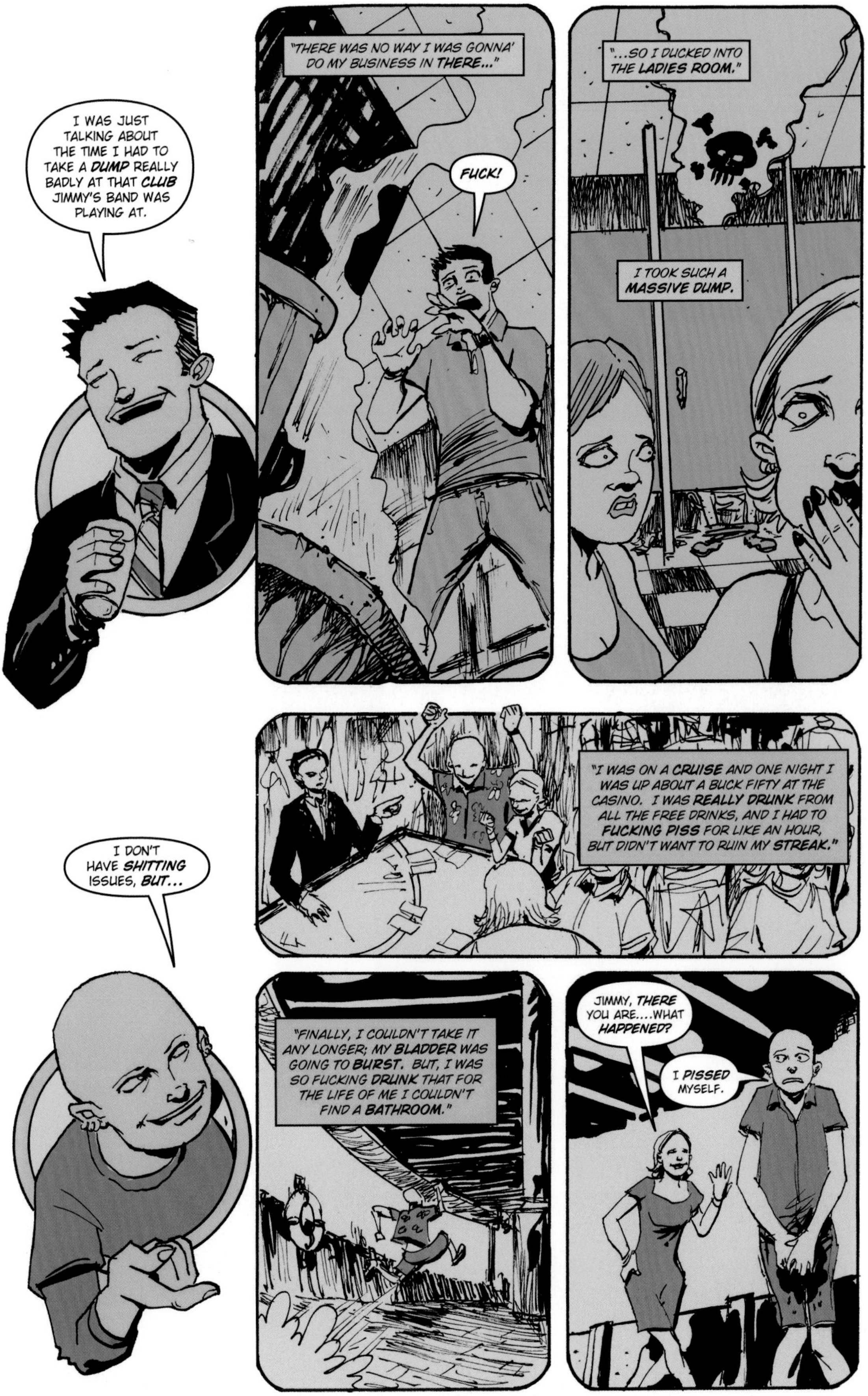
I WAS JUST TALKING ABOUT THE TIME I HAD TO TAKE A DUMP REALLY BADLY AT THAT CLUB JIMMY'S BAND WAS PLAYING AT.
"THERE WAS NO WAY I WAS GONNA' DO MY BUSINESS IN THERE..."
FUCK!
"...SO I DUCKED INTO THE LADIES ROOM."
I TOOK SUCH A MASSIVE DUMP.
I DON'T HAVE SHITTING ISSUES, BUT...
"I WAS ON A CRUISE AND ONE NIGHT I WAS UP ABOUT A BUCK FIFTY AT THE CASINO. I WAS REALLY DRUNK FROM ALL THE FREE DRINKS, AND I HAD TO FUCKING PISS FOR LIKE AN HOUR, BUT DIDN'T WANT TO RUIN MY STREAK."
"FINALLY, I COULDN'T TAKE IT ANY LONGER; MY BLADDER WAS GOING TO BURST. BUT, I WAS SO FUCKING DRUNK THAT FOR THE LIFE OF ME I COULDN'T FIND A BATHROOM."
JIMMY, THERE YOU ARE....WHAT HAPPENED?
I PISSED MYSELF.

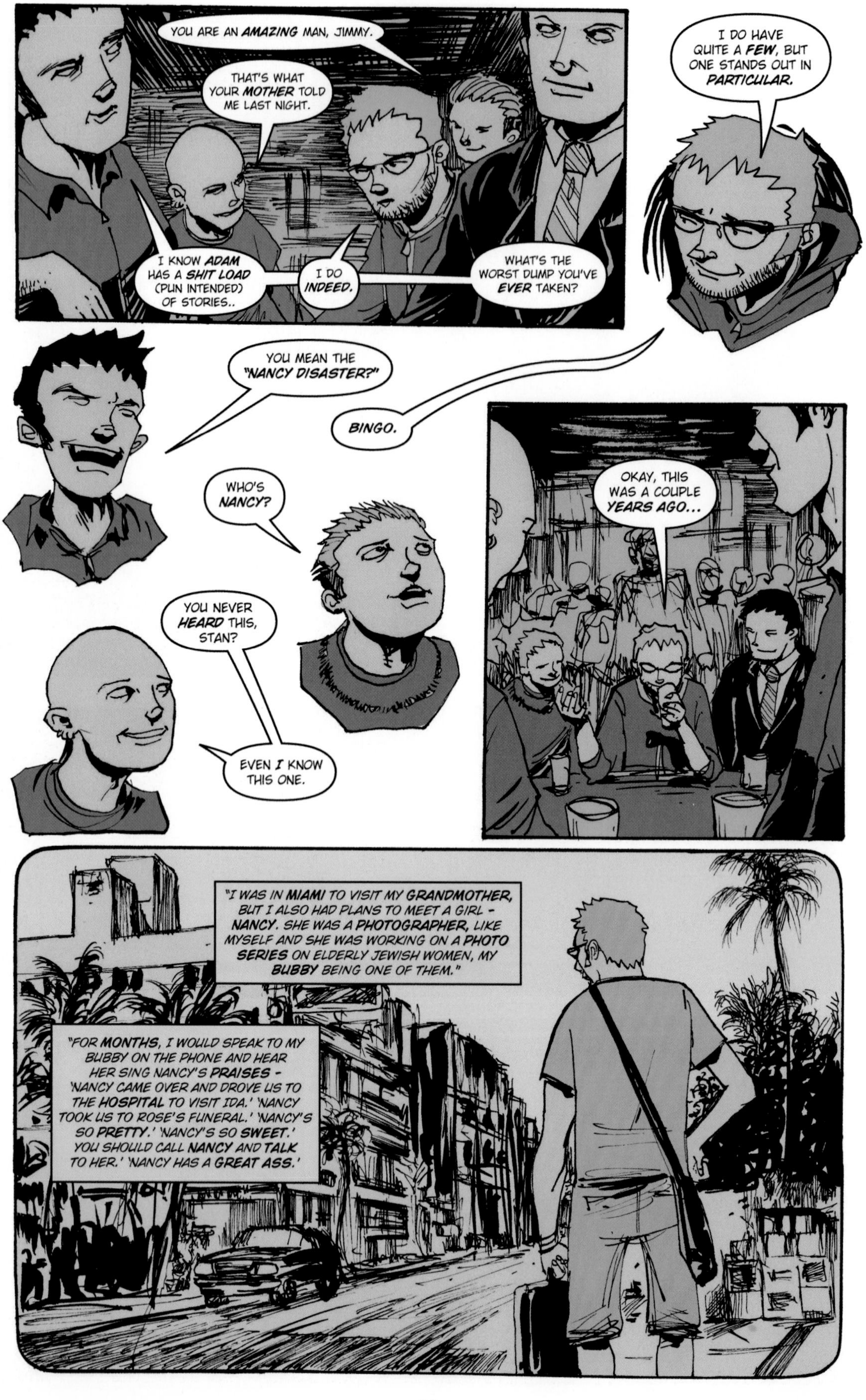
YOU ARE AN AMAZING MAN, JIMMY.
THAT'S WHAT YOUR MOTHER TOLD ME LAST NIGHT.
I KNOW ADAM HAS A SHIT LOAD (PUN INTENDED) OF STORIES..
I DO INDEED.
WHAT'S THE WORST DUMP YOU'VE EVER TAKEN?
I DO HAVE QUITE A FEW, BUT ONE STANDS OUT IN PARTICULAR.
YOU MEAN THE "NANCY DISASTER?"
BINGO.
WHO'S NANCY?
YOU NEVER HEARD THIS, STAN?
EVEN I KNOW THIS ONE.
OKAY, THIS WAS A COUPLE YEARS AGO...
"I WAS IN MIAMI TO VISIT MY GRANDMOTHER, BUT I ALSO HAD PLANS TO MEET A GIRL - NANCY. SHE WAS A PHOTOGRAPHER, LIKE MYSELF AND SHE WAS WORKING ON A PHOTO SERIES ON ELDERLY JEWISH WOMEN, MY BUBBY BEING ONE OF THEM."
"FOR MONTHS, I WOULD SPEAK TO MY BUBBY ON THE PHONE AND HEAR HER SING NANCY'S PRAISES - 'NANCY CAME OVER AND DROVE US TO THE HOSPITAL TO VISIT IDA.' 'NANCY TOOK US TO ROSE'S FUNERAL.' 'NANCY'S SO PRETTY.' 'NANCY'S SO SWEET.' YOU SHOULD CALL NANCY AND TALK TO HER.' 'NANCY HAS A GREAT ASS.'

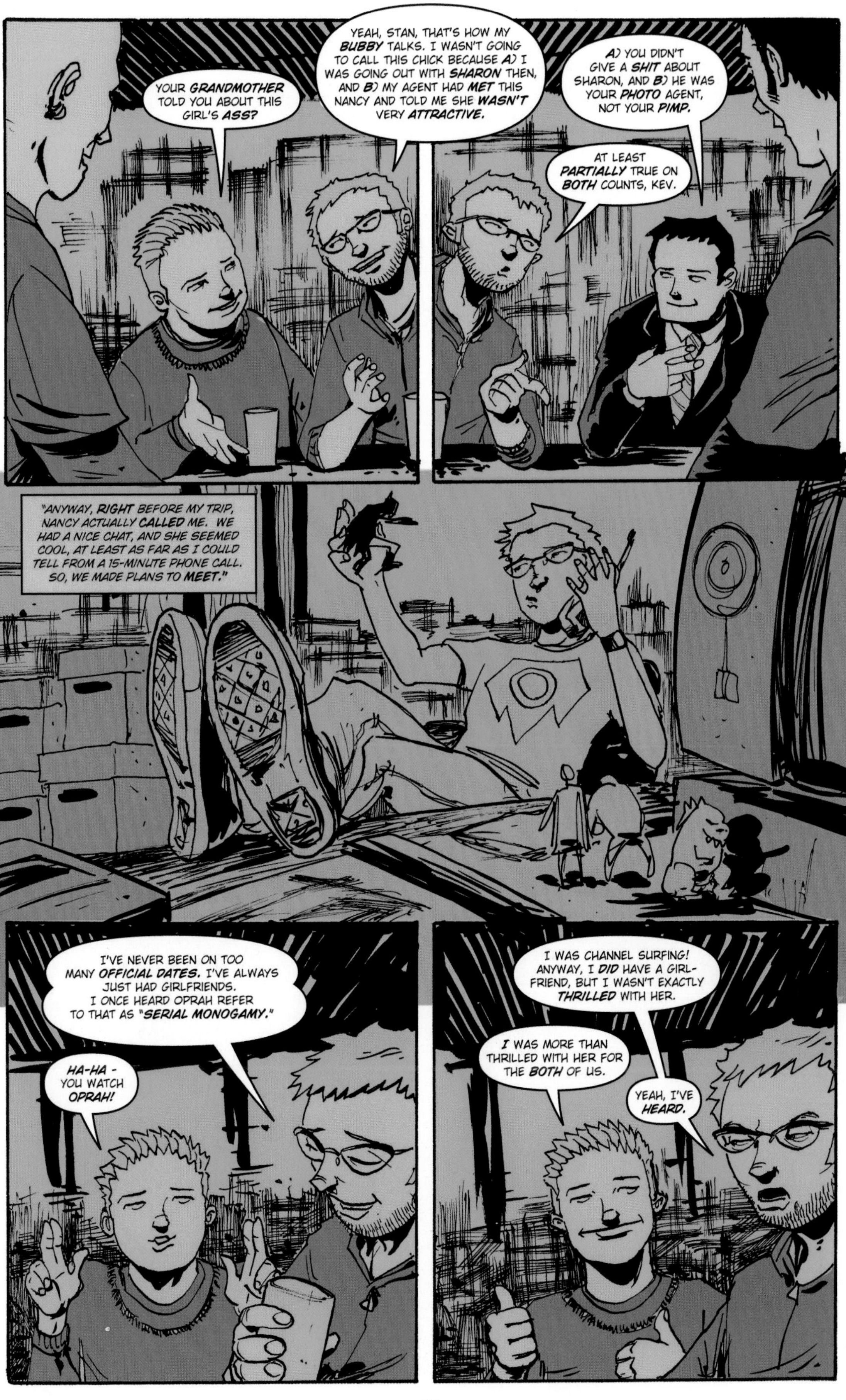
YOUR GRANDMOTHER TOLD YOU ABOUT THIS GIRL'S ASS?
YEAH, STAN, THAT'S HOW MY BUBBY TALKS. I WASN'T GOING TO CALL THIS CHICK BECAUSE A) I WAS GOING OUT WITH SHARON THEN, AND B) MY AGENT HAD MET THIS NANCY AND TOLD ME SHE WASN'T VERY ATTRACTIVE.
A) YOU DIDN'T GIVE A SHIT ABOUT SHARON, AND B) HE WAS YOUR PHOTO AGENT, NOT YOUR PIMP.
AT LEAST PARTIALLY TRUE ON BOTH COUNTS, KEV.
"ANYWAY, RIGHT BEFORE MY TRIP, NANCY ACTUALLY CALLED ME. WE HAD A NICE CHAT, AND SHE SEEMED COOL, AT LEAST AS FAR AS I COULD TELL FROM A 15-MINUTE PHONE CALL. SO, WE MADE PLANS TO MEET."
I'VE NEVER BEEN ON TOO MANY OFFICIAL DATES. I'VE ALWAYS JUST HAD GIRLFRIENDS. I ONCE HEARD OPRAH REFER TO THAT AS "SERIAL MONOGAMY."
HA-HA - YOU WATCH OPRAH!
I WAS CHANNEL SURFING! ANYWAY, I DID HAVE A GIRL-FRIEND, BUT I WASN'T EXACTLY THRILLED WITH HER.
I WAS MORE THAN THRILLED WITH HER FOR THE BOTH OF US.
YEAH, I'VE HEARD.

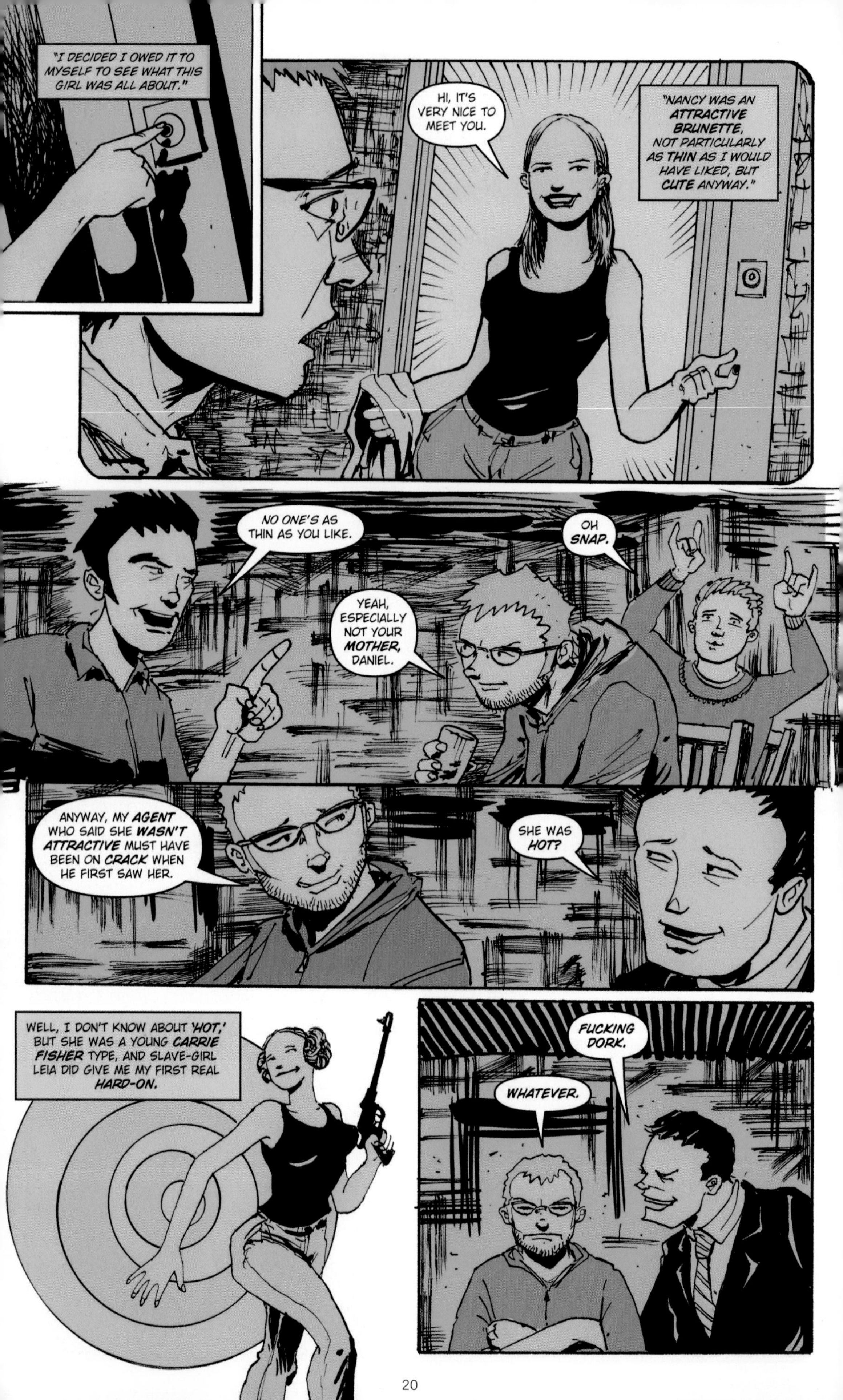
"I DECIDED I OWED IT TO MYSELF TO SEE WHAT THIS GIRL WAS ALL ABOUT."
HI, IT'S VERY NICE TO MEET YOU.
"NANCY WAS AN ATTRACTIVE BRUNETTE, NOT PARTICULARLY AS THIN AS I WOULD HAVE LIKED, BUT CUTE ANYWAY."
NO ONE'S AS THIN AS YOU LIKE.
OH SNAP.
YEAH, ESPECIALLY NOT YOUR MOTHER, DANIEL.
ANYWAY, MY AGENT WHO SAID SHE WASN'T ATTRACTIVE MUST HAVE BEEN ON CRACK WHEN HE FIRST SAW HER.
SHE WAS HOT?
WELL, I DON'T KNOW ABOUT 'HOT,' BUT SHE WAS A YOUNG CARRIE FISHER TYPE, AND SLAVE-GIRL LEIA DID GIVE ME MY FIRST REAL HARD-ON.
FUCKING DORK.
WHATEVER.

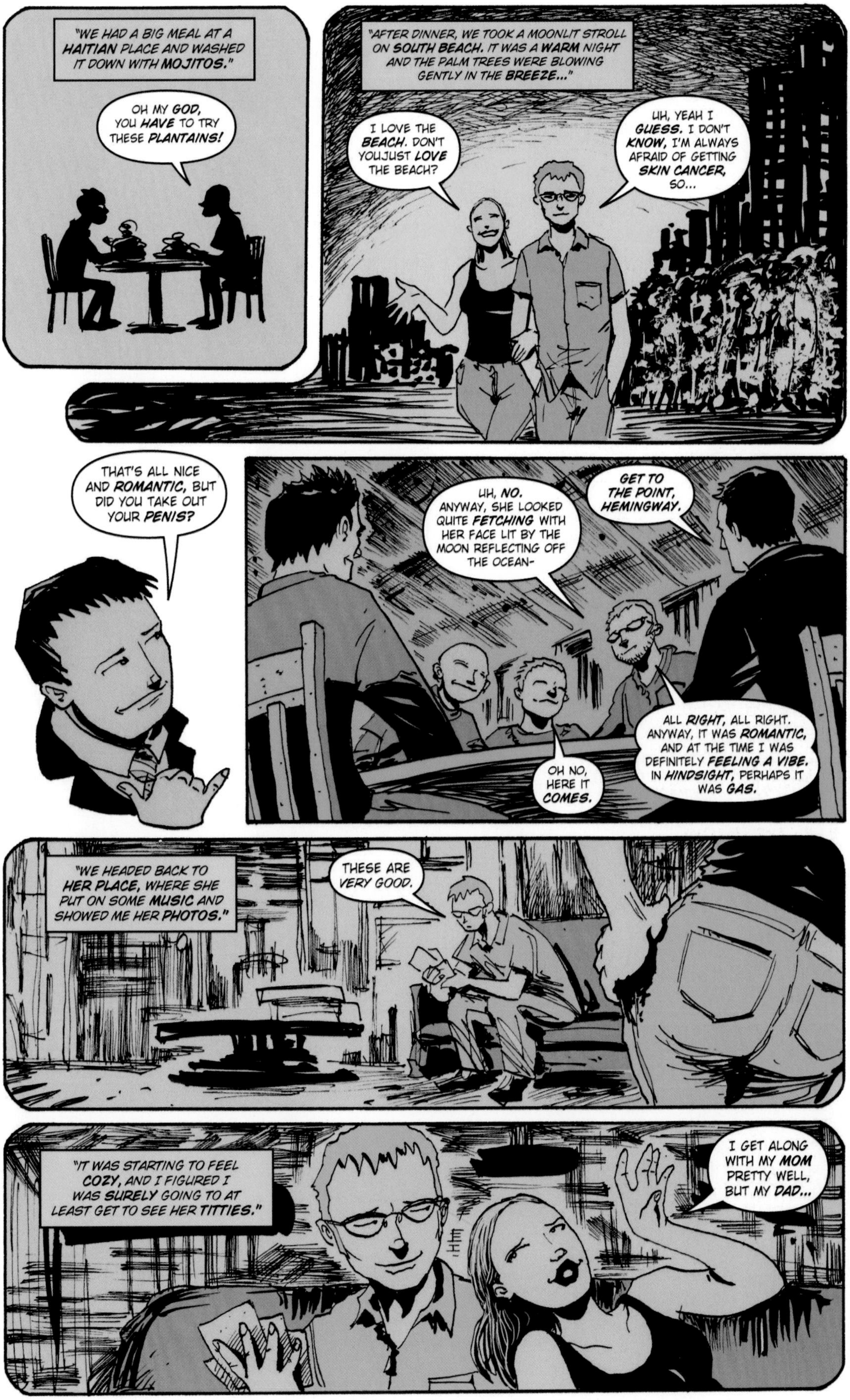
"WE HAD A BIG MEAL AT A HAITIAN PLACE AND WASHED IT DOWN WITH MOJITOS."
OH MY GOD, YOU HAVE TO TRY THESE PLANTAINS!
"AFTER DINNER, WE TOOK A MOONLIT STROLL ON SOUTH BEACH. IT WAS A WARM NIGHT AND THE PALM TREES WERE BLOWING GENTLY IN THE BREEZE..."
I LOVE THE BEACH. DON'T YOUJUST LOVE THE BEACH?
UH, YEAH I GUESS. I DON'T KNOW, I'M ALWAYS AFRAID OF GETTING SKIN CANCER, SO...
THAT'S ALL NICE AND ROMANTIC, BUT DID YOU TAKE OUT YOUR PENIS?
UH, NO. ANYWAY, SHE LOOKED QUITE FETCHING WITH HER FACE LIT BY THE MOON REFLECTING OFF THE OCEAN-
GET TO THE POINT, HEMINGWAY.
OH NO, HERE IT COMES.
ALL RIGHT, ALL RIGHT. ANYWAY, IT WAS ROMANTIC, AND AT THE TIME I WAS DEFINITELY FEELING A VIBE. IN HINDSIGHT, PERHAPS IT WAS GAS.
"WE HEADED BACK TO HER PLACE, WHERE SHE PUT ON SOME MUSIC AND SHOWED ME HER PHOTOS."
THESE ARE VERY GOOD.
"IT WAS STARTING TO FEEL COZY, AND I FIGURED I WAS SURELY GOING TO AT LEAST GET TO SEE HER TITTIES."
I GET ALONG WITH MY MOM PRETTY WELL, BUT MY DAD...

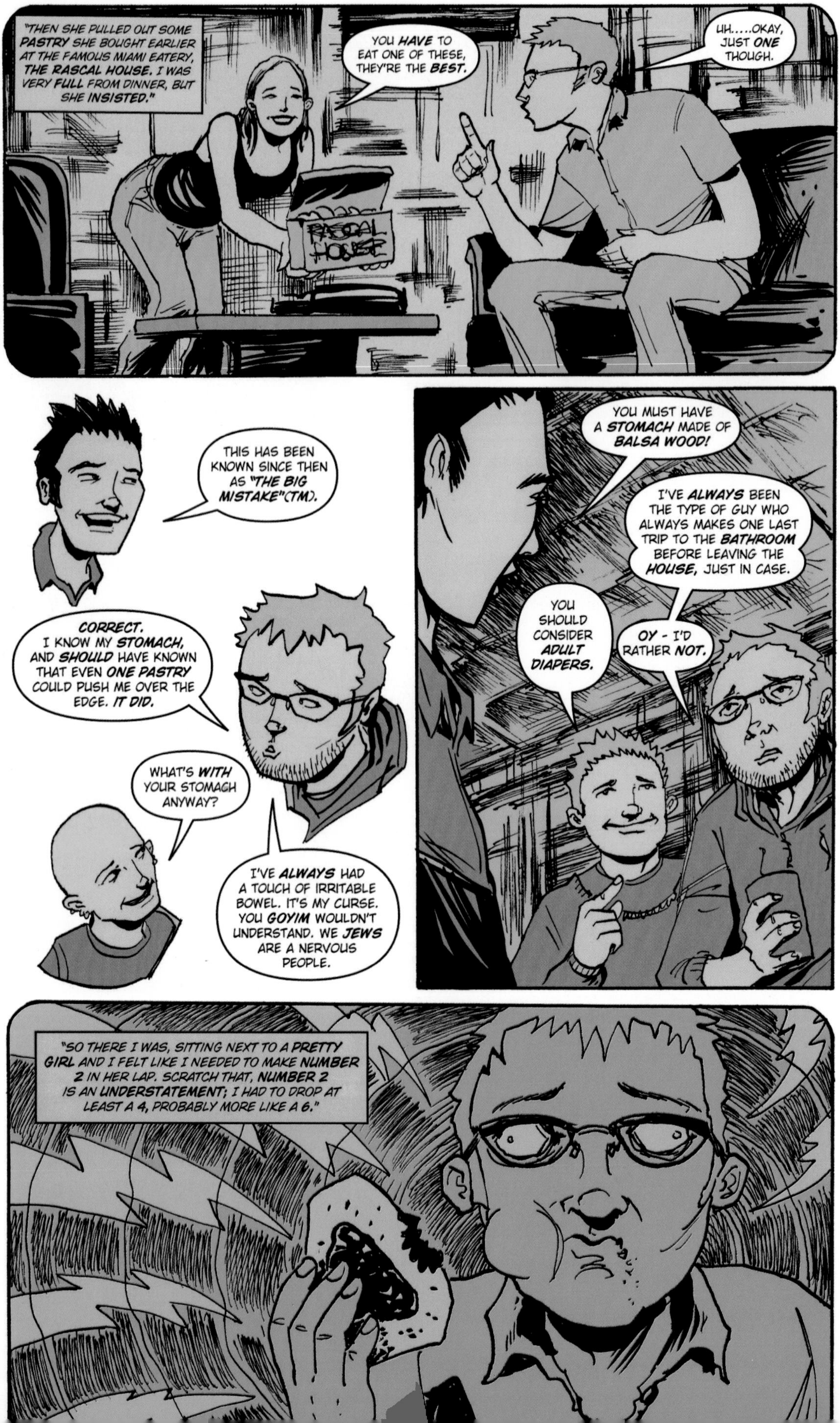
"THEN SHE PULLED OUT SOME PASTRY SHE BOUGHT EARLIER AT THE FAMOUS MIAMI EATERY, THE RASCAL HOUSE. I WAS VERY FULL FROM DINNER, BUT SHE INSISTED."
YOU HAVE TO EAT ONE OF THESE, THEY'RE THE BEST.
UH.....OKAY, JUST ONE THOUGH.
RASCAL HOUSE
THIS HAS BEEN KNOWN SINCE THEN AS "THE BIG MISTAKE"(TM).
CORRECT. I KNOW MY STOMACH, AND SHOULD HAVE KNOWN THAT EVEN ONE PASTRY COULD PUSH ME OVER THE EDGE. IT DID.
WHAT'S WITH YOUR STOMACH ANYWAY?
I'VE ALWAYS HAD A TOUCH OF IRRITABLE BOWEL. IT'S MY CURSE. YOU GOYIM WOULDN'T UNDERSTAND. WE JEWS ARE A NERVOUS PEOPLE.
YOU MUST HAVE A STOMACH MADE OF BALSA WOOD!
I'VE ALWAYS BEEN THE TYPE OF GUY WHO ALWAYS MAKES ONE LAST TRIP TO THE BATHROOM BEFORE LEAVING THE HOUSE, JUST IN CASE.
YOU SHOULD CONSIDER ADULT DIAPERS.
OY - I'D RATHER NOT.
"SO THERE I WAS, SITTING NEXT TO A PRETTY GIRL AND I FELT LIKE I NEEDED TO MAKE NUMBER 2 IN HER LAP. SCRATCH THAT, NUMBER 2 IS AN UNDERSTATEMENT; I HAD TO DROP AT LEAST A 4, PROBABLY MORE LIKE A 6."

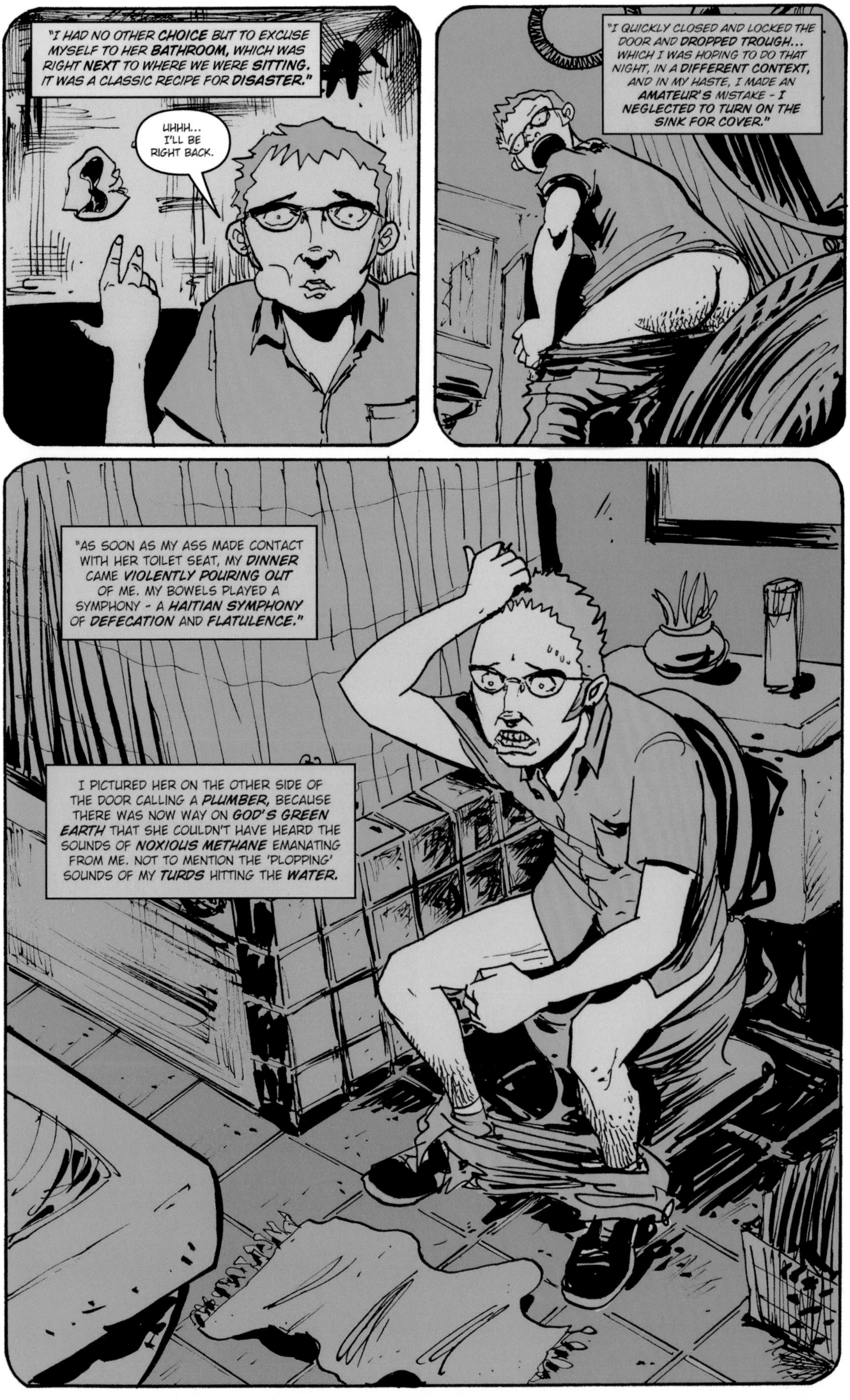
"I HAD NO OTHER CHOICE BUT TO EXCUSE MYSELF TO HER BATHROOM, WHICH WAS RIGHT NEXT TO WHERE WE WERE SITTING. IT WAS A CLASSIC RECIPE FOR DISASTER."
UHHH... I'LL BE RIGHT BACK.
"I QUICKLY CLOSED AND LOCKED THE DOOR AND DROPPED TROUGH... WHICH I WAS HOPING TO DO THAT NIGHT, IN A DIFFERENT CONTEXT, AND IN MY HASTE, I MADE AN AMATEUR'S MISTAKE - I NEGLECTED TO TURN ON THE SINK FOR COVER."
"AS SOON AS MY ASS MADE CONTACT WITH HER TOILET SEAT, MY DINNER CAME VIOLENTLY POURING OUT OF ME. MY BOWELS PLAYED A SYMPHONY - A HAITIAN SYMPHONY OF DEFECATION AND FLATULENCE."
I PICTURED HER ON THE OTHER SIDE OF THE DOOR CALLING A PLUMBER, BECAUSE THERE WAS NOW WAY ON GOD'S GREEN EARTH THAT SHE COULDN'T HAVE HEARD THE SOUNDS OF NOXIOUS METHANE EMANATING FROM ME. NOT TO MENTION THE 'PLOPPING' SOUNDS OF MY TURDS HITTING THE WATER.

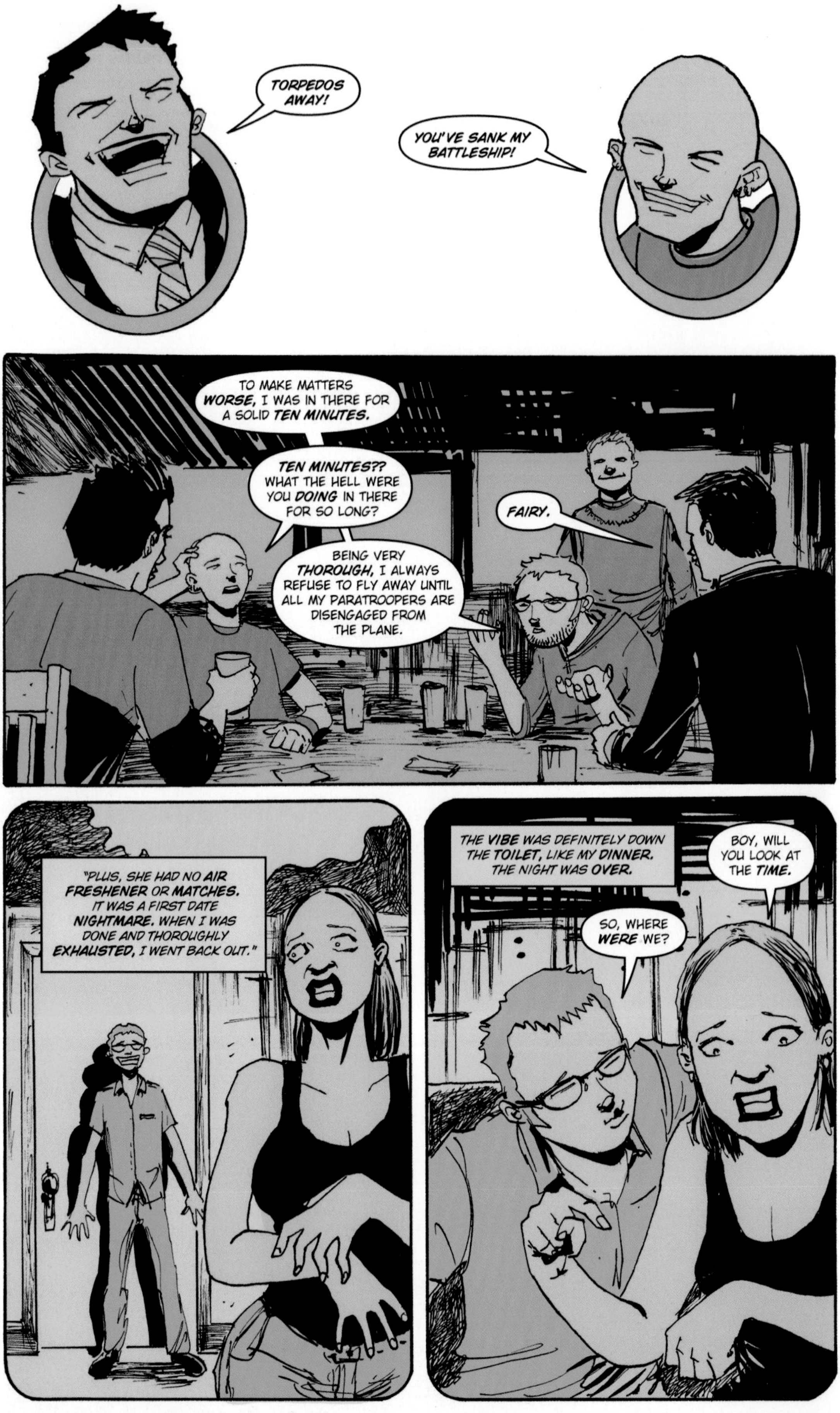
TORPEDOS AWAY!
YOU'VE SANK MY BATTLESHIP!
TO MAKE MATTERS WORSE, I WAS IN THERE FOR A SOLID TEN MINUTES.
TEN MINUTES?? WHAT THE HELL WERE YOU DOING IN THERE FOR SO LONG?
BEING VERY THOROUGH, I ALWAYS REFUSE TO FLY AWAY UNTIL ALL MY PARATROOPERS ARE DISENGAGED FROM THE PLANE.
FAIRY.
"PLUS, SHE HAD NO AIR FRESHENER OR MATCHES. IT WAS A FIRST DATE NIGHTMARE. WHEN I WAS DONE AND THOROUGHLY EXHAUSTED, I WENT BACK OUT."
THE VIBE WAS DEFINITELY DOWN THE TOILET, LIKE MY DINNER. THE NIGHT WAS OVER.
BOY, WILL YOU LOOK AT THE TIME.
SO, WHERE WERE WE?

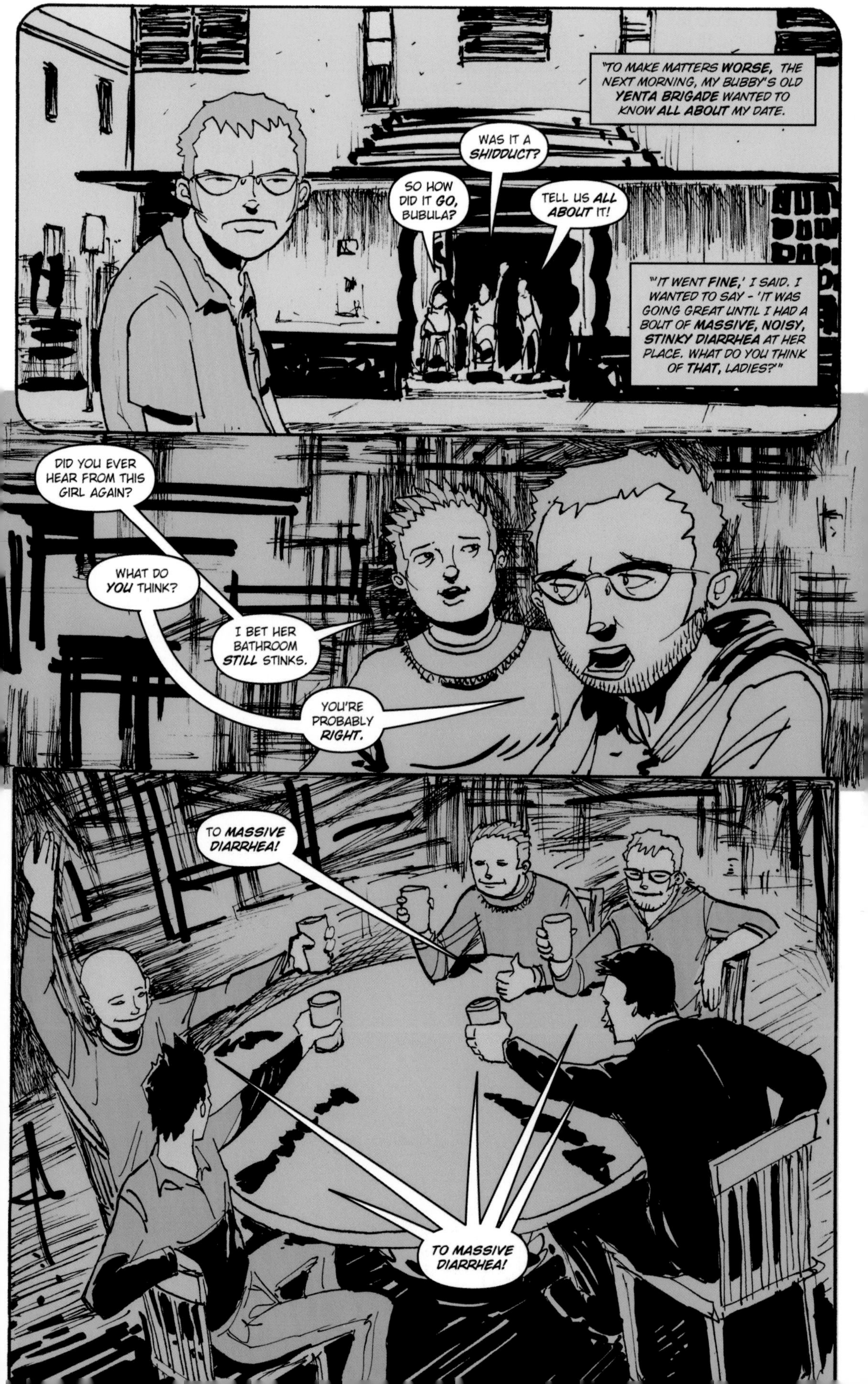
"TO MAKE MATTERS WORSE, THE NEXT MORNING, MY BUBBY'S OLD YENTA BRIGADE WANTED TO KNOW ALL ABOUT MY DATE.
SO HOW DID IT GO, BUBULA?
WAS IT A SHIDDUCT?
TELL US ALL ABOUT IT!
"'IT WENT FINE,' I SAID. I WANTED TO SAY - 'IT WAS GOING GREAT UNTIL I HAD A BOUT OF MASSIVE, NOISY, STINKY DIARRHEA AT HER PLACE. WHAT DO YOU THINK OF THAT, LADIES?'"
DID YOU EVER HEAR FROM THIS GIRL AGAIN?
WHAT DO YOU THINK?
I BET HER BATHROOM STILL STINKS.
YOU'RE PROBABLY RIGHT.
TO MASSIVE DIARRHEA!
TO MASSIVE DIARRHEA!

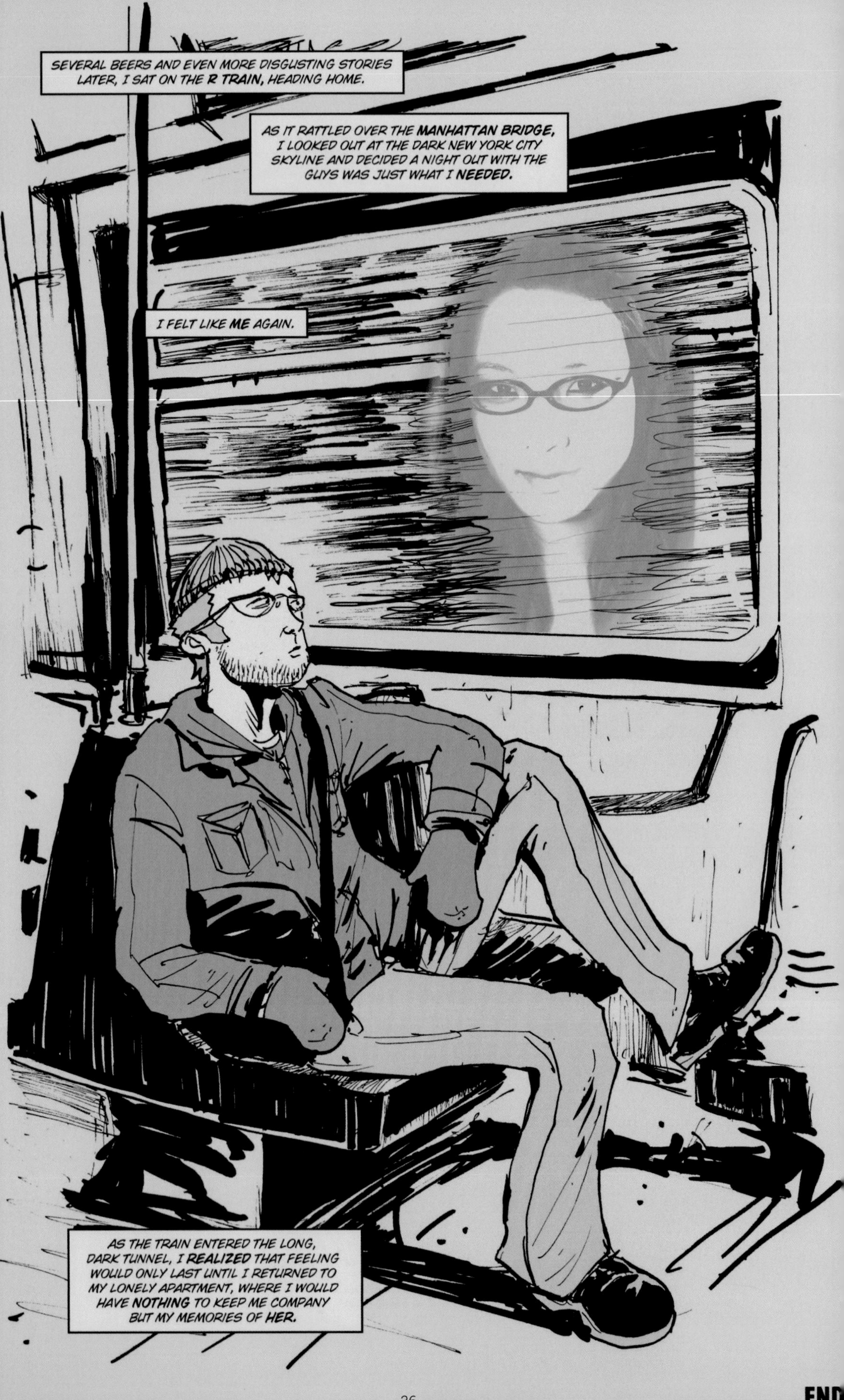
SEVERAL BEERS AND EVEN MORE DISGUSTING STORIES LATER, I SAT ON THE R TRAIN, HEADING HOME.
AS IT RATTLED OVER THE MANHATTAN BRIDGE, I LOOKED OUT AT THE DARK NEW YORK CITY SKYLINE AND DECIDED A NIGHT OUT WITH THE GUYS WAS JUST WHAT I NEEDED.
I FELT LIKE ME AGAIN.
AS THE TRAIN ENTERED THE LONG, DARK TUNNEL, I REALIZED THAT FEELING WOULD ONLY LAST UNTIL I RETURNED TO MY LONELY APARTMENT, WHERE I WOULD HAVE NOTHING TO KEEP ME COMPANY BUT MY MEMORIES OF HER.
END

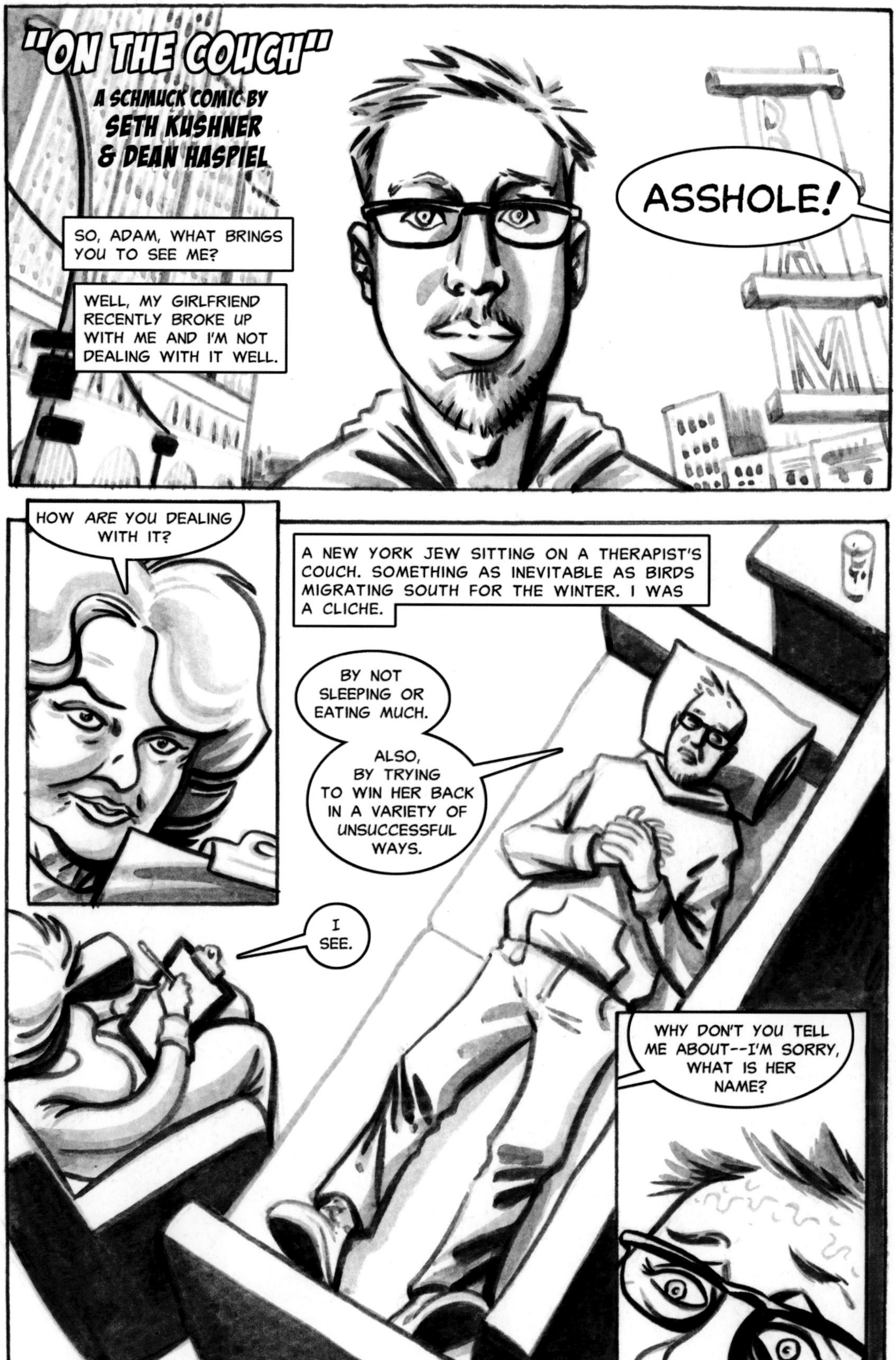
"ON THE COUCH"
A SCHMUCK COMIC BY
SETH KUSHNER
& DEAN HASPIEL
SO, ADAM, WHAT BRINGS YOU TO SEE ME?
WELL, MY GIRLFRIEND RECENTLY BROKE UP WITH ME AND I'M NOT DEALING WITH IT WELL.
ASSHOLE!
HOW ARE YOU DEALING WITH IT?
A NEW YORK JEW SITTING ON A THERAPIST'S COUCH. SOMETHING AS INEVITABLE AS BIRDS MIGRATING SOUTH FOR THE WINTER. I WAS A CLICHE.
BY NOT SLEEPING OR EATING MUCH.
ALSO, BY TRYING TO WIN HER BACK IN A VARIETY OF UNSUCCESSFUL WAYS.
I SEE.
WHY DON'T YOU TELL ME ABOUT--I'M SORRY, WHAT IS HER NAME?

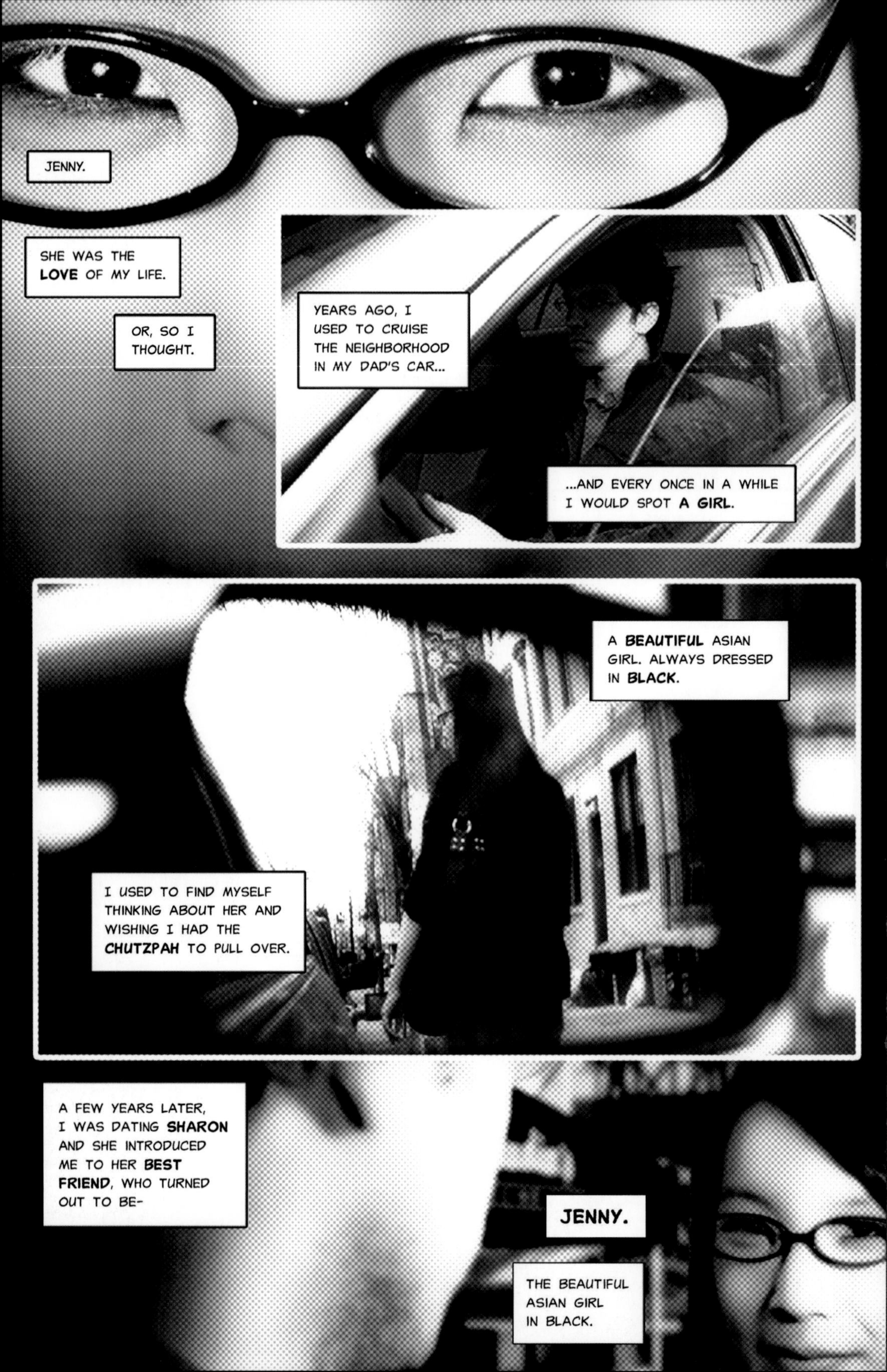
JENNY.
SHE WAS THE LOVE OF MY LIFE.
OR, SO I THOUGHT.
YEARS AGO, I USED TO CRUISE THE NEIGHBORHOOD IN MY DAD'S CAR...
...AND EVERY ONCE IN A WHILE I WOULD SPOT A GIRL.
A BEAUTIFUL ASIAN GIRL. ALWAYS DRESSED IN BLACK.
I USED TO FIND MYSELF THINKING ABOUT HER AND WISHING I HAD THE CHUTZPAH TO PULL OVER.
A FEW YEARS LATER, I WAS DATING SHARON AND SHE INTRODUCED ME TO HER BEST FRIEND, WHO TURNED OUT TO BE-
JENNY.
THE BEAUTIFUL ASIAN GIRL IN BLACK.

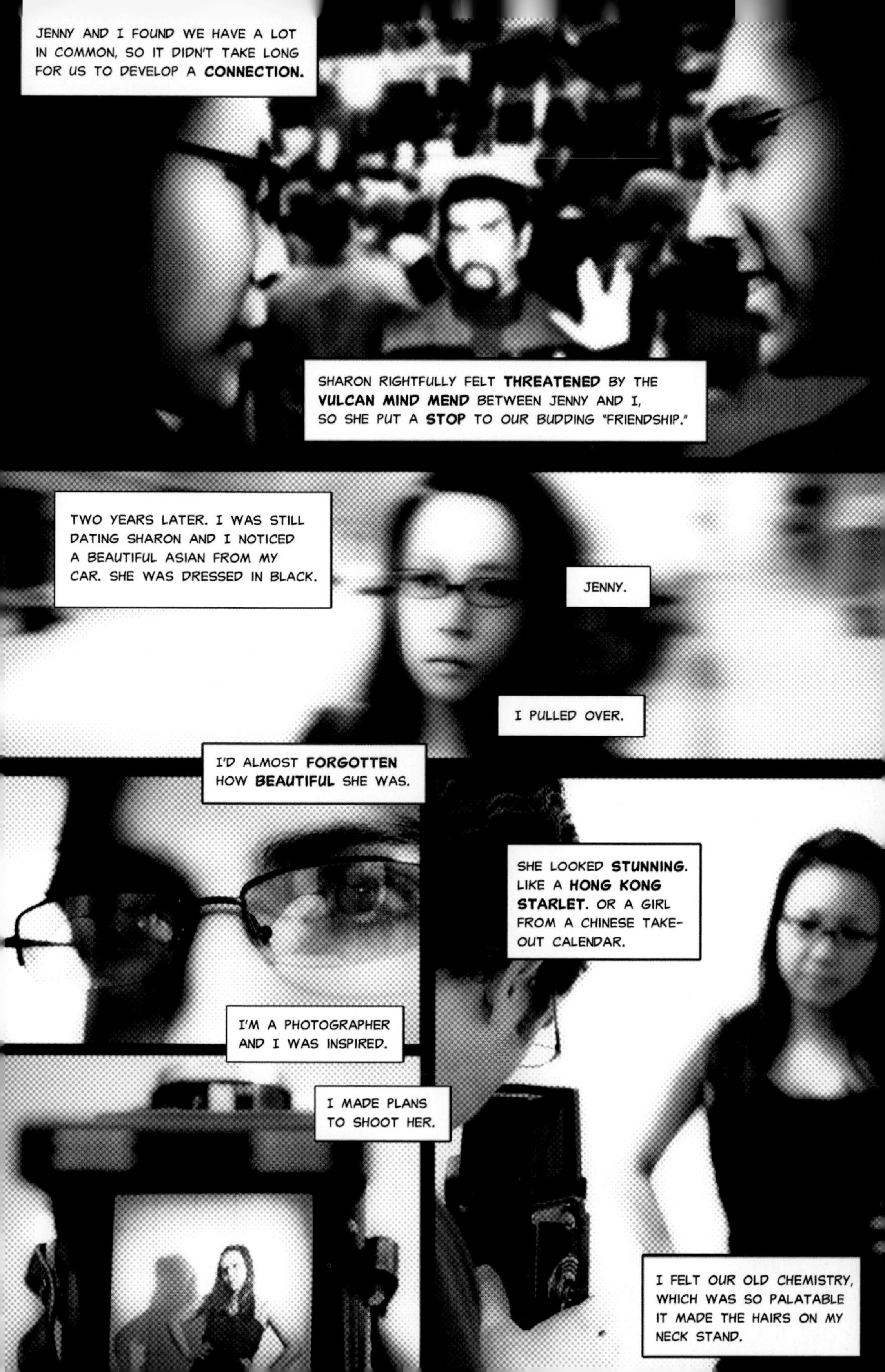
JENNY AND I FOUND WE HAVE A LOT IN COMMON, SO IT DIDN'T TAKE LONG FOR US TO DEVELOP A CONNECTION.
SHARON RIGHTFULLY FELT THREATENED BY THE VULCAN MIND MEND BETWEEN JENNY AND I, SO SHE PUT A STOP TO OUR BUDDING "FRIENDSHIP."
TWO YEARS LATER. I WAS STILL DATING SHARON AND I NOTICED A BEAUTIFUL ASIAN FROM MY CAR. SHE WAS DRESSED IN BLACK.
JENNY.
I PULLED OVER.
I'D ALMOST FORGOTTEN HOW BEAUTIFUL SHE WAS.
SHE LOOKED STUNNING. LIKE A HONG KONG STARLET. OR A GIRL FROM A CHINESE TAKE-OUT CALENDAR.
I'M A PHOTOGRAPHER AND I WAS INSPIRED.
I MADE PLANS TO SHOOT HER.
I FELT OUR OLD CHEMISTRY, WHICH WAS SO PALATABLE IT MADE THE HAIRS ON MY NECK STAND.

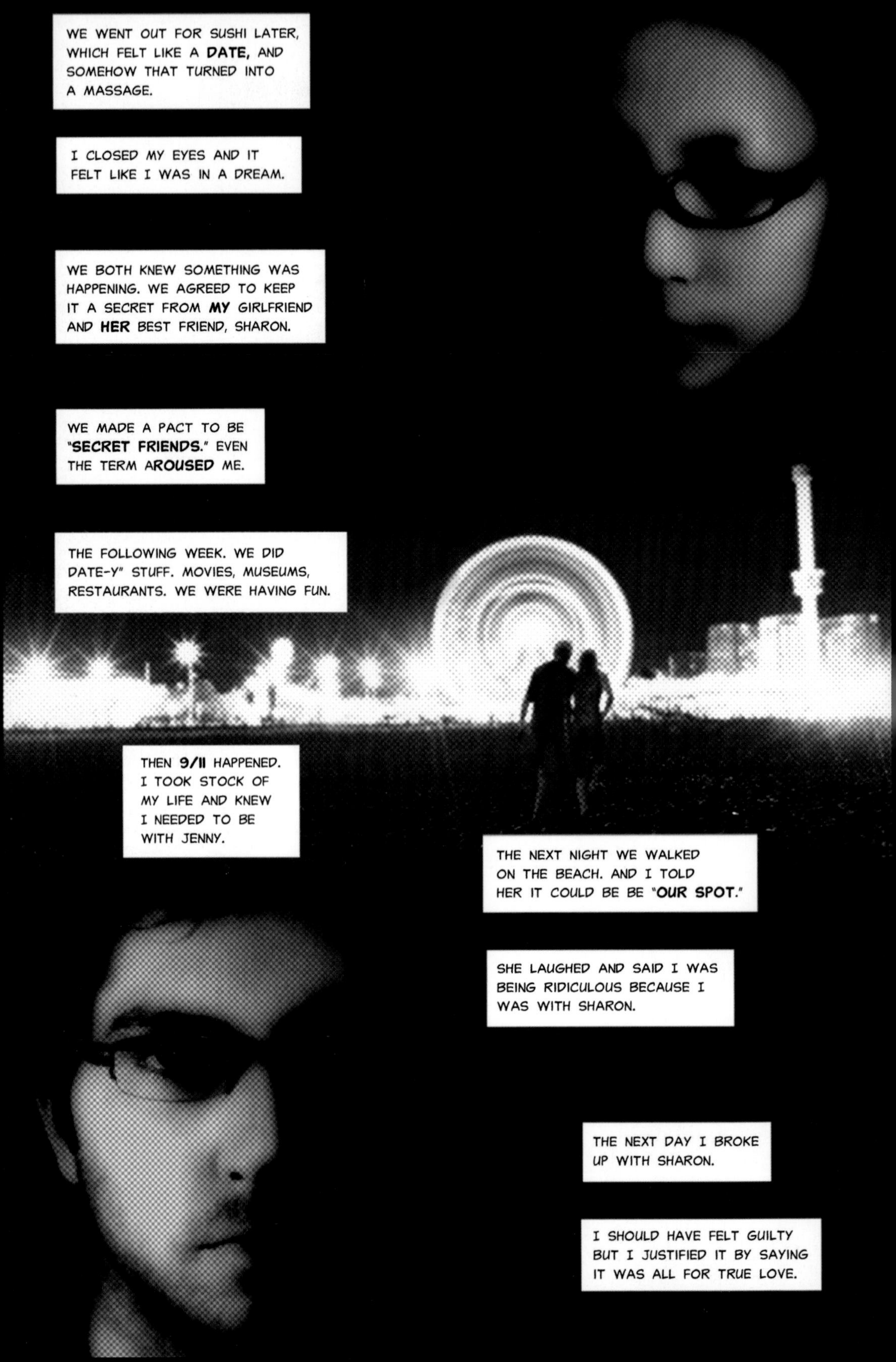
WE WENT OUT FOR SUSHI LATER, WHICH FELT LIKE A **DATE,** AND SOMEHOW THAT TURNED INTO A MASSAGE.
I CLOSED MY EYES AND IT FELT LIKE I WAS IN A DREAM.
WE BOTH KNEW SOMETHING WAS HAPPENING. WE AGREED TO KEEP IT A SECRET FROM **MY** GIRLFRIEND AND **HER** BEST FRIEND, SHARON.
WE MADE A PACT TO BE "**SECRET FRIENDS.**" EVEN THE TERM A**ROUSED** ME.
THE FOLLOWING WEEK. WE DID DATE-Y" STUFF. MOVIES, MUSEUMS, RESTAURANTS. WE WERE HAVING FUN.
THEN **9/11** HAPPENED. I TOOK STOCK OF MY LIFE AND KNEW I NEEDED TO BE WITH JENNY.
THE NEXT NIGHT WE WALKED ON THE BEACH. AND I TOLD HER IT COULD BE BE "**OUR SPOT**."
SHE LAUGHED AND SAID I WAS BEING RIDICULOUS BECAUSE I WAS WITH SHARON.
THE NEXT DAY I BROKE UP WITH SHARON.
I SHOULD HAVE FELT GUILTY BUT I JUSTIFIED IT BY SAYING IT WAS ALL FOR TRUE LOVE.

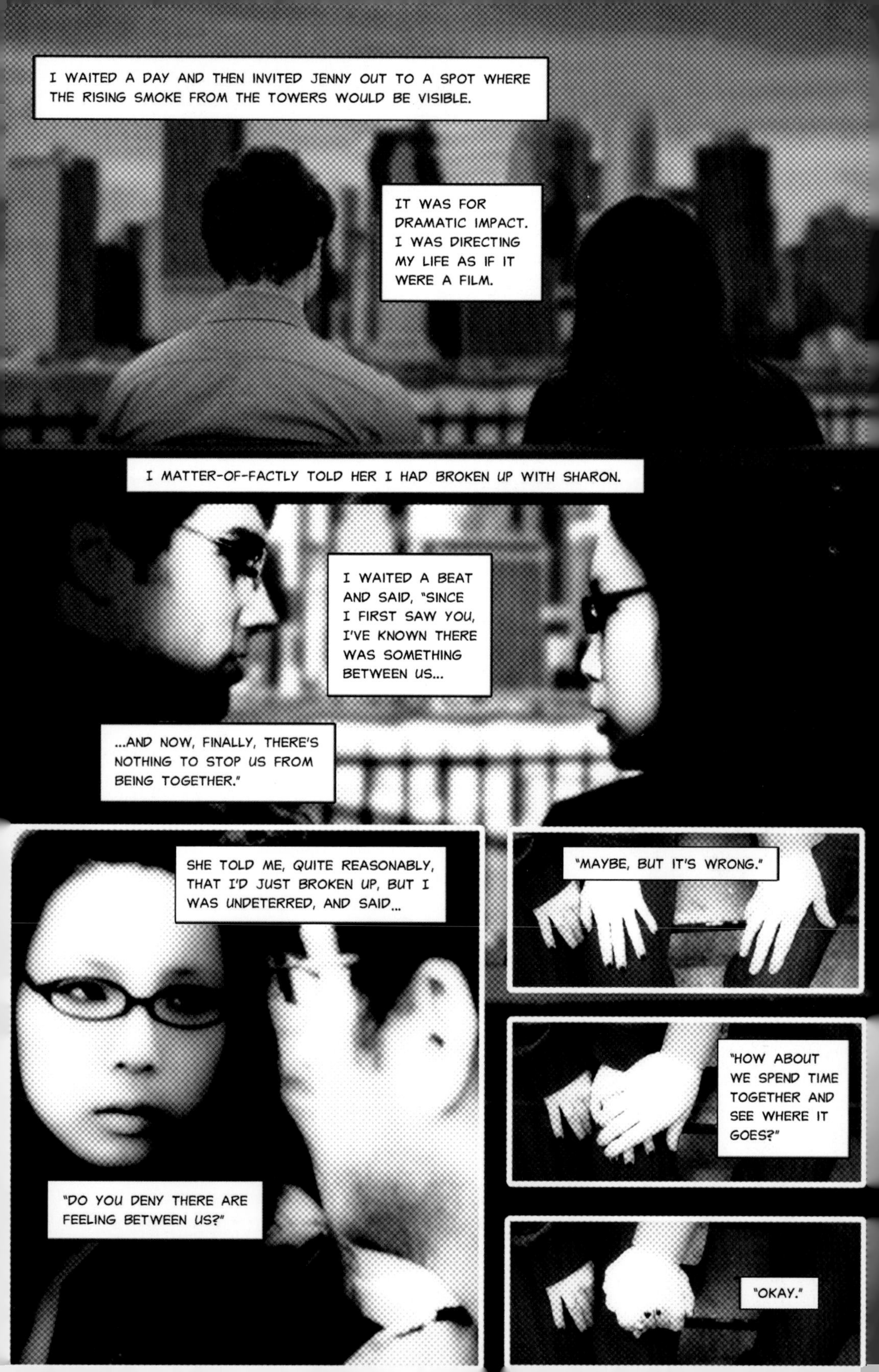
I WAITED A DAY AND THEN INVITED JENNY OUT TO A SPOT WHERE THE RISING SMOKE FROM THE TOWERS WOULD BE VISIBLE.
IT WAS FOR DRAMATIC IMPACT. I WAS DIRECTING MY LIFE AS IF IT WERE A FILM.
I MATTER-OF-FACTLY TOLD HER I HAD BROKEN UP WITH SHARON.
I WAITED A BEAT AND SAID, "SINCE I FIRST SAW YOU, I'VE KNOWN THERE WAS SOMETHING BETWEEN US...
...AND NOW, FINALLY, THERE'S NOTHING TO STOP US FROM BEING TOGETHER."
SHE TOLD ME, QUITE REASONABLY, THAT I'D JUST BROKEN UP, BUT I WAS UNDETERRED, AND SAID...
"DO YOU DENY THERE ARE FEELING BETWEEN US?"
"MAYBE, BUT IT'S WRONG."
"HOW ABOUT WE SPEND TIME TOGETHER AND SEE WHERE IT GOES?"
"OKAY."

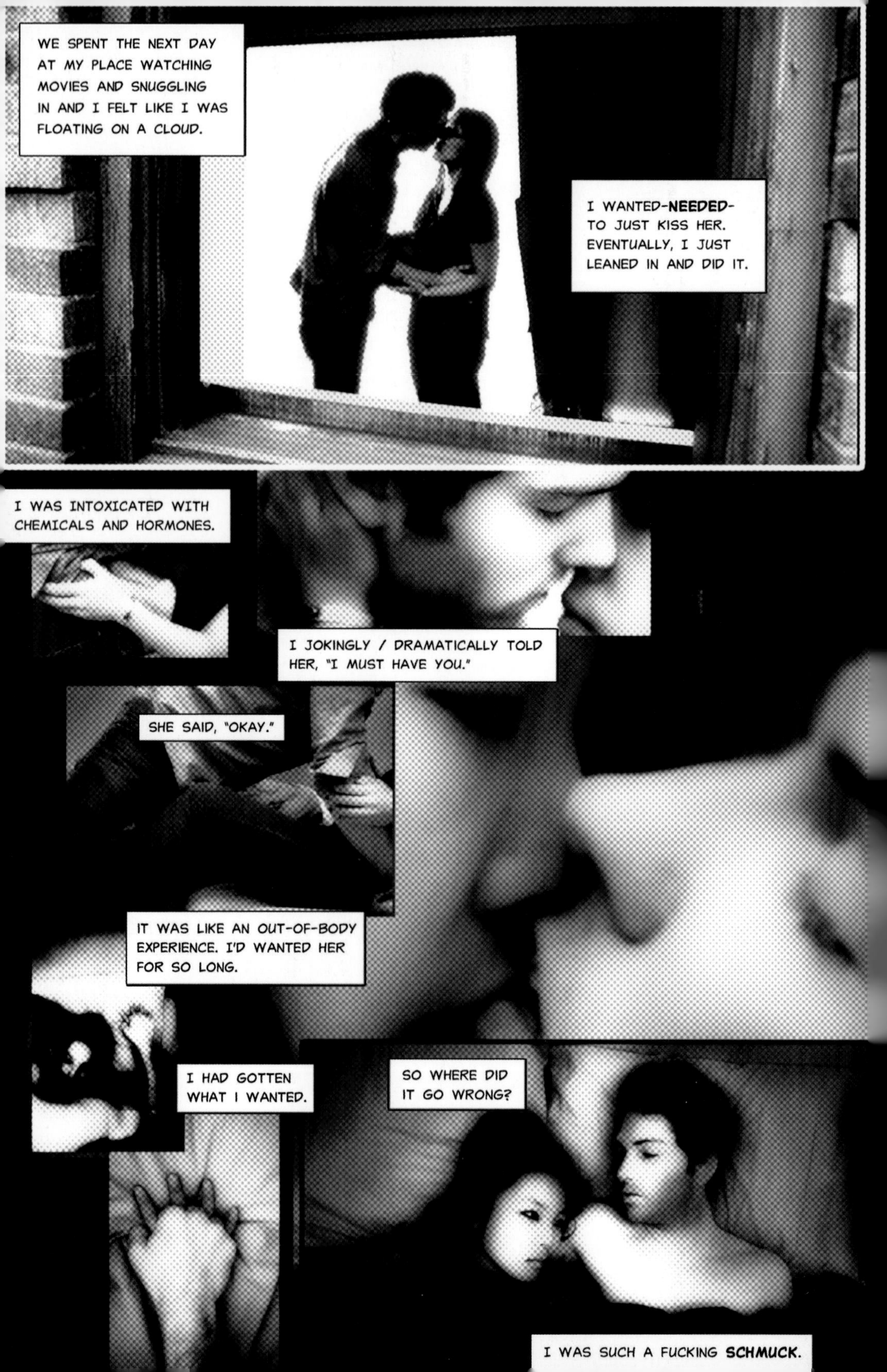

WE SPENT THE NEXT DAY AT MY PLACE WATCHING MOVIES AND SNUGGLING IN AND I FELT LIKE I WAS FLOATING ON A CLOUD.
I WANTED-**NEEDED**-TO JUST KISS HER. EVENTUALLY, I JUST LEANED IN AND DID IT.
I WAS INTOXICATED WITH CHEMICALS AND HORMONES.
I JOKINGLY / DRAMATICALLY TOLD HER, "I MUST HAVE YOU."
SHE SAID, "OKAY."
IT WAS LIKE AN OUT-OF-BODY EXPERIENCE. I'D WANTED HER FOR SO LONG.
I HAD GOTTEN WHAT I WANTED.
SO WHERE DID IT GO WRONG?
I WAS SUCH A FUCKING **SCHMUCK**.

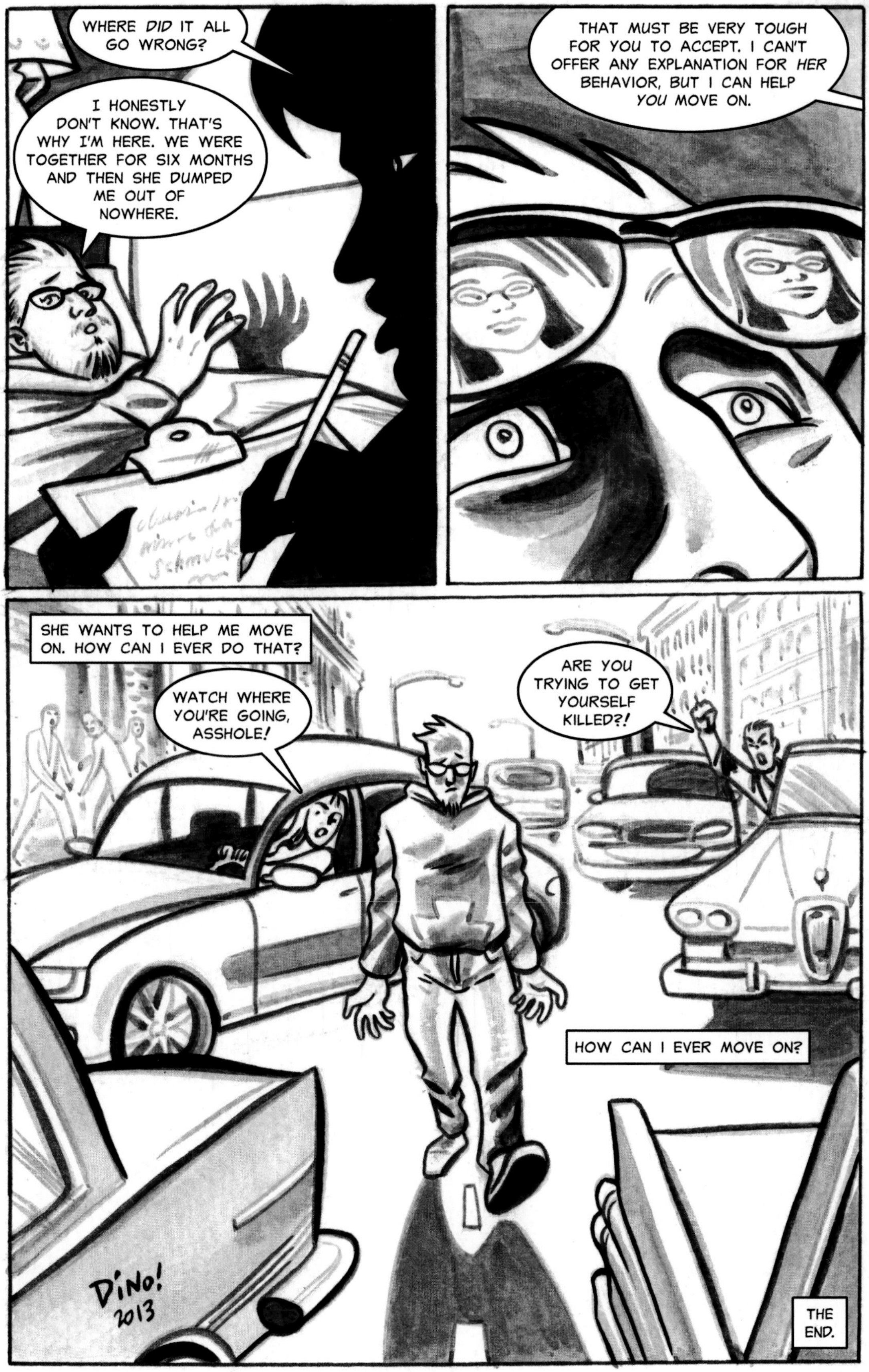
WHERE DID IT ALL GO WRONG?
I HONESTLY DON'T KNOW. THAT'S WHY I'M HERE. WE WERE TOGETHER FOR SIX MONTHS AND THEN SHE DUMPED ME OUT OF NOWHERE.
THAT MUST BE VERY TOUGH FOR YOU TO ACCEPT. I CAN'T OFFER ANY EXPLANATION FOR HER BEHAVIOR, BUT I CAN HELP YOU MOVE ON.
SHE WANTS TO HELP ME MOVE ON. HOW CAN I EVER DO THAT?
WATCH WHERE YOU'RE GOING, ASSHOLE!
ARE YOU TRYING TO GET YOURSELF KILLED?!
HOW CAN I EVER MOVE ON?
DINO! 2013
THE END.

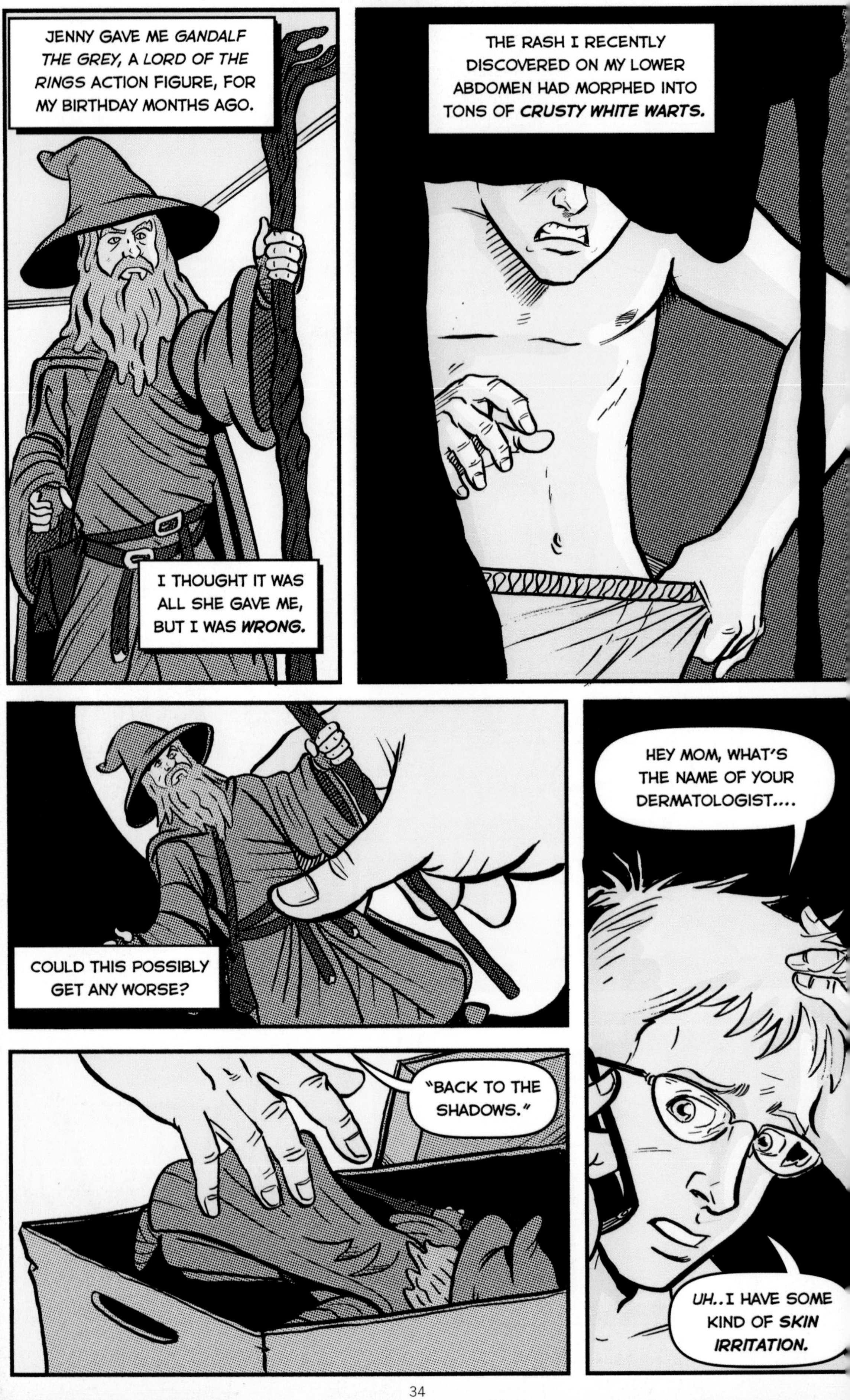
JENNY GAVE ME *GANDALF THE GREY*, A *LORD OF THE RINGS* ACTION FIGURE, FOR MY BIRTHDAY MONTHS AGO.
I THOUGHT IT WAS ALL SHE GAVE ME, BUT I WAS ***WRONG.***
THE RASH I RECENTLY DISCOVERED ON MY LOWER ABDOMEN HAD MORPHED INTO TONS OF ***CRUSTY WHITE WARTS.***
COULD THIS POSSIBLY GET ANY WORSE?
"BACK TO THE SHADOWS."
HEY MOM, WHAT'S THE NAME OF YOUR DERMATOLOGIST....
*UH..*I HAVE SOME KIND OF ***SKIN IRRITATION.***

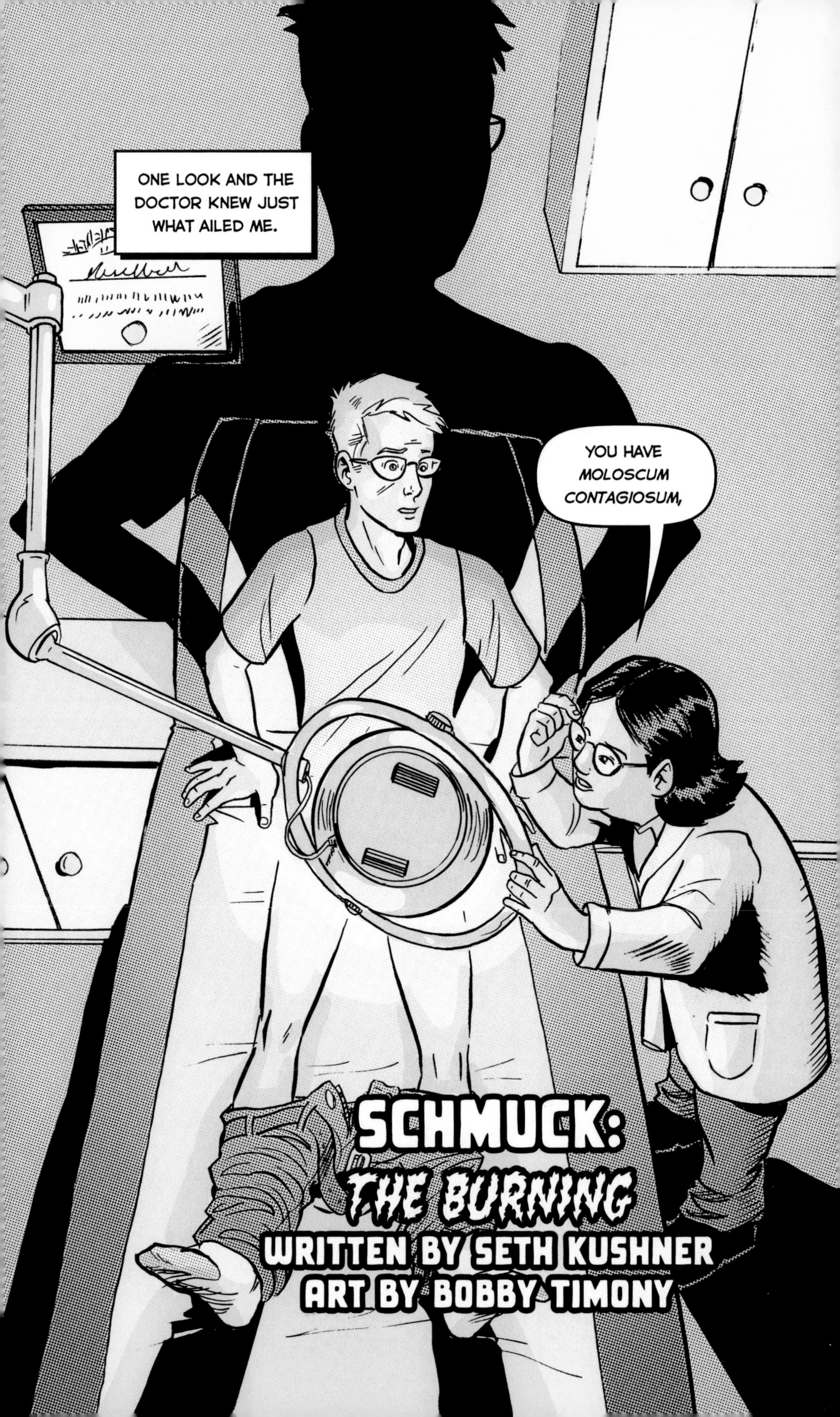
ONE LOOK AND THE DOCTOR KNEW JUST WHAT AILED ME.
YOU HAVE MOLOSCUM CONTAGIOSUM,
SCHMUCK:
THE BURNING
WRITTEN BY SETH KUSHNER
ART BY BOBBY TIMONY

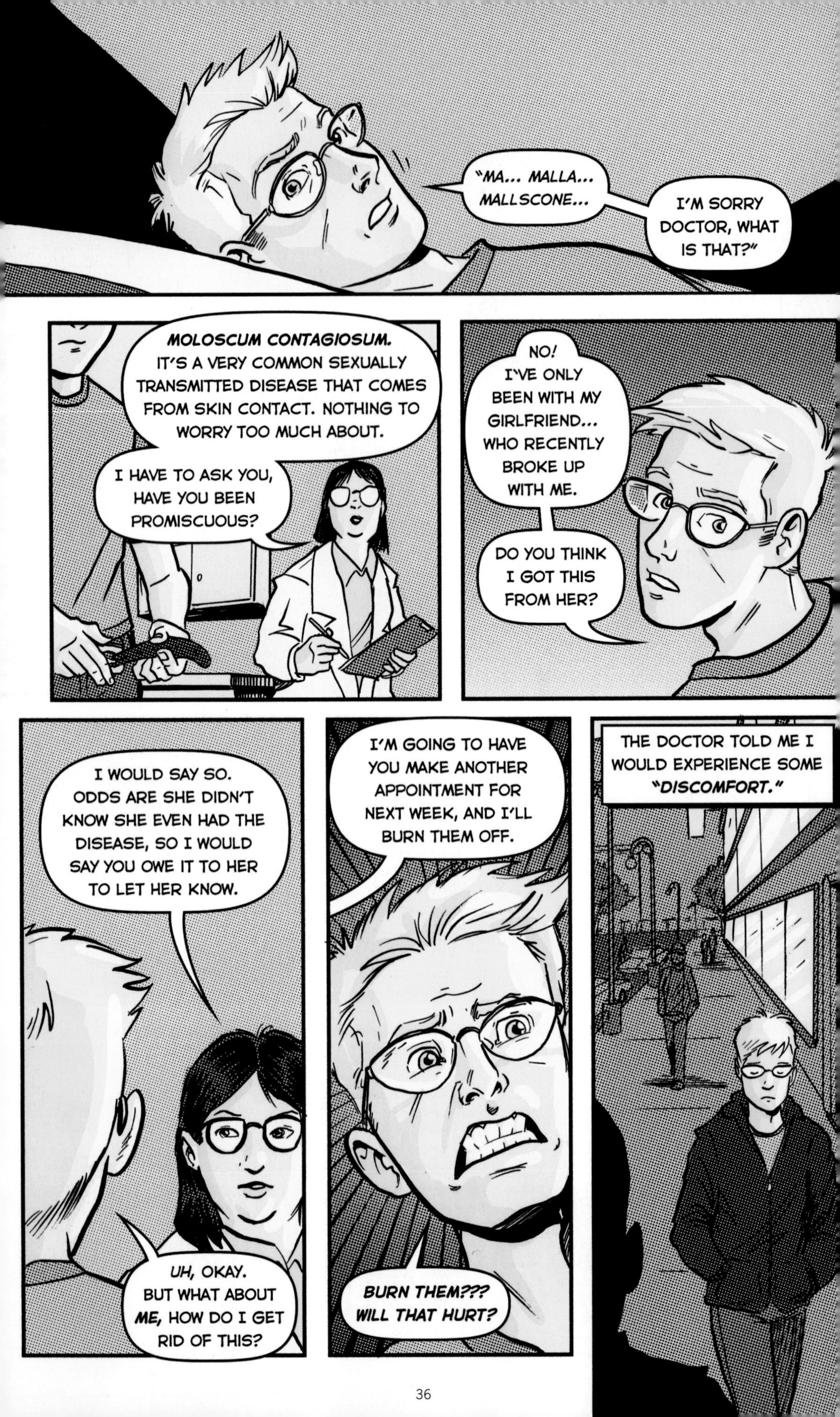
"MA... MALLA... MALLSCONE...
I'M SORRY DOCTOR, WHAT IS THAT?"
MOLOSCUM CONTAGIOSUM. IT'S A VERY COMMON SEXUALLY TRANSMITTED DISEASE THAT COMES FROM SKIN CONTACT. NOTHING TO WORRY TOO MUCH ABOUT.
I HAVE TO ASK YOU, HAVE YOU BEEN PROMISCUOUS?
NO! I'VE ONLY BEEN WITH MY GIRLFRIEND... WHO RECENTLY BROKE UP WITH ME.
DO YOU THINK I GOT THIS FROM HER?
I WOULD SAY SO. ODDS ARE SHE DIDN'T KNOW SHE EVEN HAD THE DISEASE, SO I WOULD SAY YOU OWE IT TO HER TO LET HER KNOW.
UH, OKAY. BUT WHAT ABOUT ME, HOW DO I GET RID OF THIS?
I'M GOING TO HAVE YOU MAKE ANOTHER APPOINTMENT FOR NEXT WEEK, AND I'LL BURN THEM OFF.
BURN THEM??? WILL THAT HURT?
THE DOCTOR TOLD ME I WOULD EXPERIENCE SOME "DISCOMFORT."

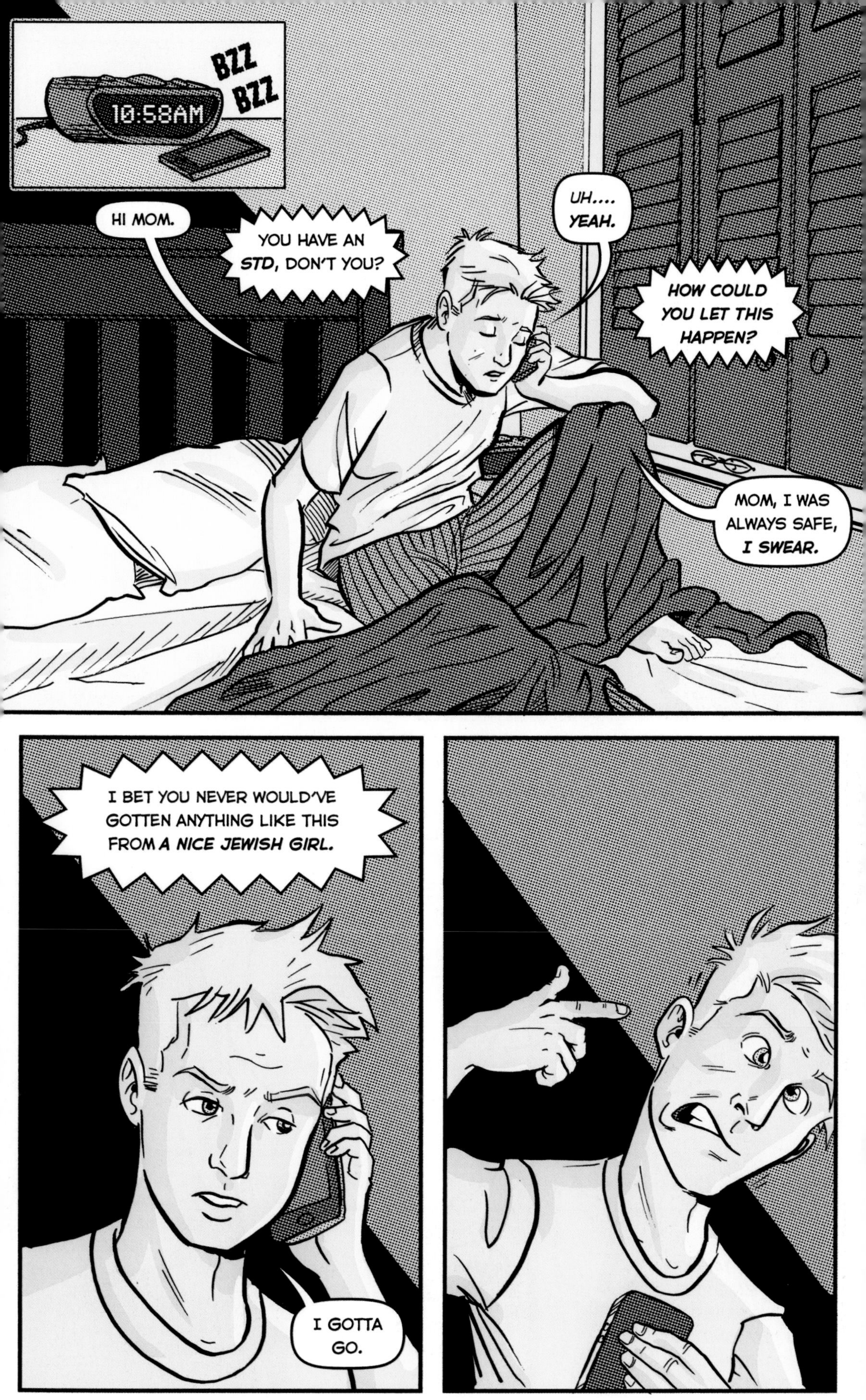
10:58AM
BZZ BZZ
HI MOM.
YOU HAVE AN STD, DON'T YOU?
UH.... YEAH.
HOW COULD YOU LET THIS HAPPEN?
MOM, I WAS ALWAYS SAFE, I SWEAR.
I BET YOU NEVER WOULD'VE GOTTEN ANYTHING LIKE THIS FROM A NICE JEWISH GIRL.
I GOTTA GO.

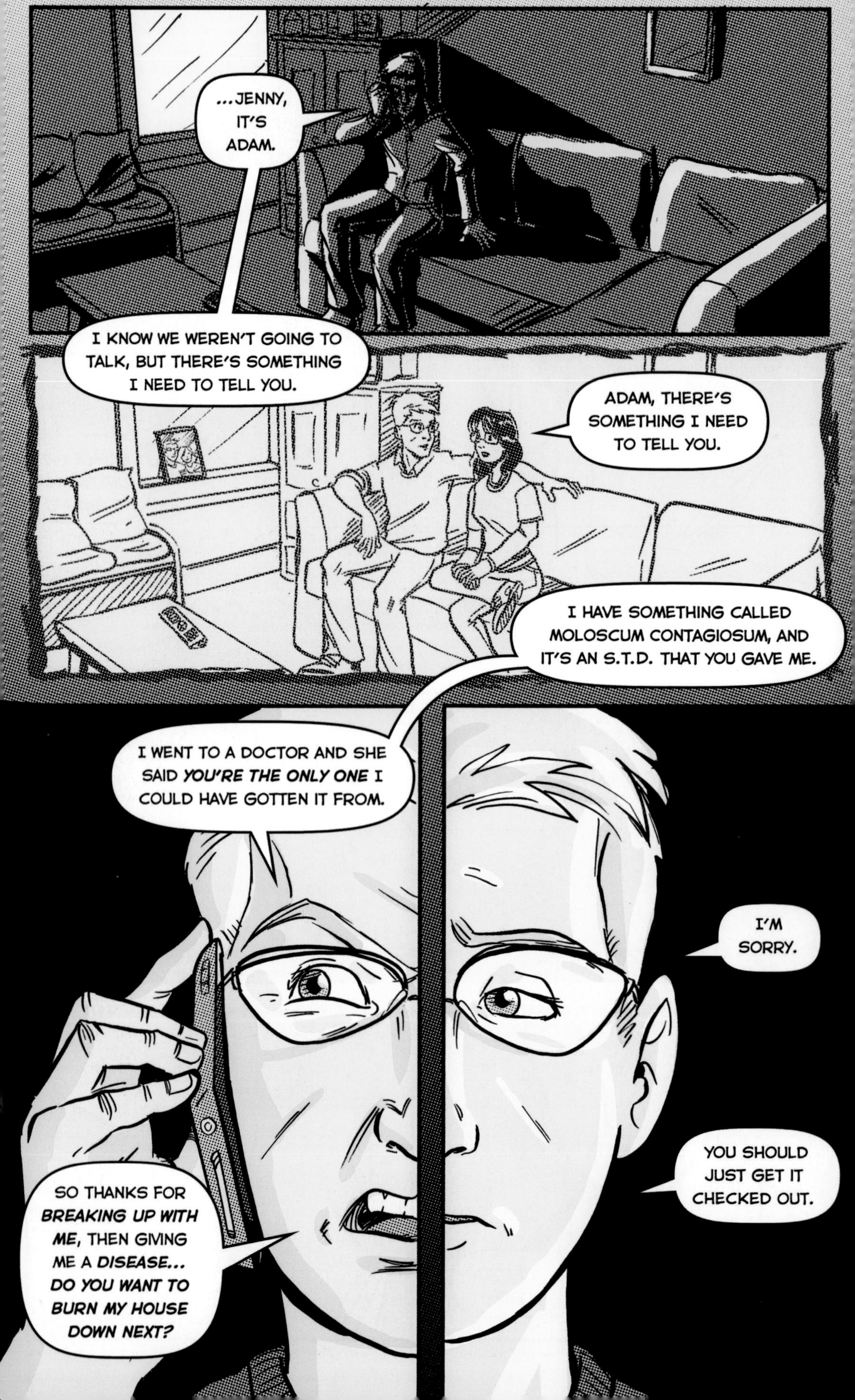
...JENNY, IT'S ADAM.
I KNOW WE WEREN'T GOING TO TALK, BUT THERE'S SOMETHING I NEED TO TELL YOU.
ADAM, THERE'S SOMETHING I NEED TO TELL YOU.
I HAVE SOMETHING CALLED MOLOSCUM CONTAGIOSUM, AND IT'S AN S.T.D. THAT YOU GAVE ME.
I WENT TO A DOCTOR AND SHE SAID *YOU'RE THE ONLY ONE* I COULD HAVE GOTTEN IT FROM.
I'M SORRY.
YOU SHOULD JUST GET IT CHECKED OUT.
SO THANKS FOR *BREAKING UP WITH ME*, THEN GIVING ME A *DISEASE... DO YOU WANT TO BURN MY HOUSE DOWN NEXT?*

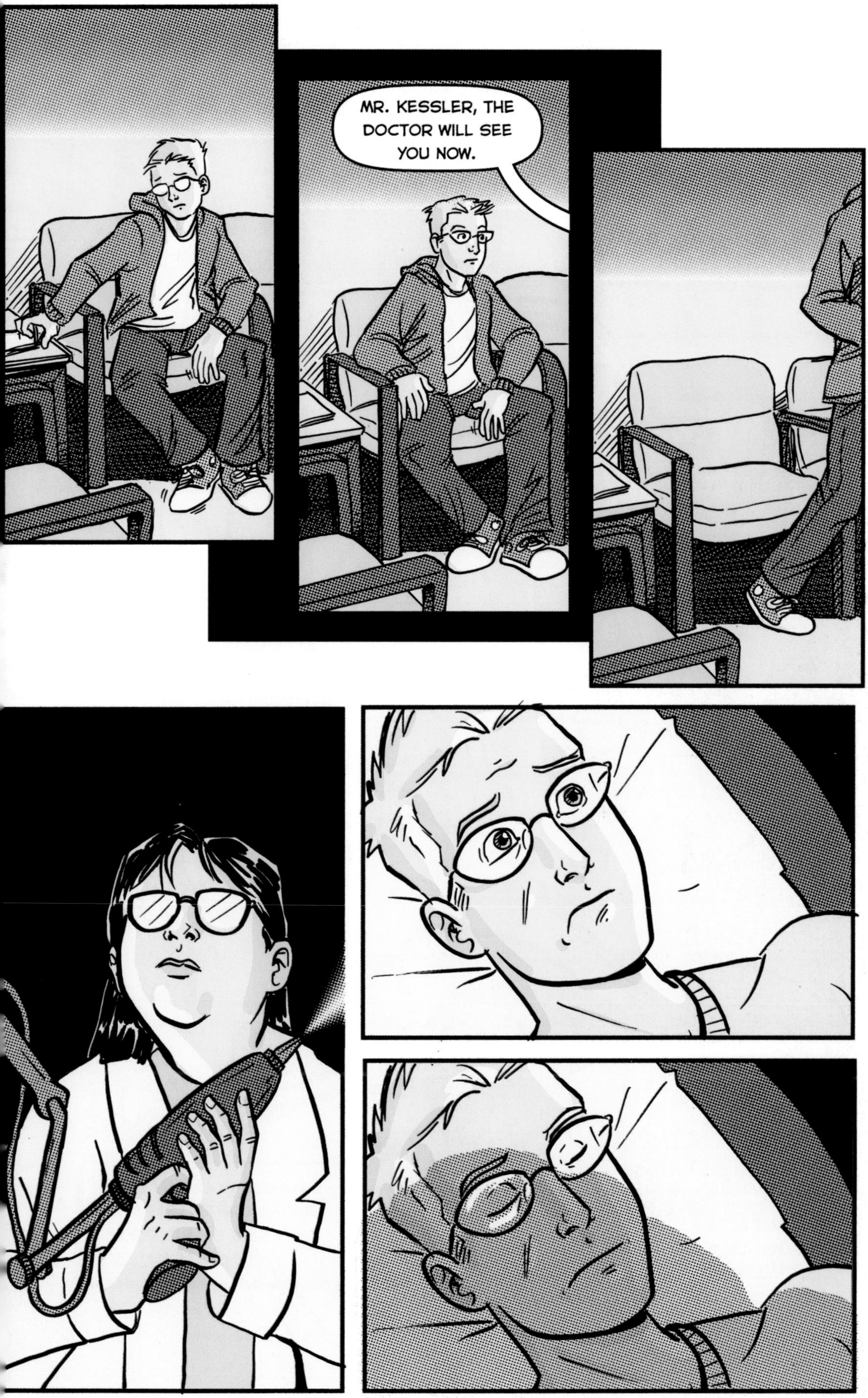
MR. KESSLER, THE DOCTOR WILL SEE YOU NOW.

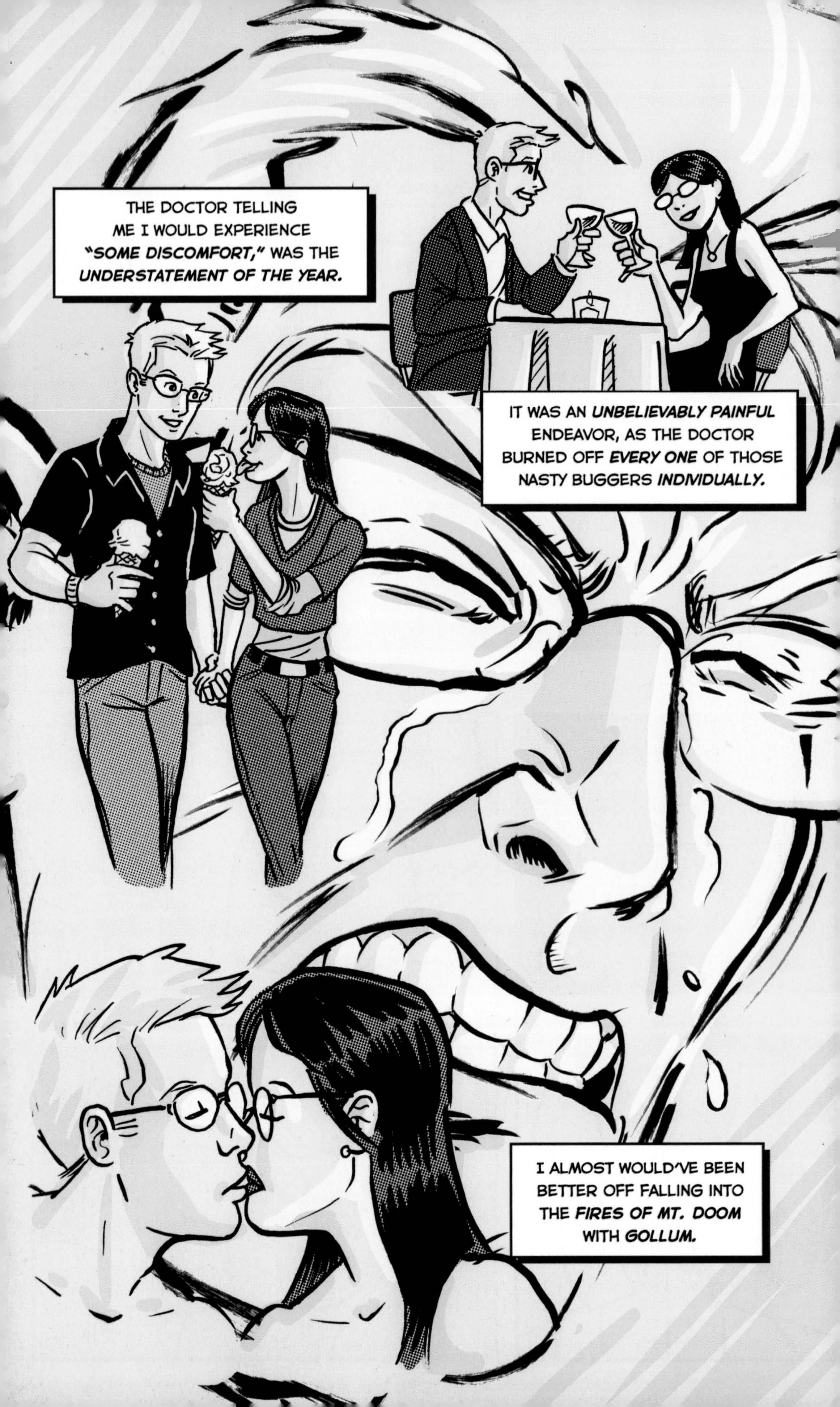
THE DOCTOR TELLING ME I WOULD EXPERIENCE "SOME DISCOMFORT," WAS THE UNDERSTATEMENT OF THE YEAR.
IT WAS AN UNBELIEVABLY PAINFUL ENDEAVOR, AS THE DOCTOR BURNED OFF EVERY ONE OF THOSE NASTY BUGGERS INDIVIDUALLY.
I ALMOST WOULD'VE BEEN BETTER OFF FALLING INTO THE FIRES OF MT. DOOM WITH GOLLUM.

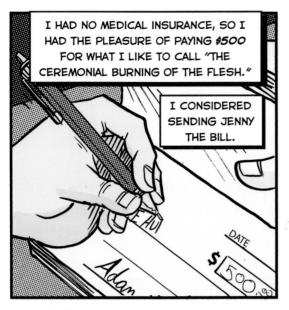

I HAD NO MEDICAL INSURANCE, SO I HAD THE PLEASURE OF PAYING *$500* FOR WHAT I LIKE TO CALL "THE CEREMONIAL BURNING OF THE FLESH."

I CONSIDERED SENDING JENNY THE BILL.

I HAD A CLEAN BILL OF HEALTH, BUT I KNEW IF I TRULY WANTED TO *"HEAL"* I HAD TO *MOVE ON* WITH MY LIFE.

I DELETED JENNY FROM MY PHONE.

AND, PUT THE PAST BEHIND ME.

Bobby Timony

After John Romita Sr.

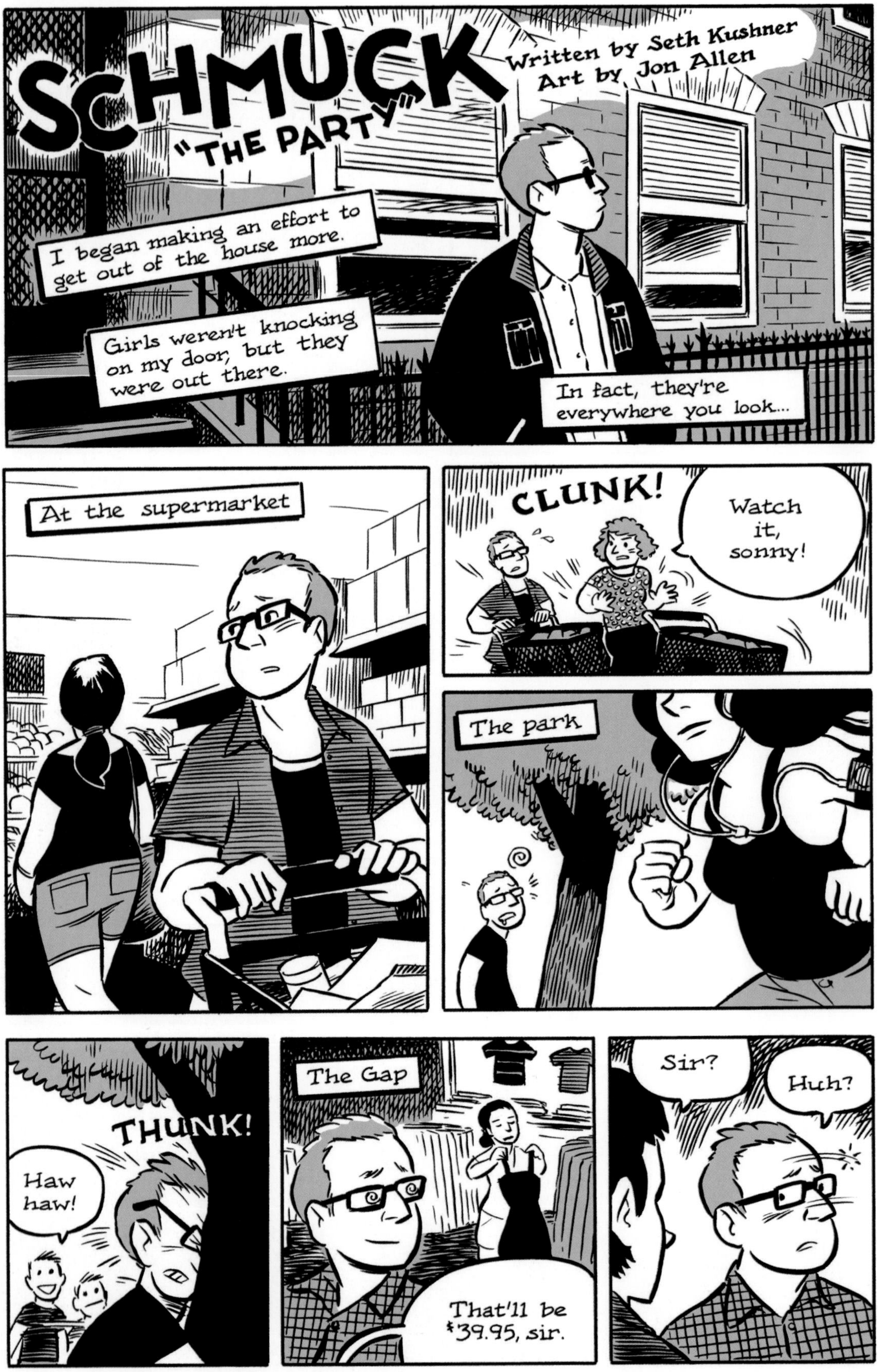

SCHMUCK
"THE PARTY"
Written by Seth Kushner
Art by Jon Allen
I began making an effort to get out of the house more.
Girls weren't knocking on my door, but they were out there.
In fact, they're everywhere you look...
At the supermarket
CLUNK!
Watch it, sonny!
The park
THUNK!
Haw haw!
The Gap
That'll be $39.95, sir.
Sir?
Huh?

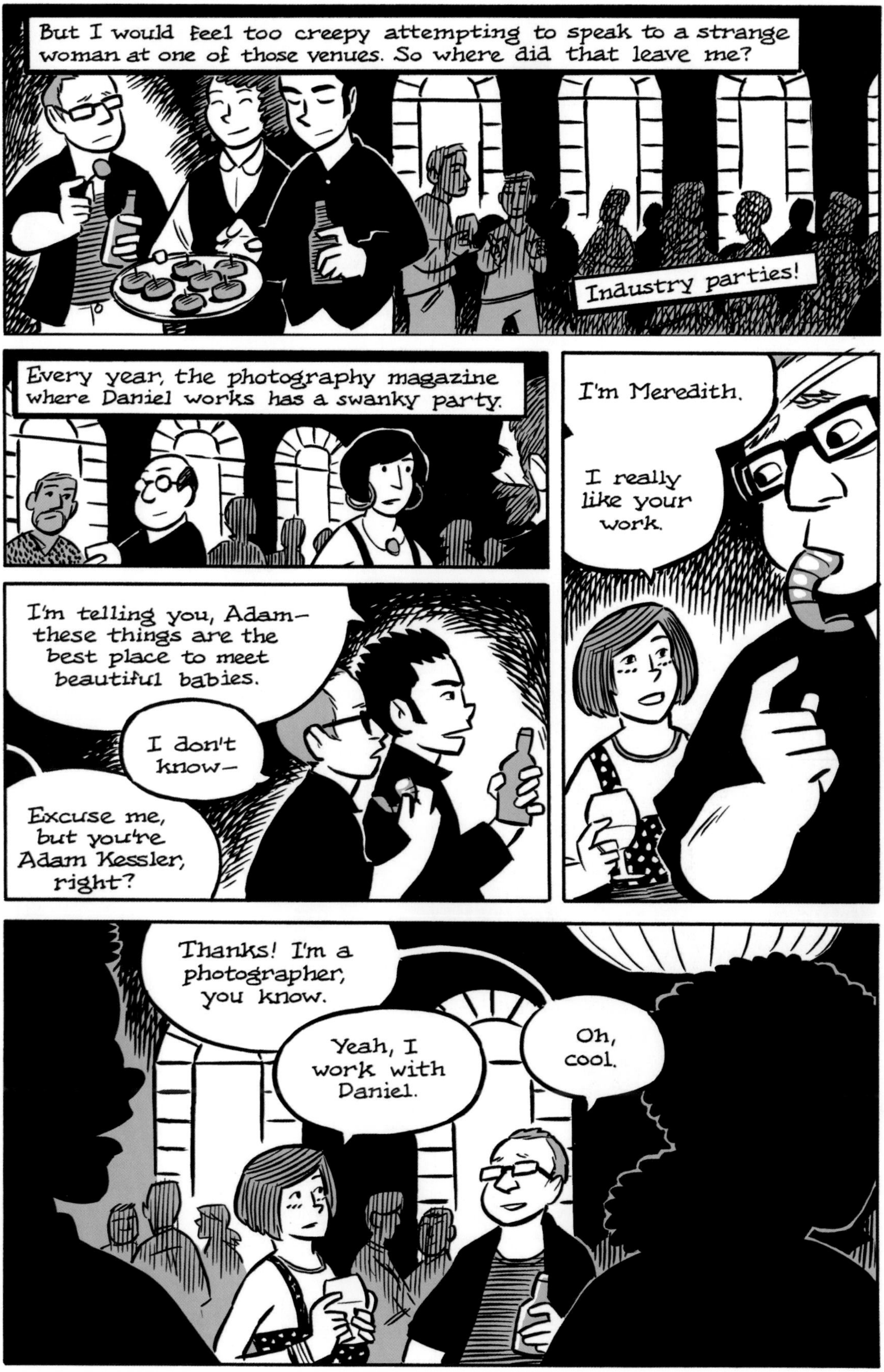

But I would feel too creepy attempting to speak to a strange woman at one of those venues. So where did that leave me?
Industry parties!
Every year, the photography magazine where Daniel works has a swanky party.
I'm telling you, Adam– these things are the best place to meet beautiful babies.
I don't know–
Excuse me, but you're Adam Kessler, right?
I'm Meredith.
I really like your work.
Thanks! I'm a photographer, you know.
Yeah, I work with Daniel.
Oh, cool.

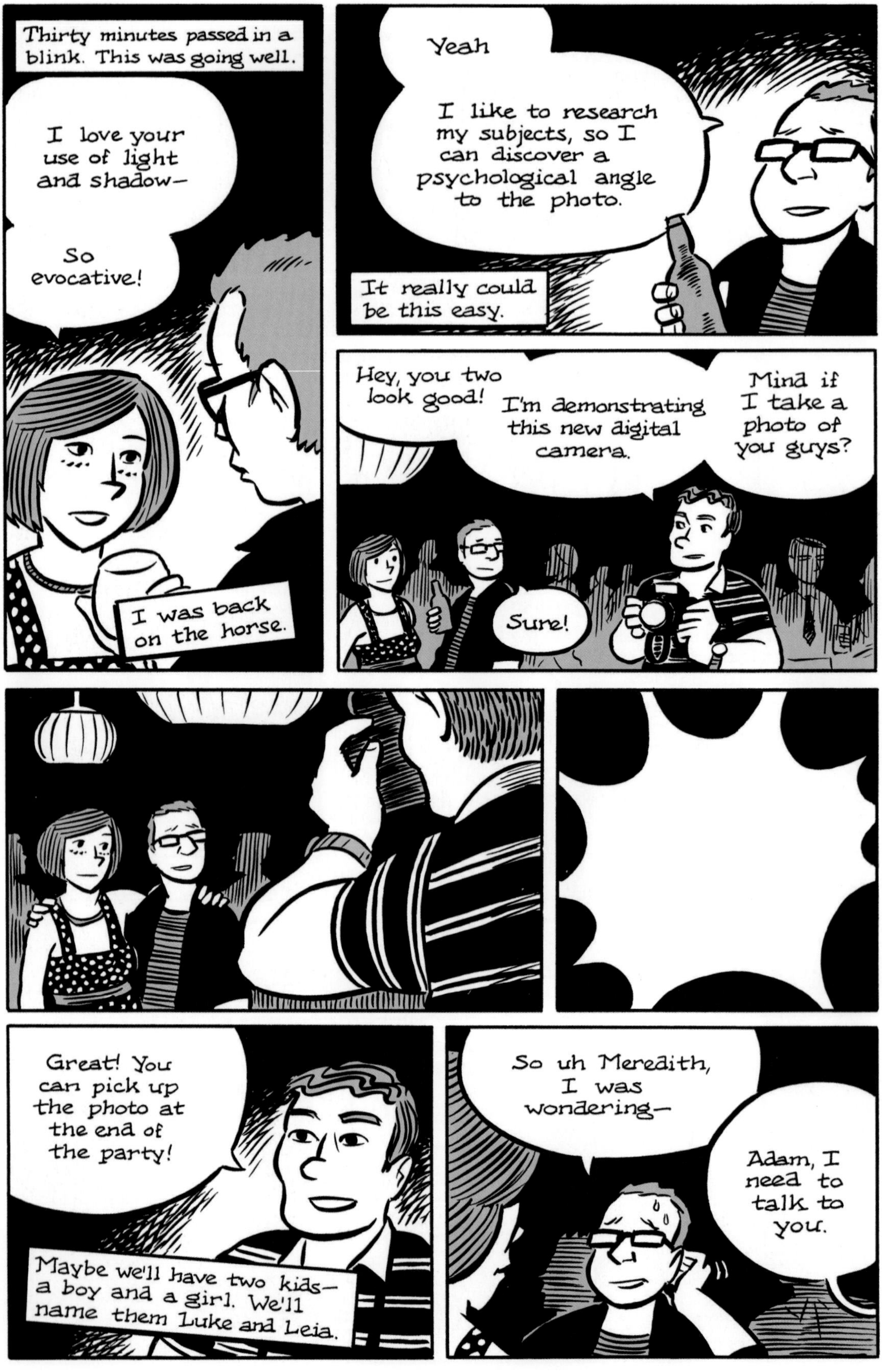
Thirty minutes passed in a blink. This was going well.
I love your use of light and shadow—
So evocative!
I was back on the horse.
Yeah
I like to research my subjects, so I can discover a psychological angle to the photo.
It really could be this easy.
Hey, you two look good!
I'm demonstrating this new digital camera.
Mind if I take a photo of you guys?
Sure!
Great! You can pick up the photo at the end of the party!
Maybe we'll have two kids—a boy and a girl. We'll name them Luke and Leia.
So uh Meredith, I was wondering—
Adam, I need to talk to you.

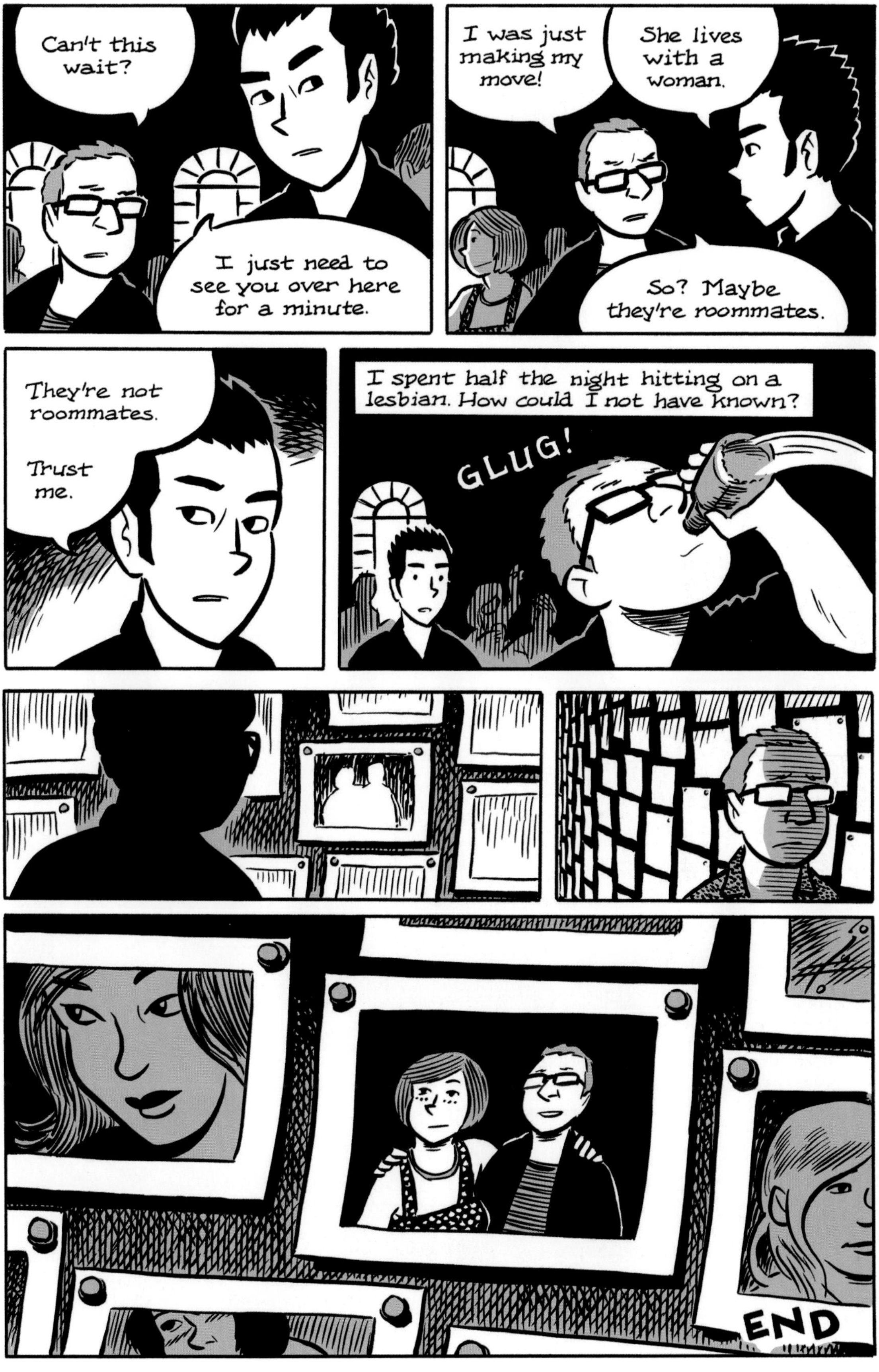
Can't this wait?
I just need to see you over here for a minute.
I was just making my move!
She lives with a woman.
So? Maybe they're roommates.
They're not roommates.
Trust me.
I spent half the night hitting on a lesbian. How could I not have known?
GLUG!
END

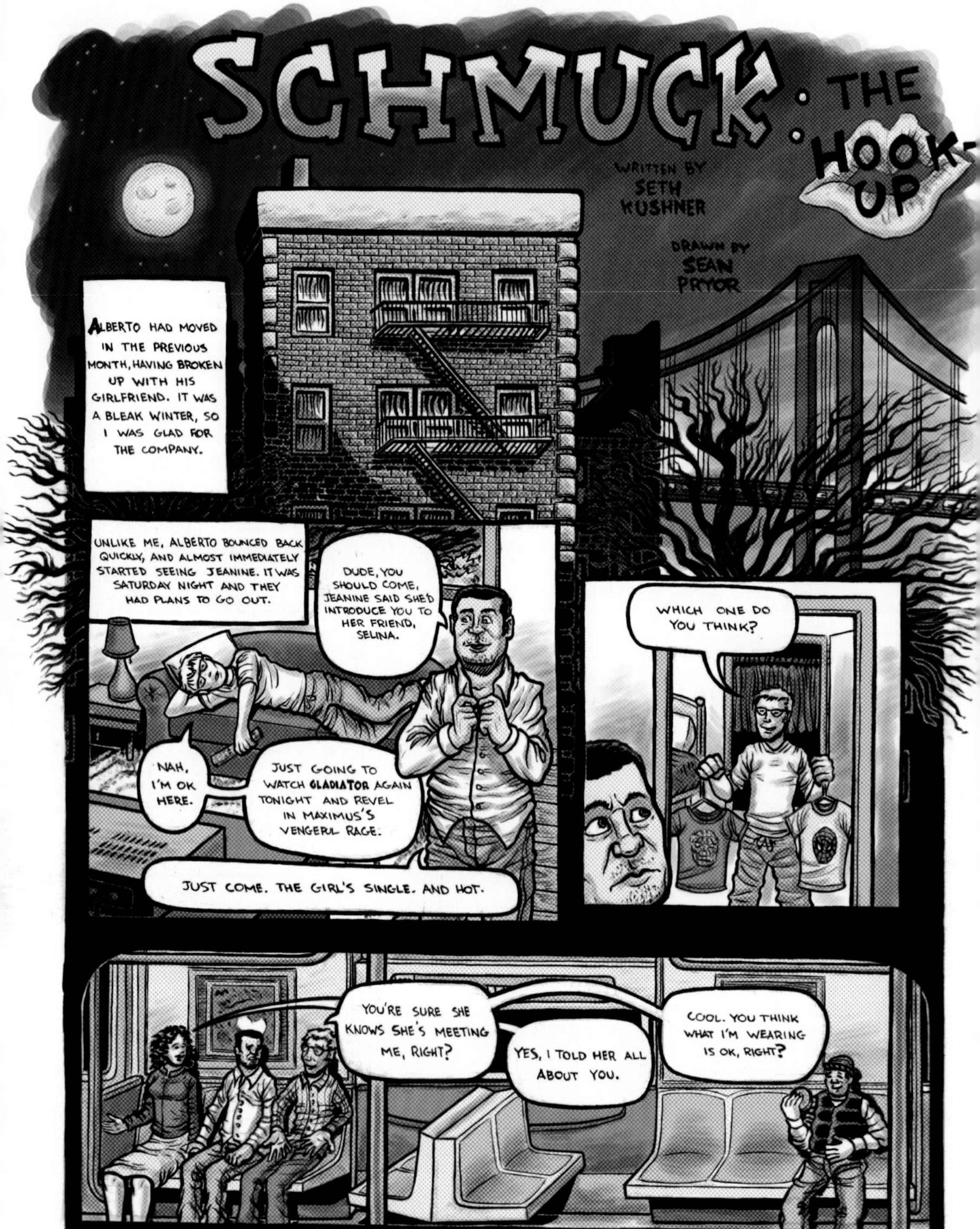
SCHMUCK: THE HOOK-UP
WRITTEN BY SETH KUSHNER
DRAWN BY SEAN PRYOR
ALBERTO HAD MOVED IN THE PREVIOUS MONTH, HAVING BROKEN UP WITH HIS GIRLFRIEND. IT WAS A BLEAK WINTER, SO I WAS GLAD FOR THE COMPANY.
UNLIKE ME, ALBERTO BOUNCED BACK QUICKLY, AND ALMOST IMMEDIATELY STARTED SEEING JEANINE. IT WAS SATURDAY NIGHT AND THEY HAD PLANS TO GO OUT.
DUDE, YOU SHOULD COME. JEANINE SAID SHE'D INTRODUCE YOU TO HER FRIEND, SELINA.
NAH, I'M OK HERE.
JUST GOING TO WATCH GLADIATOR AGAIN TONIGHT AND REVEL IN MAXIMUS'S VENGEFUL RAGE.
JUST COME. THE GIRL'S SINGLE. AND HOT.
WHICH ONE DO YOU THINK?
YOU'RE SURE SHE KNOWS SHE'S MEETING ME, RIGHT?
YES, I TOLD HER ALL ABOUT YOU.
COOL. YOU THINK WHAT I'M WEARING IS OK, RIGHT?

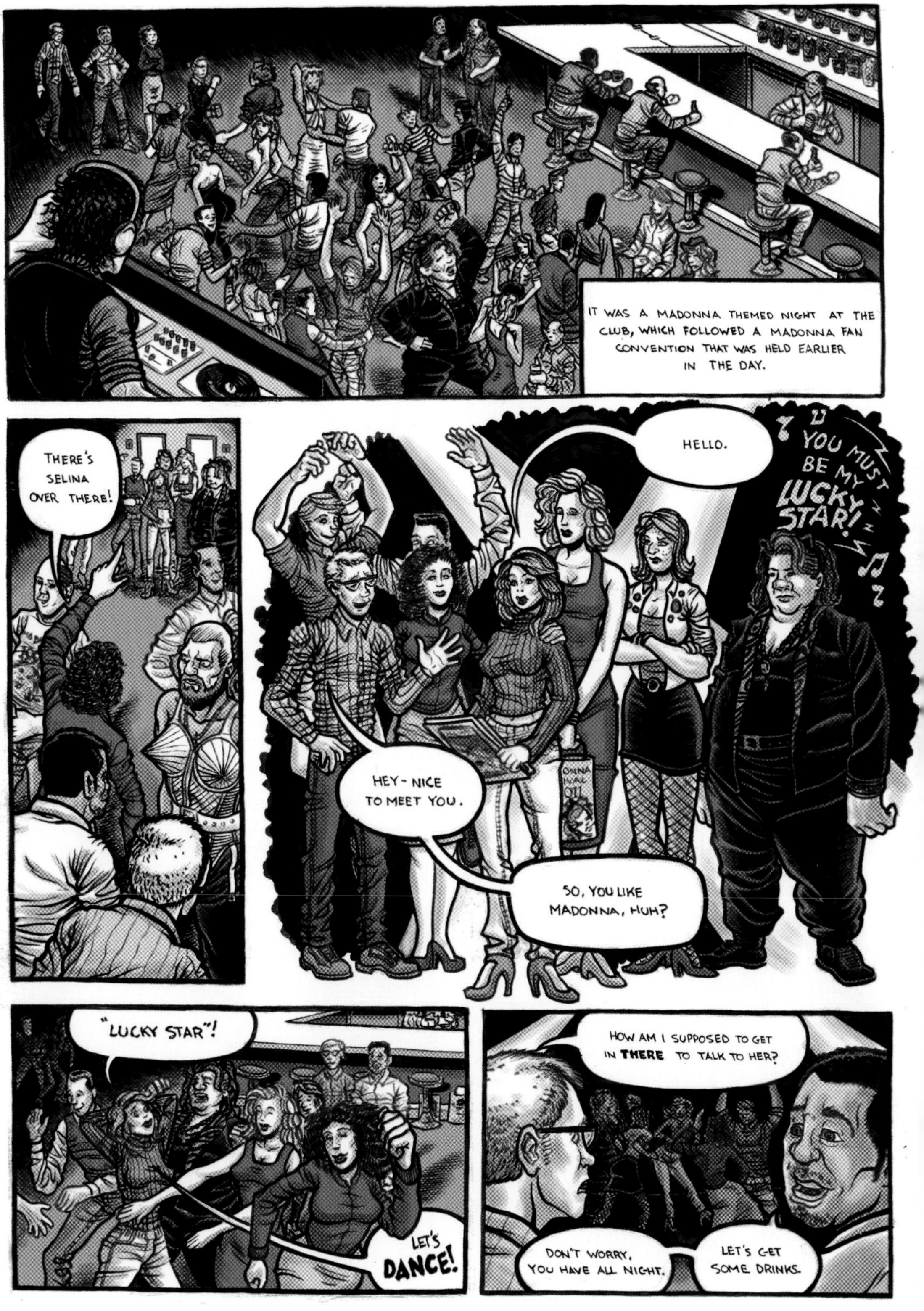

IT WAS A MADONNA THEMED NIGHT AT THE CLUB, WHICH FOLLOWED A MADONNA FAN CONVENTION THAT WAS HELD EARLIER IN THE DAY.
THERE'S SELINA OVER THERE!
HELLO.
YOU MUST BE MY LUCKY STAR!
HEY- NICE TO MEET YOU.
SO, YOU LIKE MADONNA, HUH?
"LUCKY STAR"!
LET'S DANCE!
HOW AM I SUPPOSED TO GET IN THERE TO TALK TO HER?
DON'T WORRY, YOU HAVE ALL NIGHT.
LET'S GET SOME DRINKS.

WHAT DO YOU THINK OF JEANINE'S FRIEND?

YEAH, SHE'S HOT. I'D LIKE TO GET TO KNOW HER MORE.

THE WHOLE MADONNA COMPLEX IS WIERD, BUT I GREW UP GOING TO **STAR TREK** CONVENTIONS, SO WHO AM I TO JUDGE?

BESIDES, MAYBE SHE'LL TAKE AFTER MADONNA IN THE SACK.

I'D ALWAYS HEARD STORIES ABOUT PEOPLE SNEAKING INTO CLUB BATHROOMS TO HAVE SEX. I HOPED THAT WAS IN ORDER FOR ME ON THAT NIGHT.

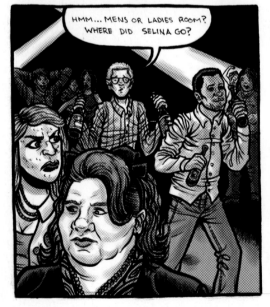

HMM... MENS OR LADIES ROOM? WHERE DID SELINA GO?

WOOSH WOOSH

48

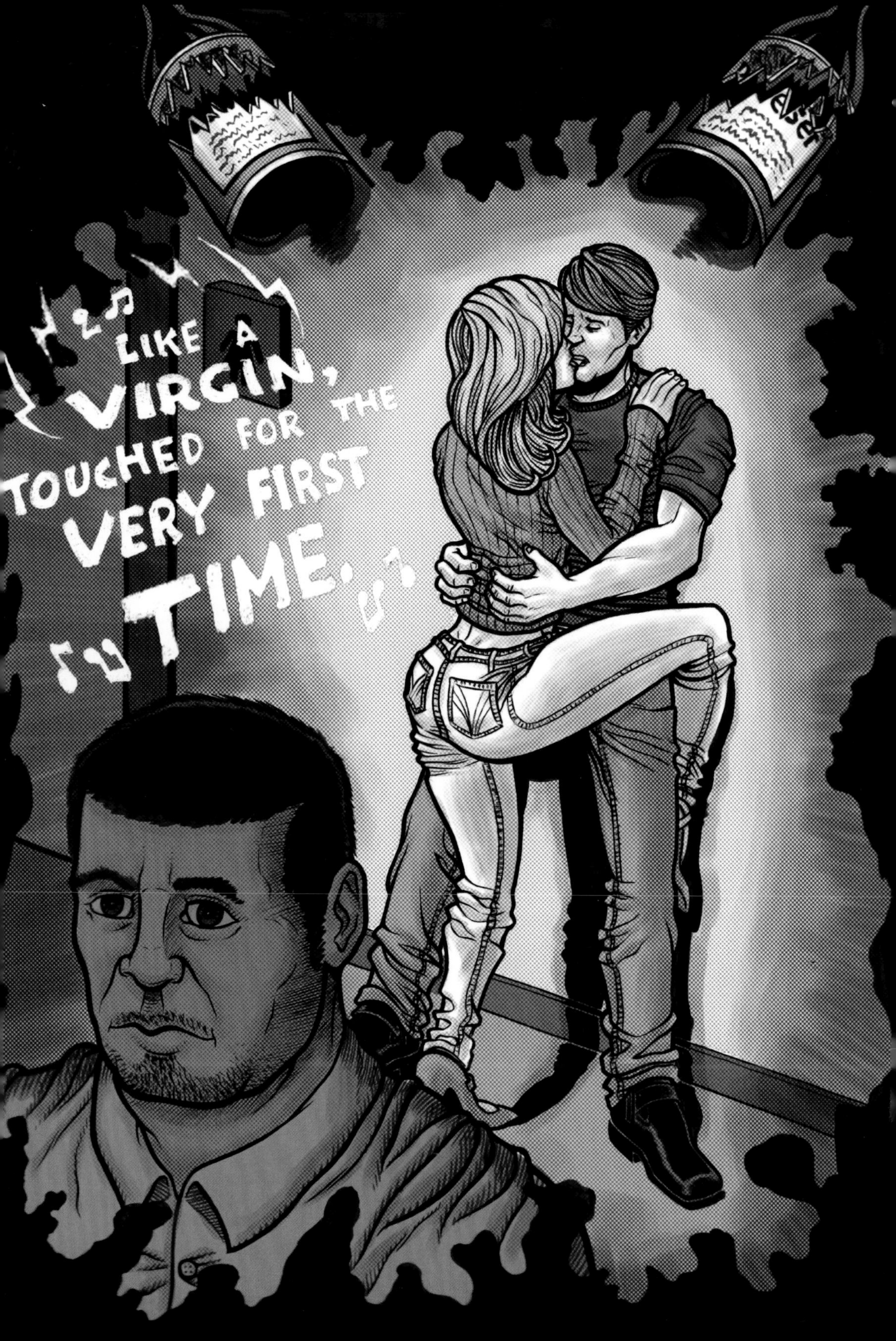
LIKE A VIRGIN, TOUCHED FOR THE VERY FIRST TIME.

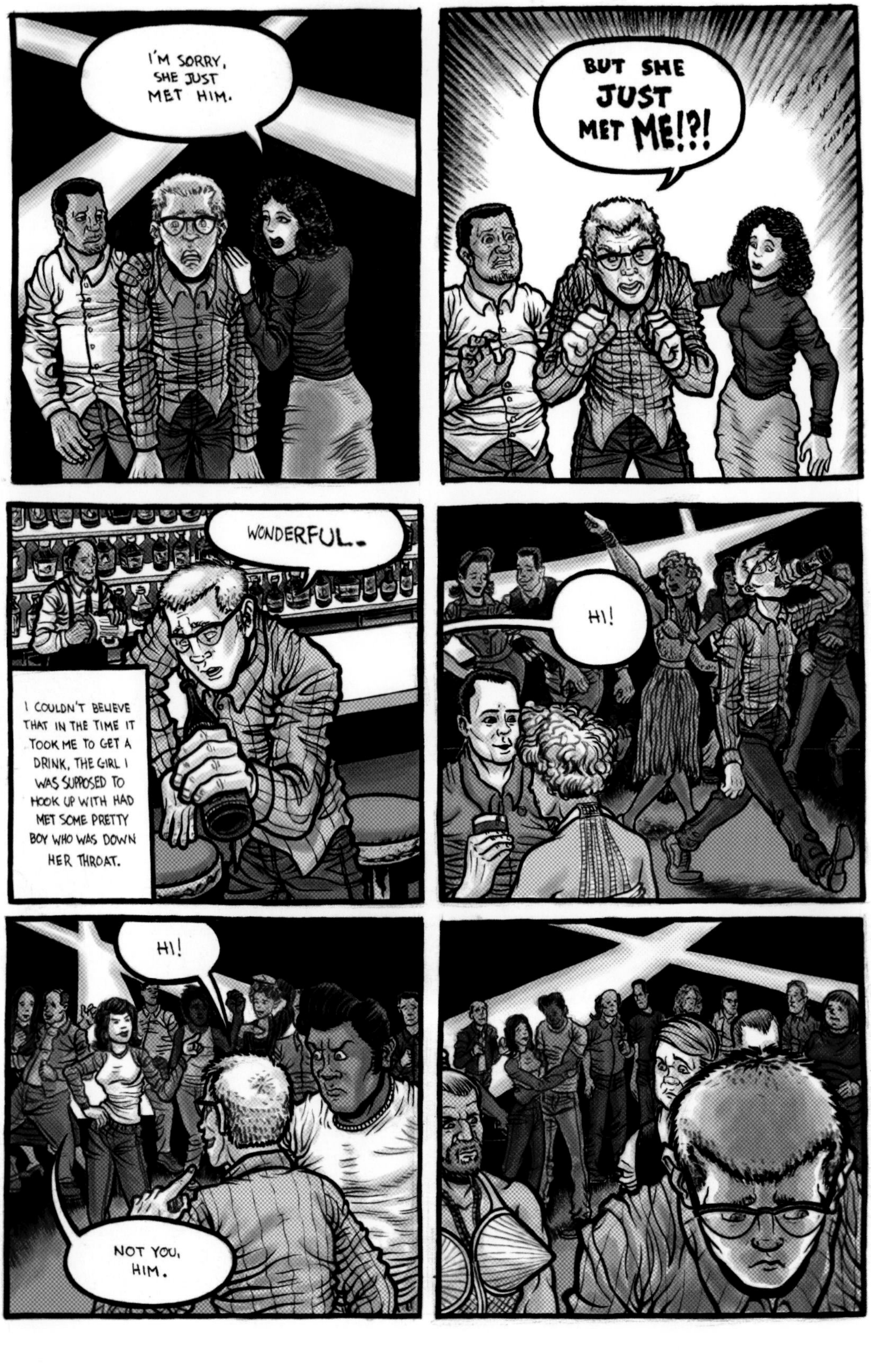
I'M SORRY, SHE JUST MET HIM.
BUT SHE JUST MET ME!?!
WONDERFUL.
I COULDN'T BELIEVE THAT IN THE TIME IT TOOK ME TO GET A DRINK, THE GIRL I WAS SUPPOSED TO HOOK UP WITH HAD MET SOME PRETTY BOY WHO WAS DOWN HER THROAT.
HI!
HI!
NOT YOU, HIM.

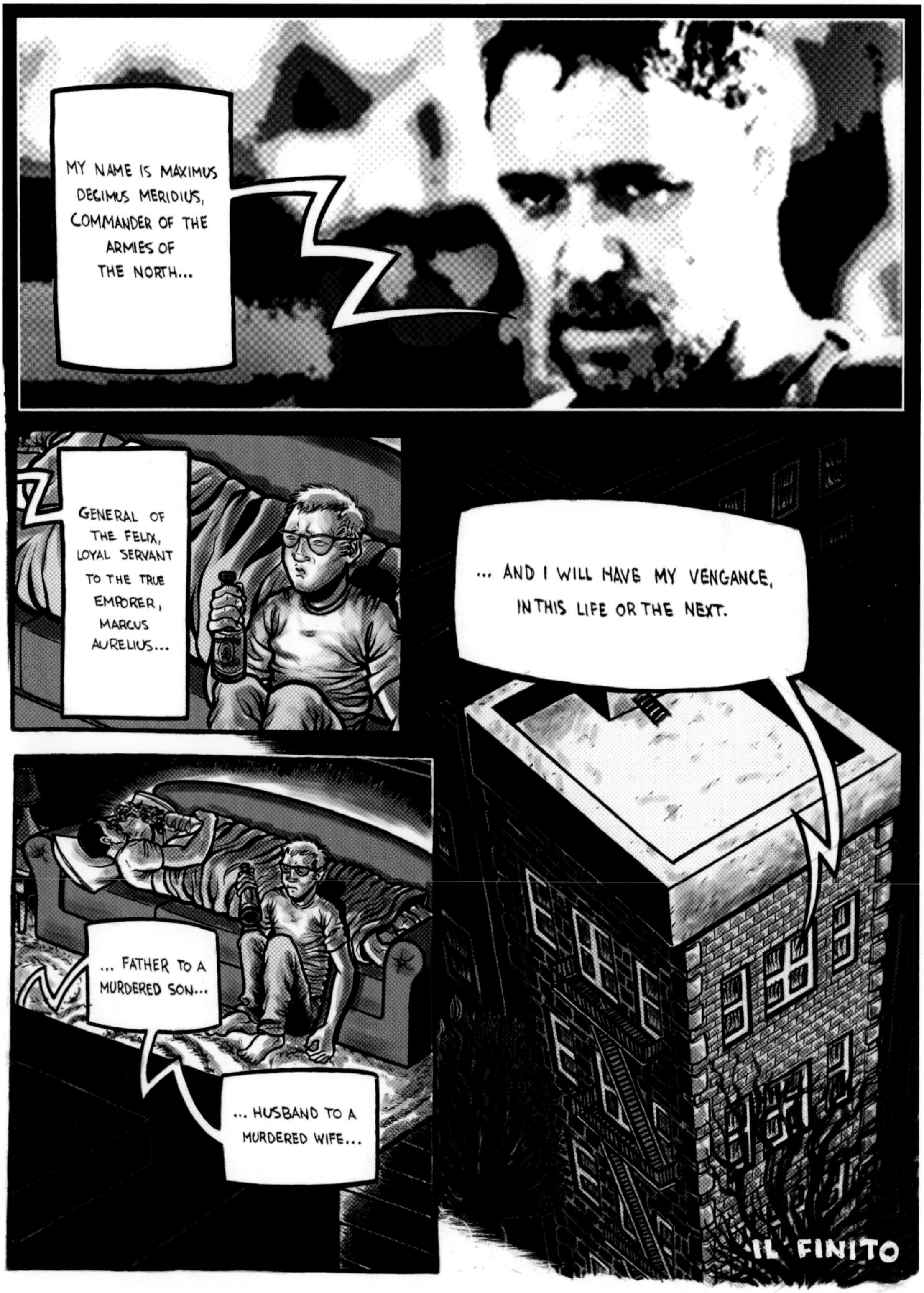
MY NAME IS MAXIMUS DECIMUS MERIDIUS, COMMANDER OF THE ARMIES OF THE NORTH...
GENERAL OF THE FELIX, LOYAL SERVANT TO THE TRUE EMPORER, MARCUS AURELIUS...
... FATHER TO A MURDERED SON...
... HUSBAND TO A MURDERED WIFE...
... AND I WILL HAVE MY VENGANCE, IN THIS LIFE OR THE NEXT.
IL FINITO

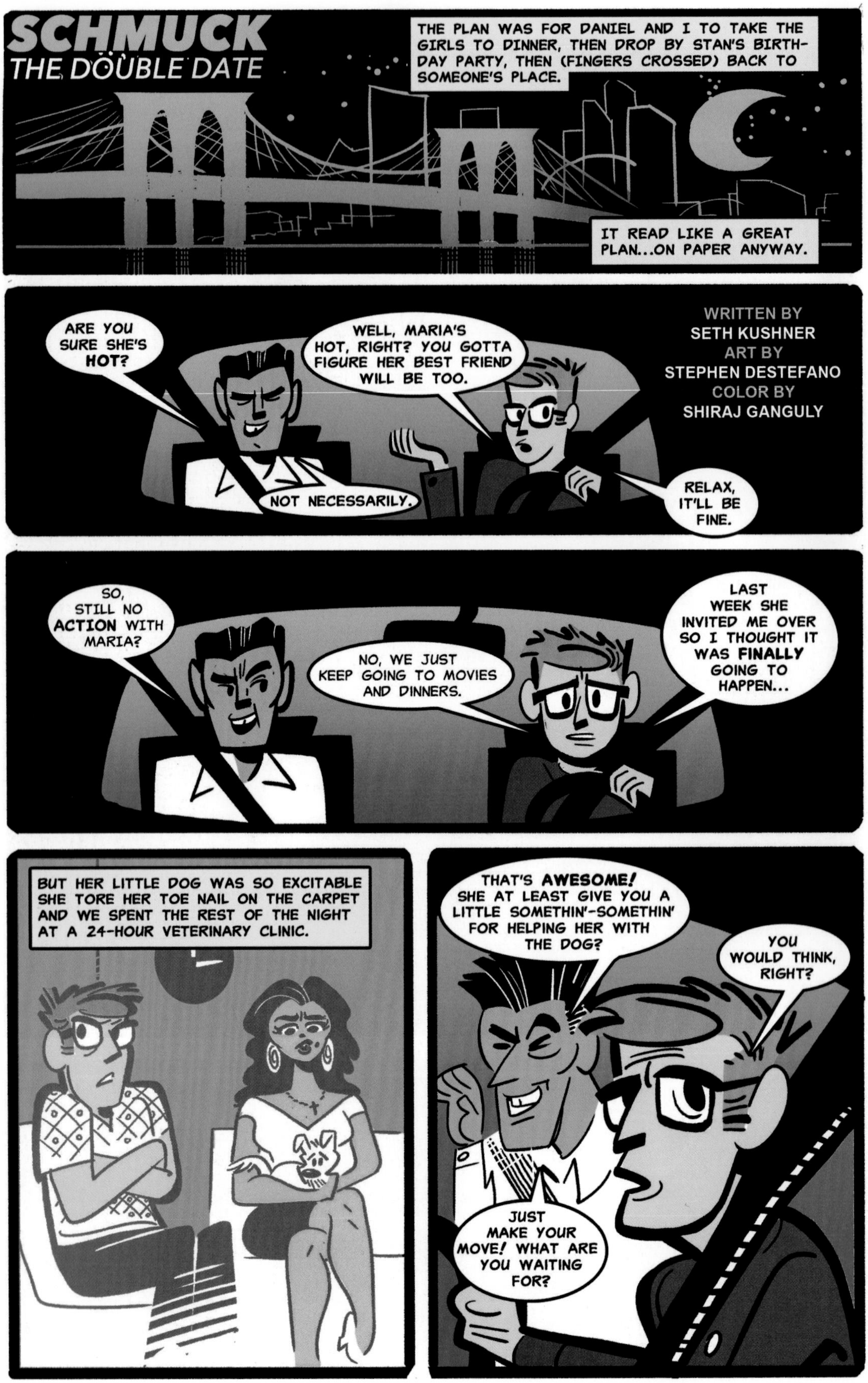
SCHMUCK
THE DOUBLE DATE
THE PLAN WAS FOR DANIEL AND I TO TAKE THE GIRLS TO DINNER, THEN DROP BY STAN'S BIRTHDAY PARTY, THEN (FINGERS CROSSED) BACK TO SOMEONE'S PLACE.
IT READ LIKE A GREAT PLAN...ON PAPER ANYWAY.
WRITTEN BY SETH KUSHNER
ART BY STEPHEN DESTEFANO
COLOR BY SHIRAJ GANGULY
ARE YOU SURE SHE'S HOT?
WELL, MARIA'S HOT, RIGHT? YOU GOTTA FIGURE HER BEST FRIEND WILL BE TOO.
NOT NECESSARILY.
RELAX, IT'LL BE FINE.
SO, STILL NO ACTION WITH MARIA?
NO, WE JUST KEEP GOING TO MOVIES AND DINNERS.
LAST WEEK SHE INVITED ME OVER SO I THOUGHT IT WAS FINALLY GOING TO HAPPEN...
BUT HER LITTLE DOG WAS SO EXCITABLE SHE TORE HER TOE NAIL ON THE CARPET AND WE SPENT THE REST OF THE NIGHT AT A 24-HOUR VETERINARY CLINIC.
THAT'S AWESOME! SHE AT LEAST GIVE YOU A LITTLE SOMETHIN'-SOMETHIN' FOR HELPING HER WITH THE DOG?
YOU WOULD THINK, RIGHT?
JUST MAKE YOUR MOVE! WHAT ARE YOU WAITING FOR?

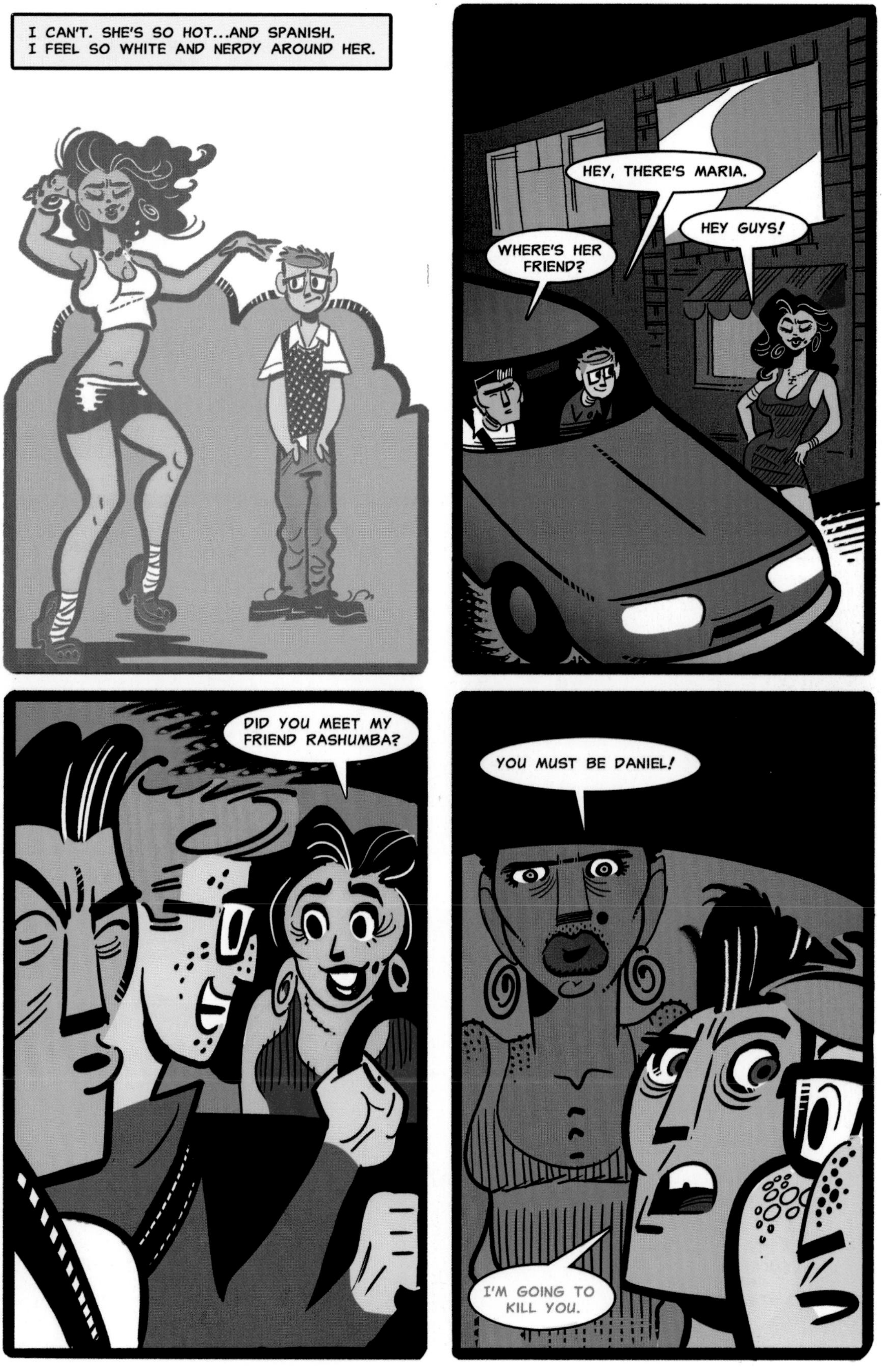

I CAN'T. SHE'S SO HOT...AND SPANISH. I FEEL SO WHITE AND NERDY AROUND HER.
HEY, THERE'S MARIA.
WHERE'S HER FRIEND?
HEY GUYS!
DID YOU MEET MY FRIEND RASHUMBA?
YOU MUST BE DANIEL!
I'M GOING TO KILL YOU.

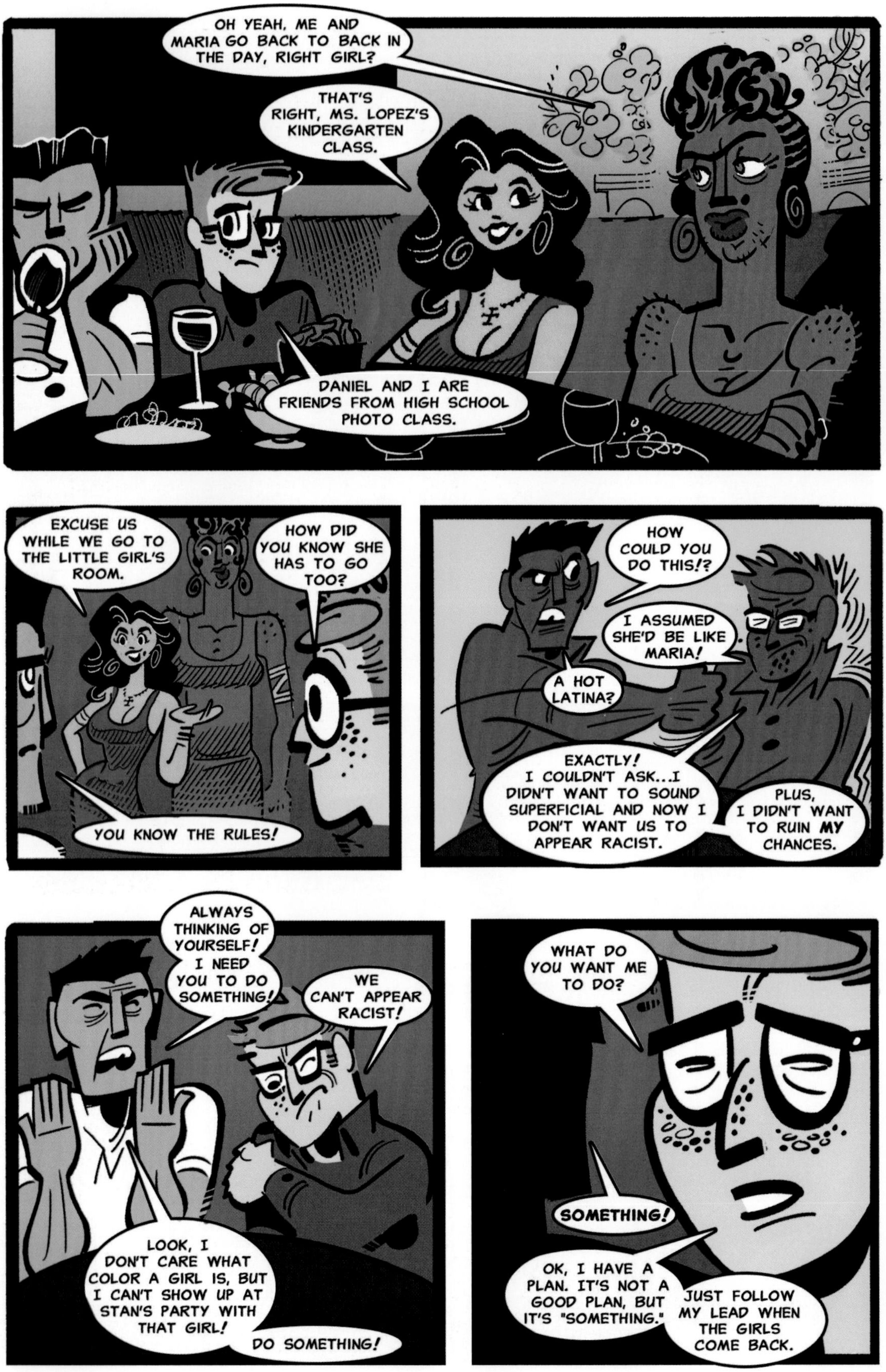
OH YEAH, ME AND MARIA GO BACK TO BACK IN THE DAY, RIGHT GIRL?
THAT'S RIGHT, MS. LOPEZ'S KINDERGARTEN CLASS.
DANIEL AND I ARE FRIENDS FROM HIGH SCHOOL PHOTO CLASS.
EXCUSE US WHILE WE GO TO THE LITTLE GIRL'S ROOM.
HOW DID YOU KNOW SHE HAS TO GO TOO?
YOU KNOW THE RULES!
HOW COULD YOU DO THIS!?
I ASSUMED SHE'D BE LIKE MARIA!
A HOT LATINA?
EXACTLY! I COULDN'T ASK...I DIDN'T WANT TO SOUND SUPERFICIAL AND NOW I DON'T WANT US TO APPEAR RACIST.
PLUS, I DIDN'T WANT TO RUIN MY CHANCES.
ALWAYS THINKING OF YOURSELF! I NEED YOU TO DO SOMETHING!
WE CAN'T APPEAR RACIST!
LOOK, I DON'T CARE WHAT COLOR A GIRL IS, BUT I CAN'T SHOW UP AT STAN'S PARTY WITH THAT GIRL!
DO SOMETHING!
WHAT DO YOU WANT ME TO DO?
SOMETHING!
OK, I HAVE A PLAN. IT'S NOT A GOOD PLAN, BUT IT'S "SOMETHING."
JUST FOLLOW MY LEAD WHEN THE GIRLS COME BACK.

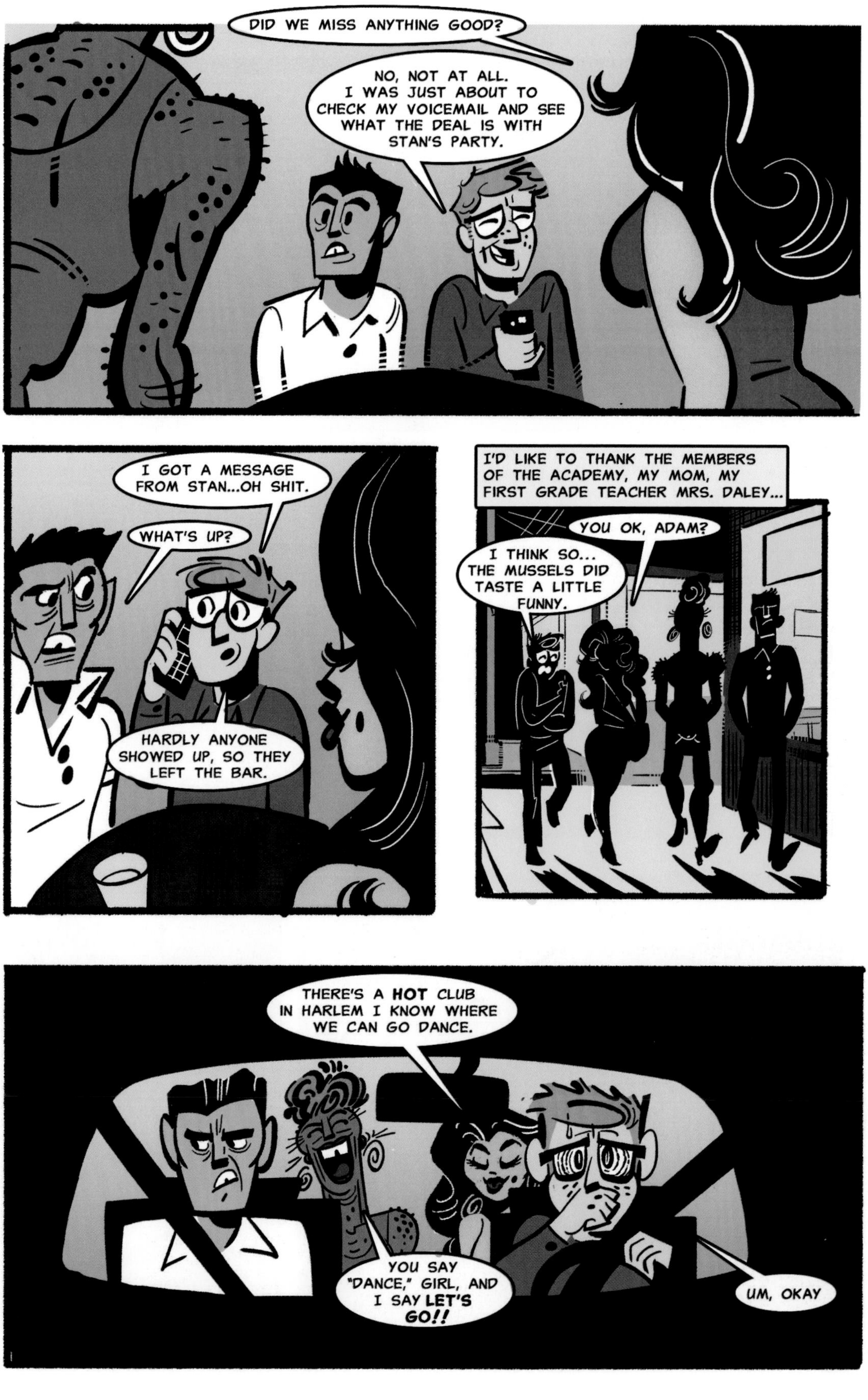
DID WE MISS ANYTHING GOOD?
NO, NOT AT ALL. I WAS JUST ABOUT TO CHECK MY VOICEMAIL AND SEE WHAT THE DEAL IS WITH STAN'S PARTY.
I GOT A MESSAGE FROM STAN...OH SHIT.
WHAT'S UP?
HARDLY ANYONE SHOWED UP, SO THEY LEFT THE BAR.
I'D LIKE TO THANK THE MEMBERS OF THE ACADEMY, MY MOM, MY FIRST GRADE TEACHER MRS. DALEY...
YOU OK, ADAM?
I THINK SO... THE MUSSELS DID TASTE A LITTLE FUNNY.
THERE'S A HOT CLUB IN HARLEM I KNOW WHERE WE CAN GO DANCE.
YOU SAY "DANCE," GIRL, AND I SAY LET'S GO!!
UM, OKAY

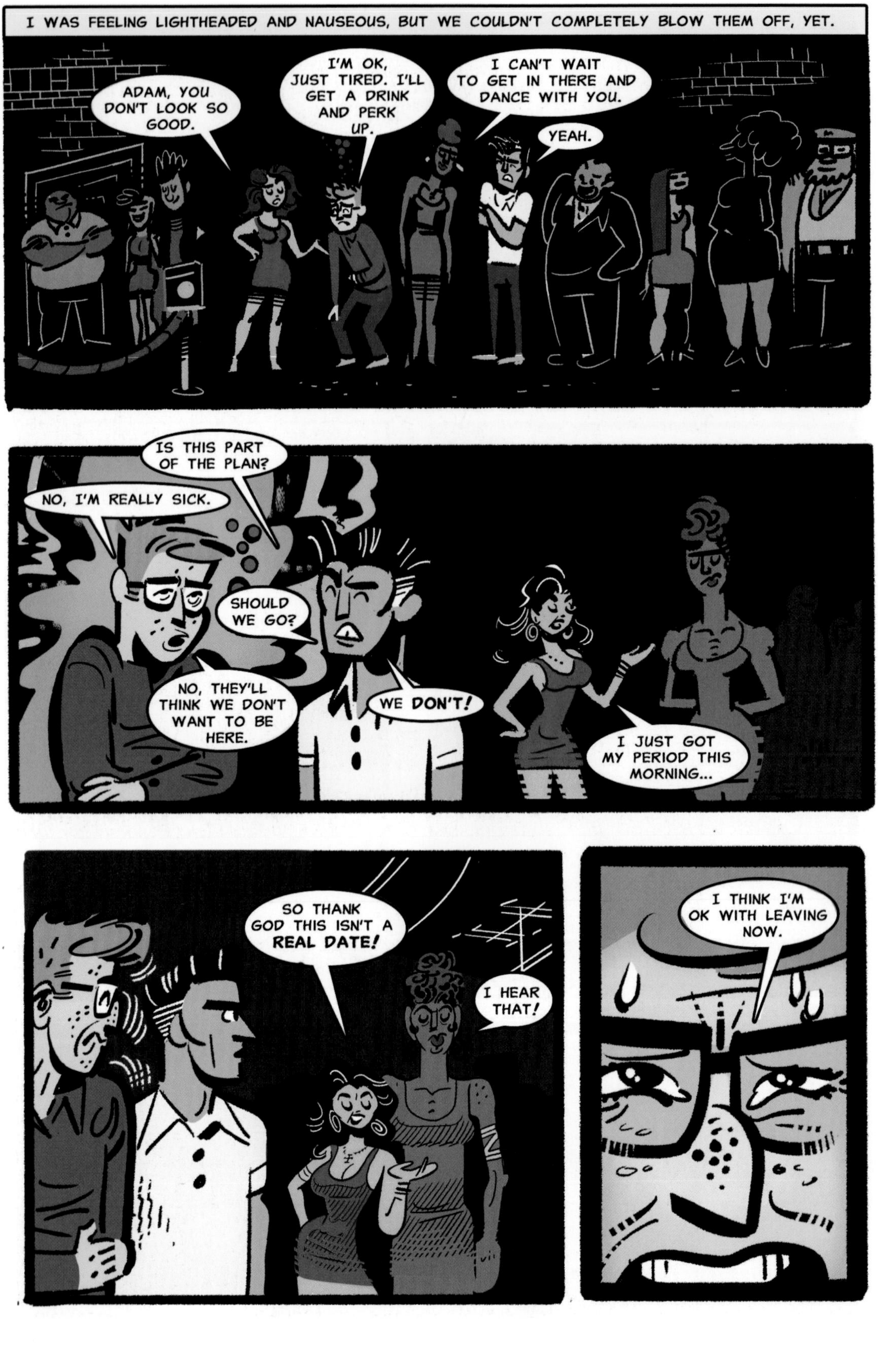
I WAS FEELING LIGHTHEADED AND NAUSEOUS, BUT WE COULDN'T COMPLETELY BLOW THEM OFF, YET.
ADAM, YOU DON'T LOOK SO GOOD.
I'M OK, JUST TIRED. I'LL GET A DRINK AND PERK UP.
I CAN'T WAIT TO GET IN THERE AND DANCE WITH YOU.
YEAH.
IS THIS PART OF THE PLAN?
NO, I'M REALLY SICK.
SHOULD WE GO?
NO, THEY'LL THINK WE DON'T WANT TO BE HERE.
WE DON'T!
I JUST GOT MY PERIOD THIS MORNING...
SO THANK GOD THIS ISN'T A REAL DATE!
I HEAR THAT!
I THINK I'M OK WITH LEAVING NOW.

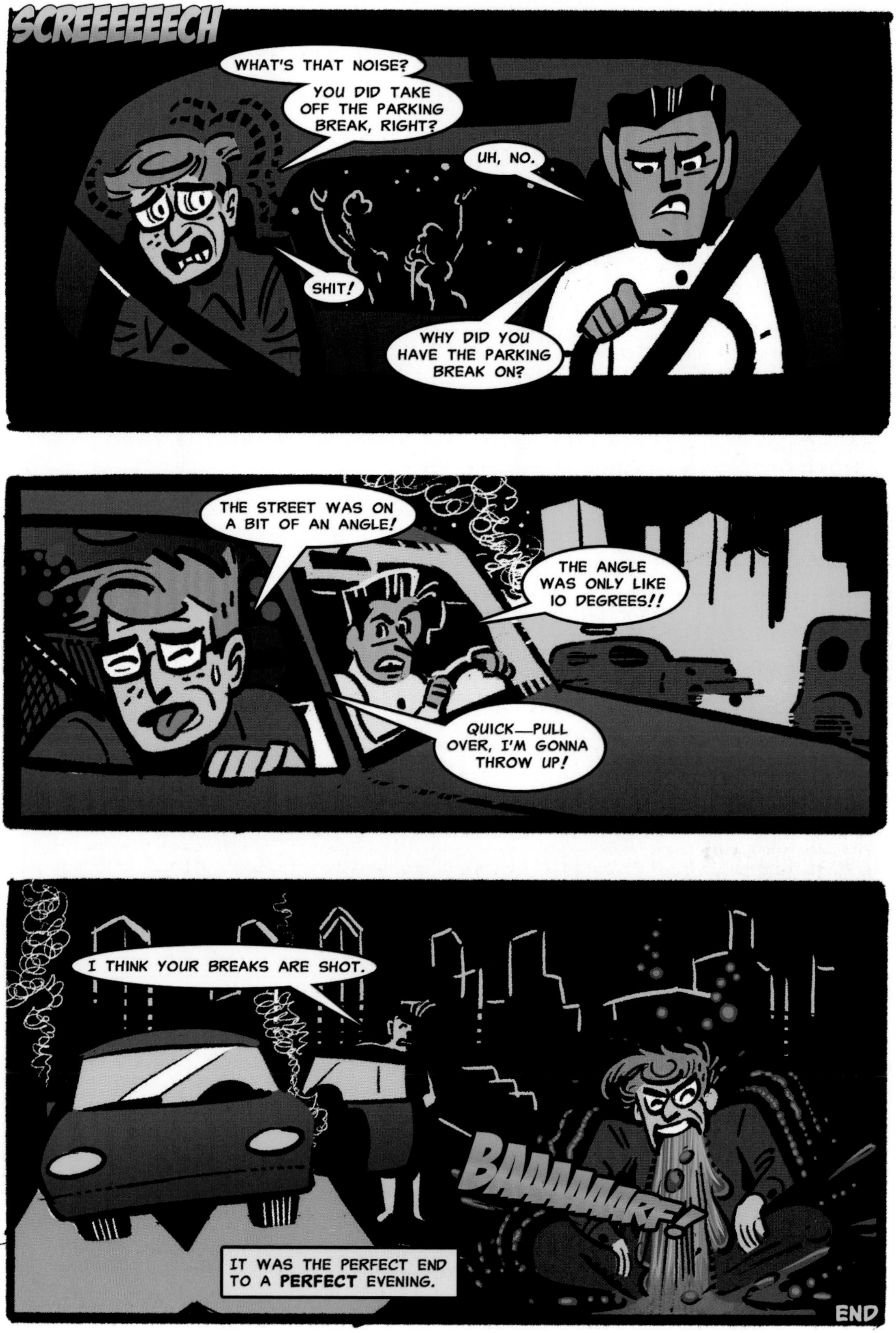
SCREEEEEEECH
WHAT'S THAT NOISE?
YOU DID TAKE OFF THE PARKING BREAK, RIGHT?
UH, NO.
SHIT!
WHY DID YOU HAVE THE PARKING BREAK ON?
THE STREET WAS ON A BIT OF AN ANGLE!
THE ANGLE WAS ONLY LIKE 10 DEGREES!!
QUICK—PULL OVER, I'M GONNA THROW UP!
I THINK YOUR BREAKS ARE SHOT.
BAAAAAAARF!
IT WAS THE PERFECT END TO A PERFECT EVENING.
END

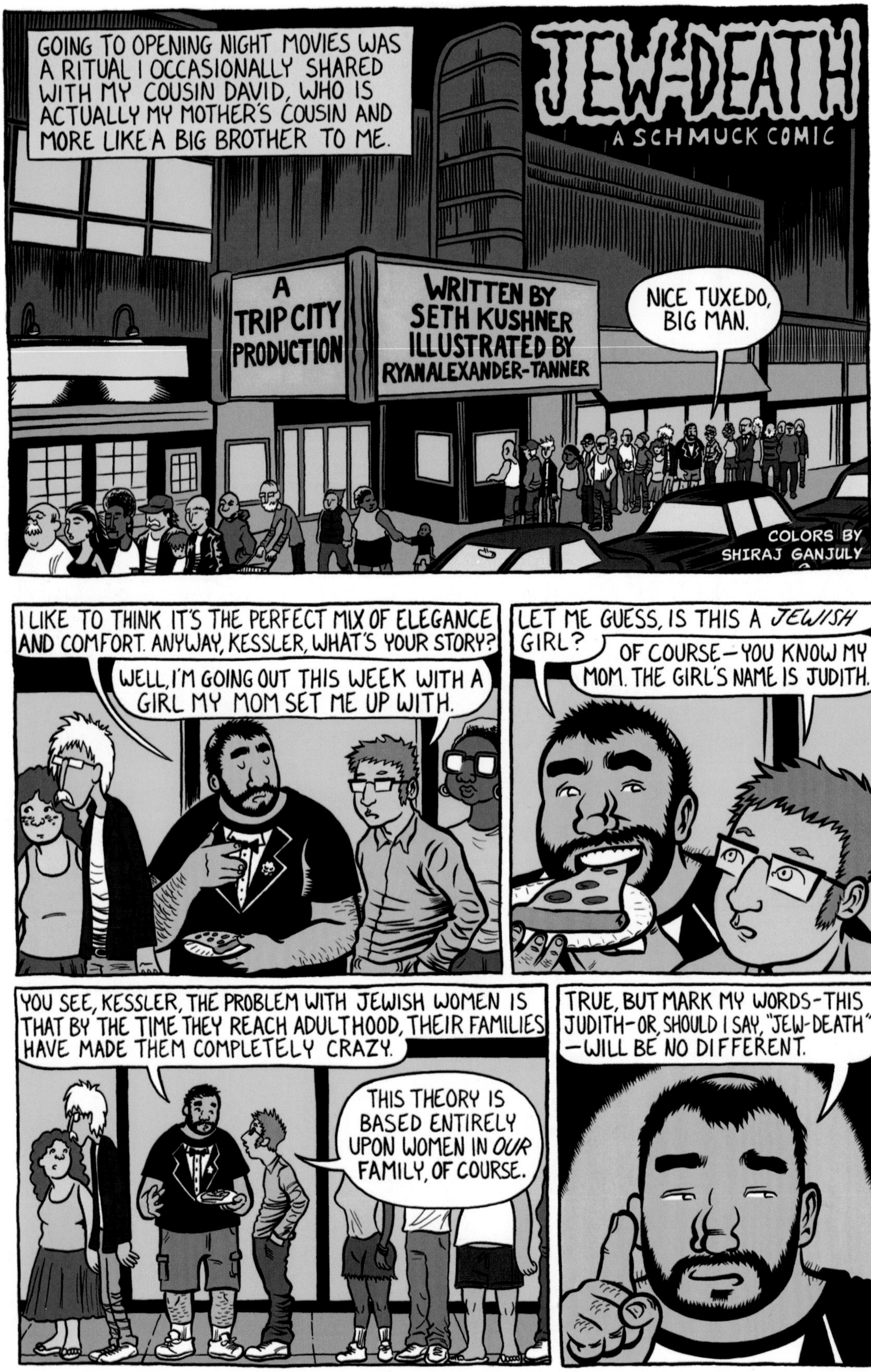

JEW-DEATH
A SCHMUCK COMIC
GOING TO OPENING NIGHT MOVIES WAS A RITUAL I OCCASIONALLY SHARED WITH MY COUSIN DAVID, WHO IS ACTUALLY MY MOTHER'S COUSIN AND MORE LIKE A BIG BROTHER TO ME.
A TRIP CITY PRODUCTION
WRITTEN BY SETH KUSHNER ILLUSTRATED BY RYAN ALEXANDER-TANNER
NICE TUXEDO, BIG MAN.
COLORS BY SHIRAJ GANJULY
I LIKE TO THINK IT'S THE PERFECT MIX OF ELEGANCE AND COMFORT. ANYWAY, KESSLER, WHAT'S YOUR STORY?
WELL, I'M GOING OUT THIS WEEK WITH A GIRL MY MOM SET ME UP WITH.
LET ME GUESS, IS THIS A *JEWISH* GIRL?
OF COURSE—YOU KNOW MY MOM. THE GIRL'S NAME IS JUDITH.
YOU SEE, KESSLER, THE PROBLEM WITH JEWISH WOMEN IS THAT BY THE TIME THEY REACH ADULTHOOD, THEIR FAMILIES HAVE MADE THEM COMPLETELY CRAZY.
THIS THEORY IS BASED ENTIRELY UPON WOMEN IN *OUR* FAMILY, OF COURSE.
TRUE, BUT MARK MY WORDS-THIS JUDITH-OR, SHOULD I SAY, "JEW-DEATH" —WILL BE NO DIFFERENT.

I COULDN'T COMPLETELY DISAGREE WITH MY SINGLE, NEVER-MARRIED OLDER COUSIN. REGARDLESS OF HIS WORDS OF WARNING, I OWED IT TO MYSELF TO GIVE "JEW-DEATH" A SHOT.

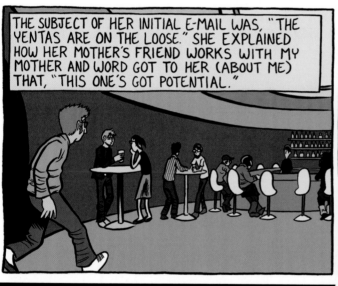

THE SUBJECT OF HER INITIAL E-MAIL WAS, "THE YENTAS ARE ON THE LOOSE." SHE EXPLAINED HOW HER MOTHER'S FRIEND WORKS WITH MY MOTHER AND WORD GOT TO HER (ABOUT ME) THAT, "THIS ONE'S GOT POTENTIAL."

HI, I'M JUDITH. WELCOME TO THE SPACE STATION.

HI. SORRY I'M LATE. TRAFFIC WAS CRAWLING BY ALPHA CENTURI.

SHE WAS WHAT I LIKE TO CALL A "DOT-ORG." AN INTELLIGENT, WELL-EDUCATED YOUNG LADY WHO WORKED FOR A NON-PROFIT ORGANIZATION, LISTENED TO LOTS OF NPR AND EITHER OWNED A VERY SMALL TV, OR NO TV AT ALL. THIS CITY IS FILLED WITH THEM.

IT'S WARM IN HERE, HUH?

ANYWAY, AS I WAS SAYING...

MY ROOMMATE LEFT WITH ZERO NOTICE, BUT SHE LEFT ALL OF HER STUFF...

...AND I HAD NO IDEA WHAT TO DO WITH IT ALL, SO...

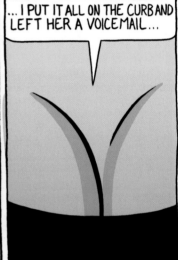

...I PUT IT ALL ON THE CURB AND LEFT HER A VOICEMAIL...

EYES UP, SCHMUCK... SHE'S GOING TO CATCH YOU LEERING.

HI.

SORRY.

SHE WAS COOL ABOUT CATCHING ME, BUT I FELT BADLY WHEN SHE TOLD ME SHE HEARD MY MOTHER SAID I ONLY LIKE TALL, THIN GIRLS. MAYBE THAT MADE HER FEEL SELF-CONSCIOUS AND WAS THE REASON FOR THE CLEAVAGE. BUT, THAT'S JUST CONJECTURE FROM A SCHMUCK.

IT WAS NICE MEETING YOU.

YEAH, YOU TOO. LET'S DO THIS AGAIN.

SURE, I'VE ALWAYS BEEN ATTRACTED TO THIN GIRLS, BUT "TALL" WAS NEVER A PREREQUISITE. I AM OF COURSE AWARE OF HOW SUPERFICIAL I SOUND. I CHOOSE TO BLAME SOCIETY AND THE MEDIA.

I WAS NERVOUS TO ASK HER OUT AGAIN, BUT THE WEEKEND WAS COMING AND I HAD NO PLANS. PLUS, I REALLY WANTED TO SEE THOSE BREASTS AGAIN!

HEY JUDITH,
    I HAD A GREAT TIME WITH YOU THE OTHER NIGHT. I KNOW THE ODDS OF A COOL GIRL LIKE YOU BEING AVAILABLE ON A SATURDAY, ONLY TWO DAYS AWAY, ARE VIRTUALLY NIL, BUT PERHAPS YOUR PLANS HAVE FALLEN THROUGH AND YOU MIGHT WANT TO HAVE SOME DINNER?
                                        ADAM

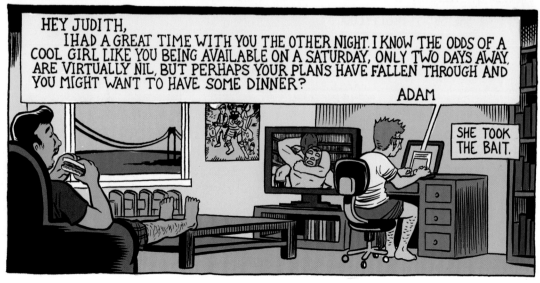

SHE TOOK THE BAIT.

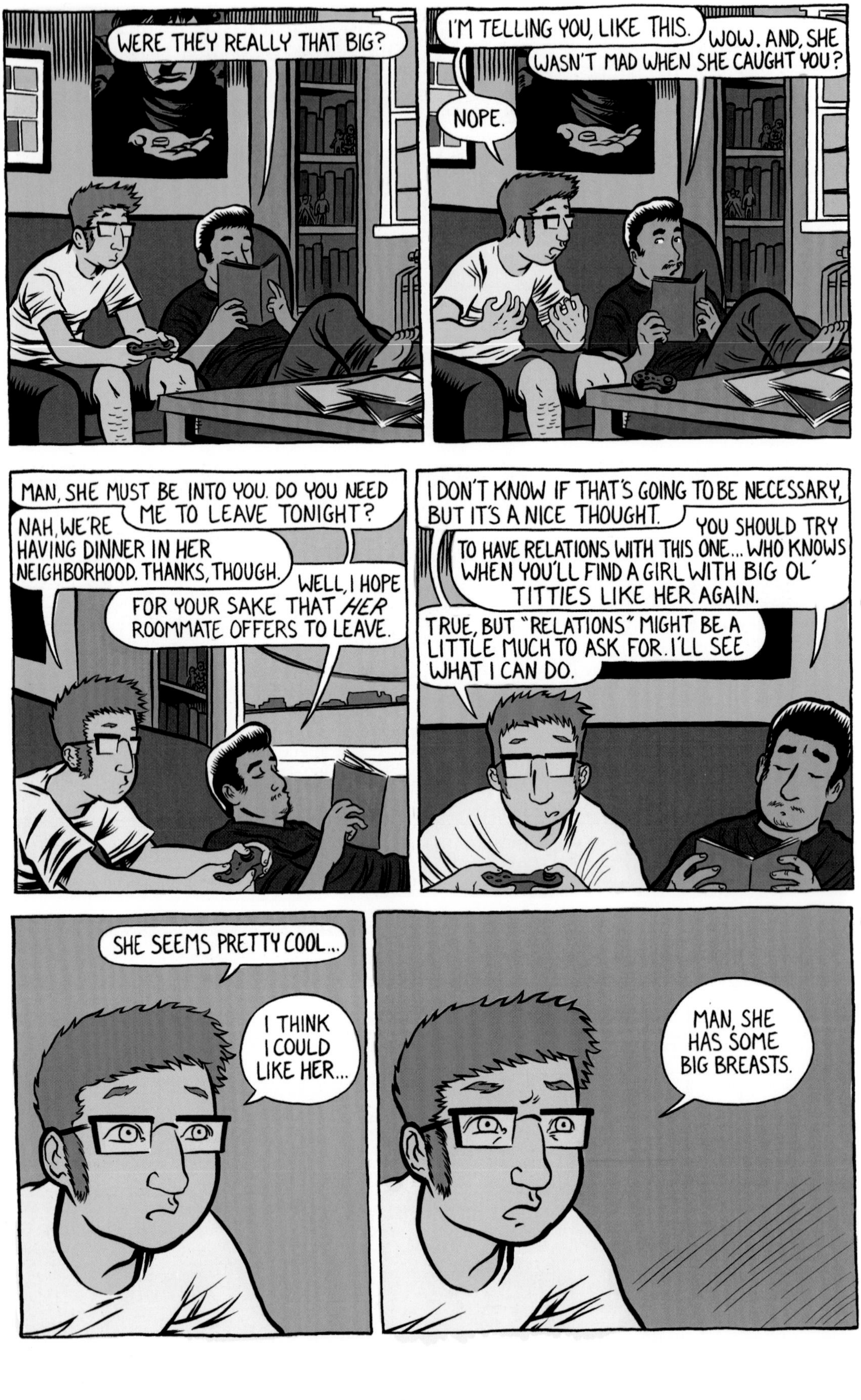
WERE THEY REALLY THAT BIG?
I'M TELLING YOU, LIKE THIS.
WOW. AND, SHE WASN'T MAD WHEN SHE CAUGHT YOU?
NOPE.
MAN, SHE MUST BE INTO YOU. DO YOU NEED ME TO LEAVE TONIGHT?
NAH, WE'RE HAVING DINNER IN HER NEIGHBORHOOD. THANKS, THOUGH.
WELL, I HOPE FOR YOUR SAKE THAT *HER* ROOMMATE OFFERS TO LEAVE.
I DON'T KNOW IF THAT'S GOING TO BE NECESSARY, BUT IT'S A NICE THOUGHT.
YOU SHOULD TRY TO HAVE RELATIONS WITH THIS ONE... WHO KNOWS WHEN YOU'LL FIND A GIRL WITH BIG OL' TITTIES LIKE HER AGAIN.
TRUE, BUT "RELATIONS" MIGHT BE A LITTLE MUCH TO ASK FOR. I'LL SEE WHAT I CAN DO.
SHE SEEMS PRETTY COOL...
I THINK I COULD LIKE HER...
MAN, SHE HAS SOME BIG BREASTS.

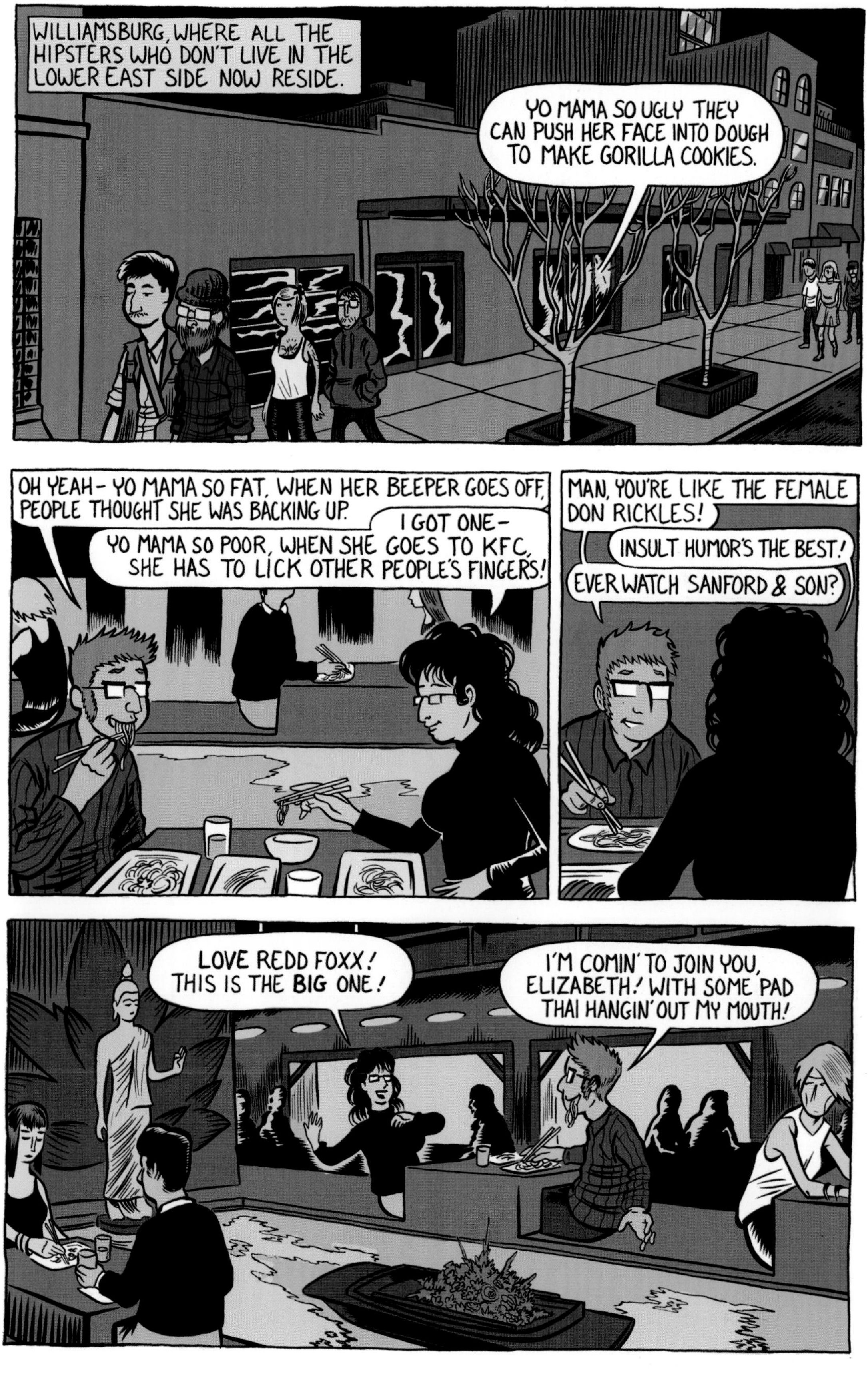
WILLIAMSBURG, WHERE ALL THE HIPSTERS WHO DON'T LIVE IN THE LOWER EAST SIDE NOW RESIDE.
YO MAMA SO UGLY THEY CAN PUSH HER FACE INTO DOUGH TO MAKE GORILLA COOKIES.
OH YEAH– YO MAMA SO FAT, WHEN HER BEEPER GOES OFF, PEOPLE THOUGHT SHE WAS BACKING UP.
I GOT ONE– YO MAMA SO POOR, WHEN SHE GOES TO KFC, SHE HAS TO LICK OTHER PEOPLE'S FINGERS!
MAN, YOU'RE LIKE THE FEMALE DON RICKLES!
INSULT HUMOR'S THE BEST!
EVER WATCH SANFORD & SON?
LOVE REDD FOXX! THIS IS THE **BIG** ONE!
I'M COMIN' TO JOIN YOU, ELIZABETH! WITH SOME PAD THAI HANGIN' OUT MY MOUTH!

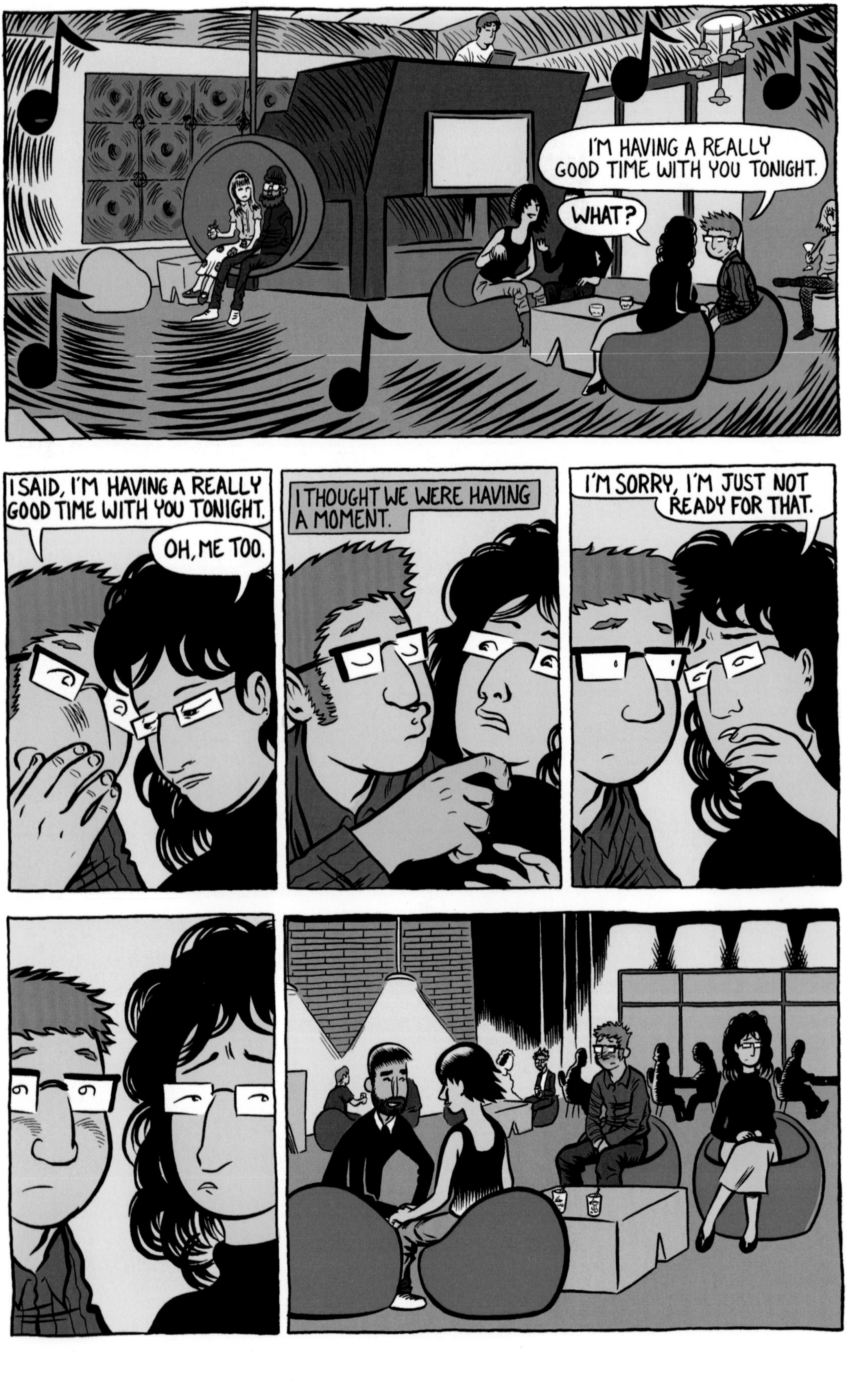

I'M HAVING A REALLY GOOD TIME WITH YOU TONIGHT.
WHAT?
I SAID, I'M HAVING A REALLY GOOD TIME WITH YOU TONIGHT.
OH, ME TOO.
I THOUGHT WE WERE HAVING A MOMENT.
I'M SORRY, I'M JUST NOT READY FOR THAT.

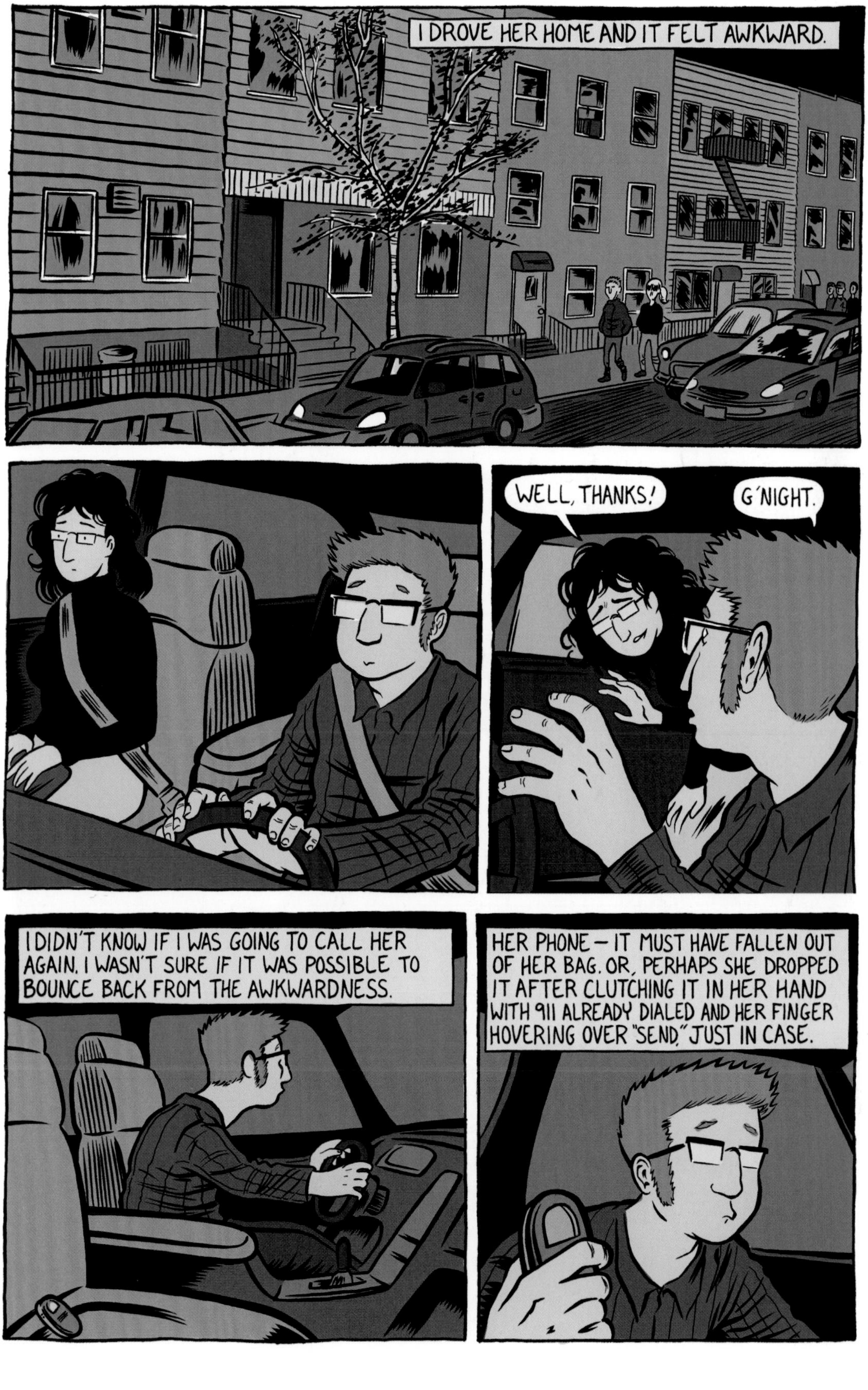
I DROVE HER HOME AND IT FELT AWKWARD.
WELL, THANKS!
G'NIGHT.
I DIDN'T KNOW IF I WAS GOING TO CALL HER AGAIN. I WASN'T SURE IF IT WAS POSSIBLE TO BOUNCE BACK FROM THE AWKWARDNESS.
HER PHONE — IT MUST HAVE FALLEN OUT OF HER BAG. OR, PERHAPS SHE DROPPED IT AFTER CLUTCHING IT IN HER HAND WITH 911 ALREADY DIALED AND HER FINGER HOVERING OVER "SEND," JUST IN CASE.

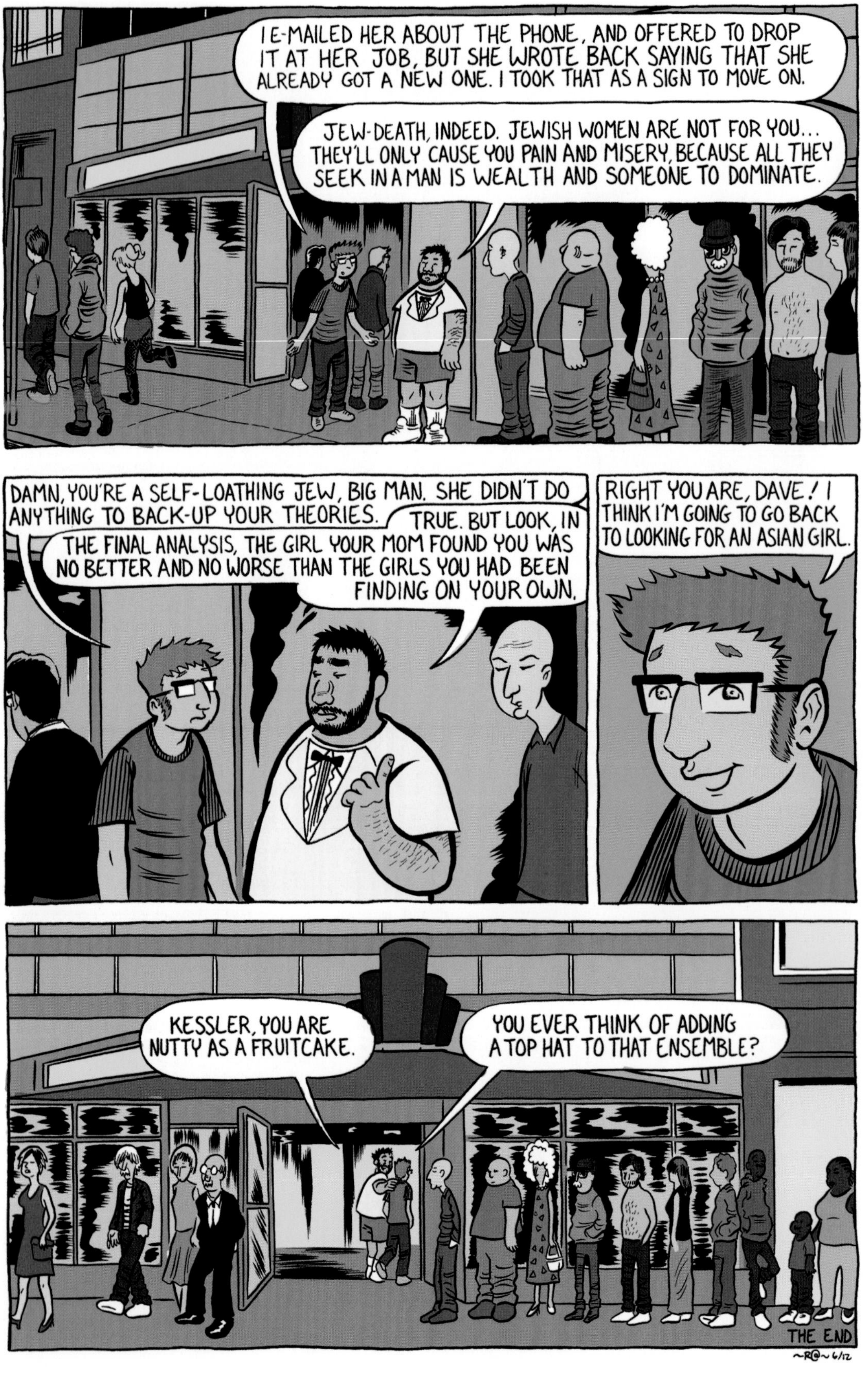

I E-MAILED HER ABOUT THE PHONE, AND OFFERED TO DROP IT AT HER JOB, BUT SHE WROTE BACK SAYING THAT SHE ALREADY GOT A NEW ONE. I TOOK THAT AS A SIGN TO MOVE ON.
JEW-DEATH, INDEED. JEWISH WOMEN ARE NOT FOR YOU... THEY'LL ONLY CAUSE YOU PAIN AND MISERY, BECAUSE ALL THEY SEEK IN A MAN IS WEALTH AND SOMEONE TO DOMINATE.
DAMN, YOU'RE A SELF-LOATHING JEW, BIG MAN. SHE DIDN'T DO ANYTHING TO BACK-UP YOUR THEORIES.
TRUE. BUT LOOK, IN THE FINAL ANALYSIS, THE GIRL YOUR MOM FOUND YOU WAS NO BETTER AND NO WORSE THAN THE GIRLS YOU HAD BEEN FINDING ON YOUR OWN.
RIGHT YOU ARE, DAVE! I THINK I'M GOING TO GO BACK TO LOOKING FOR AN ASIAN GIRL.
KESSLER, YOU ARE NUTTY AS A FRUITCAKE.
YOU EVER THINK OF ADDING A TOP HAT TO THAT ENSEMBLE?
THE END
~R@~ 6/12

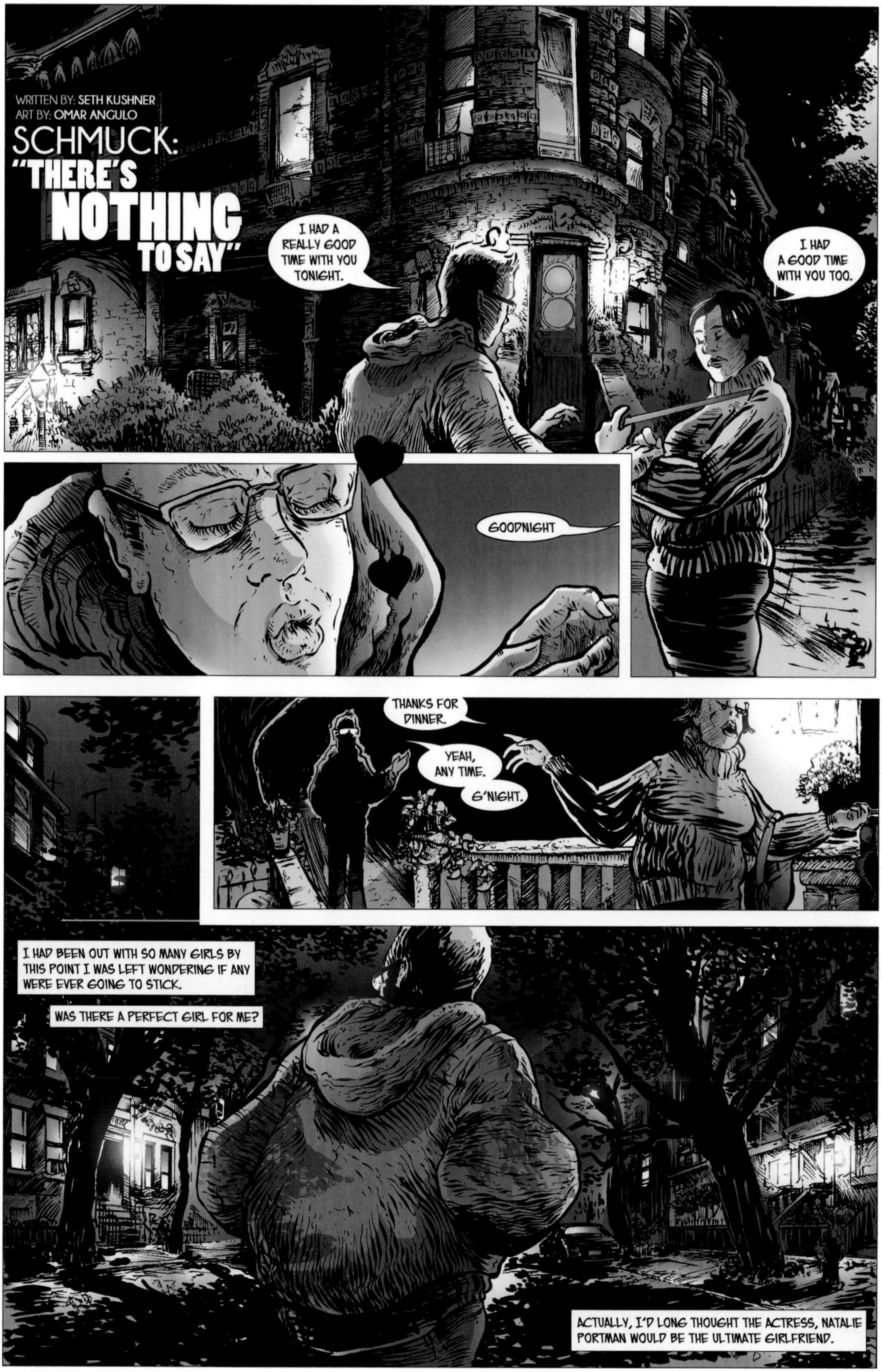
WRITTEN BY: SETH KUSHNER
ART BY: OMAR ANGULO
SCHMUCK: "THERE'S NOTHING TO SAY"
I HAD A REALLY GOOD TIME WITH YOU TONIGHT.
I HAD A GOOD TIME WITH YOU TOO.
GOODNIGHT
THANKS FOR DINNER.
YEAH, ANY TIME.
G'NIGHT.
I HAD BEEN OUT WITH SO MANY GIRLS BY THIS POINT I WAS LEFT WONDERING IF ANY WERE EVER GOING TO STICK.
WAS THERE A PERFECT GIRL FOR ME?
ACTUALLY, I'D LONG THOUGHT THE ACTRESS, NATALIE PORTMAN WOULD BE THE ULTIMATE GIRLFRIEND.

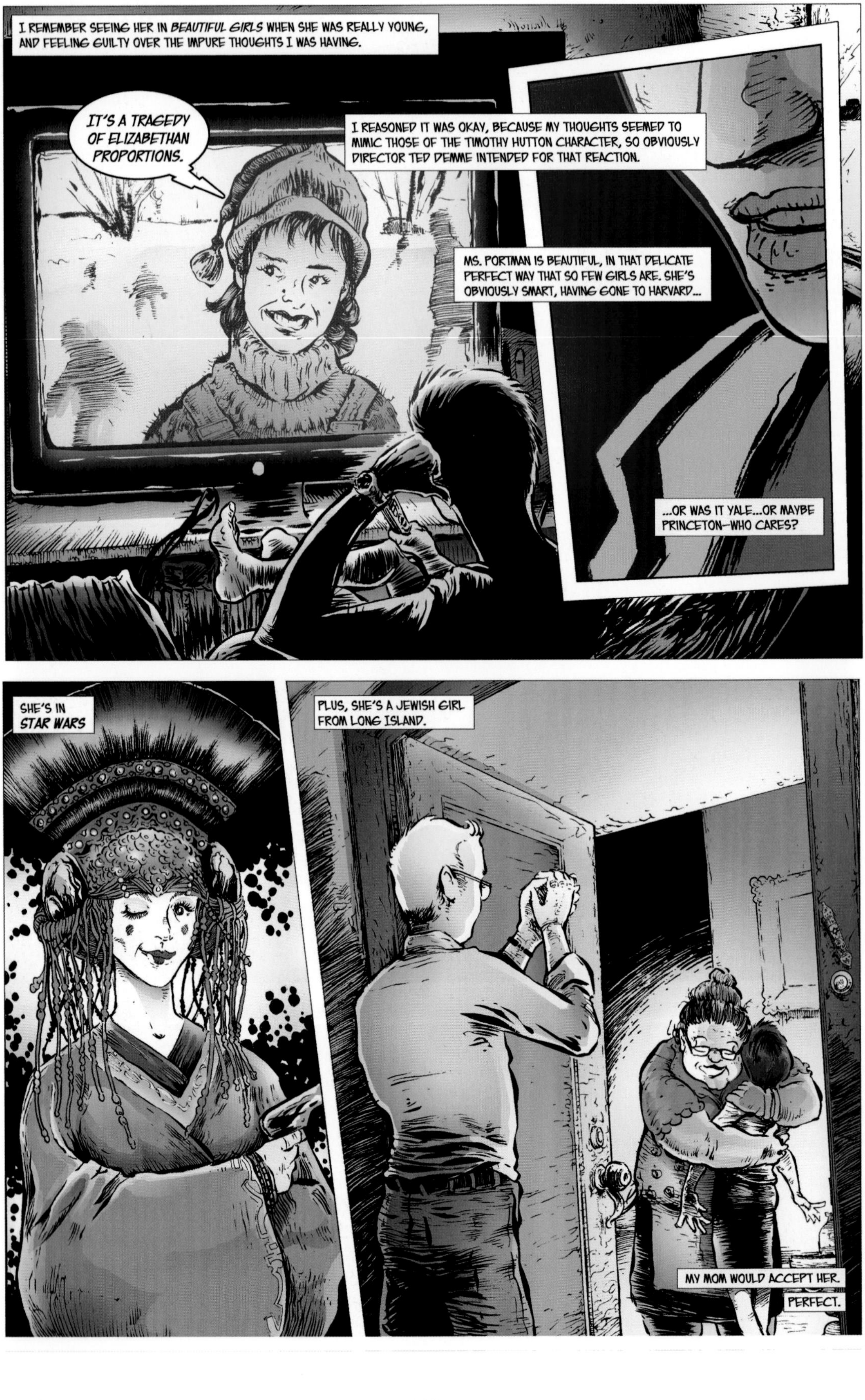
I REMEMBER SEEING HER IN *BEAUTIFUL GIRLS* WHEN SHE WAS REALLY YOUNG, AND FEELING GUILTY OVER THE IMPURE THOUGHTS I WAS HAVING.
IT'S A TRAGEDY OF ELIZABETHAN PROPORTIONS.
I REASONED IT WAS OKAY, BECAUSE MY THOUGHTS SEEMED TO MIMIC THOSE OF THE TIMOTHY HUTTON CHARACTER, SO OBVIOUSLY DIRECTOR TED DEMME INTENDED FOR THAT REACTION.
MS. PORTMAN IS BEAUTIFUL, IN THAT DELICATE PERFECT WAY THAT SO FEW GIRLS ARE. SHE'S OBVIOUSLY SMART, HAVING GONE TO HARVARD...
...OR WAS IT YALE...OR MAYBE PRINCETON—WHO CARES?
SHE'S IN *STAR WARS*
PLUS, SHE'S A JEWISH GIRL FROM LONG ISLAND.
MY MOM WOULD ACCEPT HER.
PERFECT.

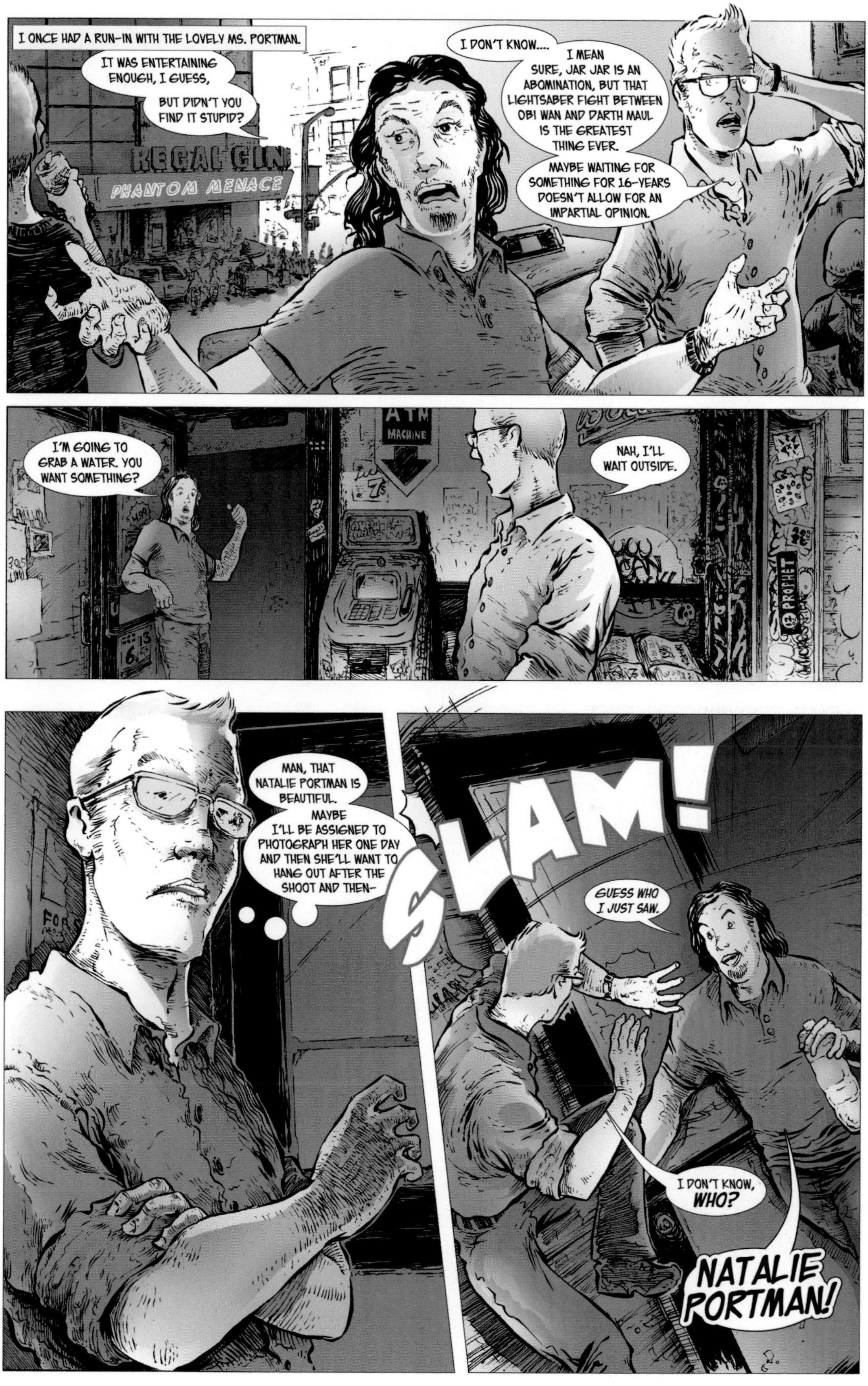
I ONCE HAD A RUN-IN WITH THE LOVELY MS. PORTMAN.
IT WAS ENTERTAINING ENOUGH, I GUESS,
BUT DIDN'T YOU FIND IT STUPID?
REGAL CIN
PHANTOM MENACE
I DON'T KNOW....
I MEAN SURE, JAR JAR IS AN ABOMINATION, BUT THAT LIGHTSABER FIGHT BETWEEN OBI WAN AND DARTH MAUL IS THE GREATEST THING EVER.
MAYBE WAITING FOR SOMETHING FOR 16-YEARS DOESN'T ALLOW FOR AN IMPARTIAL OPINION.
I'M GOING TO GRAB A WATER. YOU WANT SOMETHING?
ATM MACHINE
NAH, I'LL WAIT OUTSIDE.
PROPHET
MAN, THAT NATALIE PORTMAN IS BEAUTIFUL.
MAYBE I'LL BE ASSIGNED TO PHOTOGRAPH HER ONE DAY AND THEN SHE'LL WANT TO HANG OUT AFTER THE SHOOT AND THEN-
SLAM!
GUESS WHO I JUST SAW.
I DON'T KNOW, WHO?
NATALIE PORTMAN!

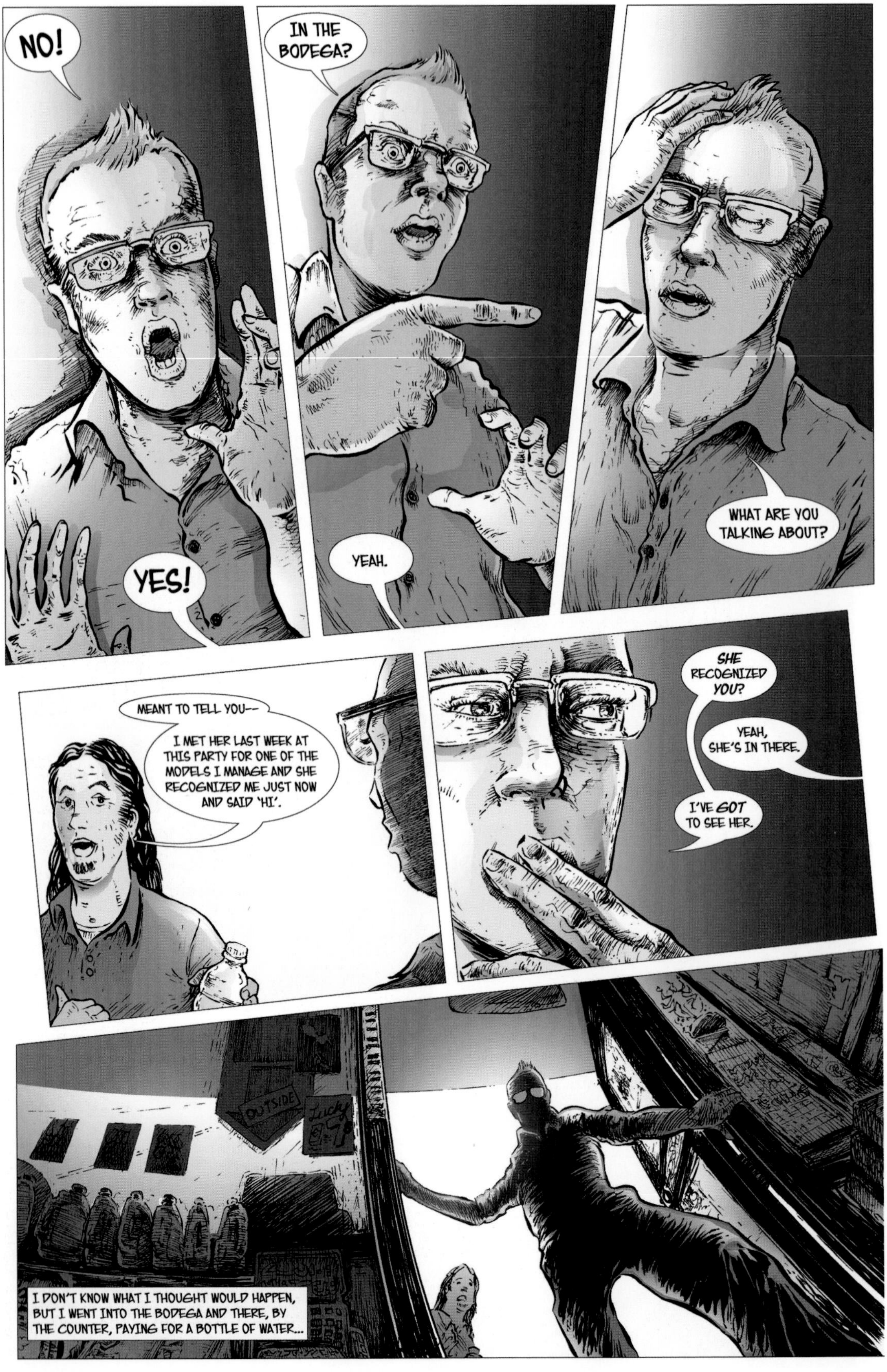
NO!
YES!
IN THE BODEGA?
YEAH.
WHAT ARE YOU TALKING ABOUT?
MEANT TO TELL YOU--
I MET HER LAST WEEK AT THIS PARTY FOR ONE OF THE MODELS I MANAGE AND SHE RECOGNIZED ME JUST NOW AND SAID 'HI'.
SHE RECOGNIZED YOU?
YEAH, SHE'S IN THERE.
I'VE GOT TO SEE HER.
OUTSIDE
I DON'T KNOW WHAT I THOUGHT WOULD HAPPEN, BUT I WENT INTO THE BODEGA AND THERE, BY THE COUNTER, PAYING FOR A BOTTLE OF WATER...

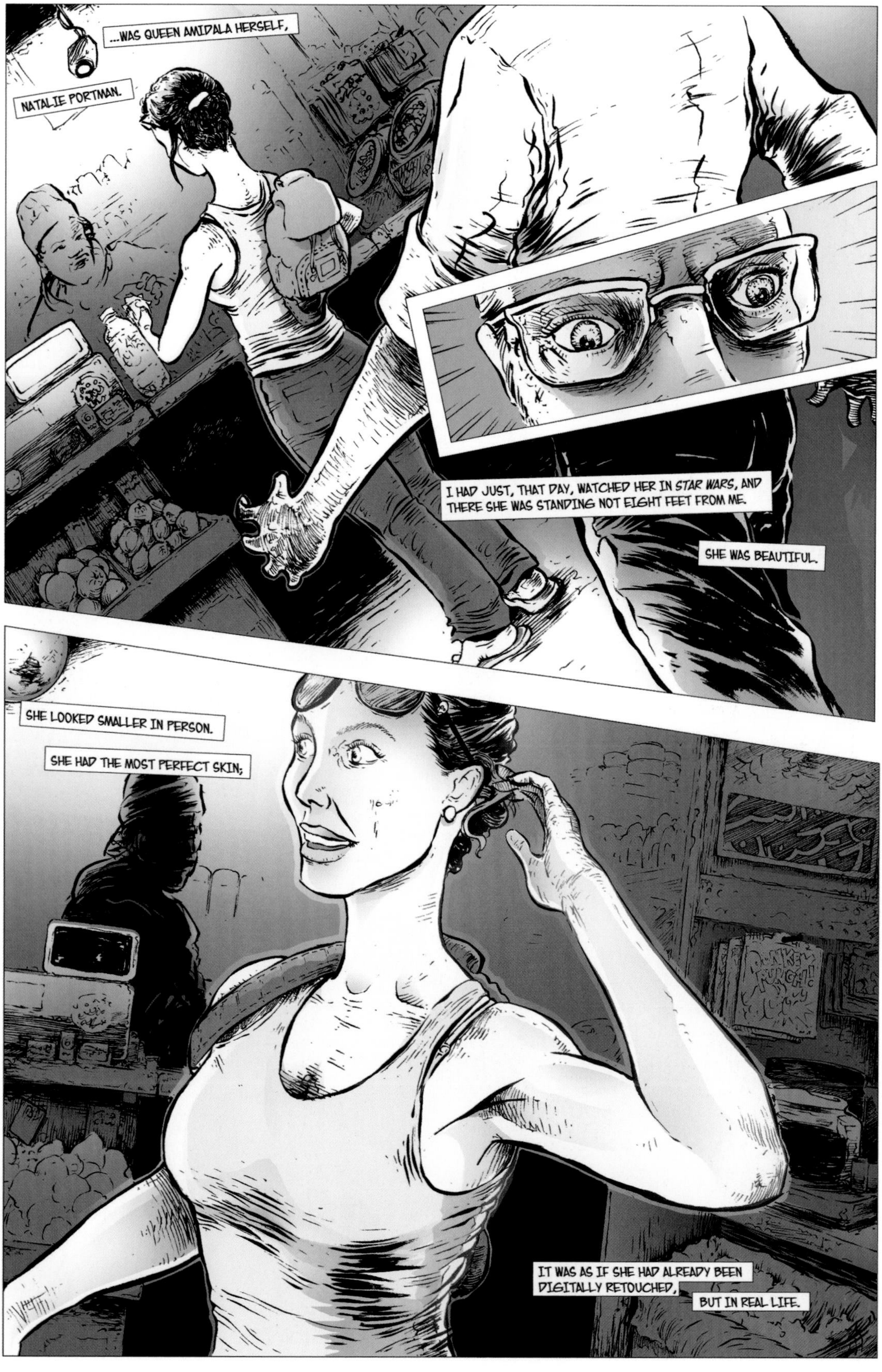

...WAS QUEEN AMIDALA HERSELF,
NATALIE PORTMAN.
I HAD JUST, THAT DAY, WATCHED HER IN STAR WARS, AND THERE SHE WAS STANDING NOT EIGHT FEET FROM ME.
SHE WAS BEAUTIFUL.
SHE LOOKED SMALLER IN PERSON.
SHE HAD THE MOST PERFECT SKIN;
IT WAS AS IF SHE HAD ALREADY BEEN DIGITALLY RETOUCHED,
BUT IN REAL LIFE.

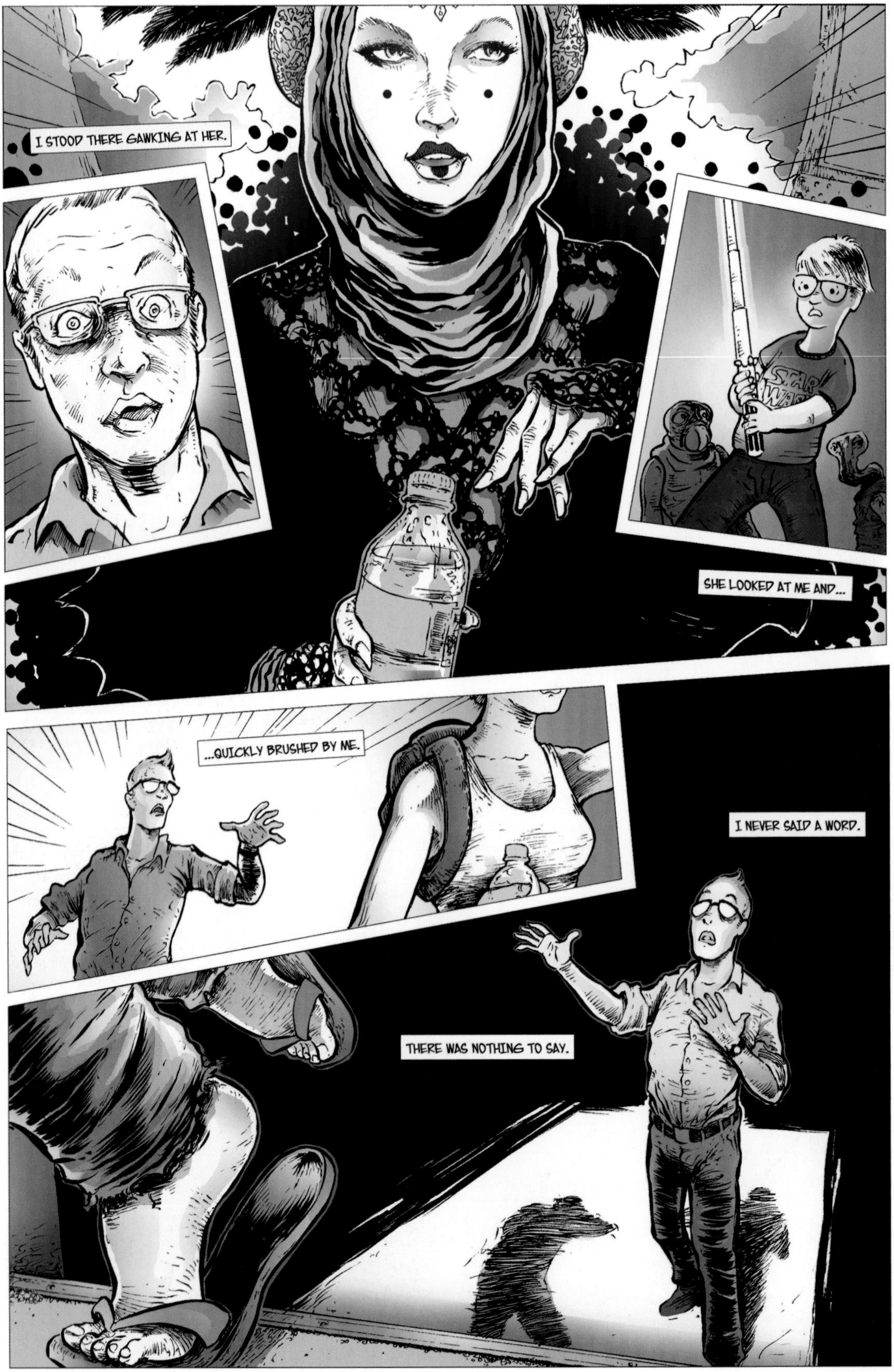

I STOOD THERE GAWKING AT HER.
STAR WARS
SHE LOOKED AT ME AND...
...QUICKLY BRUSHED BY ME.
I NEVER SAID A WORD.
THERE WAS NOTHING TO SAY.

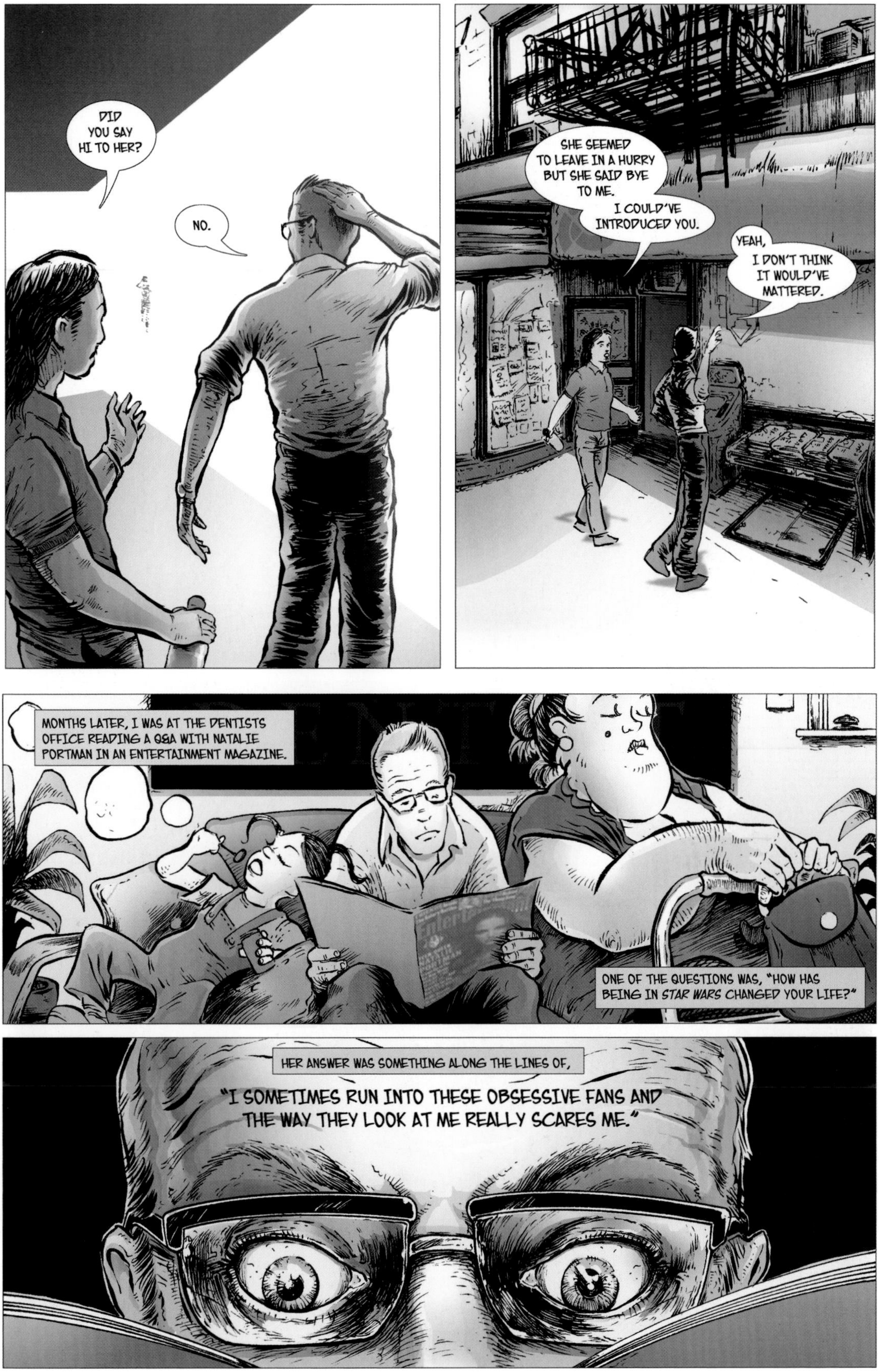
DID YOU SAY HI TO HER?
NO.
SHE SEEMED TO LEAVE IN A HURRY BUT SHE SAID BYE TO ME.
I COULD'VE INTRODUCED YOU.
YEAH, I DON'T THINK IT WOULD'VE MATTERED.
MONTHS LATER, I WAS AT THE DENTISTS OFFICE READING A Q&A WITH NATALIE PORTMAN IN AN ENTERTAINMENT MAGAZINE.
ONE OF THE QUESTIONS WAS, "HOW HAS BEING IN *STAR WARS* CHANGED YOUR LIFE?"
HER ANSWER WAS SOMETHING ALONG THE LINES OF,
"I SOMETIMES RUN INTO THESE OBSESSIVE FANS AND THE WAY THEY LOOK AT ME REALLY SCARES ME."

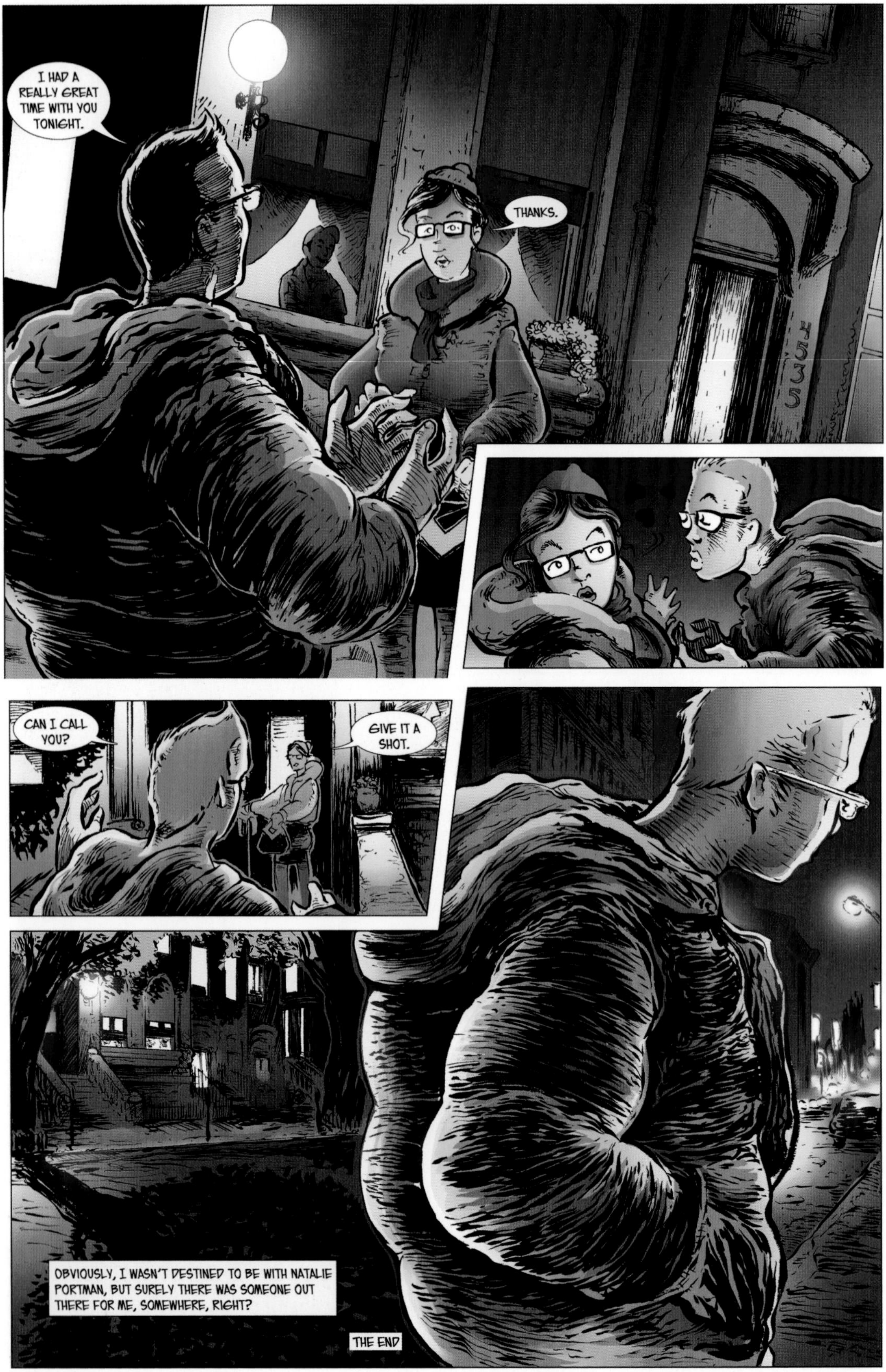
I HAD A REALLY GREAT TIME WITH YOU TONIGHT.
THANKS.
4535
CAN I CALL YOU?
GIVE IT A SHOT.
OBVIOUSLY, I WASN'T DESTINED TO BE WITH NATALIE PORTMAN, BUT SURELY THERE WAS SOMEONE OUT THERE FOR ME, SOMEWHERE, RIGHT?
THE END

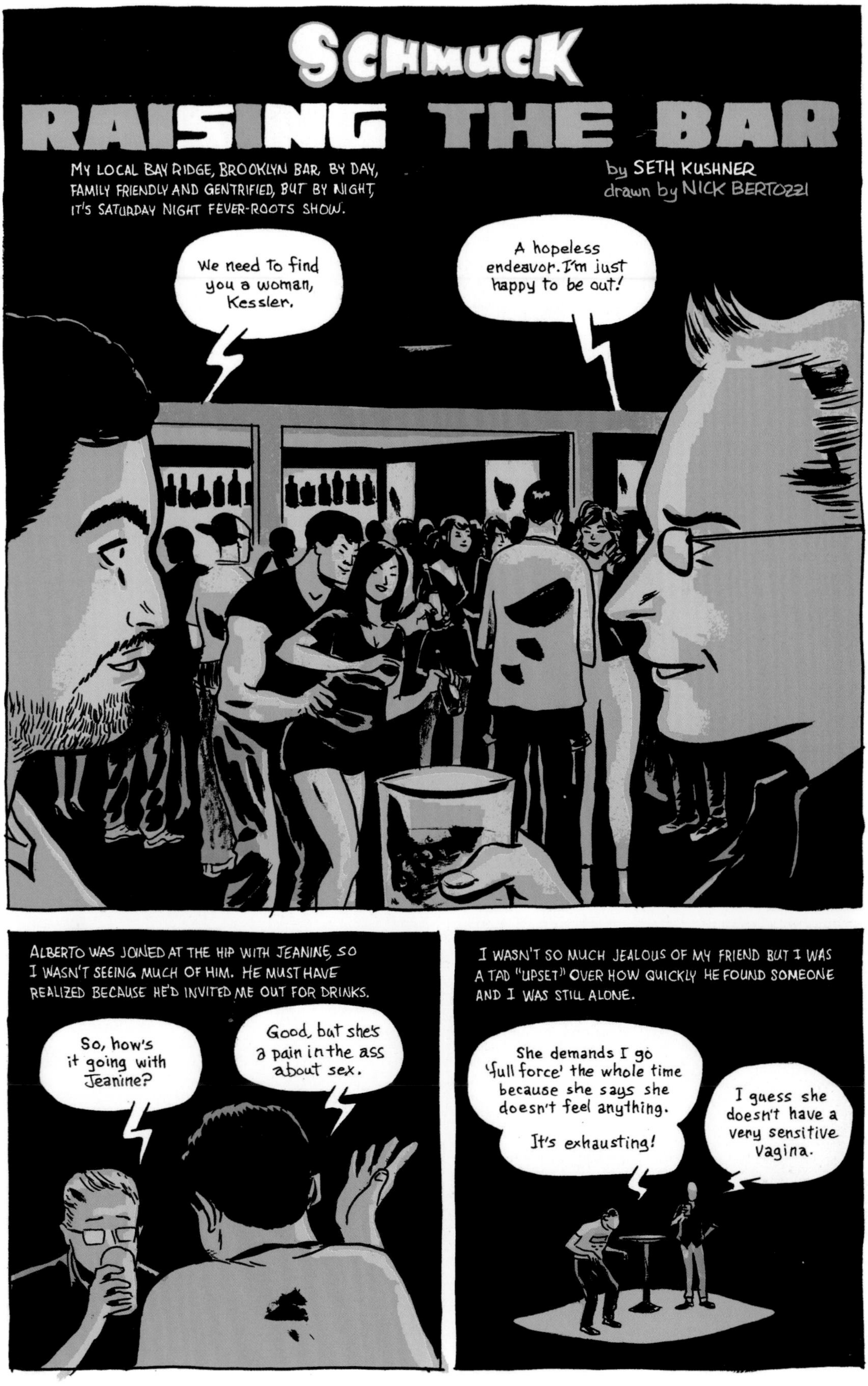
SCHMUCK
RAISING THE BAR
MY LOCAL BAY RIDGE, BROOKLYN BAR. BY DAY, FAMILY FRIENDLY AND GENTRIFIED, BUT BY NIGHT, IT'S SATURDAY NIGHT FEVER-ROOTS SHOW.
by SETH KUSHNER
drawn by NICK BERTOZZI
We need to find you a woman, Kessler.
A hopeless endeavor. I'm just happy to be out!
ALBERTO WAS JOINED AT THE HIP WITH JEANINE, SO I WASN'T SEEING MUCH OF HIM. HE MUST HAVE REALIZED BECAUSE HE'D INVITED ME OUT FOR DRINKS.
So, how's it going with Jeanine?
Good, but she's a pain in the ass about sex.
I WASN'T SO MUCH JEALOUS OF MY FRIEND BUT I WAS A TAD "UPSET" OVER HOW QUICKLY HE FOUND SOMEONE AND I WAS STILL ALONE.
She demands I go 'full force' the whole time because she says she doesn't feel anything.
It's exhausting!
I guess she doesn't have a very sensitive vagina.

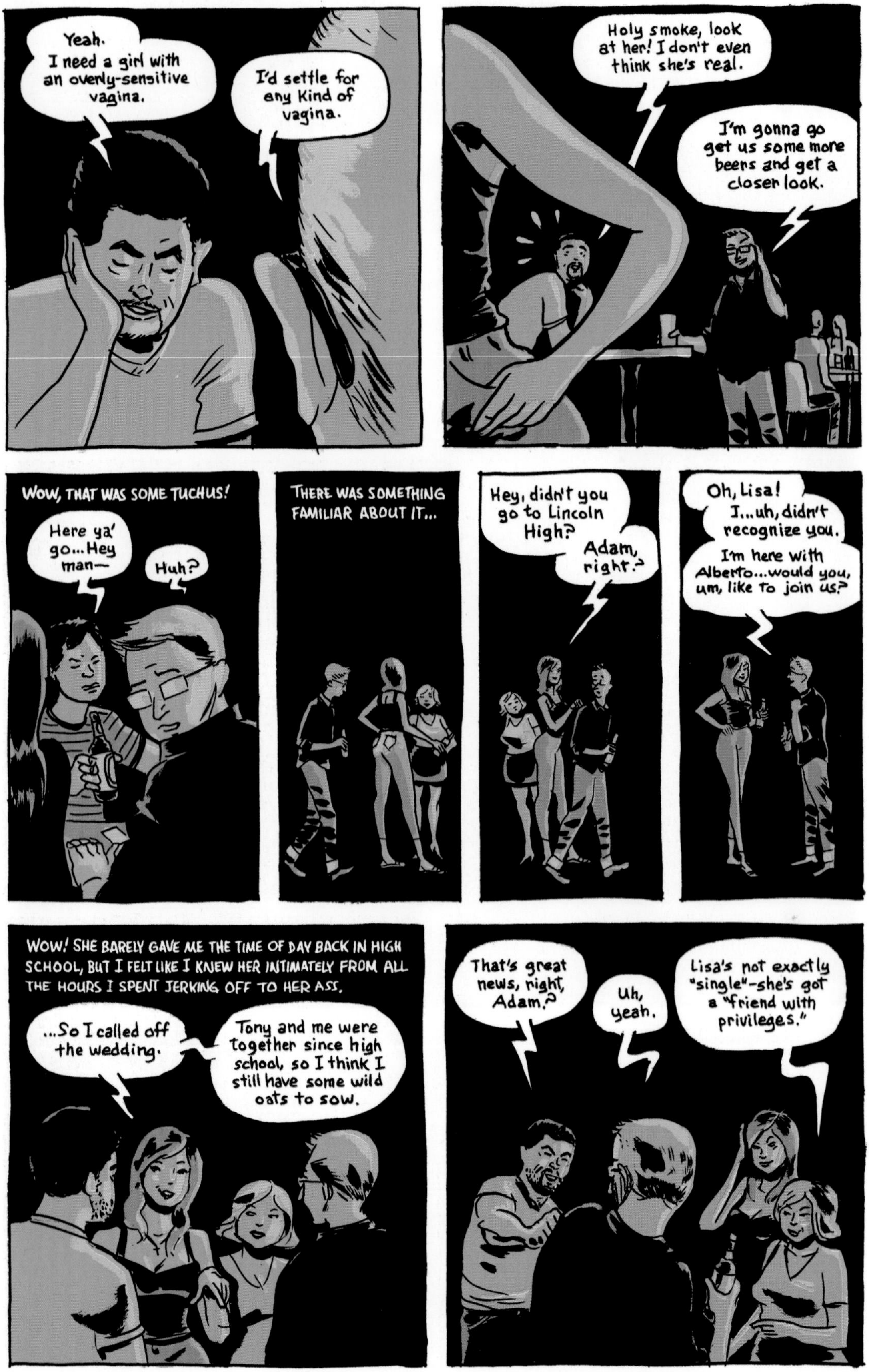

Yeah. I need a girl with an overly-sensitive vagina.
I'd settle for any kind of vagina.
Holy smoke, look at her! I don't even think she's real.
I'm gonna go get us some more beers and get a closer look.
WOW, THAT WAS SOME TUCHUS!
Here ya' go...Hey man—
Huh?
THERE WAS SOMETHING FAMILIAR ABOUT IT...
Hey, didn't you go to Lincoln High?
Adam, right?
Oh, Lisa! I...uh, didn't recognize you.
I'm here with Alberto...would you, um, like to join us?
WOW! SHE BARELY GAVE ME THE TIME OF DAY BACK IN HIGH SCHOOL, BUT I FELT LIKE I KNEW HER INTIMATELY FROM ALL THE HOURS I SPENT JERKING OFF TO HER ASS.
...So I called off the wedding.
Tony and me were together since high school, so I think I still have some wild oats to sow.
That's great news, right, Adam?
Uh, yeah.
Lisa's not exactly "single"-she's got a "friend with privileges."

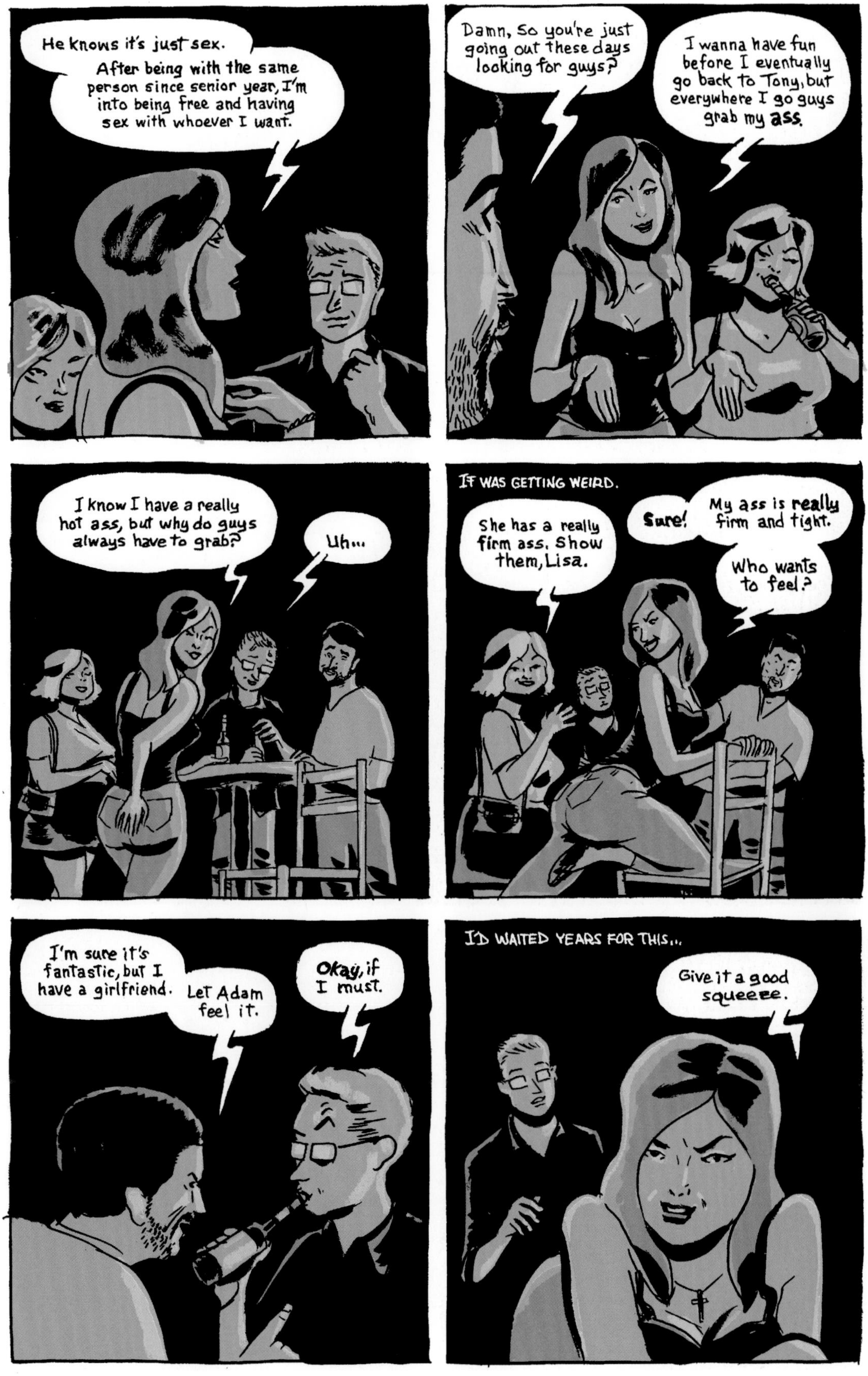
He knows it's just sex.
After being with the same person since senior year, I'm into being free and having sex with whoever I want.
Damn, so you're just going out these days looking for guys?
I wanna have fun before I eventually go back to Tony, but everywhere I go guys grab my ass.
I know I have a really hot ass, but why do guys always have to grab?
Uh...
IT WAS GETTING WEIRD.
She has a really firm ass. Show them, Lisa.
Sure!
My ass is really firm and tight.
Who wants to feel?
I'm sure it's fantastic, but I have a girlfriend.
Let Adam feel it.
Okay, if I must.
I'D WAITED YEARS FOR THIS...
Give it a good squeeze.

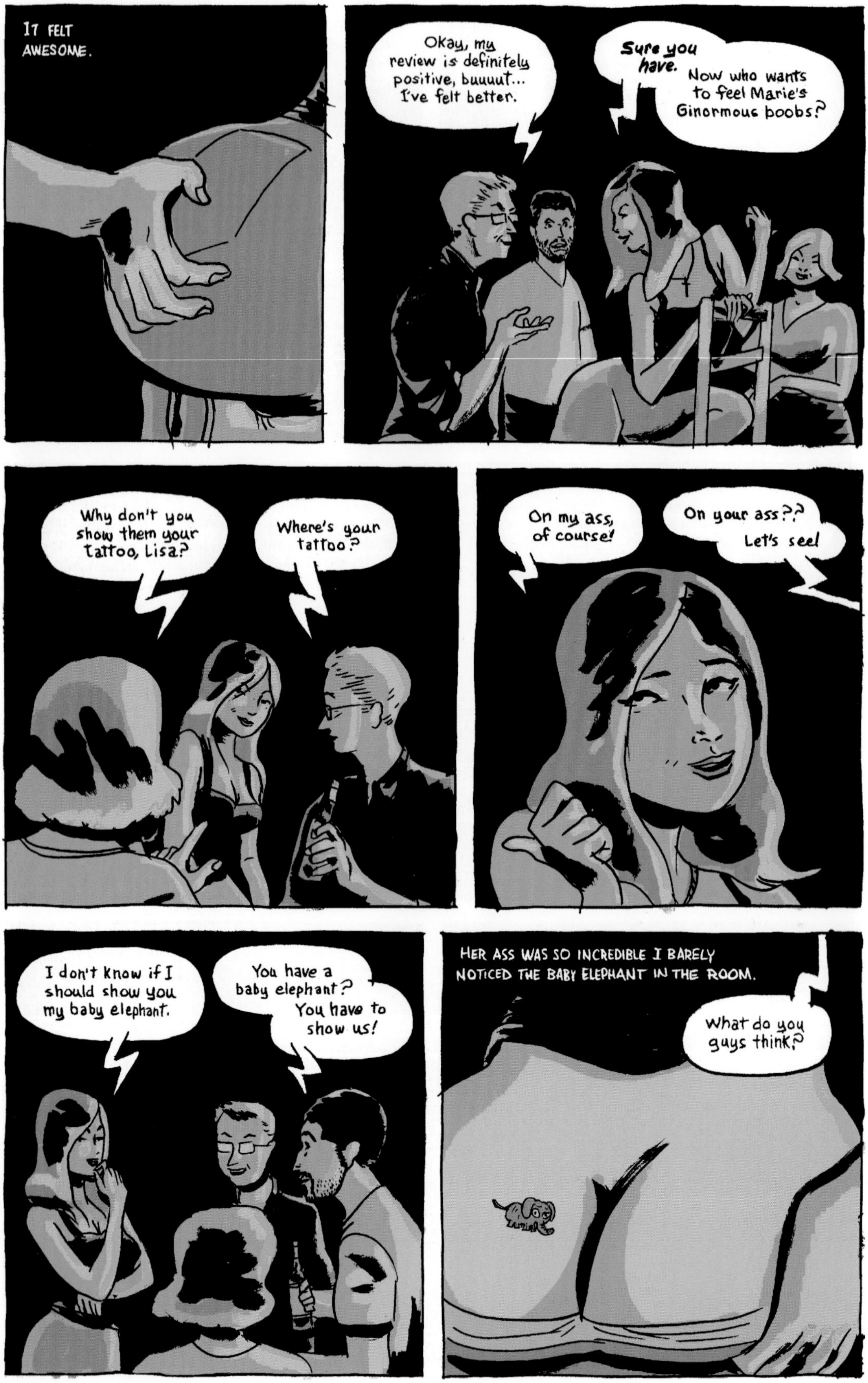

IT FELT AWESOME.
Okay, my review is definitely positive, buuuut... I've felt better.
Sure you have.
Now who wants to feel Marie's Ginormous boobs?
Why don't you show them your tattoo, Lisa?
Where's your tattoo?
On my ass, of course!
On your ass?!? Let's see!
I don't know if I should show you my baby elephant.
You have a baby elephant? You have to show us!
HER ASS WAS SO INCREDIBLE I BARELY NOTICED THE BABY ELEPHANT IN THE ROOM.
What do you guys think?

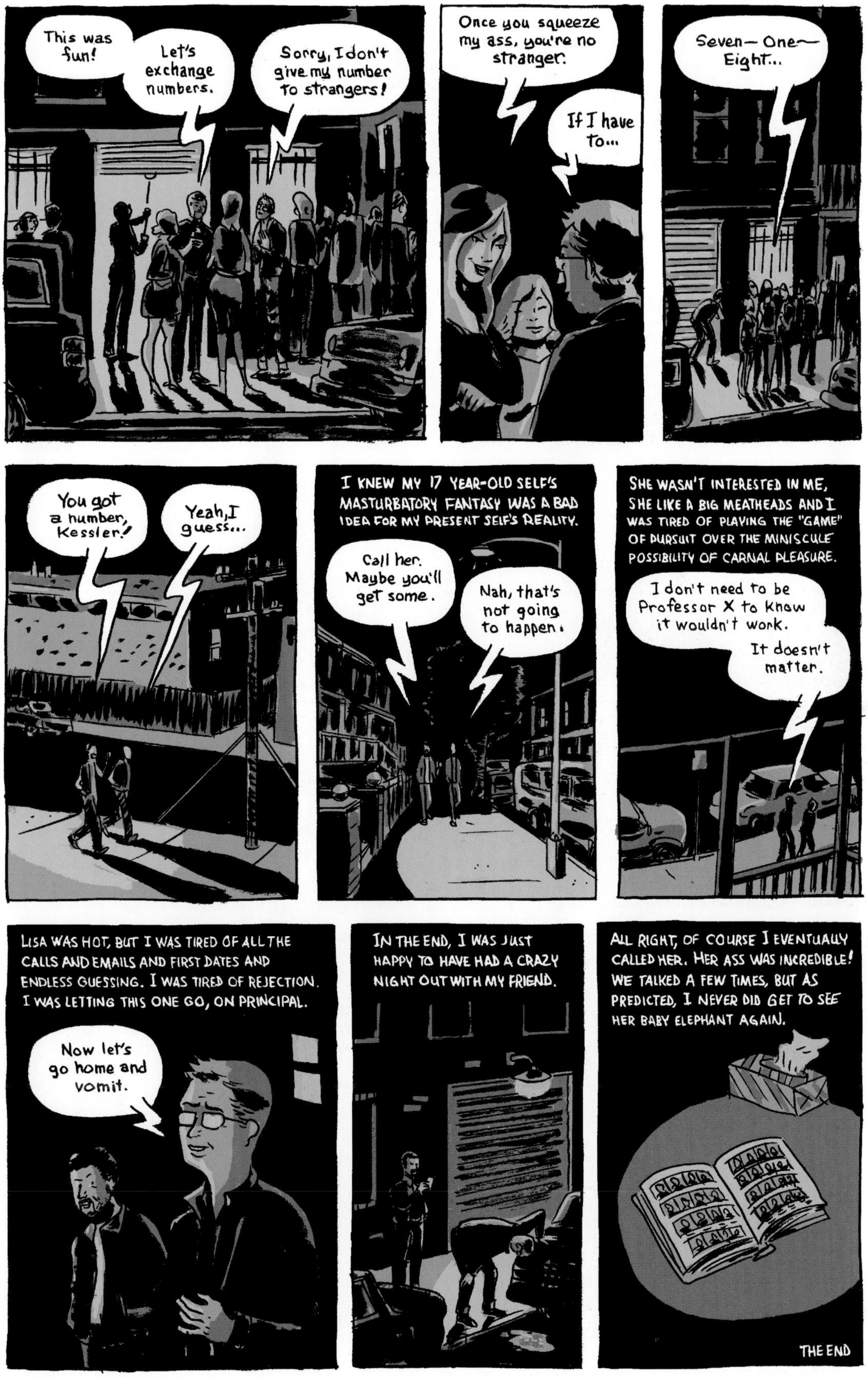
This was fun!
Let's exchange numbers.
Sorry, I don't give my number to strangers!
Once you squeeze my ass, you're no stranger.
If I have to...
Seven—One—Eight...
You got a number, Kessler!
Yeah, I guess...
I KNEW MY 17 YEAR-OLD SELF'S MASTURBATORY FANTASY WAS A BAD IDEA FOR MY PRESENT SELF'S REALITY.
Call her. Maybe you'll get some.
Nah, that's not going to happen.
SHE WASN'T INTERESTED IN ME, SHE LIKE A BIG MEATHEADS AND I WAS TIRED OF PLAYING THE "GAME" OF PURSUIT OVER THE MINISCULE POSSIBILITY OF CARNAL PLEASURE.
I don't need to be Professor X to know it wouldn't work.
It doesn't matter.
LISA WAS HOT, BUT I WAS TIRED OF ALL THE CALLS AND EMAILS AND FIRST DATES AND ENDLESS GUESSING. I WAS TIRED OF REJECTION. I WAS LETTING THIS ONE GO, ON PRINCIPAL.
Now let's go home and vomit.
IN THE END, I WAS JUST HAPPY TO HAVE HAD A CRAZY NIGHT OUT WITH MY FRIEND.
ALL RIGHT, OF COURSE I EVENTUALLY CALLED HER. HER ASS WAS INCREDIBLE! WE TALKED A FEW TIMES, BUT AS PREDICTED, I NEVER DID GET TO SEE HER BABY ELEPHANT AGAIN.
THE END

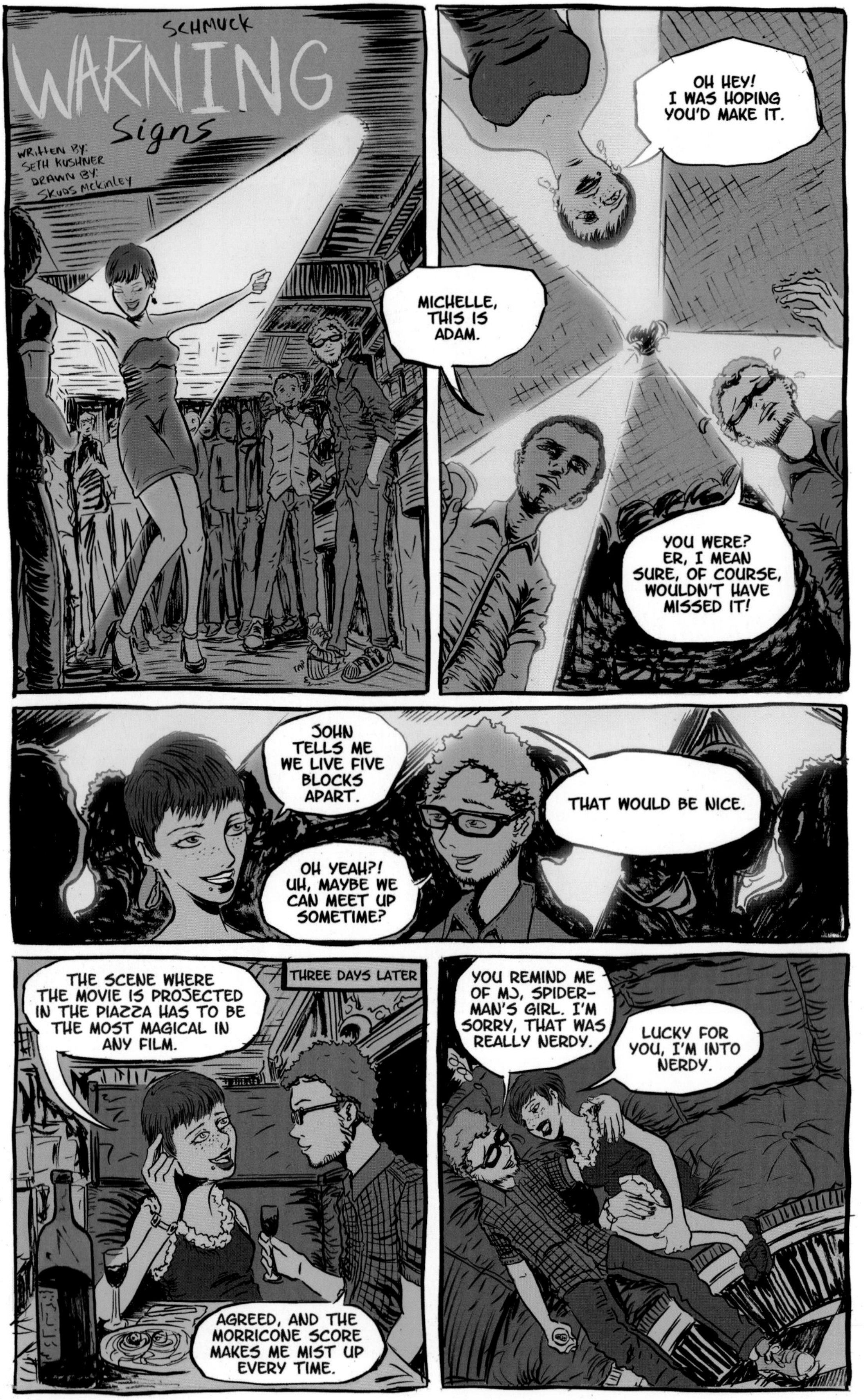
SCHMUCK
WARNING
Signs
Written by: Seth Kushner
Drawn by: Skuds McKinley
OH HEY! I WAS HOPING YOU'D MAKE IT.
MICHELLE, THIS IS ADAM.
YOU WERE? ER, I MEAN SURE, OF COURSE, WOULDN'T HAVE MISSED IT!
JOHN TELLS ME WE LIVE FIVE BLOCKS APART.
OH YEAH?! UH, MAYBE WE CAN MEET UP SOMETIME?
THAT WOULD BE NICE.
THREE DAYS LATER
THE SCENE WHERE THE MOVIE IS PROJECTED IN THE PIAZZA HAS TO BE THE MOST MAGICAL IN ANY FILM.
AGREED, AND THE MORRICONE SCORE MAKES ME MIST UP EVERY TIME.
YOU REMIND ME OF MJ, SPIDER-MAN'S GIRL. I'M SORRY, THAT WAS REALLY NERDY.
LUCKY FOR YOU, I'M INTO NERDY.

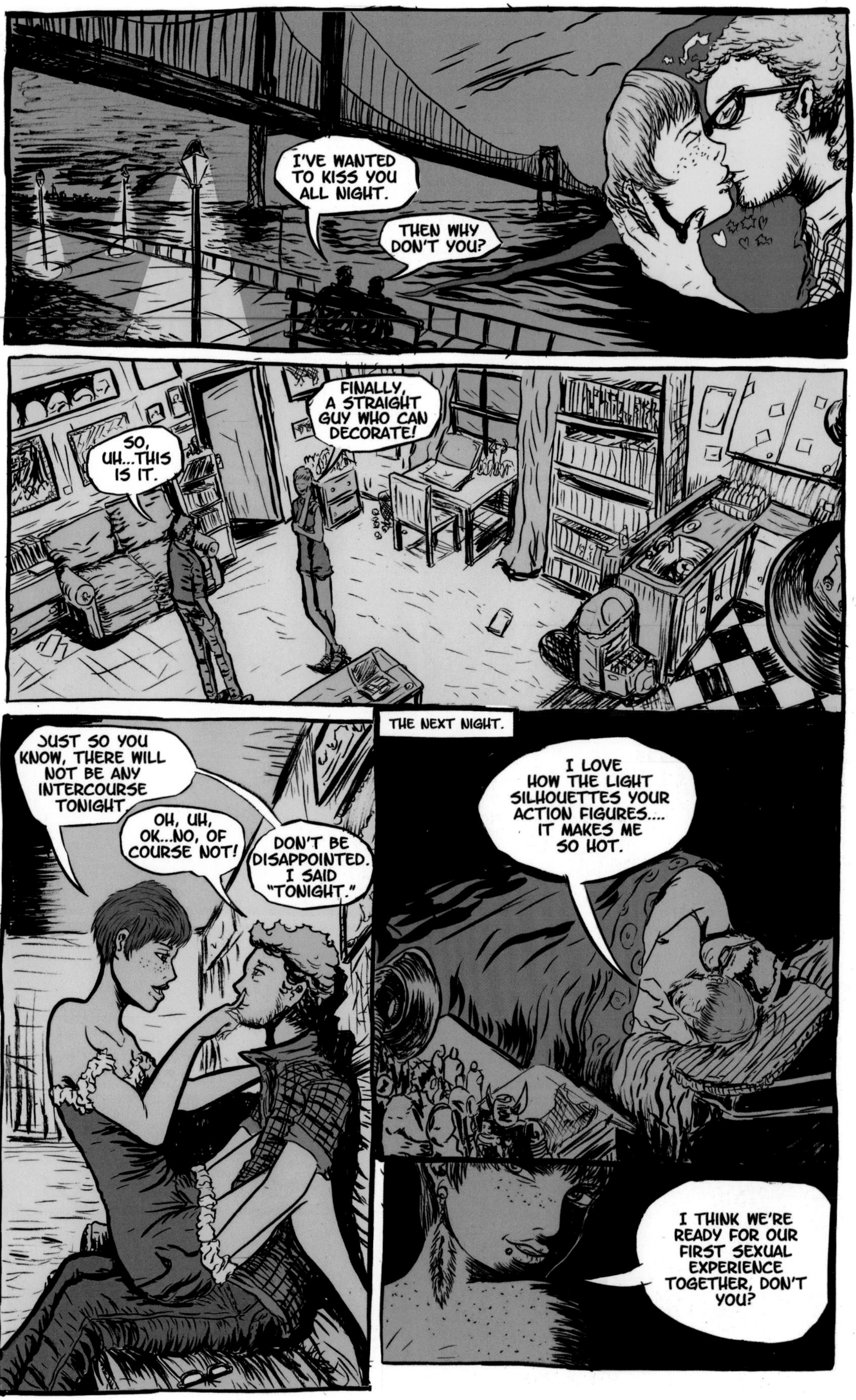
I'VE WANTED TO KISS YOU ALL NIGHT.
THEN WHY DON'T YOU?
SO, UH...THIS IS IT.
FINALLY, A STRAIGHT GUY WHO CAN DECORATE!
JUST SO YOU KNOW, THERE WILL NOT BE ANY INTERCOURSE TONIGHT.
OH, UH, OK...NO, OF COURSE NOT!
DON'T BE DISAPPOINTED. I SAID "TONIGHT."
THE NEXT NIGHT.
I LOVE HOW THE LIGHT SILHOUETTES YOUR ACTION FIGURES.... IT MAKES ME SO HOT.
I THINK WE'RE READY FOR OUR FIRST SEXUAL EXPERIENCE TOGETHER, DON'T YOU?

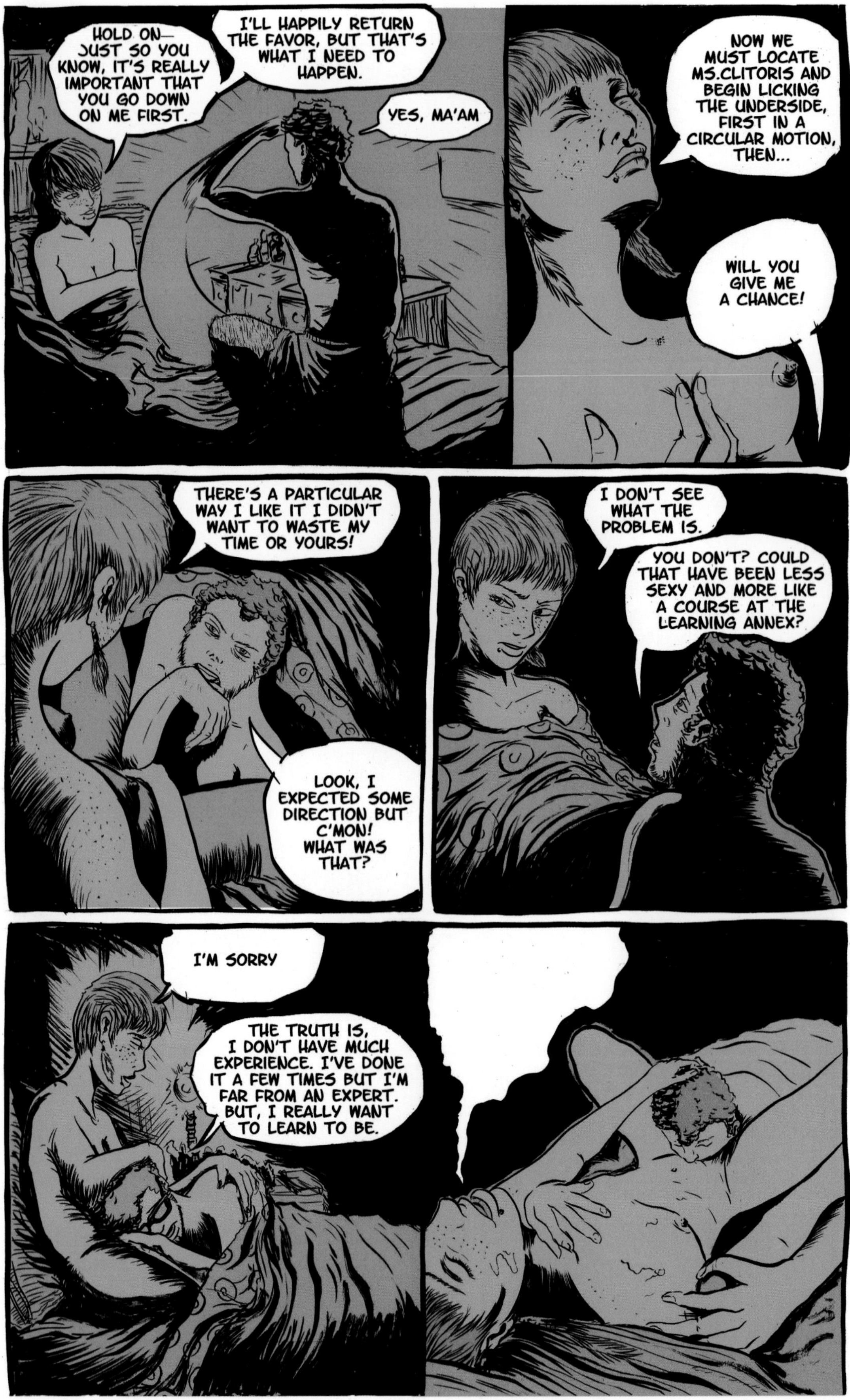
HOLD ON— JUST SO YOU KNOW, IT'S REALLY IMPORTANT THAT YOU GO DOWN ON ME FIRST.
I'LL HAPPILY RETURN THE FAVOR, BUT THAT'S WHAT I NEED TO HAPPEN.
YES, MA'AM
NOW WE MUST LOCATE MS.CLITORIS AND BEGIN LICKING THE UNDERSIDE, FIRST IN A CIRCULAR MOTION, THEN...
WILL YOU GIVE ME A CHANCE!
THERE'S A PARTICULAR WAY I LIKE IT I DIDN'T WANT TO WASTE MY TIME OR YOURS!
LOOK, I EXPECTED SOME DIRECTION BUT C'MON! WHAT WAS THAT?
I DON'T SEE WHAT THE PROBLEM IS.
YOU DON'T? COULD THAT HAVE BEEN LESS SEXY AND MORE LIKE A COURSE AT THE LEARNING ANNEX?
I'M SORRY
THE TRUTH IS, I DON'T HAVE MUCH EXPERIENCE. I'VE DONE IT A FEW TIMES BUT I'M FAR FROM AN EXPERT. BUT, I REALLY WANT TO LEARN TO BE.

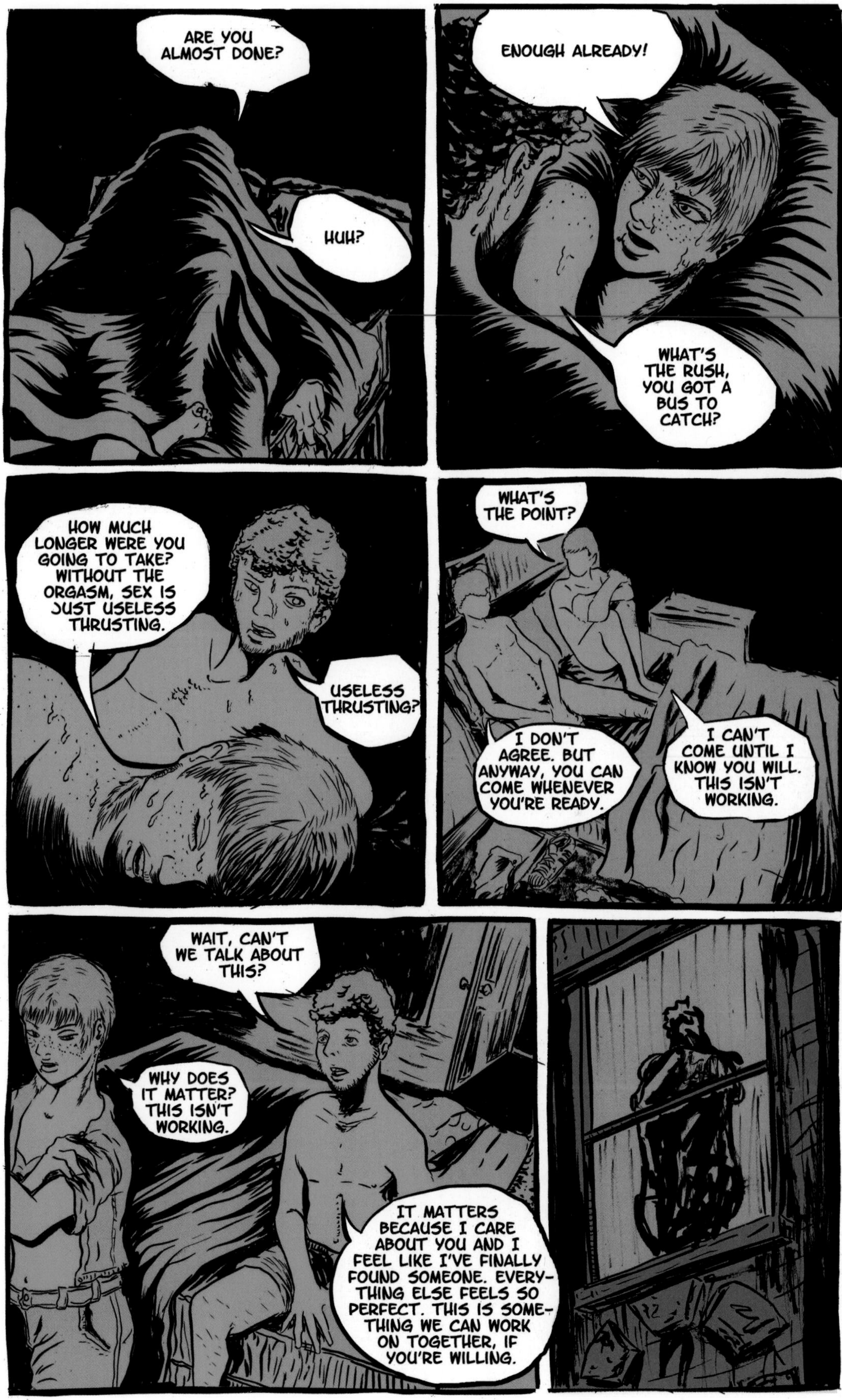
ARE YOU ALMOST DONE?
HUH?
ENOUGH ALREADY!
WHAT'S THE RUSH, YOU GOT A BUS TO CATCH?
HOW MUCH LONGER WERE YOU GOING TO TAKE? WITHOUT THE ORGASM, SEX IS JUST USELESS THRUSTING.
USELESS THRUSTING?
WHAT'S THE POINT?
I DON'T AGREE. BUT ANYWAY, YOU CAN COME WHENEVER YOU'RE READY.
I CAN'T COME UNTIL I KNOW YOU WILL. THIS ISN'T WORKING.
WAIT, CAN'T WE TALK ABOUT THIS?
WHY DOES IT MATTER? THIS ISN'T WORKING.
IT MATTERS BECAUSE I CARE ABOUT YOU AND I FEEL LIKE I'VE FINALLY FOUND SOMEONE. EVERYTHING ELSE FEELS SO PERFECT. THIS IS SOMETHING WE CAN WORK ON TOGETHER, IF YOU'RE WILLING.

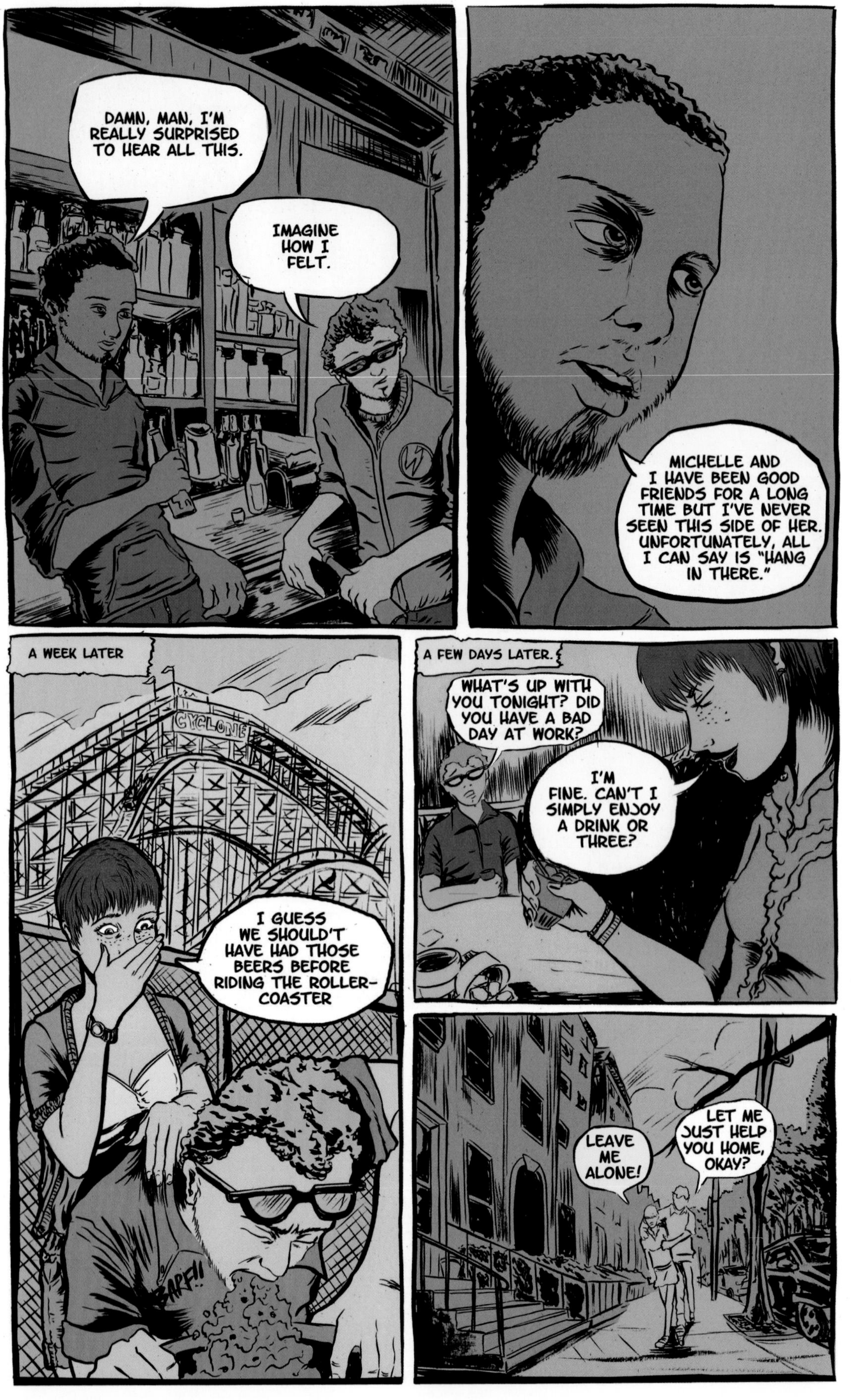
DAMN, MAN, I'M REALLY SURPRISED TO HEAR ALL THIS.
IMAGINE HOW I FELT.
MICHELLE AND I HAVE BEEN GOOD FRIENDS FOR A LONG TIME BUT I'VE NEVER SEEN THIS SIDE OF HER. UNFORTUNATELY, ALL I CAN SAY IS "HANG IN THERE."
A WEEK LATER
CYCLONE
I GUESS WE SHOULD'T HAVE HAD THOSE BEERS BEFORE RIDING THE ROLLER-COASTER
BARF!!
A FEW DAYS LATER.
WHAT'S UP WITH YOU TONIGHT? DID YOU HAVE A BAD DAY AT WORK?
I'M FINE. CAN'T I SIMPLY ENJOY A DRINK OR THREE?
LEAVE ME ALONE!
LET ME JUST HELP YOU HOME, OKAY?

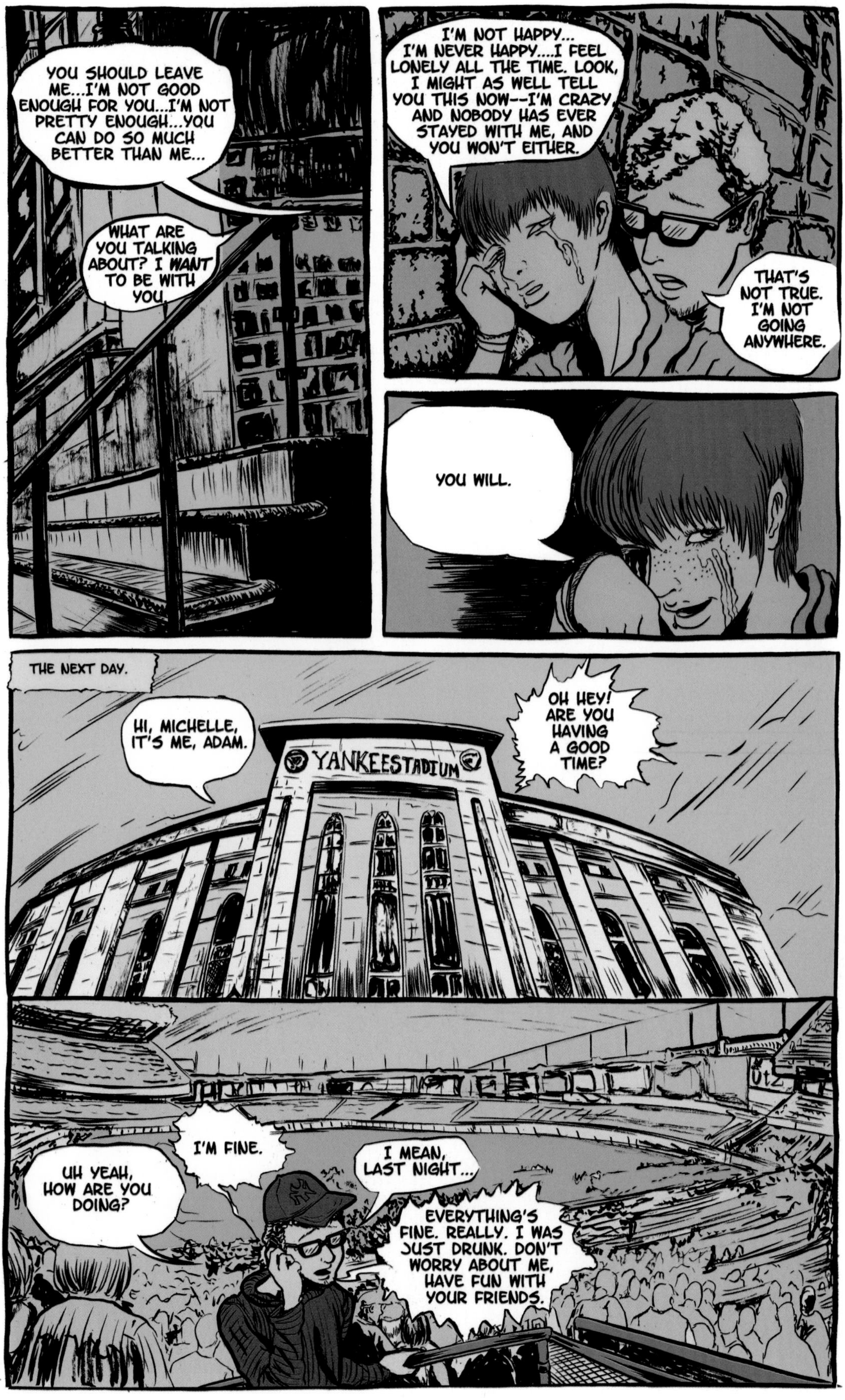
YOU SHOULD LEAVE ME...I'M NOT GOOD ENOUGH FOR YOU...I'M NOT PRETTY ENOUGH...YOU CAN DO SO MUCH BETTER THAN ME...
WHAT ARE YOU TALKING ABOUT? I WANT TO BE WITH YOU.
I'M NOT HAPPY... I'M NEVER HAPPY....I FEEL LONELY ALL THE TIME. LOOK, I MIGHT AS WELL TELL YOU THIS NOW--I'M CRAZY, AND NOBODY HAS EVER STAYED WITH ME, AND YOU WON'T EITHER.
THAT'S NOT TRUE. I'M NOT GOING ANYWHERE.
YOU WILL.
THE NEXT DAY.
HI, MICHELLE, IT'S ME, ADAM.
YANKEESTADIUM
OH HEY! ARE YOU HAVING A GOOD TIME?
UH YEAH, HOW ARE YOU DOING?
I'M FINE.
I MEAN, LAST NIGHT...
EVERYTHING'S FINE. REALLY. I WAS JUST DRUNK. DON'T WORRY ABOUT ME, HAVE FUN WITH YOUR FRIENDS.

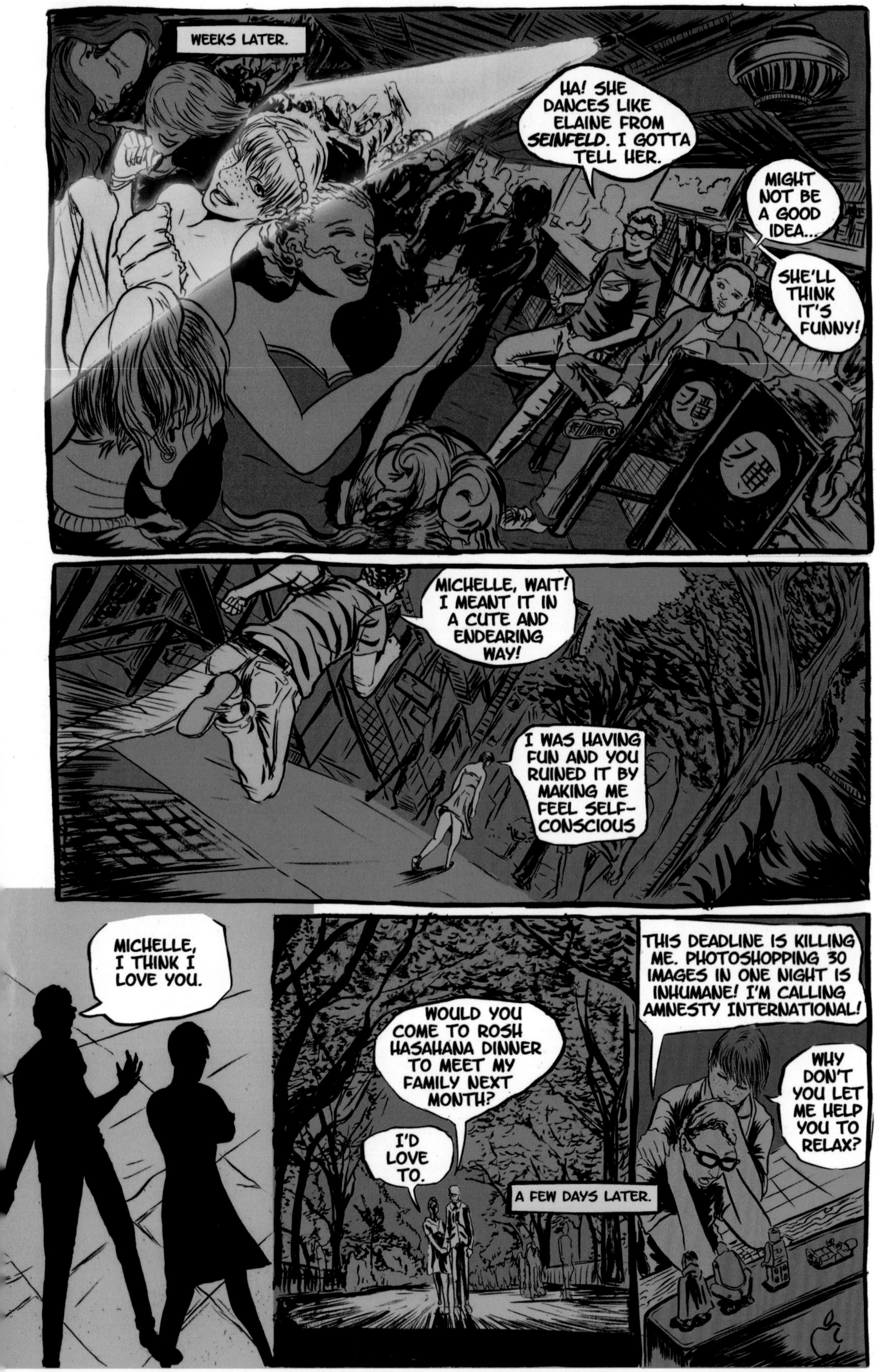
WEEKS LATER.
HA! SHE DANCES LIKE ELAINE FROM SEINFELD. I GOTTA TELL HER.
MIGHT NOT BE A GOOD IDEA...
SHE'LL THINK IT'S FUNNY!
MICHELLE, WAIT! I MEANT IT IN A CUTE AND ENDEARING WAY!
I WAS HAVING FUN AND YOU RUINED IT BY MAKING ME FEEL SELF-CONSCIOUS
MICHELLE, I THINK I LOVE YOU.
WOULD YOU COME TO ROSH HASAHANA DINNER TO MEET MY FAMILY NEXT MONTH?
I'D LOVE TO.
A FEW DAYS LATER.
THIS DEADLINE IS KILLING ME. PHOTOSHOPPING 30 IMAGES IN ONE NIGHT IS INHUMANE! I'M CALLING AMNESTY INTERNATIONAL!
WHY DON'T YOU LET ME HELP YOU TO RELAX?

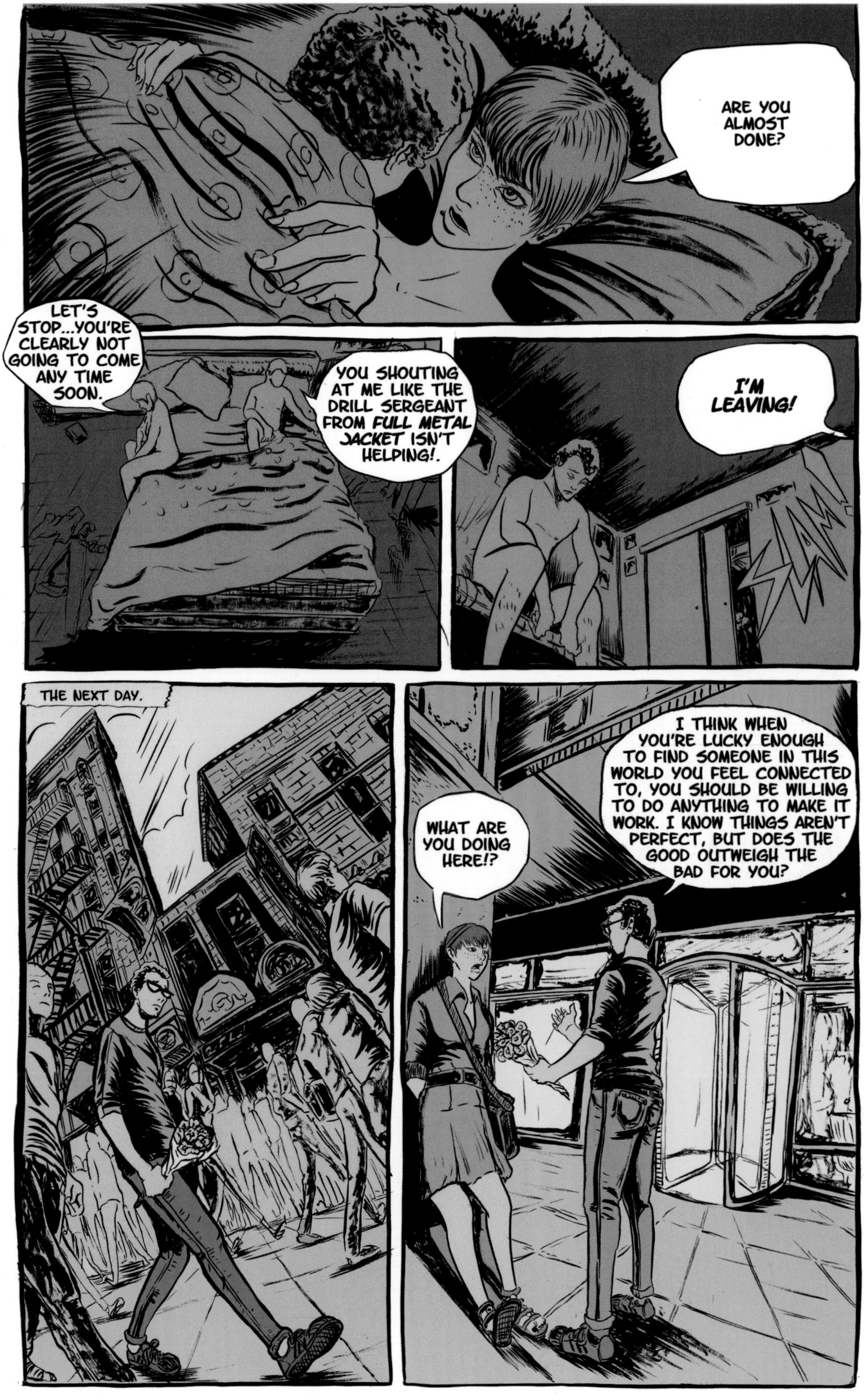
ARE YOU ALMOST DONE?
LET'S STOP...YOU'RE CLEARLY NOT GOING TO COME ANY TIME SOON.
YOU SHOUTING AT ME LIKE THE DRILL SERGEANT FROM FULL METAL JACKET ISN'T HELPING!.
I'M LEAVING!
SLAM
THE NEXT DAY.
WHAT ARE YOU DOING HERE!?
I THINK WHEN YOU'RE LUCKY ENOUGH TO FIND SOMEONE IN THIS WORLD YOU FEEL CONNECTED TO, YOU SHOULD BE WILLING TO DO ANYTHING TO MAKE IT WORK. I KNOW THINGS AREN'T PERFECT, BUT DOES THE GOOD OUTWEIGH THE BAD FOR YOU?

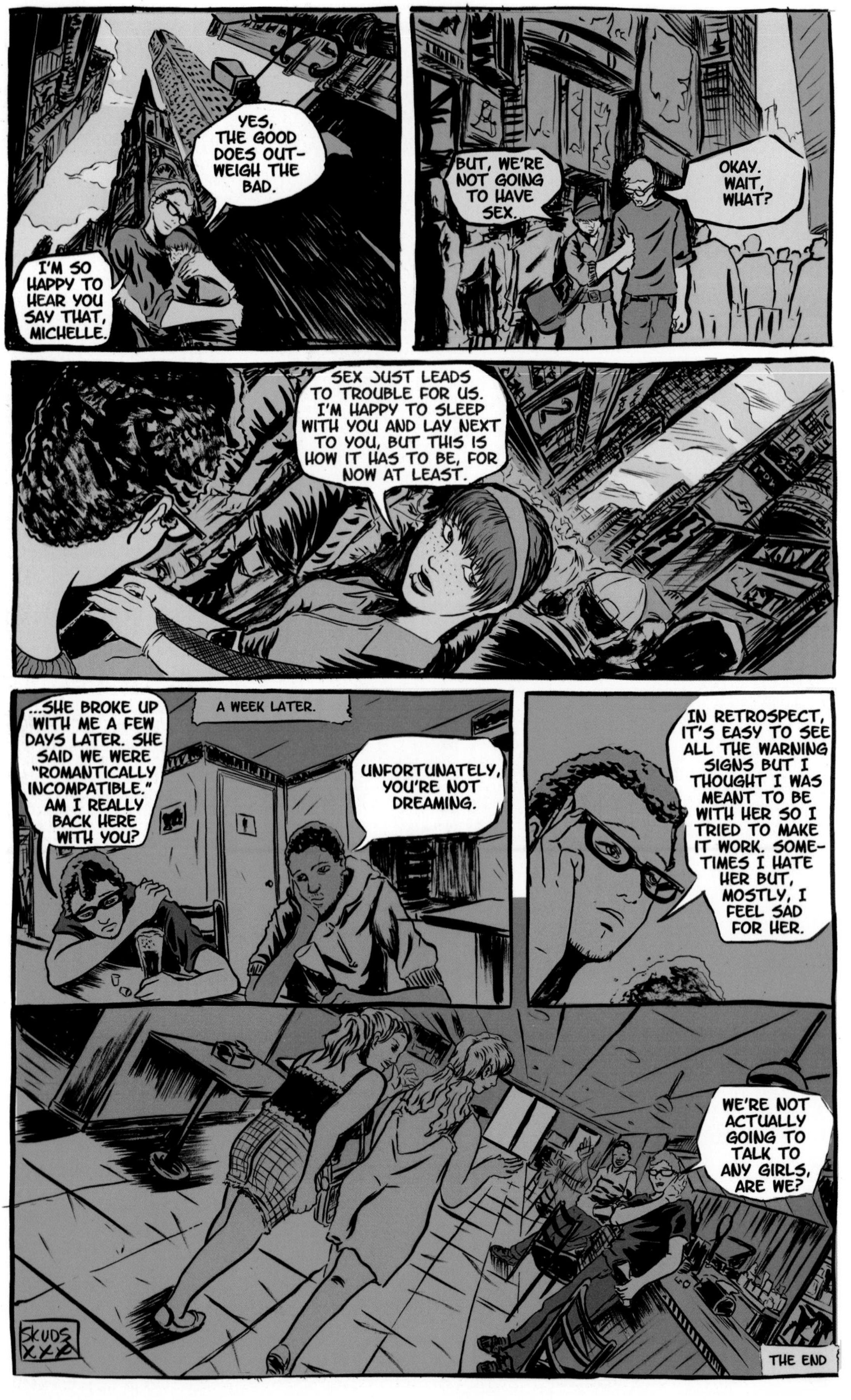
I'M SO HAPPY TO HEAR YOU SAY THAT, MICHELLE.
YES, THE GOOD DOES OUT-WEIGH THE BAD.
BUT, WE'RE NOT GOING TO HAVE SEX.
OKAY. WAIT, WHAT?
SEX JUST LEADS TO TROUBLE FOR US. I'M HAPPY TO SLEEP WITH YOU AND LAY NEXT TO YOU, BUT THIS IS HOW IT HAS TO BE, FOR NOW AT LEAST.
A WEEK LATER.
...SHE BROKE UP WITH ME A FEW DAYS LATER. SHE SAID WE WERE "ROMANTICALLY INCOMPATIBLE." AM I REALLY BACK HERE WITH YOU?
UNFORTUNATELY, YOU'RE NOT DREAMING.
IN RETROSPECT, IT'S EASY TO SEE ALL THE WARNING SIGNS BUT I THOUGHT I WAS MEANT TO BE WITH HER SO I TRIED TO MAKE IT WORK. SOME-TIMES I HATE HER BUT, MOSTLY, I FEEL SAD FOR HER.
WE'RE NOT ACTUALLY GOING TO TALK TO ANY GIRLS, ARE WE?
SKUDS XXX
THE END

SCHMUCK
THE LAPDATE

Written by Seth Kushner
Drawn by Christa Cassano

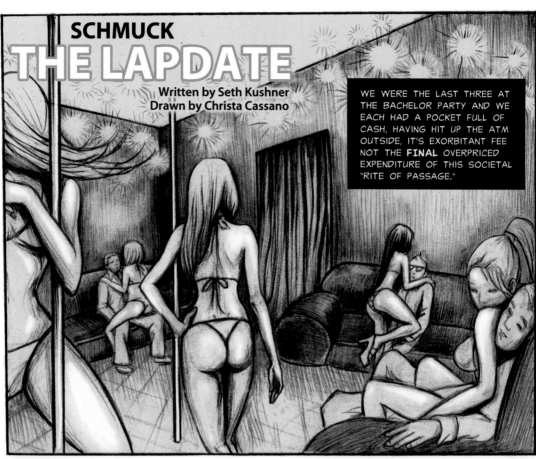

WE WERE THE LAST THREE AT THE BACHELOR PARTY AND WE EACH HAD A POCKET FULL OF CASH, HAVING HIT UP THE ATM OUTSIDE, IT'S EXORBITANT FEE NOT THE **FINAL** OVERPRICED EXPENDITURE OF THIS SOCIETAL "RITE OF PASSAGE."

HOW MUCH TO **MARRY** HIM?

I DON'T KNOW HIM WELL ENOUGH YET.

IT'D BEEN MONTHS SINCE A HUMAN FEMALE HAD TOUCHED ME, AND I WAS IN A PLACE WHERE IT WAS A WOMEN'S **JOB** TO **PRETEND** SHE'S INTERESTED.

I WAS VULNERABLE.

YEAH, THAT SOUNDS GREAT.... BUT THAT MIGHT BE OUT OF MY BUDGET.

CAN YOU AFFORD A HUNDRED DOLLARS?

I NEEDED TO REMIND MYSELF THAT I WAS JUST ANOTHER CUSTOMER WITH A BULGE IN HIS PANTS...

AND MORE IMPORTANTLY, ONE IN MY WALLET.

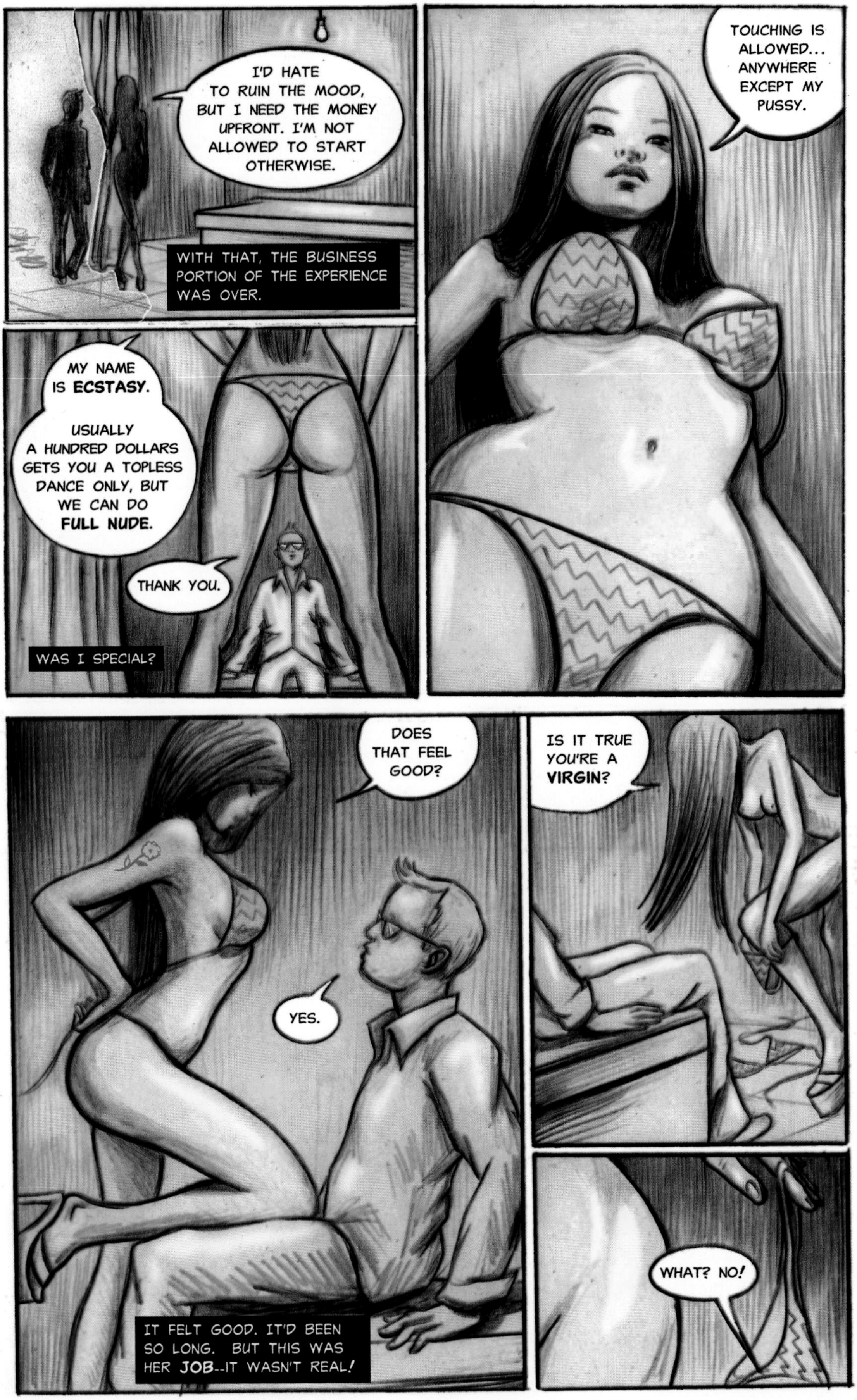
I'D HATE TO RUIN THE MOOD, BUT I NEED THE MONEY UPFRONT. I'M NOT ALLOWED TO START OTHERWISE.
WITH THAT, THE BUSINESS PORTION OF THE EXPERIENCE WAS OVER.
TOUCHING IS ALLOWED... ANYWHERE EXCEPT MY PUSSY.
MY NAME IS **ECSTASY**.
USUALLY A HUNDRED DOLLARS GETS YOU A TOPLESS DANCE ONLY, BUT WE CAN DO **FULL NUDE**.
THANK YOU.
WAS I SPECIAL?
DOES THAT FEEL GOOD?
YES.
IT FELT GOOD. IT'D BEEN SO LONG. BUT THIS WAS HER **JOB**--IT WASN'T REAL!
IS IT TRUE YOU'RE A **VIRGIN**?
WHAT? NO!

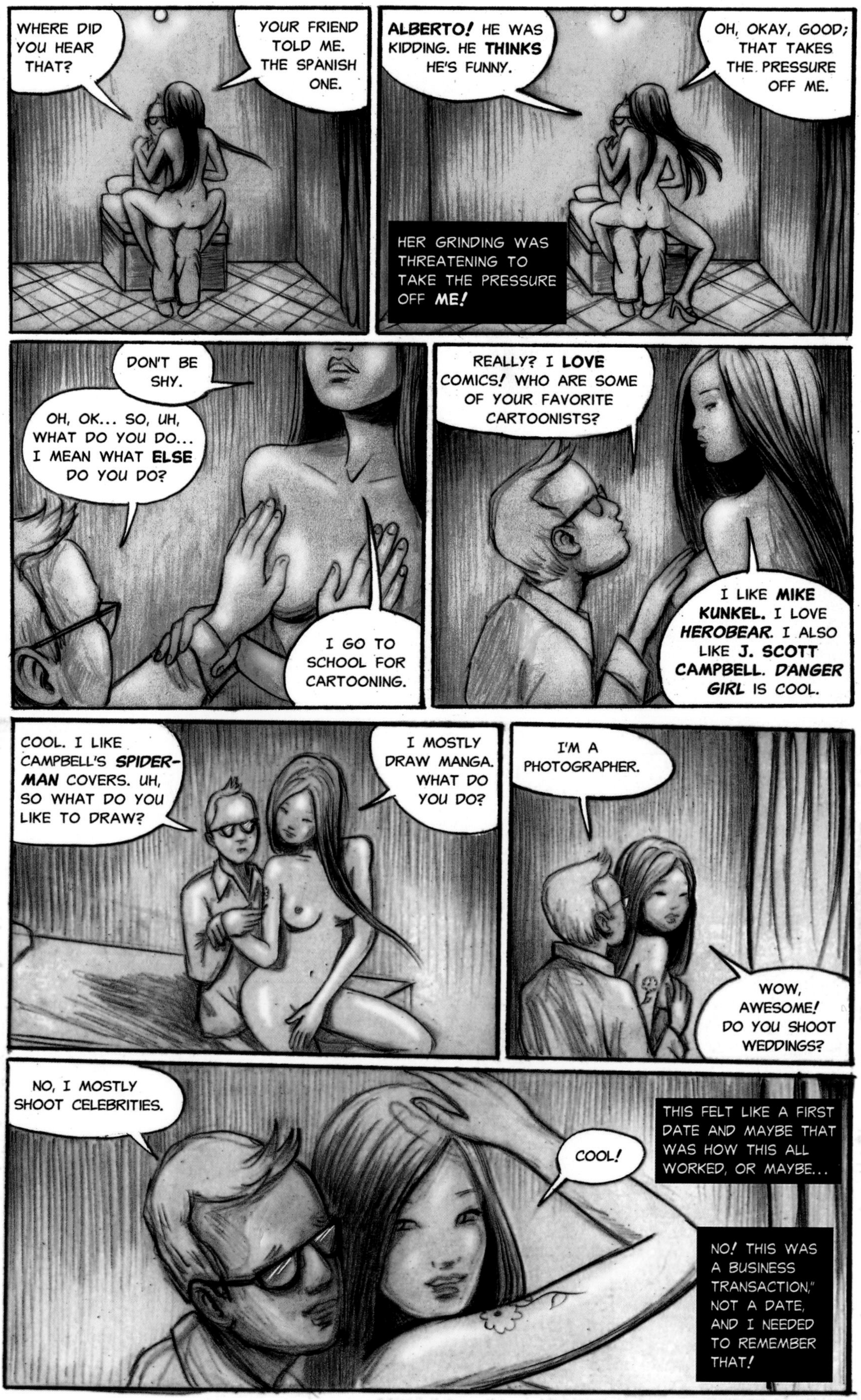

WHERE DID YOU HEAR THAT?
YOUR FRIEND TOLD ME. THE SPANISH ONE.
ALBERTO! HE WAS KIDDING. HE THINKS HE'S FUNNY.
OH, OKAY, GOOD; THAT TAKES THE PRESSURE OFF ME.
HER GRINDING WAS THREATENING TO TAKE THE PRESSURE OFF ME!
DON'T BE SHY.
OH, OK... SO, UH, WHAT DO YOU DO... I MEAN WHAT ELSE DO YOU DO?
I GO TO SCHOOL FOR CARTOONING.
REALLY? I LOVE COMICS! WHO ARE SOME OF YOUR FAVORITE CARTOONISTS?
I LIKE MIKE KUNKEL. I LOVE HEROBEAR. I ALSO LIKE J. SCOTT CAMPBELL. DANGER GIRL IS COOL.
COOL. I LIKE CAMPBELL'S SPIDER-MAN COVERS. UH, SO WHAT DO YOU LIKE TO DRAW?
I MOSTLY DRAW MANGA. WHAT DO YOU DO?
I'M A PHOTOGRAPHER.
WOW, AWESOME! DO YOU SHOOT WEDDINGS?
NO, I MOSTLY SHOOT CELEBRITIES.
COOL!
THIS FELT LIKE A FIRST DATE AND MAYBE THAT WAS HOW THIS ALL WORKED, OR MAYBE...
NO! THIS WAS A BUSINESS TRANSACTION," NOT A DATE, AND I NEEDED TO REMEMBER THAT!

WOULD YOU LIKE TO LAY BACK?

DO YOU EVER SHOOT MODELS?

SOMETIMES. I THINK **YOU'D** MAKE A GREAT MODEL.

I'D BEEN ON PLENTY OF DATES WHERE I'D SPENT **WAY** MORE THAN A HUNDRED DOLLARS FOR DINNER OR DRINKS AND THEY NEVER WENT ANYWHERE NEAR **THIS** FAR.

YOU'RE SURE YOU'RE NOT A VIRGIN?

I'M SURE.

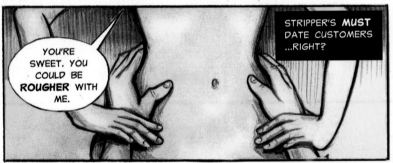

YOU'RE SWEET. YOU COULD BE **ROUGHER** WITH ME.

STRIPPER'S **MUST** DATE CUSTOMERS ...RIGHT?

SHE SEEMED TO CLIMAX, BUT I WASN'T GOING TO FALL FOR THAT CLASSIC STRIPPER **RUSE**.

Mooaaaan!

STILL, THAT SURE **SEEMED** REAL...

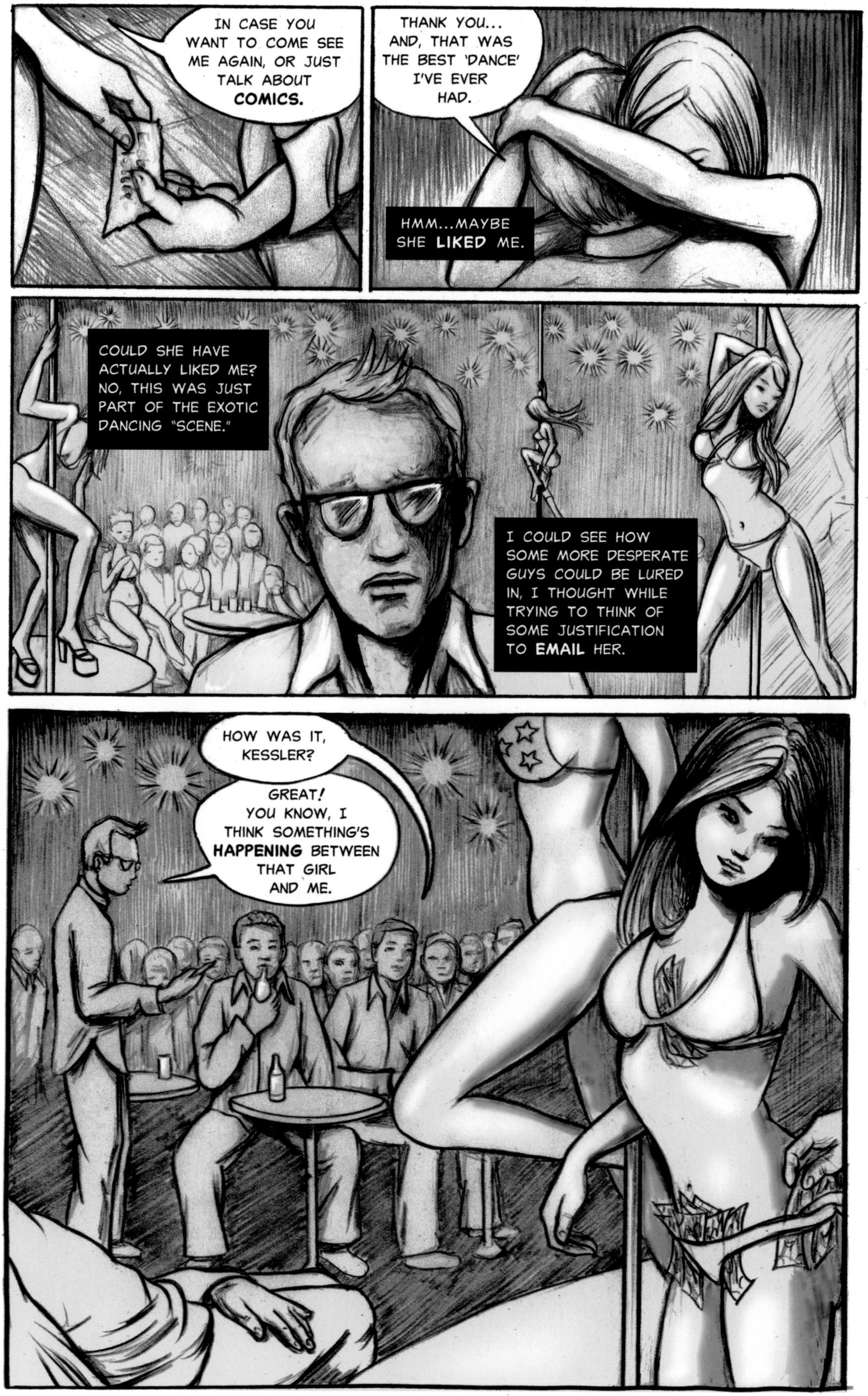
IN CASE YOU WANT TO COME SEE ME AGAIN, OR JUST TALK ABOUT **COMICS.**
THANK YOU... AND, THAT WAS THE BEST 'DANCE' I'VE EVER HAD.
HMM...MAYBE SHE **LIKED** ME.
COULD SHE HAVE ACTUALLY LIKED ME? NO, THIS WAS JUST PART OF THE EXOTIC DANCING "SCENE."
I COULD SEE HOW SOME MORE DESPERATE GUYS COULD BE LURED IN, I THOUGHT WHILE TRYING TO THINK OF SOME JUSTIFICATION TO **EMAIL** HER.
HOW WAS IT, KESSLER?
GREAT! YOU KNOW, I THINK SOMETHING'S **HAPPENING** BETWEEN THAT GIRL AND ME.

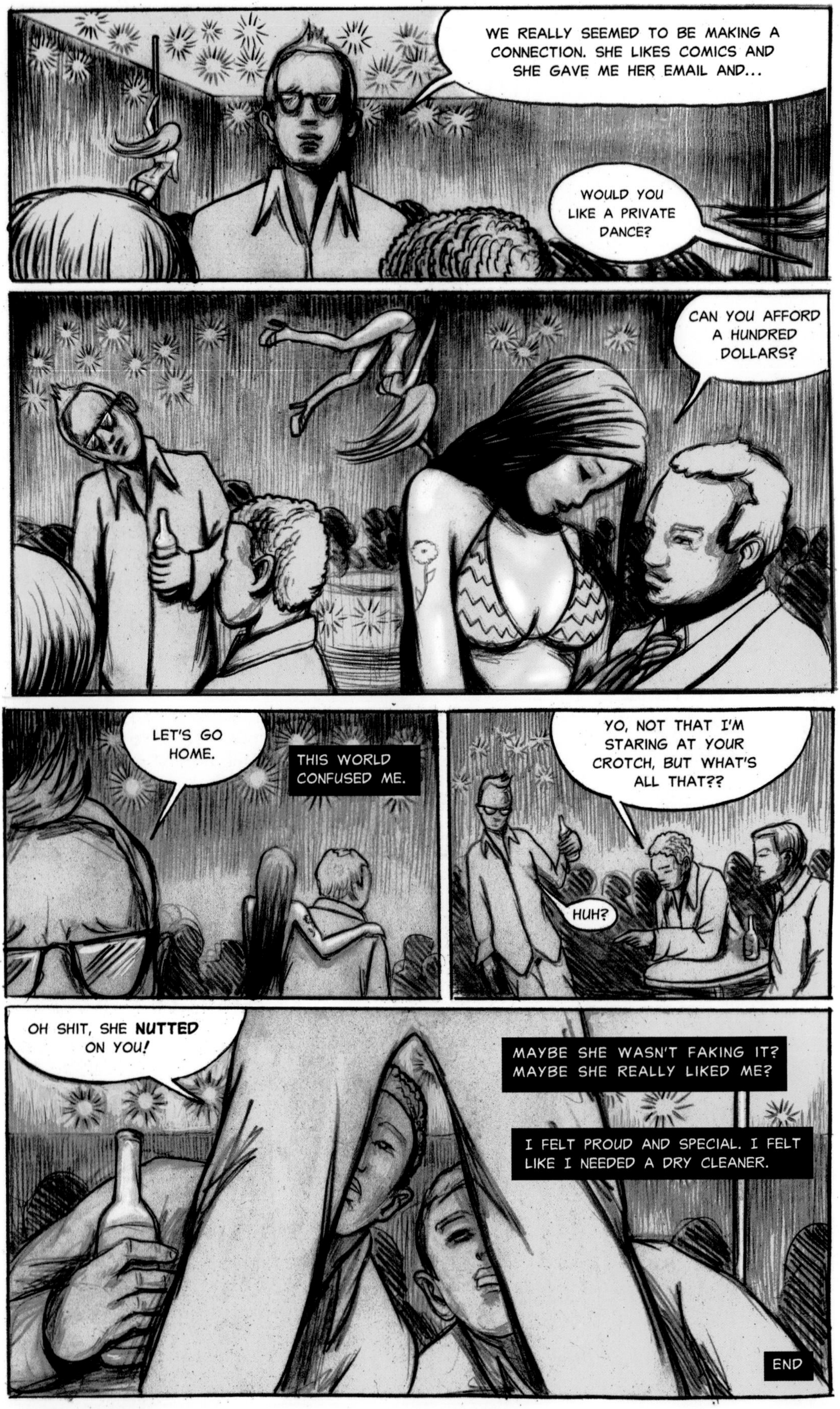
WE REALLY SEEMED TO BE MAKING A CONNECTION. SHE LIKES COMICS AND SHE GAVE ME HER EMAIL AND...
WOULD YOU LIKE A PRIVATE DANCE?
CAN YOU AFFORD A HUNDRED DOLLARS?
LET'S GO HOME.
THIS WORLD CONFUSED ME.
YO, NOT THAT I'M STARING AT YOUR CROTCH, BUT WHAT'S ALL THAT??
HUH?
OH SHIT, SHE **NUTTED** ON YOU!
MAYBE SHE WASN'T FAKING IT? MAYBE SHE REALLY LIKED ME?
I FELT PROUD AND SPECIAL. I FELT LIKE I NEEDED A DRY CLEANER.
END

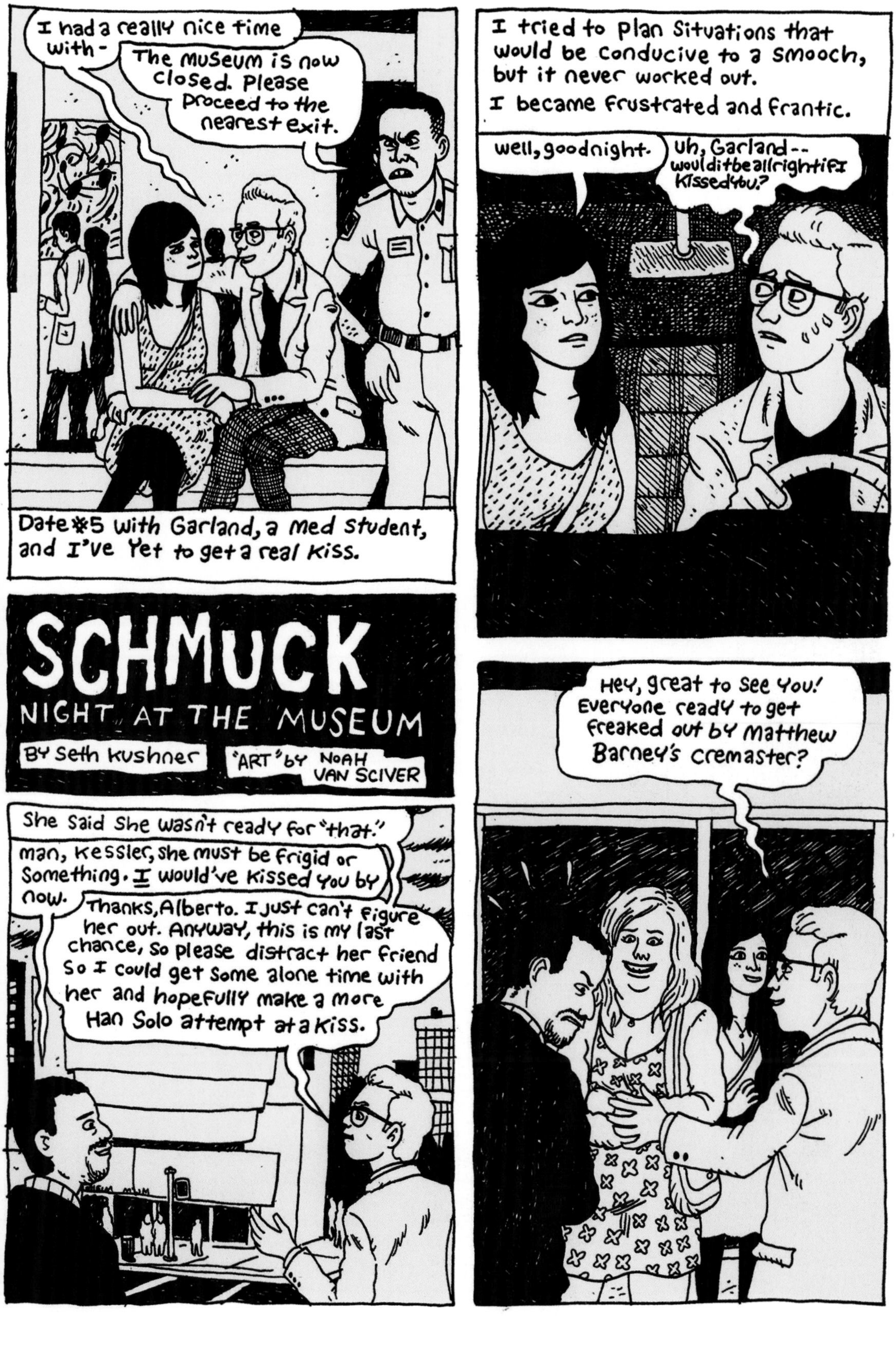

I had a really nice time with-
The museum is now closed. Please proceed to the nearest exit.
Date #5 with Garland, a med student, and I've yet to get a real kiss.
I tried to plan situations that would be conducive to a smooch, but it never worked out.
I became frustrated and frantic.
Well, goodnight.
Uh, Garland-- wouldit be allright if I kissed you?
SCHMUCK
NIGHT AT THE MUSEUM
BY Seth Kushner
"ART" by NOAH VAN SCIVER
She said she wasn't ready for "that."
Man, Kessler, she must be frigid or something. I would've kissed you by now.
Thanks, Alberto. I just can't figure her out. Anyway, this is my last chance, so please distract her friend so I could get some alone time with her and hopefully make a more Han Solo attempt at a kiss.
Hey, great to see you! Everyone ready to get freaked out by Matthew Barney's Cremaster?

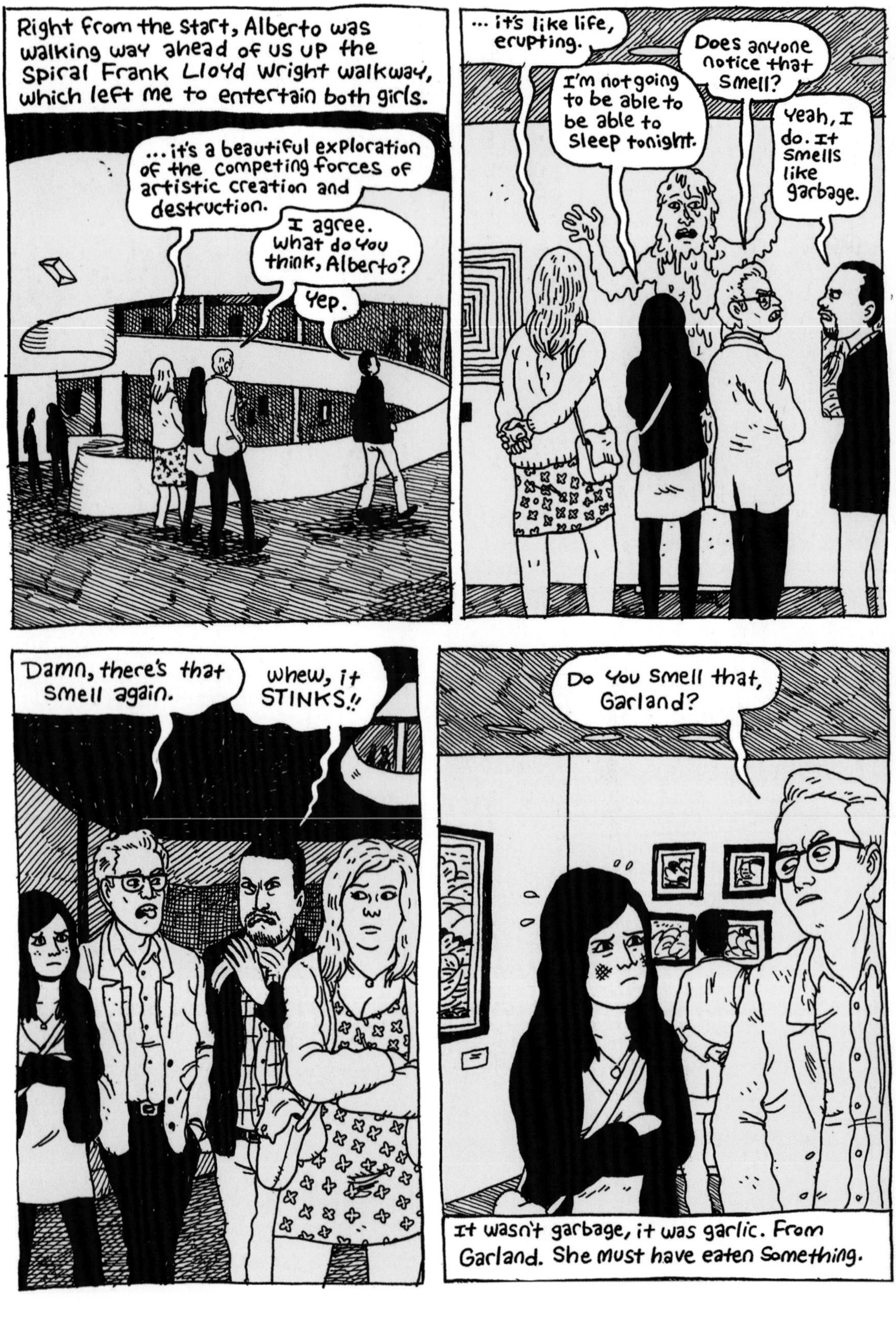

Right from the start, Alberto was walking way ahead of us up the Spiral Frank Lloyd Wright walkway, which left me to entertain both girls.
...it's a beautiful exploration of the competing forces of artistic creation and destruction.
I agree. What do you think, Alberto?
Yep.
... it's like life, erupting.
I'm not going to be able to be able to Sleep tonight.
Does anyone notice that smell?
Yeah, I do. It smells like garbage.
Damn, there's that smell again.
Whew, it STINKS!!
Do you smell that, Garland?
It wasn't garbage, it was garlic. From Garland. She must have eaten Something.

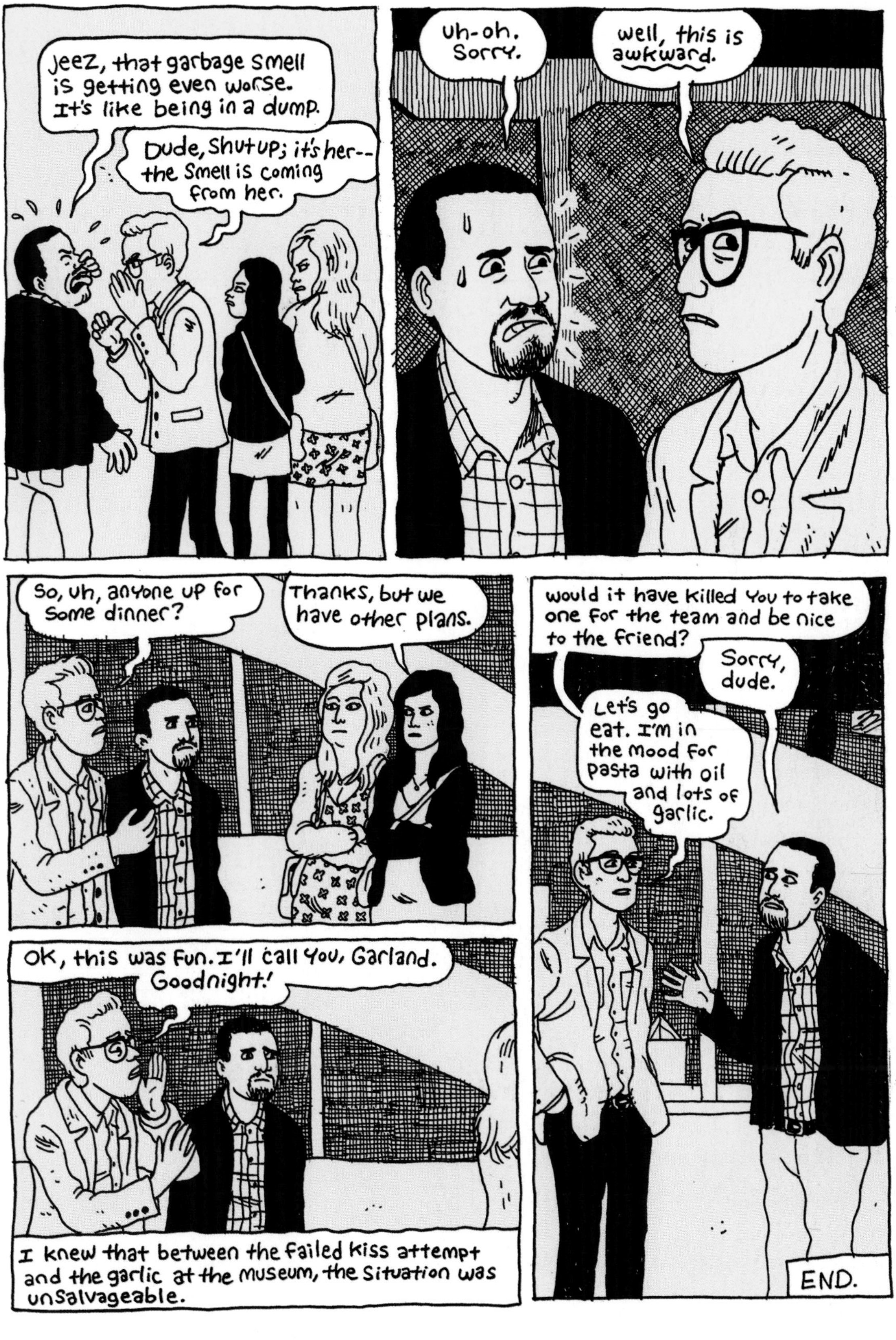
Jeez, that garbage smell is getting even worse. It's like being in a dump.
Dude, shut up; it's her-- the smell is coming from her.
Uh-oh. Sorry.
Well, this is awkward.
So, uh, anyone up for some dinner?
Thanks, but we have other plans.
OK, this was fun. I'll call you, Garland. Goodnight!
I knew that between the failed kiss attempt and the garlic at the museum, the situation was unsalvageable.
Would it have killed you to take one for the team and be nice to the friend?
Sorry, dude.
Let's go eat. I'm in the mood for pasta with oil and lots of garlic.
END.

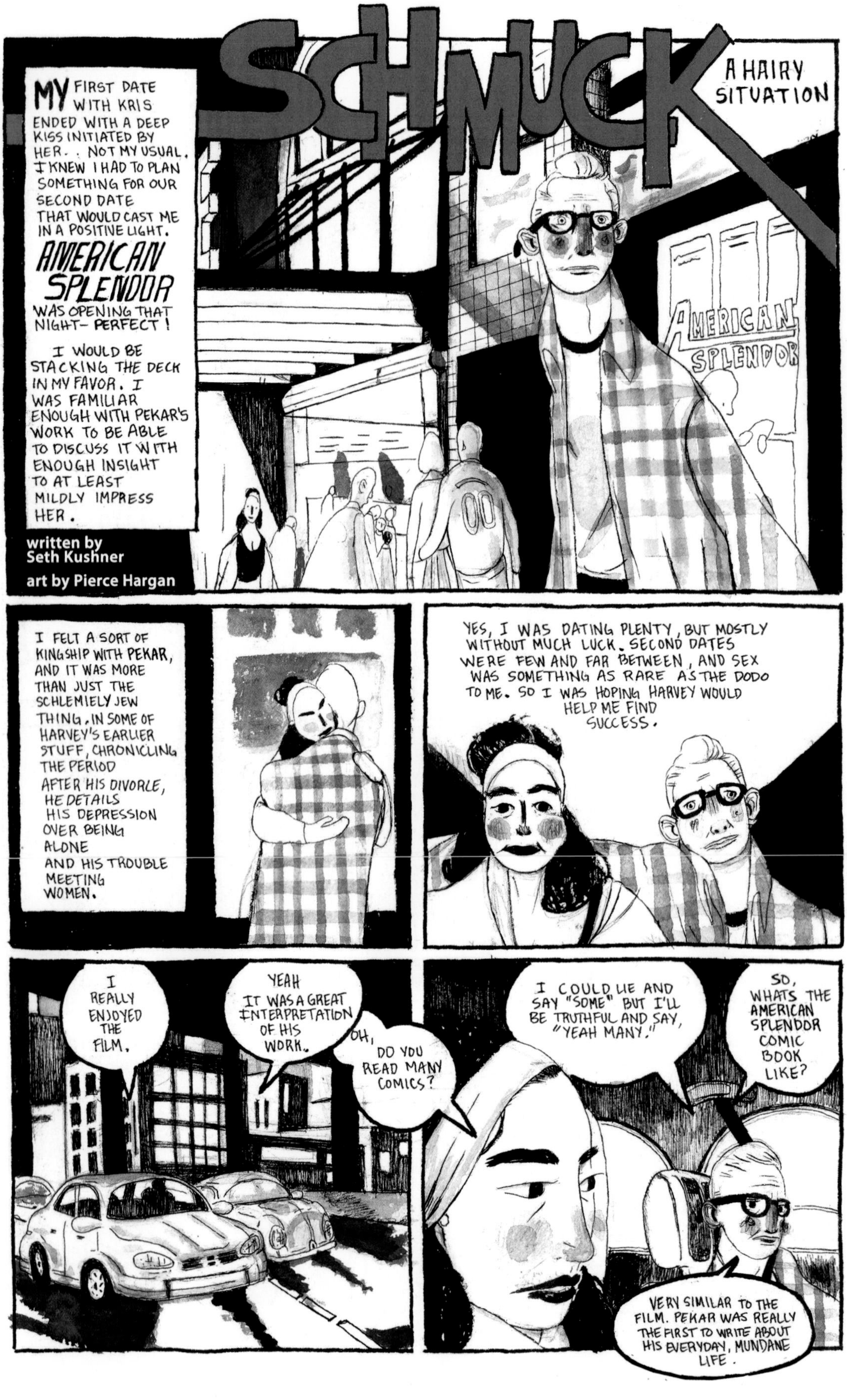
SCHMUCK
A HAIRY SITUATION
MY FIRST DATE WITH KRIS ENDED WITH A DEEP KISS INITIATED BY HER. . NOT MY USUAL. I KNEW I HAD TO PLAN SOMETHING FOR OUR SECOND DATE THAT WOULD CAST ME IN A POSITIVE LIGHT.
AMERICAN SPLENDOR WAS OPENING THAT NIGHT– PERFECT!
I WOULD BE STACKING THE DECK IN MY FAVOR. I WAS FAMILIAR ENOUGH WITH PEKAR'S WORK TO BE ABLE TO DISCUSS IT WITH ENOUGH INSIGHT TO AT LEAST MILDLY IMPRESS HER.
written by Seth Kushner
art by Pierce Hargan
AMERICAN SPLENDOR
I FELT A SORT OF KINGSHIP WITH PEKAR, AND IT WAS MORE THAN JUST THE SCHLEMIELY JEW THING. IN SOME OF HARVEY'S EARLIER STUFF, CHRONICLING THE PERIOD AFTER HIS DIVORCE, HE DETAILS HIS DEPRESSION OVER BEING ALONE AND HIS TROUBLE MEETING WOMEN.
YES, I WAS DATING PLENTY, BUT MOSTLY WITHOUT MUCH LUCK. SECOND DATES WERE FEW AND FAR BETWEEN, AND SEX WAS SOMETHING AS RARE AS THE DODO TO ME. SO I WAS HOPING HARVEY WOULD HELP ME FIND SUCCESS.
I REALLY ENJOYED THE FILM.
YEAH IT WAS A GREAT INTERPRETATION OF HIS WORK.
OH, DO YOU READ MANY COMICS?
I COULD LIE AND SAY "SOME" BUT I'LL BE TRUTHFUL AND SAY, "YEAH MANY."
SO, WHATS THE AMERICAN SPLENDOR COMIC BOOK LIKE?
VERY SIMILAR TO THE FILM. PEKAR WAS REALLY THE FIRST TO WRITE ABOUT HIS EVERYDAY, MUNDANE LIFE.

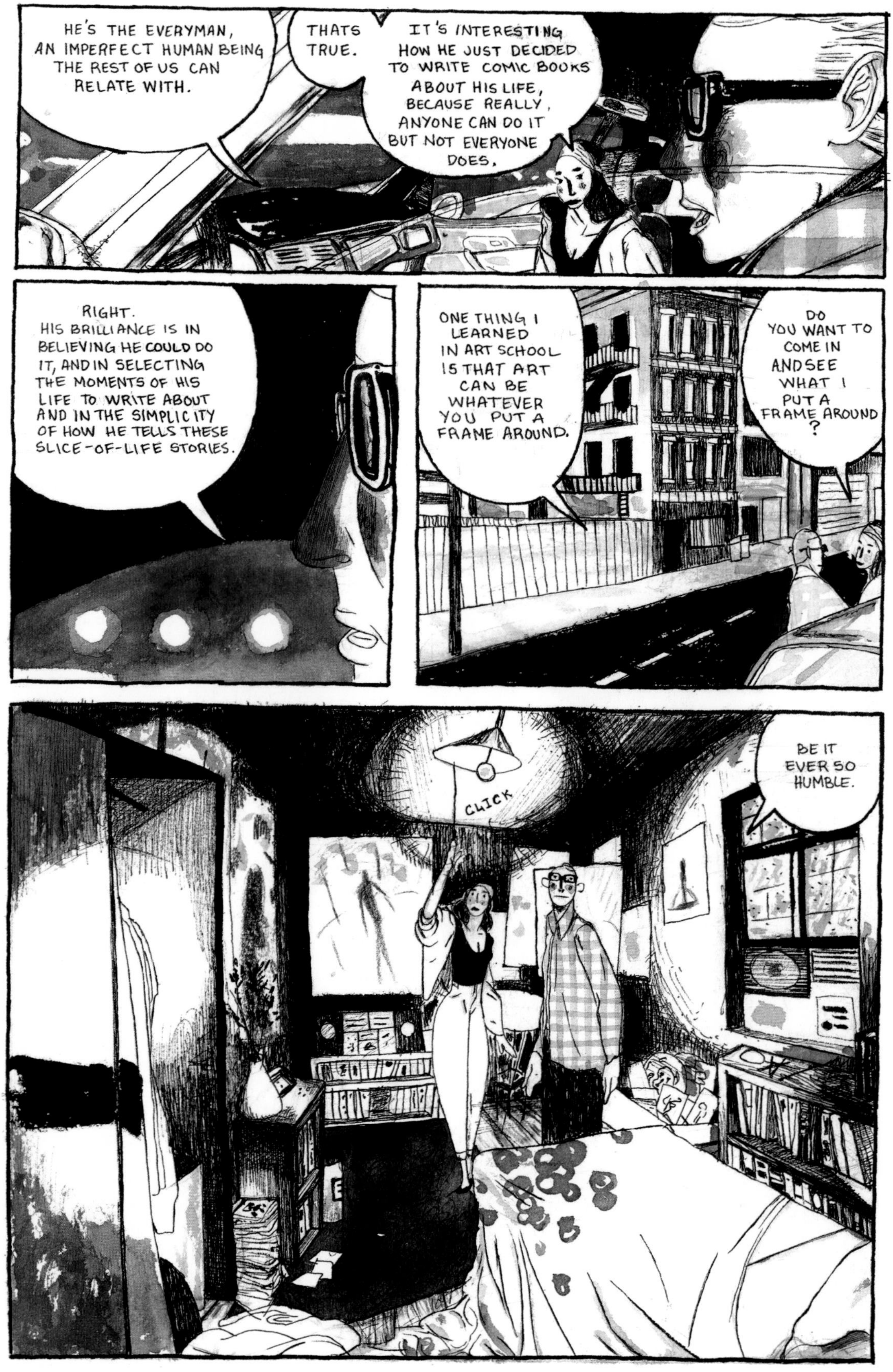
HE'S THE EVERYMAN, AN IMPERFECT HUMAN BEING THE REST OF US CAN RELATE WITH.
THATS TRUE.
IT'S INTERESTING HOW HE JUST DECIDED TO WRITE COMIC BOOKS ABOUT HIS LIFE, BECAUSE REALLY, ANYONE CAN DO IT BUT NOT EVERYONE DOES.
RIGHT. HIS BRILLIANCE IS IN BELIEVING HE COULD DO IT, AND IN SELECTING THE MOMENTS OF HIS LIFE TO WRITE ABOUT AND IN THE SIMPLICITY OF HOW HE TELLS THESE SLICE-OF-LIFE STORIES.
ONE THING I LEARNED IN ART SCHOOL IS THAT ART CAN BE WHATEVER YOU PUT A FRAME AROUND.
DO YOU WANT TO COME IN AND SEE WHAT I PUT A FRAME AROUND?
CLICK
BE IT EVER SO HUMBLE.

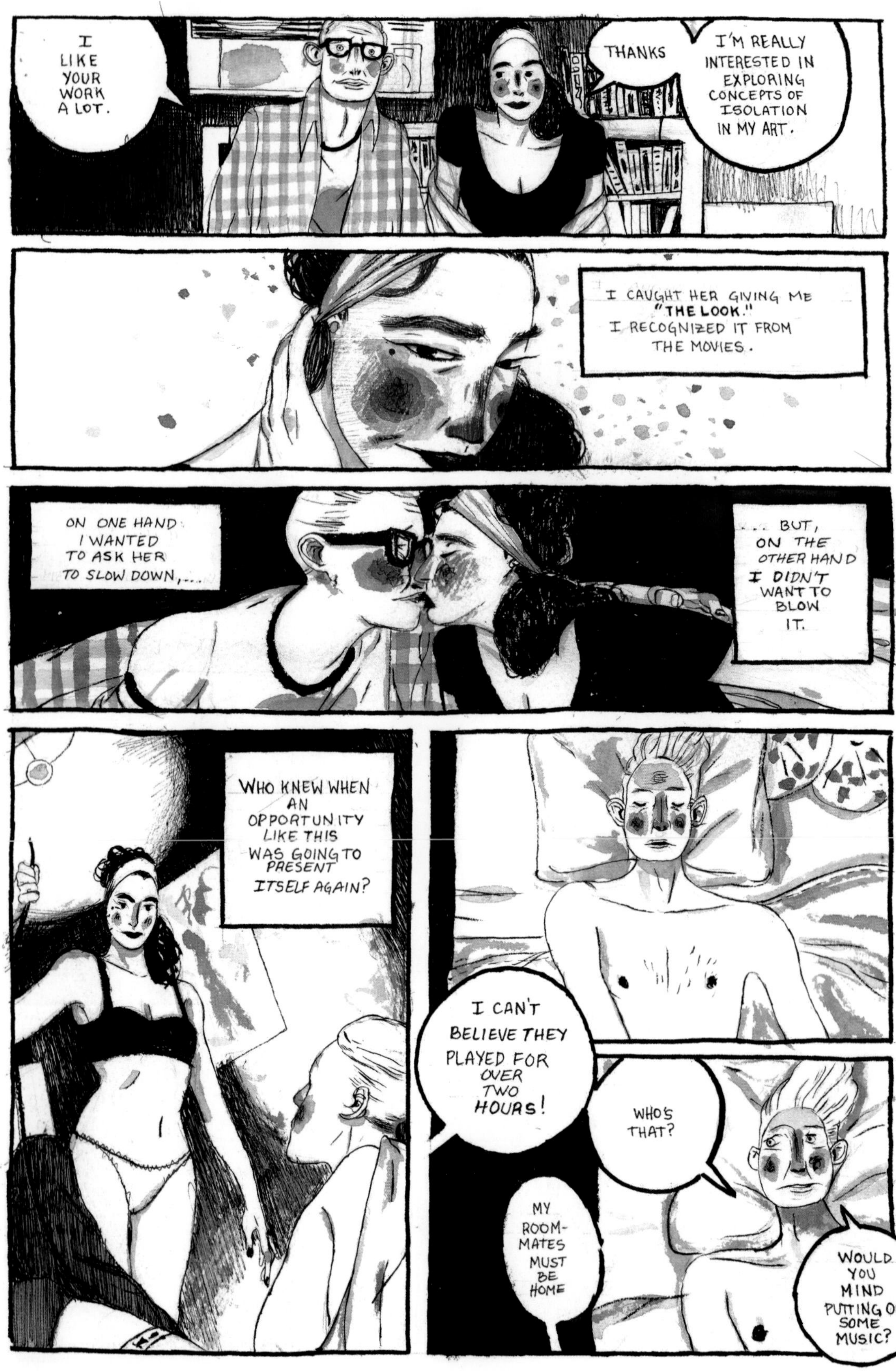
I LIKE YOUR WORK A LOT.
THANKS
I'M REALLY INTERESTED IN EXPLORING CONCEPTS OF ISOLATION IN MY ART.
I CAUGHT HER GIVING ME "THE LOOK." I RECOGNIZED IT FROM THE MOVIES.
ON ONE HAND I WANTED TO ASK HER TO SLOW DOWN,...
... BUT, ON THE OTHER HAND I DIDN'T WANT TO BLOW IT.
WHO KNEW WHEN AN OPPORTUNITY LIKE THIS WAS GOING TO PRESENT ITSELF AGAIN?
I CAN'T BELIEVE THEY PLAYED FOR OVER TWO HOURS!
WHO'S THAT?
MY ROOMMATES MUST BE HOME
WOULD YOU MIND PUTTING ON SOME MUSIC?

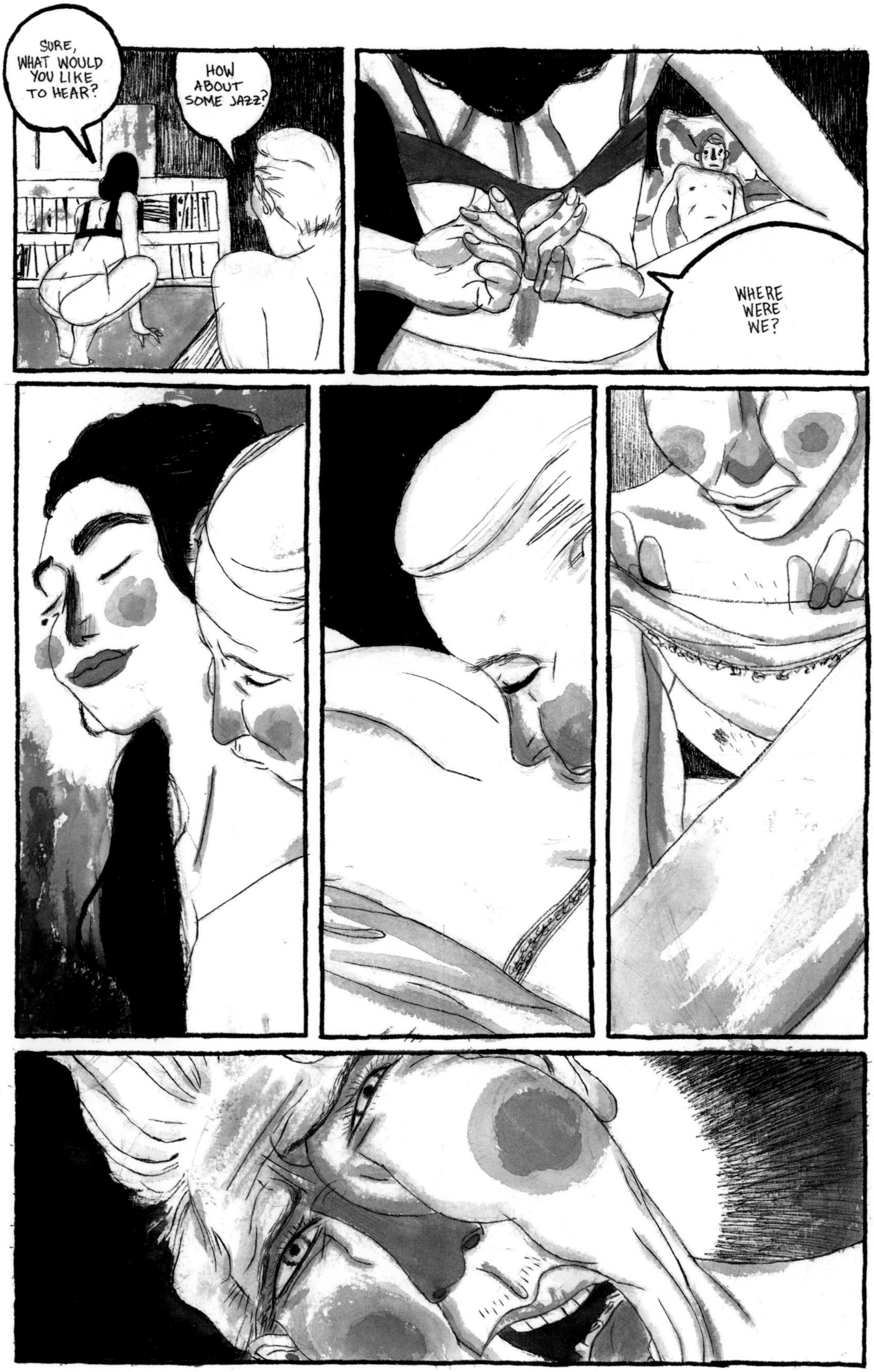
SURE, WHAT WOULD YOU LIKE TO HEAR?
HOW ABOUT SOME JAZZ?
WHERE WERE WE?

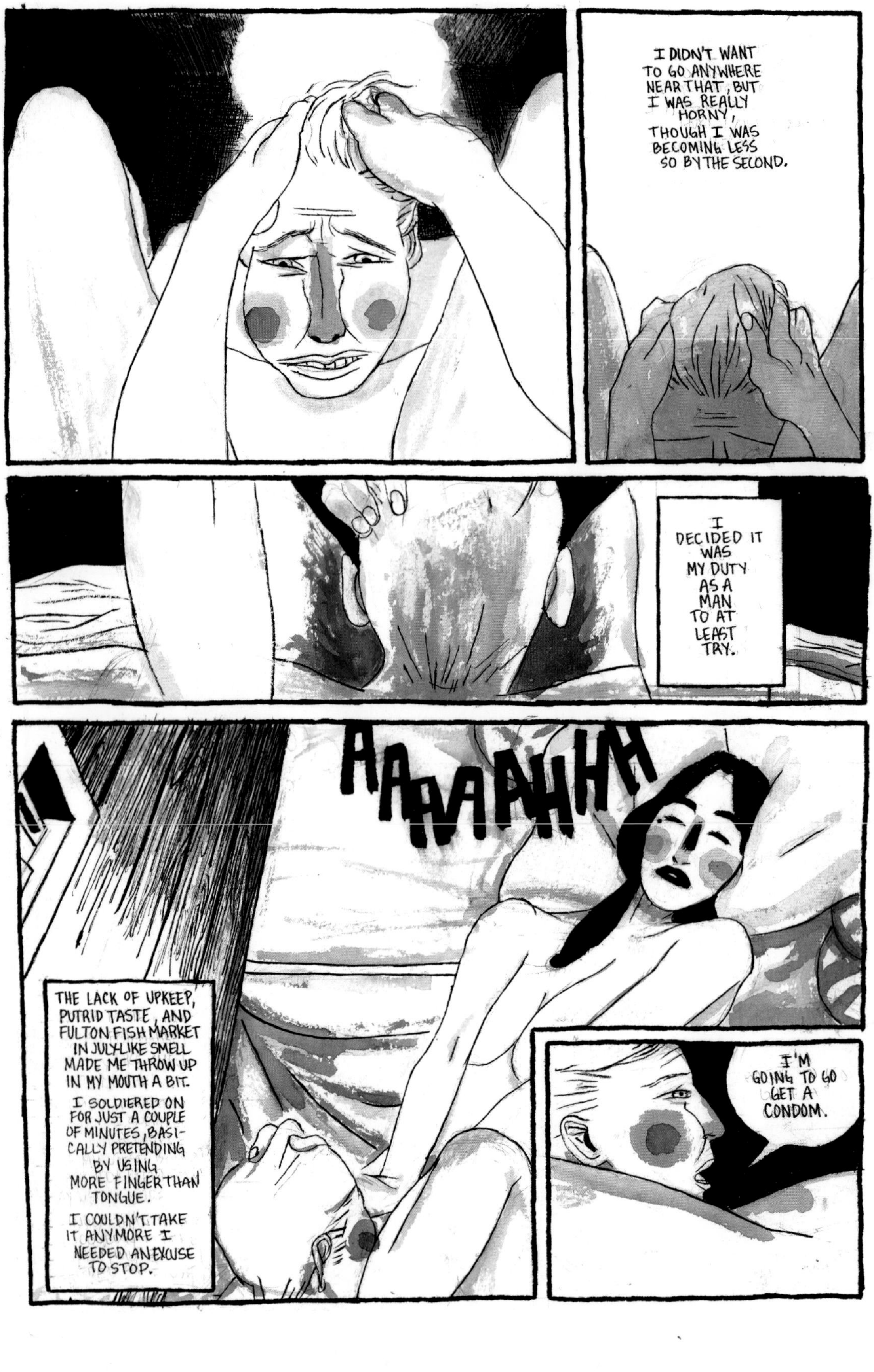
I DIDN'T WANT TO GO ANYWHERE NEAR THAT, BUT I WAS REALLY HORNY, THOUGH I WAS BECOMING LESS SO BY THE SECOND.
I DECIDED IT WAS MY DUTY AS A MAN TO AT LEAST TRY.
AAAAAHHH
THE LACK OF UPKEEP, PUTRID TASTE, AND FULTON FISH MARKET IN JULY-LIKE SMELL MADE ME THROW UP IN MY MOUTH A BIT.
I SOLDIERED ON FOR JUST A COUPLE OF MINUTES, BASICALLY PRETENDING BY USING MORE FINGER THAN TONGUE.
I COULDN'T TAKE IT ANYMORE I NEEDED AN EXCUSE TO STOP.
I'M GOING TO GO GET A CONDOM.

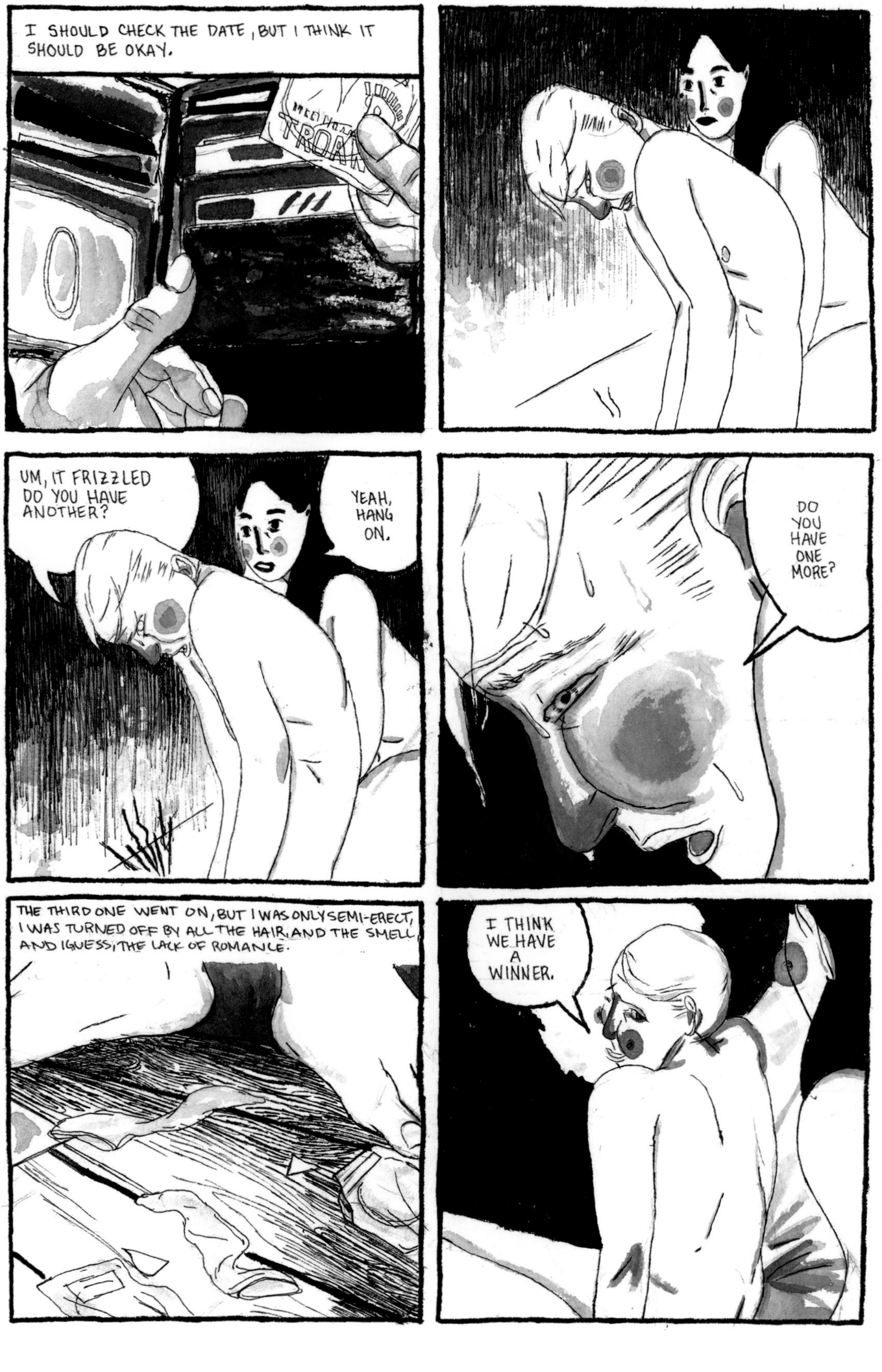
I SHOULD CHECK THE DATE, BUT I THINK IT SHOULD BE OKAY.
UM, IT FRIZZLED DO YOU HAVE ANOTHER?
YEAH, HANG ON.
DO YOU HAVE ONE MORE?
THE THIRD ONE WENT ON, BUT I WAS ONLY SEMI-ERECT, I WAS TURNED OFF BY ALL THE HAIR, AND THE SMELL AND I GUESS, THE LACK OF ROMANCE.
I THINK WE HAVE A WINNER.

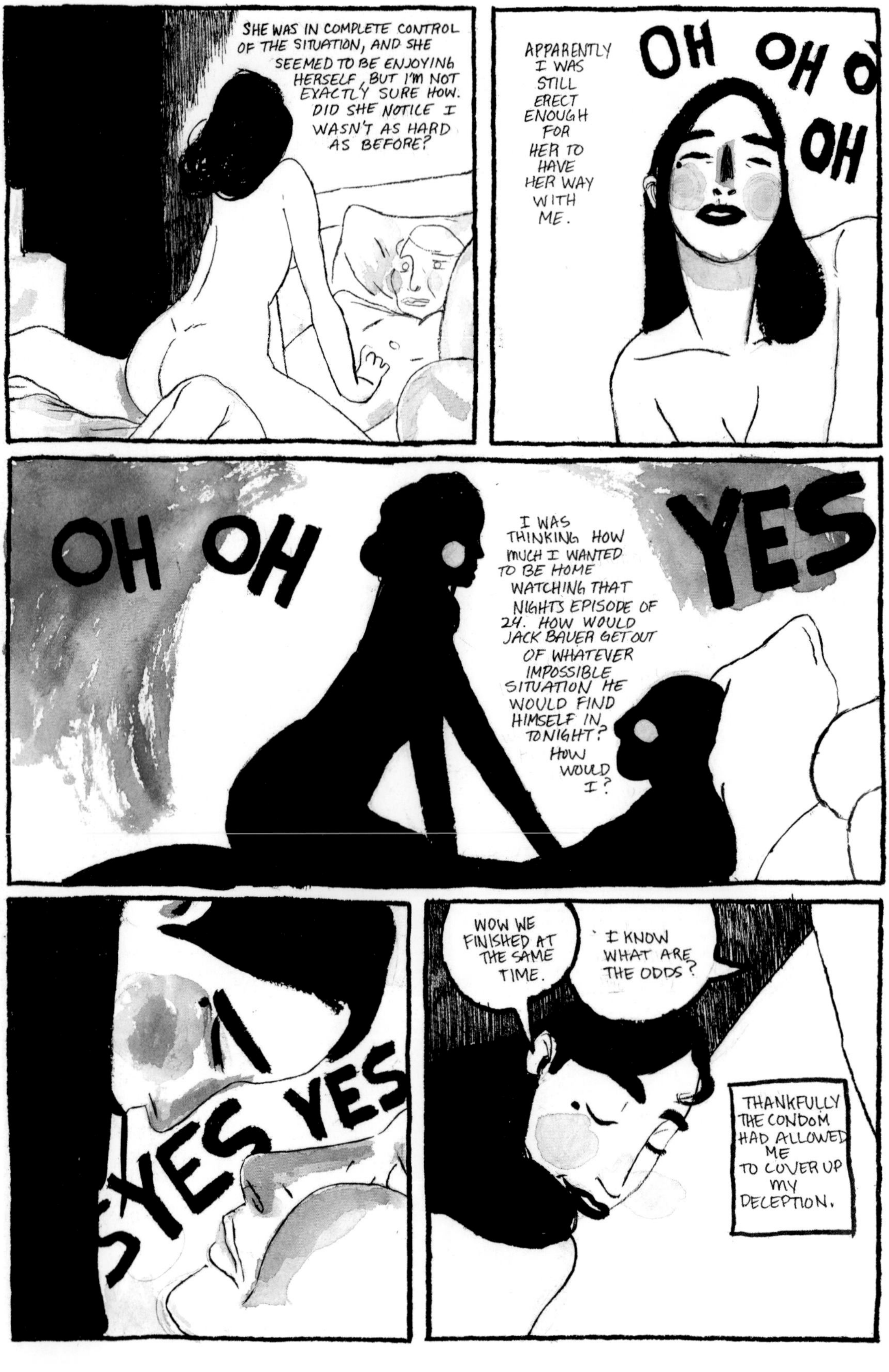
SHE WAS IN COMPLETE CONTROL OF THE SITUATION, AND SHE SEEMED TO BE ENJOYING HERSELF, BUT I'M NOT EXACTLY SURE HOW. DID SHE NOTICE I WASN'T AS HARD AS BEFORE?
APPARENTLY I WAS STILL ERECT ENOUGH FOR HER TO HAVE HER WAY WITH ME.
OH OH OH
OH
OH OH
I WAS THINKING HOW MUCH I WANTED TO BE HOME WATCHING THAT NIGHTS EPISODE OF 24. HOW WOULD JACK BAUER GET OUT OF WHATEVER IMPOSSIBLE SITUATION HE WOULD FIND HIMSELF IN TONIGHT? HOW WOULD I?
YES
YES YES
WOW WE FINISHED AT THE SAME TIME.
I KNOW WHAT ARE THE ODDS?
THANKFULLY THE CONDOM HAD ALLOWED ME TO COVER UP MY DECEPTION.

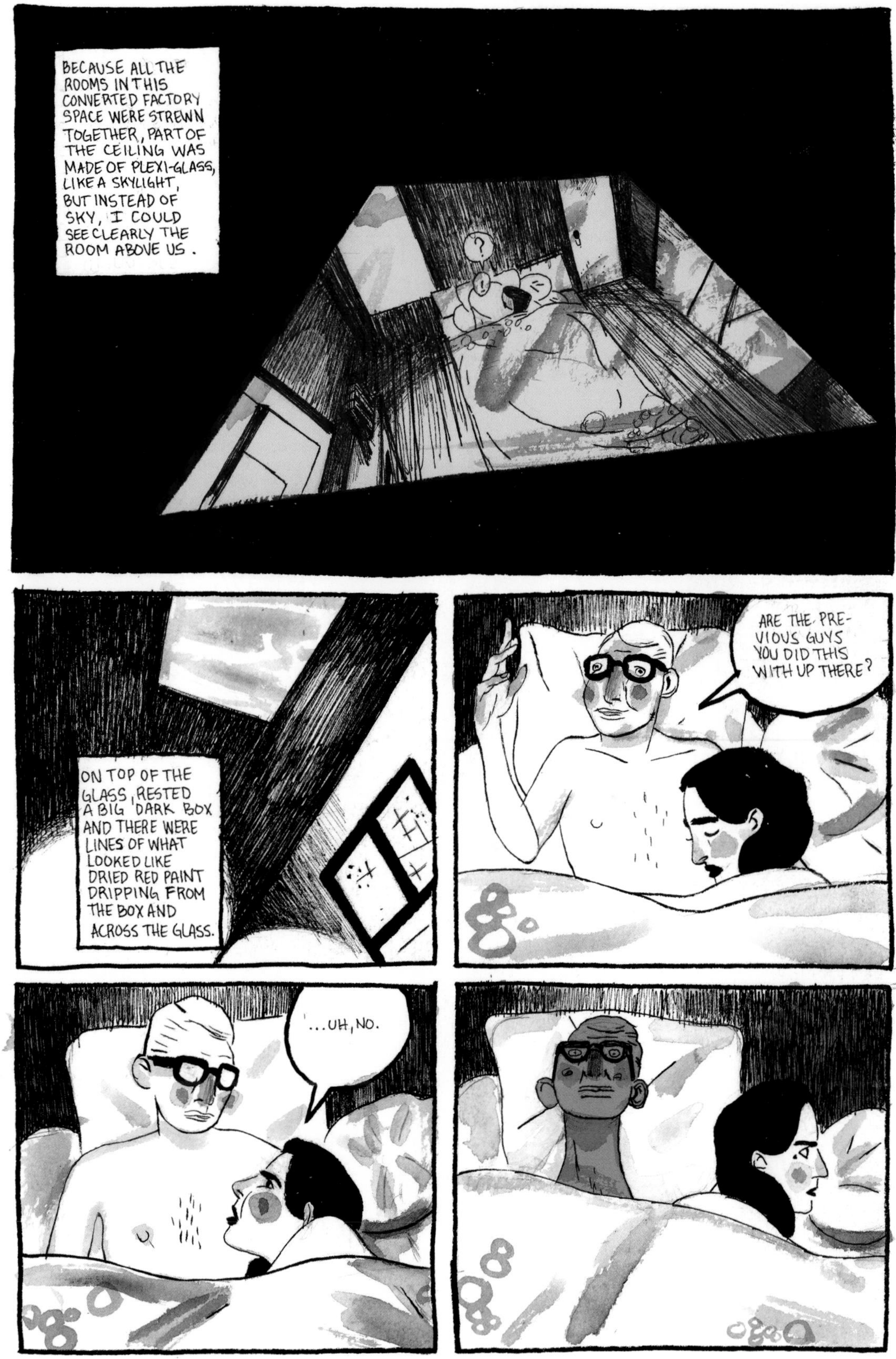
BECAUSE ALL THE ROOMS IN THIS CONVERTED FACTORY SPACE WERE STREWN TOGETHER, PART OF THE CEILING WAS MADE OF PLEXI-GLASS, LIKE A SKYLIGHT, BUT INSTEAD OF SKY, I COULD SEE CLEARLY THE ROOM ABOVE US.
ON TOP OF THE GLASS, RESTED A BIG DARK BOX AND THERE WERE LINES OF WHAT LOOKED LIKE DRIED RED PAINT DRIPPING FROM THE BOX AND ACROSS THE GLASS.
ARE THE PREVIOUS GUYS YOU DID THIS WITH UP THERE?
...UH, NO.

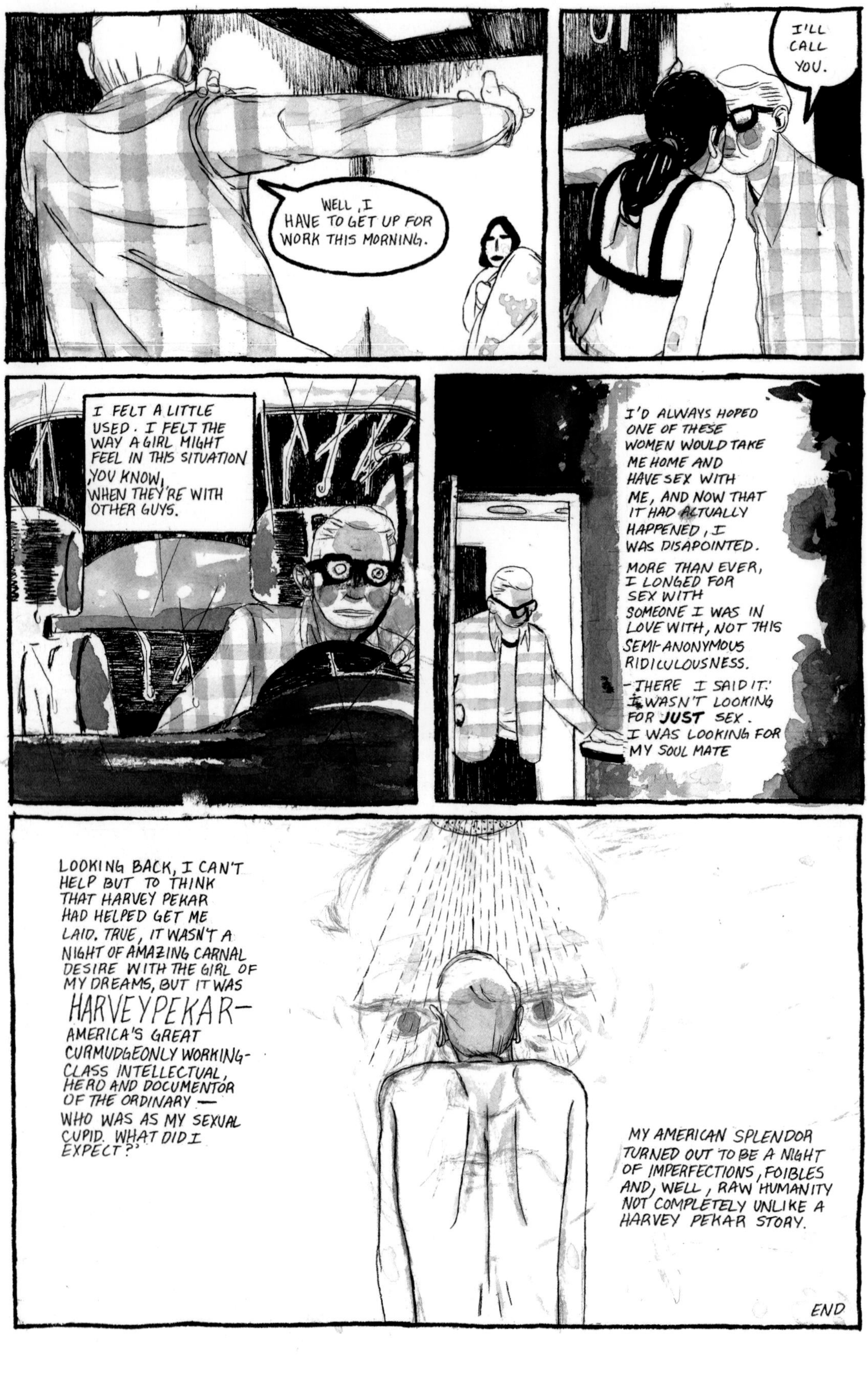
WELL, I HAVE TO GET UP FOR WORK THIS MORNING.
I'LL CALL YOU.
I FELT A LITTLE USED. I FELT THE WAY A GIRL MIGHT FEEL IN THIS SITUATION, YOU KNOW, WHEN THEY'RE WITH OTHER GUYS.
I'D ALWAYS HOPED ONE OF THESE WOMEN WOULD TAKE ME HOME AND HAVE SEX WITH ME, AND NOW THAT IT HAD ACTUALLY HAPPENED, I WAS DISAPOINTED.
MORE THAN EVER, I LONGED FOR SEX WITH SOMEONE I WAS IN LOVE WITH, NOT THIS SEMI-ANONYMOUS RIDICULOUSNESS.
-THERE I SAID IT.' I WASN'T LOOKING FOR JUST SEX. I WAS LOOKING FOR MY SOUL MATE
LOOKING BACK, I CAN'T HELP BUT TO THINK THAT HARVEY PEKAR HAD HELPED GET ME LAID. TRUE, IT WASN'T A NIGHT OF AMAZING CARNAL DESIRE WITH THE GIRL OF MY DREAMS, BUT IT WAS HARVEY PEKAR— AMERICA'S GREAT CURMUDGEONLY WORKING-CLASS INTELLECTUAL, HERO AND DOCUMENTOR OF THE ORDINARY — WHO WAS AS MY SEXUAL CUPID. WHAT DID I EXPECT?'
MY AMERICAN SPLENDOR TURNED OUT TO BE A NIGHT OF IMPERFECTIONS, FOIBLES AND, WELL, RAW HUMANITY NOT COMPLETELY UNLIKE A HARVEY PEKAR STORY.
END

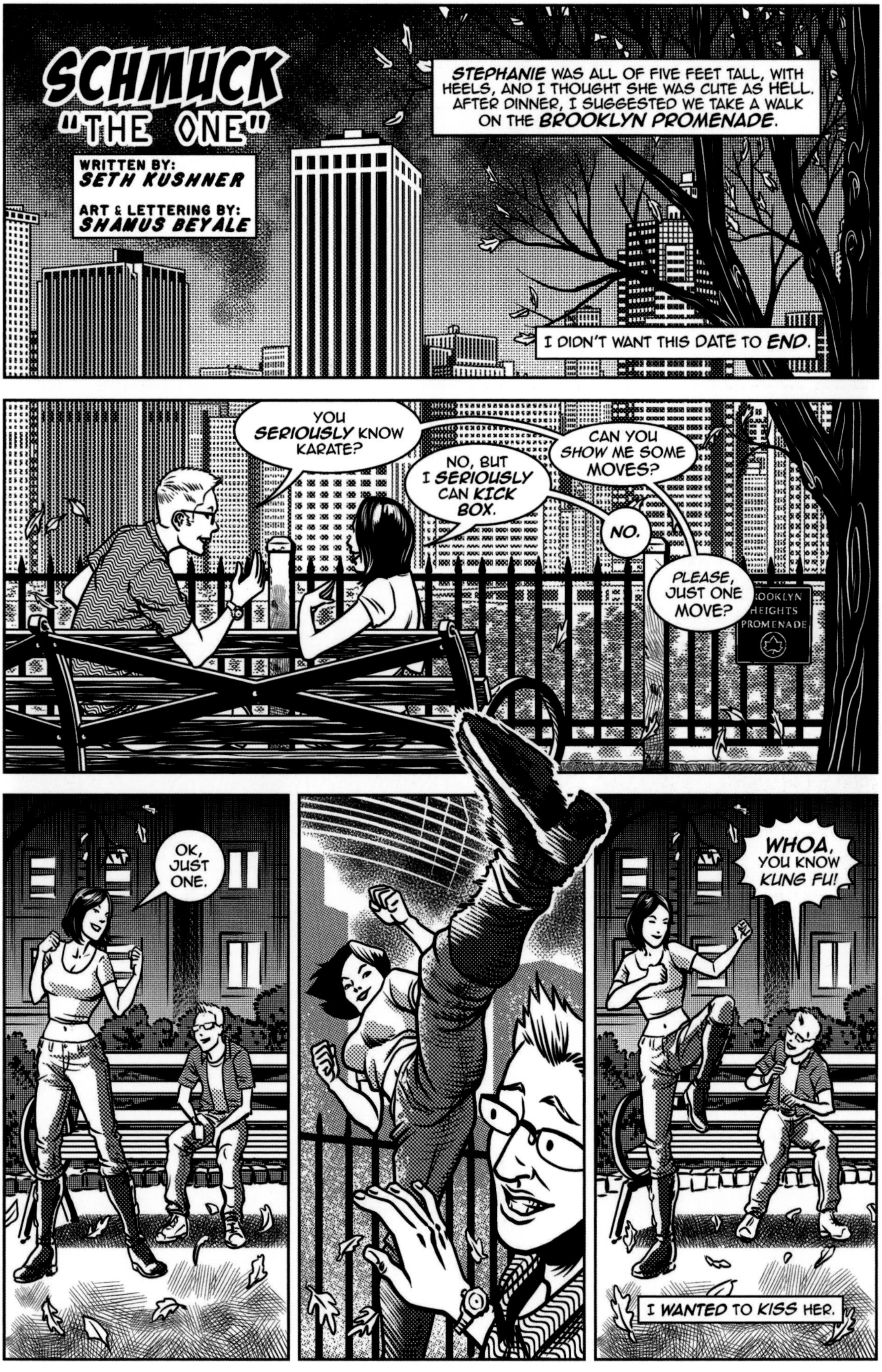
SCHMUCK
"THE ONE"
WRITTEN BY: SETH KUSHNER
ART & LETTERING BY: SHAMUS BEYALE
STEPHANIE WAS ALL OF FIVE FEET TALL, WITH HEELS, AND I THOUGHT SHE WAS CUTE AS HELL. AFTER DINNER, I SUGGESTED WE TAKE A WALK ON THE BROOKLYN PROMENADE.
I DIDN'T WANT THIS DATE TO END.
YOU SERIOUSLY KNOW KARATE?
NO, BUT I SERIOUSLY CAN KICK BOX.
CAN YOU SHOW ME SOME MOVES?
NO.
PLEASE, JUST ONE MOVE?
BROOKLYN HEIGHTS PROMENADE
OK, JUST ONE.
WHOA, YOU KNOW KUNG FU!
I WANTED TO KISS HER.

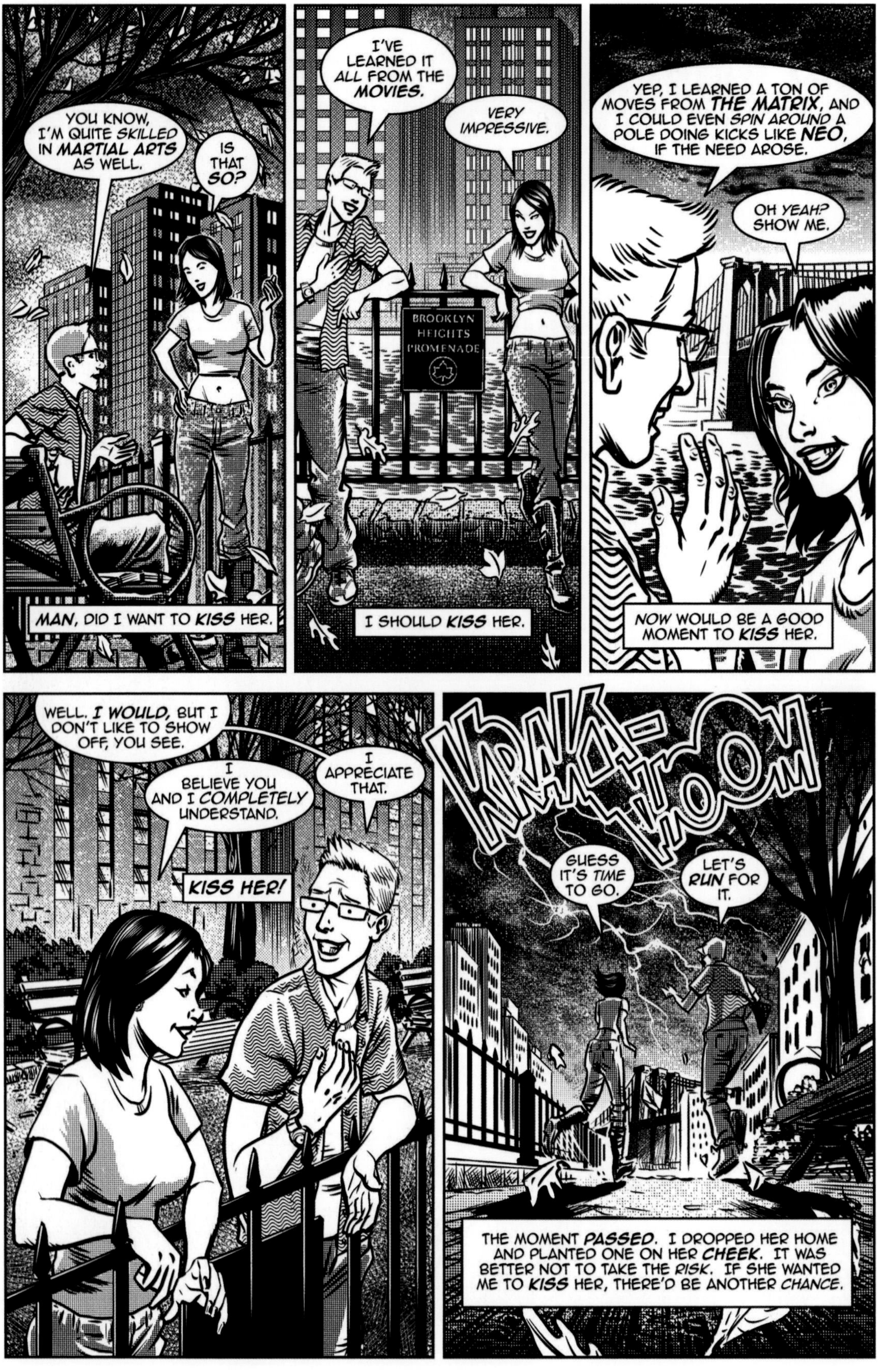

YOU KNOW, I'M QUITE SKILLED IN MARTIAL ARTS AS WELL.
IS THAT SO?
MAN, DID I WANT TO KISS HER.
I'VE LEARNED IT ALL FROM THE MOVIES.
VERY IMPRESSIVE.
BROOKLYN HEIGHTS PROMENADE
I SHOULD KISS HER.
YEP, I LEARNED A TON OF MOVES FROM THE MATRIX, AND I COULD EVEN SPIN AROUND A POLE DOING KICKS LIKE NEO, IF THE NEED AROSE.
OH YEAH? SHOW ME.
NOW WOULD BE A GOOD MOMENT TO KISS HER.
WELL. I WOULD, BUT I DON'T LIKE TO SHOW OFF, YOU SEE.
I BELIEVE YOU AND I COMPLETELY UNDERSTAND.
I APPRECIATE THAT.
KISS HER!
KRAKA-THOOM
GUESS IT'S TIME TO GO.
LET'S RUN FOR IT.
THE MOMENT PASSED. I DROPPED HER HOME AND PLANTED ONE ON HER CHEEK. IT WAS BETTER NOT TO TAKE THE RISK. IF SHE WANTED ME TO KISS HER, THERE'D BE ANOTHER CHANCE.

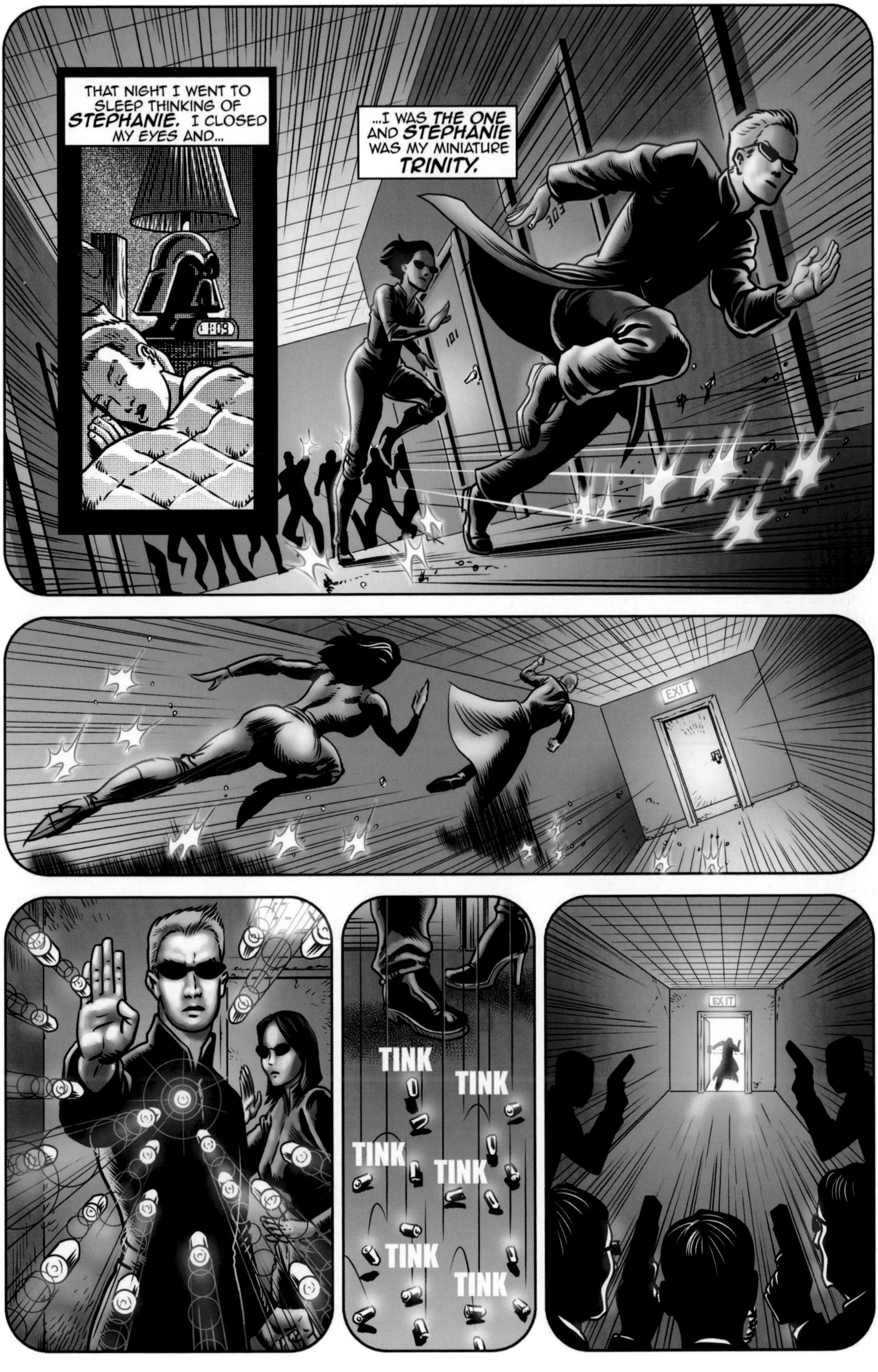
THAT NIGHT I WENT TO SLEEP THINKING OF STEPHANIE. I CLOSED MY EYES AND...
...I WAS THE ONE AND STEPHANIE WAS MY MINIATURE TRINITY.
EXIT
EXIT
TINK
TINK
TINK
TINK
TINK
TINK

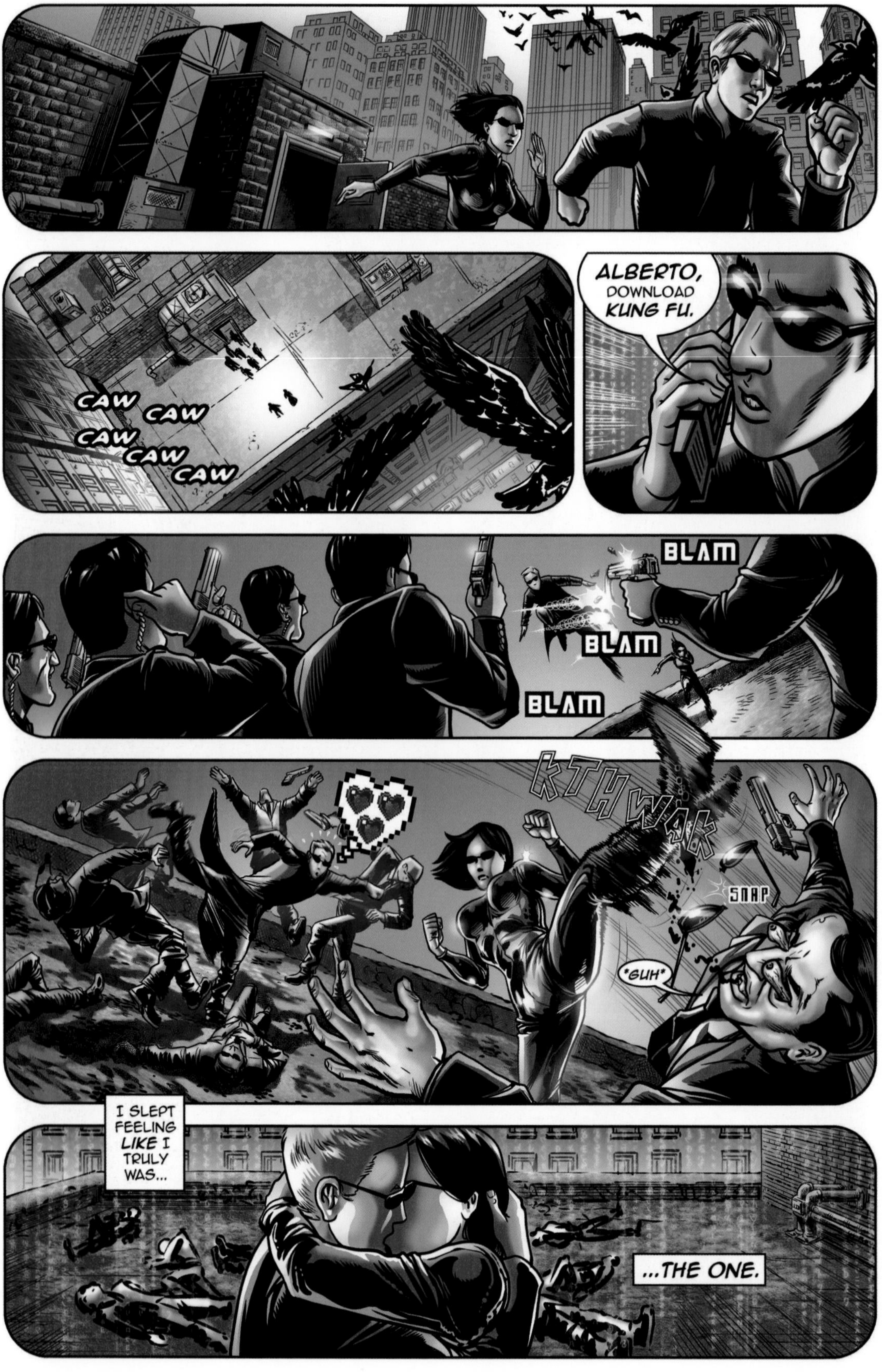
ALBERTO, DOWNLOAD KUNG FU.
CAW CAW
CAW CAW CAW
BLAM
BLAM
BLAM
KTHWAK
SNAP
GUH
I SLEPT FEELING LIKE I TRULY WAS...
...THE ONE.

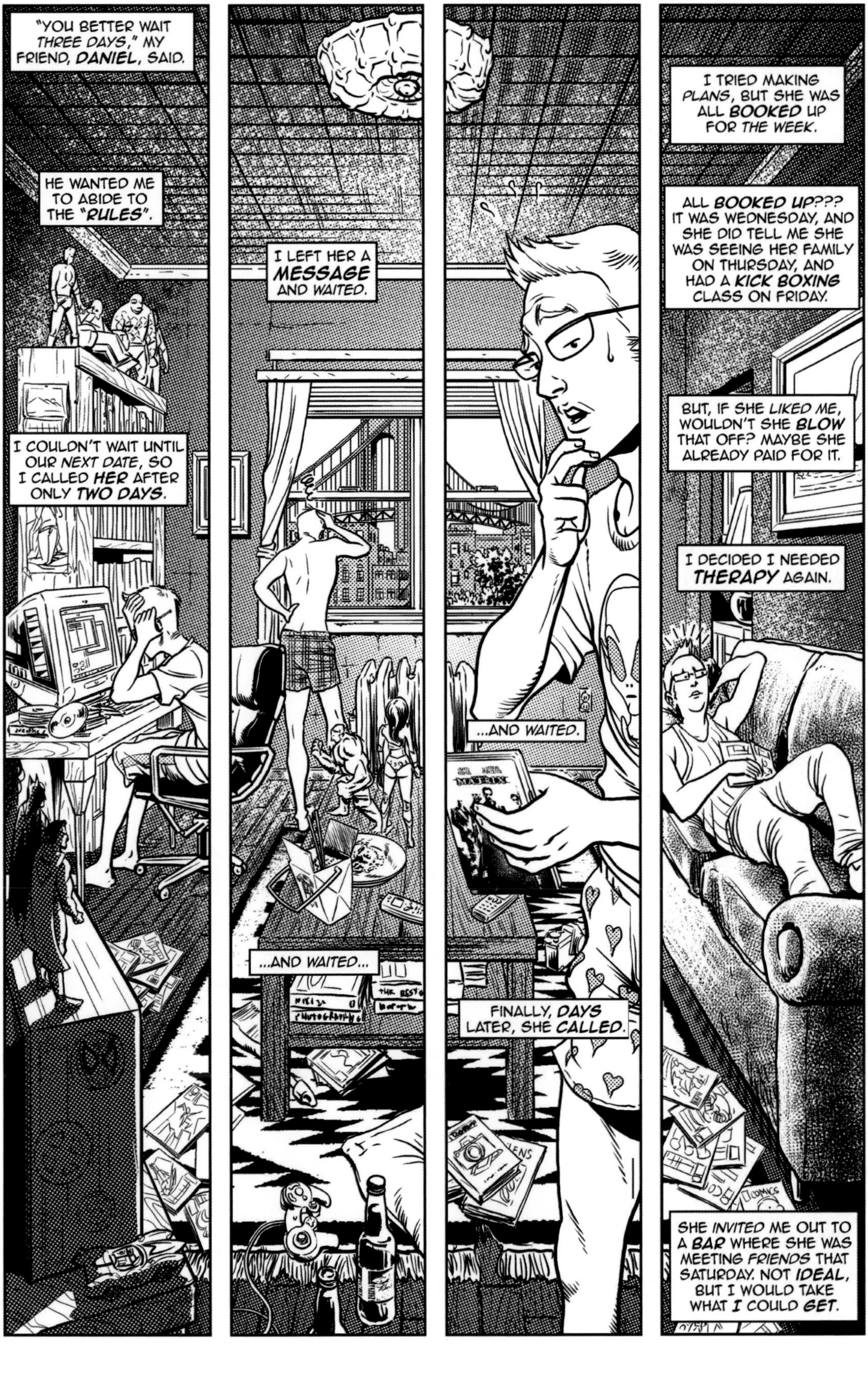
"YOU BETTER WAIT THREE DAYS," MY FRIEND, DANIEL, SAID.
HE WANTED ME TO ABIDE TO THE "RULES".
I COULDN'T WAIT UNTIL OUR NEXT DATE, SO I CALLED HER AFTER ONLY TWO DAYS.
I LEFT HER A MESSAGE AND WAITED.
...AND WAITED...
...AND WAITED.
FINALLY, DAYS LATER, SHE CALLED.
I TRIED MAKING PLANS, BUT SHE WAS ALL BOOKED UP FOR THE WEEK.
ALL BOOKED UP??? IT WAS WEDNESDAY, AND SHE DID TELL ME SHE WAS SEEING HER FAMILY ON THURSDAY, AND HAD A KICK BOXING CLASS ON FRIDAY.
BUT, IF SHE LIKED ME, WOULDN'T SHE BLOW THAT OFF? MAYBE SHE ALREADY PAID FOR IT.
I DECIDED I NEEDED THERAPY AGAIN.
SHE INVITED ME OUT TO A BAR WHERE SHE WAS MEETING FRIENDS THAT SATURDAY. NOT IDEAL, BUT I WOULD TAKE WHAT I COULD GET.

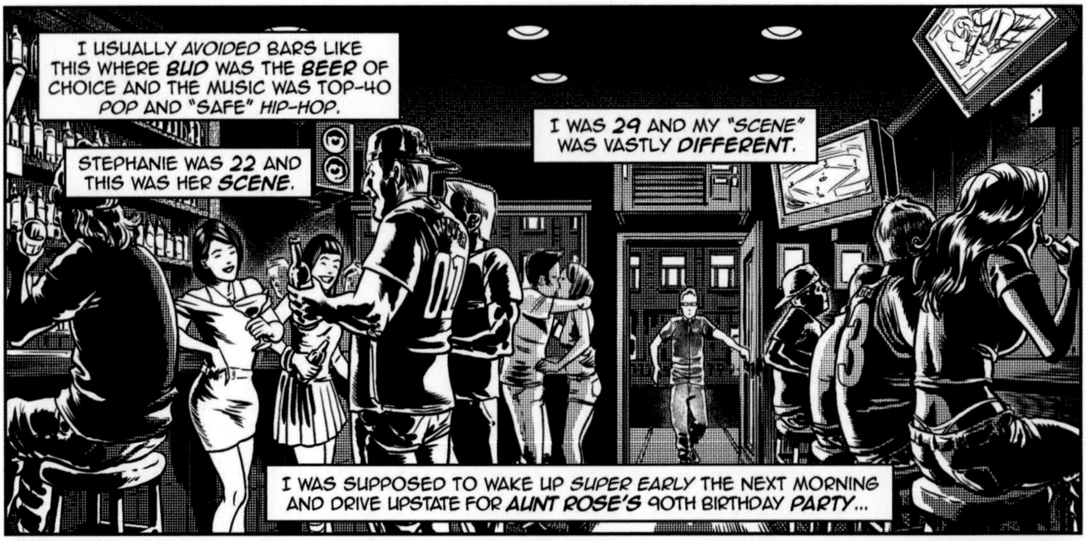
I USUALLY AVOIDED BARS LIKE THIS WHERE BUD WAS THE BEER OF CHOICE AND THE MUSIC WAS TOP-40 POP AND "SAFE" HIP-HOP.
STEPHANIE WAS 22 AND THIS WAS HER SCENE.
I WAS 29 AND MY "SCENE" WAS VASTLY DIFFERENT.
I WAS SUPPOSED TO WAKE UP SUPER EARLY THE NEXT MORNING AND DRIVE UPSTATE FOR AUNT ROSE'S 90TH BIRTHDAY PARTY...

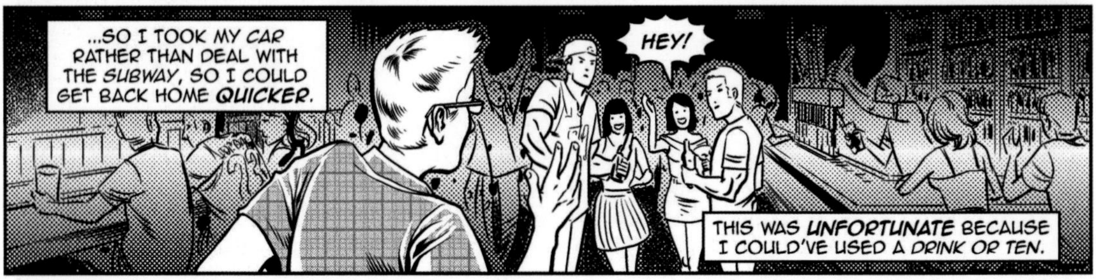
...SO I TOOK MY CAR RATHER THAN DEAL WITH THE SUBWAY, SO I COULD GET BACK HOME QUICKER.
HEY!
THIS WAS UNFORTUNATE BECAUSE I COULD'VE USED A DRINK OR TEN.

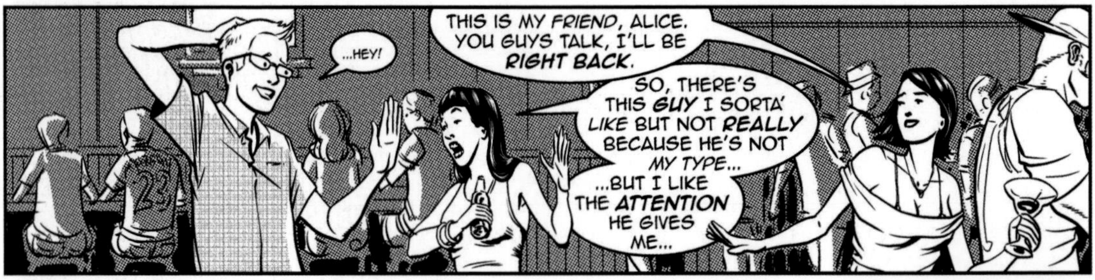
THIS IS MY FRIEND, ALICE. YOU GUYS TALK, I'LL BE RIGHT BACK.
...HEY!
SO, THERE'S THIS GUY I SORTA' LIKE BUT NOT REALLY BECAUSE HE'S NOT MY TYPE...
...BUT I LIKE THE ATTENTION HE GIVES ME...

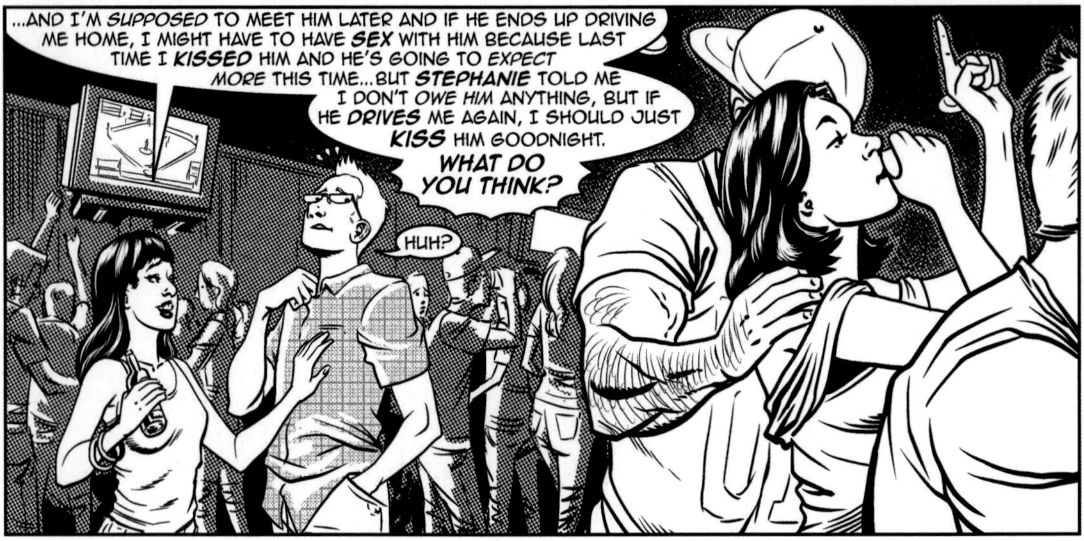
...AND I'M SUPPOSED TO MEET HIM LATER AND IF HE ENDS UP DRIVING ME HOME, I MIGHT HAVE TO HAVE SEX WITH HIM BECAUSE LAST TIME I KISSED HIM AND HE'S GOING TO EXPECT MORE THIS TIME...BUT STEPHANIE TOLD ME I DON'T OWE HIM ANYTHING, BUT IF HE DRIVES ME AGAIN, I SHOULD JUST KISS HIM GOODNIGHT.
WHAT DO YOU THINK?
HUH?

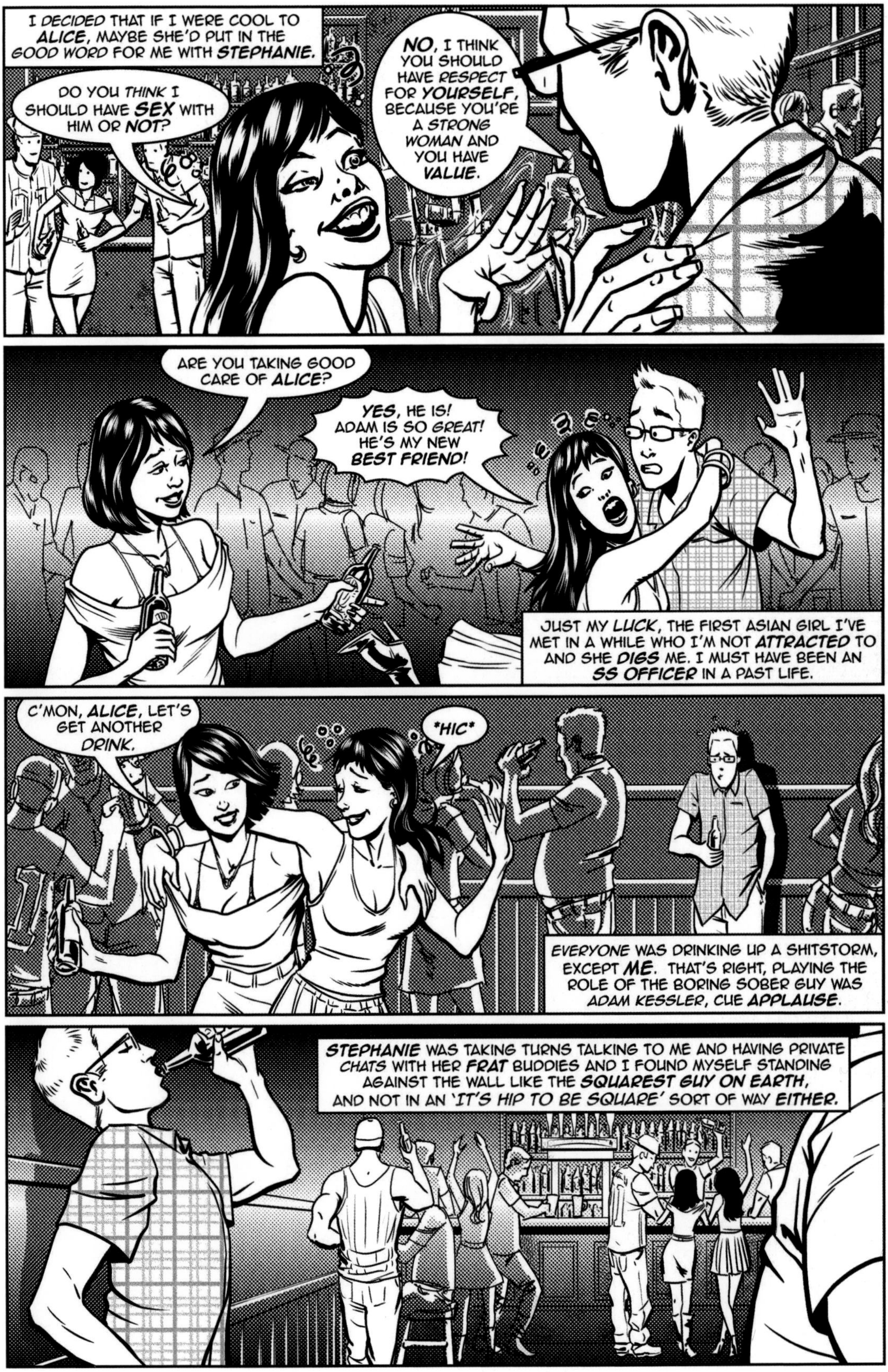
I DECIDED THAT IF I WERE COOL TO ALICE, MAYBE SHE'D PUT IN THE GOOD WORD FOR ME WITH STEPHANIE.
DO YOU THINK I SHOULD HAVE SEX WITH HIM OR NOT?
NO, I THINK YOU SHOULD HAVE RESPECT FOR YOURSELF, BECAUSE YOU'RE A STRONG WOMAN AND YOU HAVE VALUE.
ARE YOU TAKING GOOD CARE OF ALICE?
YES, HE IS! ADAM IS SO GREAT! HE'S MY NEW BEST FRIEND!
JUST MY LUCK, THE FIRST ASIAN GIRL I'VE MET IN A WHILE WHO I'M NOT ATTRACTED TO AND SHE DIGS ME. I MUST HAVE BEEN AN SS OFFICER IN A PAST LIFE.
C'MON, ALICE, LET'S GET ANOTHER DRINK.
HIC
EVERYONE WAS DRINKING UP A SHITSTORM, EXCEPT ME. THAT'S RIGHT, PLAYING THE ROLE OF THE BORING SOBER GUY WAS ADAM KESSLER, CUE APPLAUSE.
STEPHANIE WAS TAKING TURNS TALKING TO ME AND HAVING PRIVATE CHATS WITH HER FRAT BUDDIES AND I FOUND MYSELF STANDING AGAINST THE WALL LIKE THE SQUAREST GUY ON EARTH, AND NOT IN AN 'IT'S HIP TO BE SQUARE' SORT OF WAY EITHER.

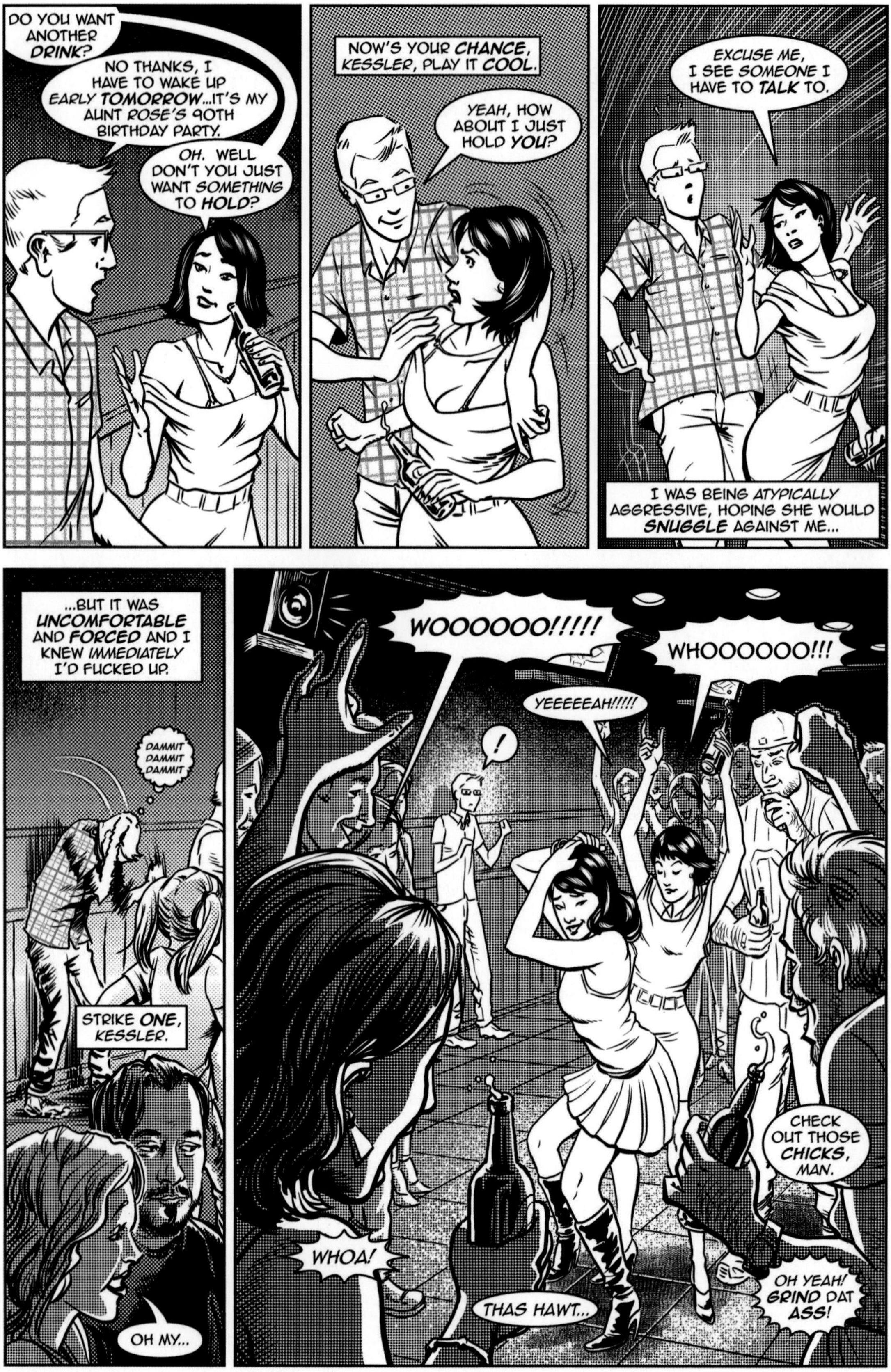
DO YOU WANT ANOTHER DRINK?
NO THANKS, I HAVE TO WAKE UP EARLY TOMORROW...IT'S MY AUNT ROSE'S 90TH BIRTHDAY PARTY.
OH. WELL DON'T YOU JUST WANT SOMETHING TO HOLD?
NOW'S YOUR CHANCE, KESSLER, PLAY IT COOL.
YEAH, HOW ABOUT I JUST HOLD YOU?
EXCUSE ME, I SEE SOMEONE I HAVE TO TALK TO.
I WAS BEING ATYPICALLY AGGRESSIVE, HOPING SHE WOULD SNUGGLE AGAINST ME...
...BUT IT WAS UNCOMFORTABLE AND FORCED AND I KNEW IMMEDIATELY I'D FUCKED UP.
DAMMIT DAMMIT DAMMIT
STRIKE ONE, KESSLER.
OH MY...
WOOOOOO!!!!!
WHOOOOOO!!!
YEEEEEAH!!!!!
!
CHECK OUT THOSE CHICKS, MAN.
WHOA!
THAS HAWT...
OH YEAH! GRIND DAT ASS!

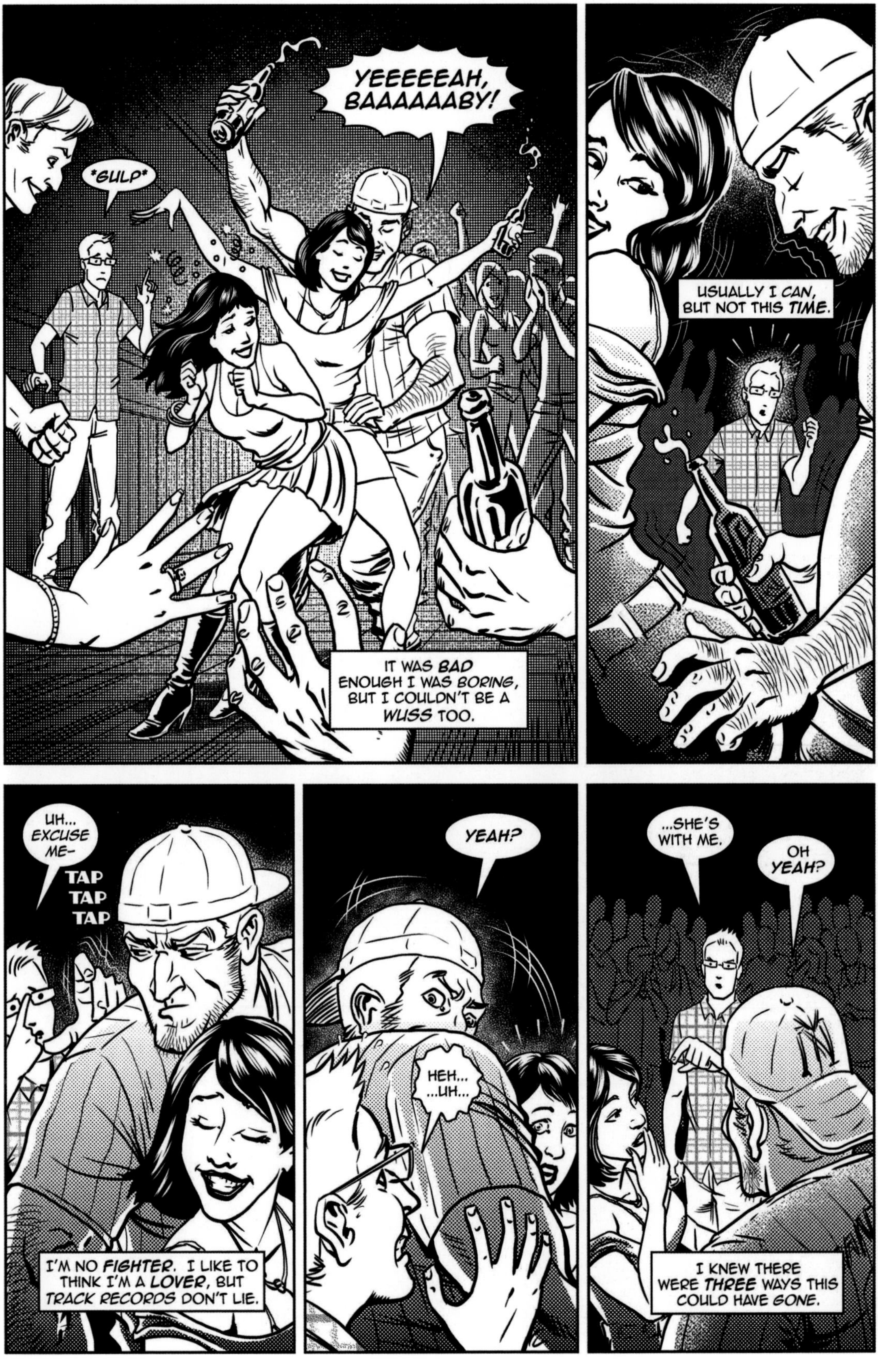
YEEEEEAH, BAAAAAABY!
GULP
IT WAS BAD ENOUGH I WAS BORING, BUT I COULDN'T BE A WUSS TOO.
USUALLY I CAN, BUT NOT THIS TIME.
UH... EXCUSE ME-
TAP TAP TAP
I'M NO FIGHTER. I LIKE TO THINK I'M A LOVER, BUT TRACK RECORDS DON'T LIE.
YEAH?
HEH... ...UH...
...SHE'S WITH ME.
OH YEAH?
I KNEW THERE WERE THREE WAYS THIS COULD HAVE GONE.

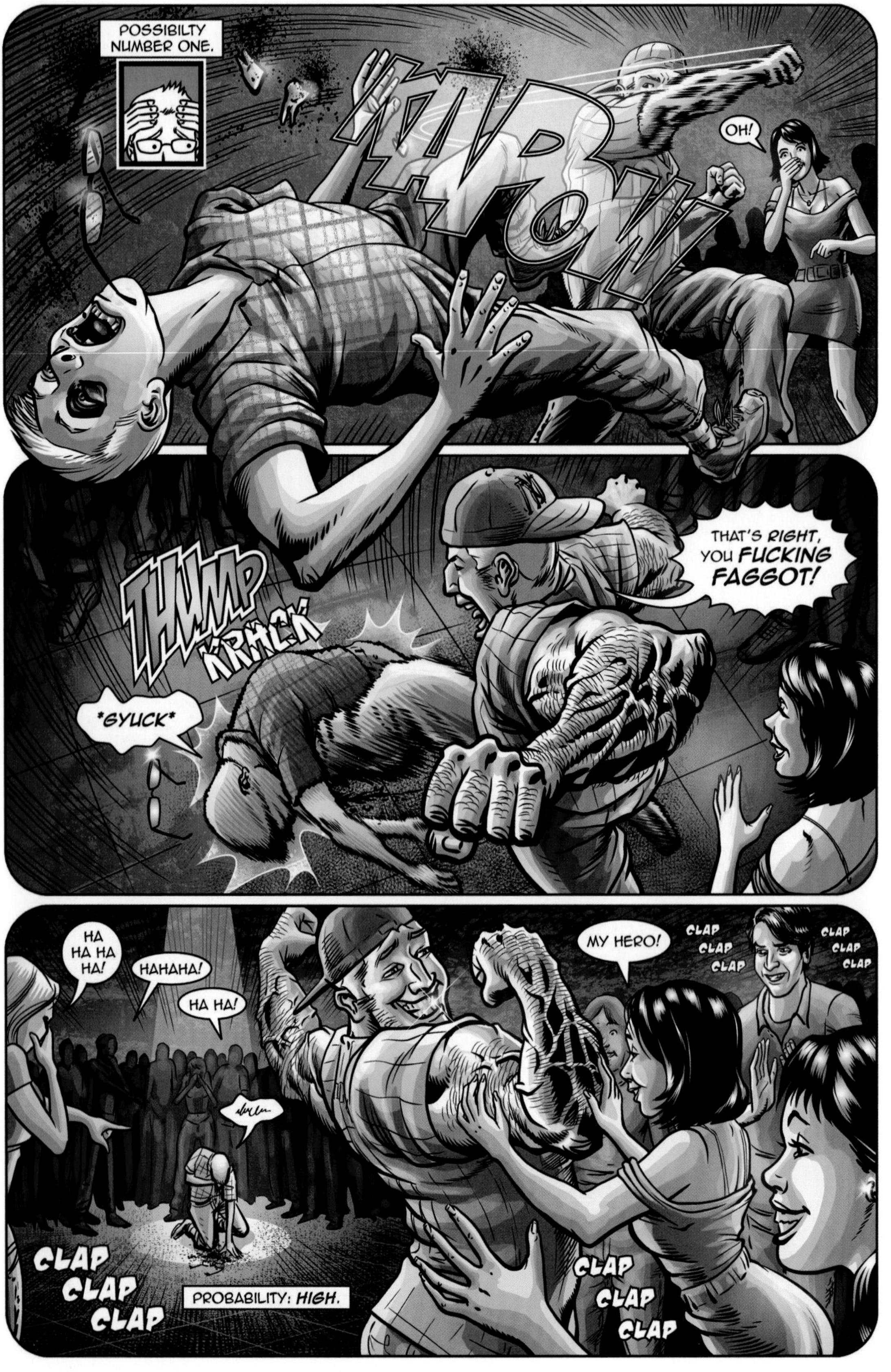
POSSIBILTY NUMBER ONE.
KRAK
OH!
THAT'S RIGHT, YOU FUCKING FAGGOT!
THUMP
KRACK
GYUCK
HA HA HA HA!
HAHAHA!
HA HA!
MY HERO!
CLAP CLAP CLAP
CLAP CLAP CLAP
CLAP CLAP CLAP
PROBABILITY: HIGH.
CLAP CLAP CLAP

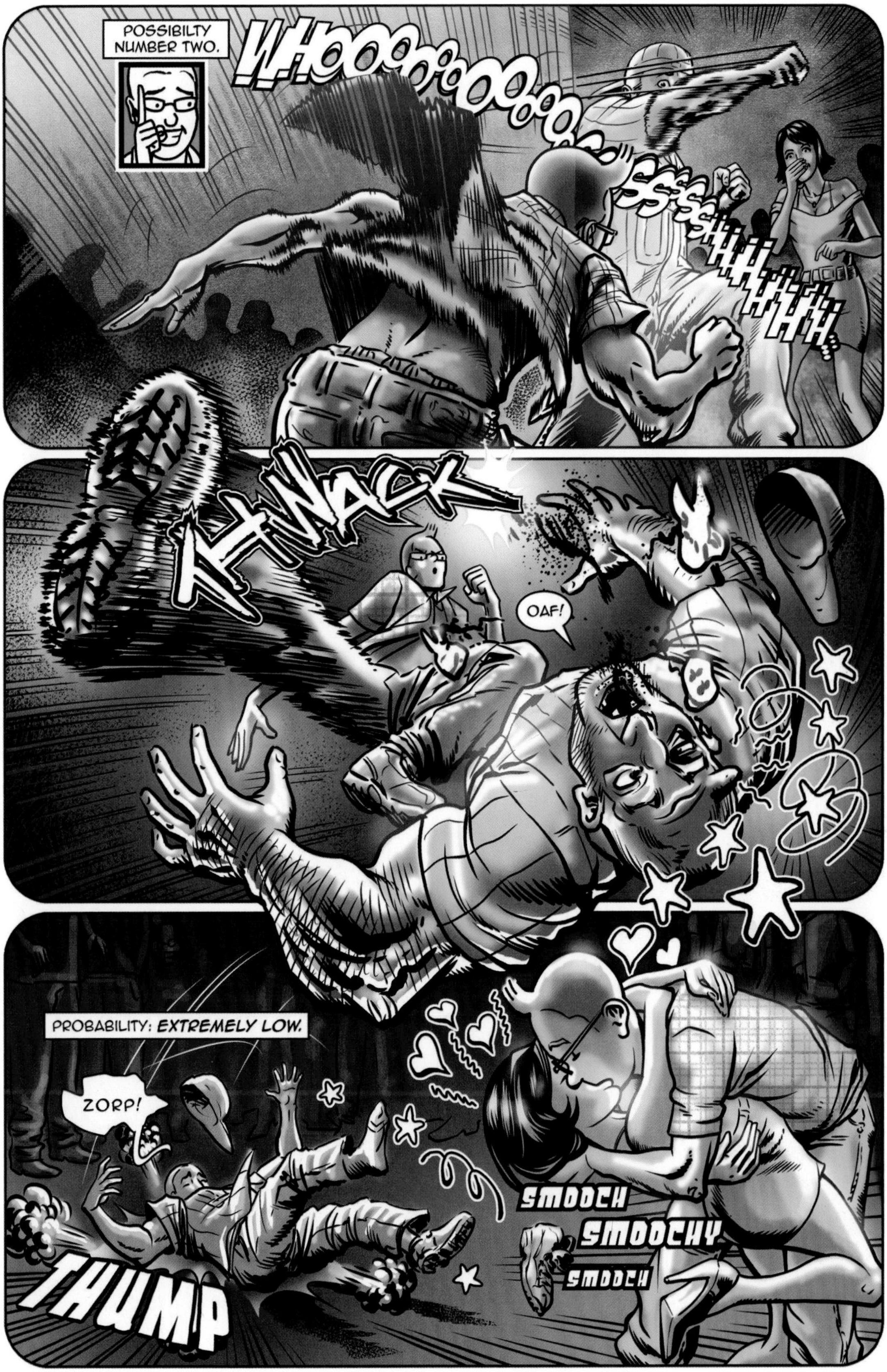
POSSIBILTY NUMBER TWO.
WHOOOOOOOOOOSSSHHHHHH
THWACK
OAF!
PROBABILITY: EXTREMELY LOW.
ZORP!
THUMP
SMOOCH
SMOOCHY
SMOOCH

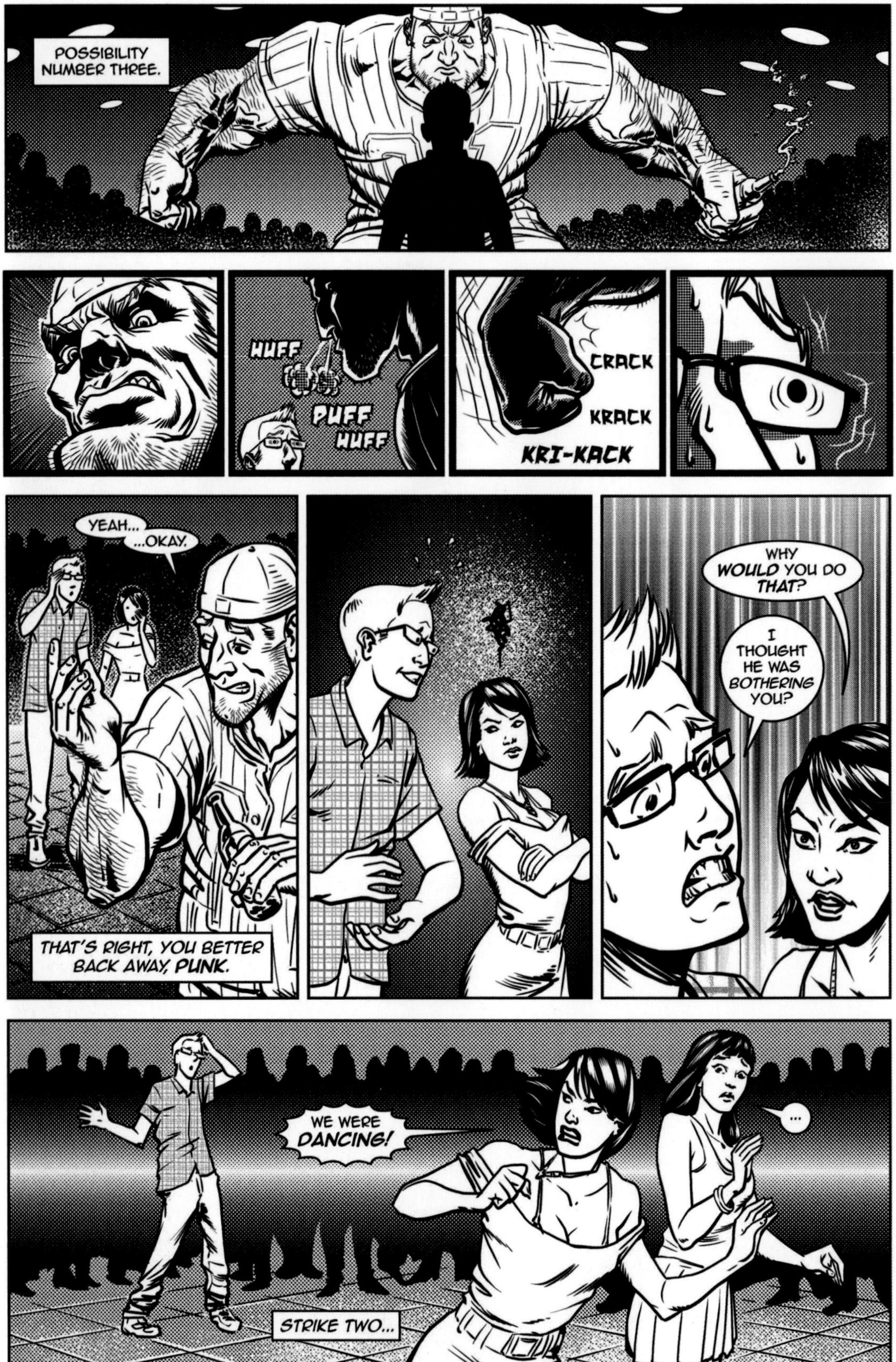

POSSIBILITY NUMBER THREE.
HUFF
PUFF
HUFF
CRACK
KRACK
KRI-KACK
YEAH... ...OKAY.
THAT'S RIGHT, YOU BETTER BACK AWAY, PUNK.
WHY WOULD YOU DO THAT?
I THOUGHT HE WAS BOTHERING YOU?
WE WERE DANCING!
...
STRIKE TWO...

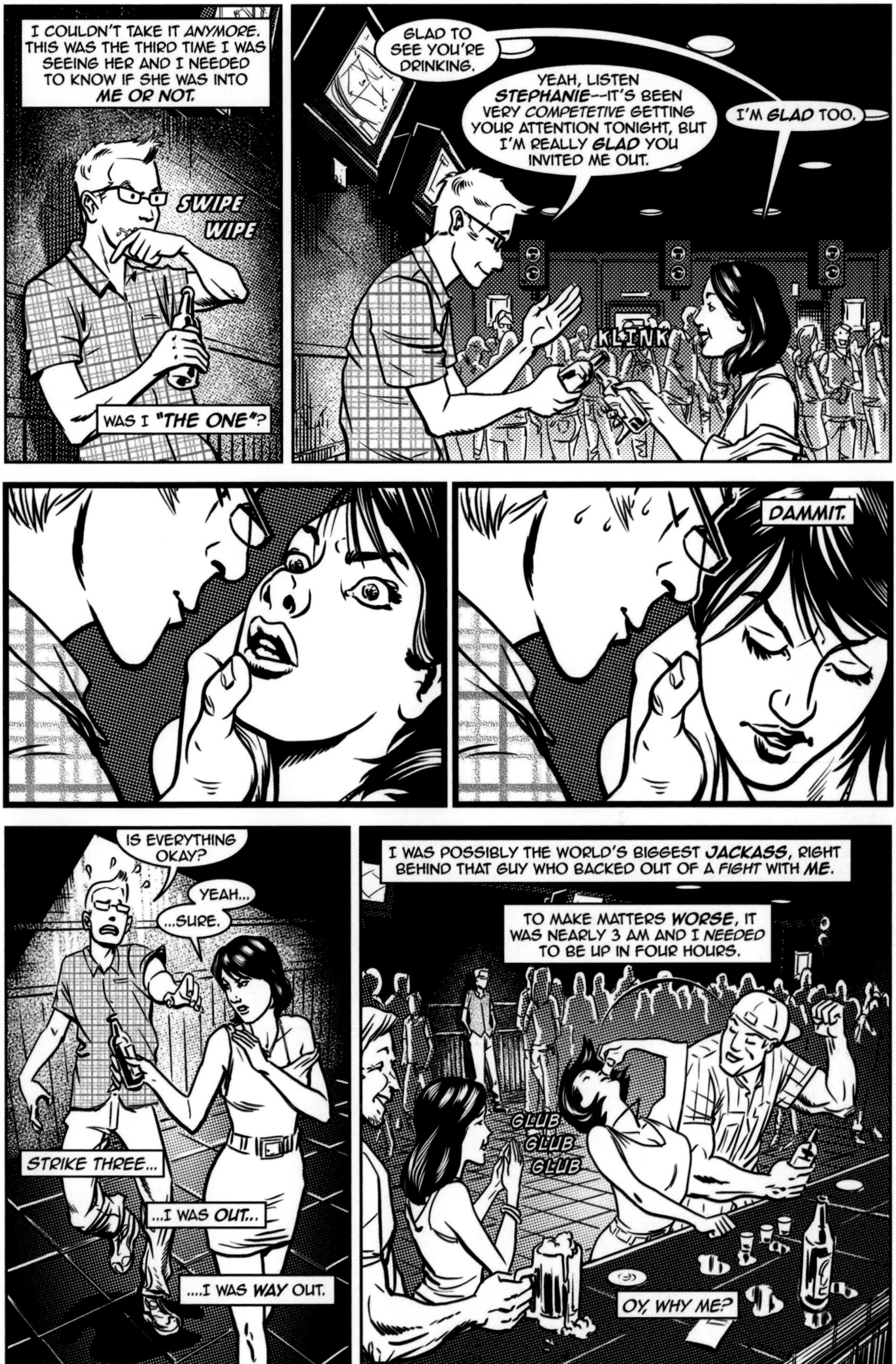

I COULDN'T TAKE IT ANYMORE. THIS WAS THE THIRD TIME I WAS SEEING HER AND I NEEDED TO KNOW IF SHE WAS INTO ME OR NOT.
SWIPE
WIPE
WAS I "THE ONE"?
GLAD TO SEE YOU'RE DRINKING.
YEAH, LISTEN STEPHANIE--IT'S BEEN VERY COMPETETIVE GETTING YOUR ATTENTION TONIGHT, BUT I'M REALLY GLAD YOU INVITED ME OUT.
I'M GLAD TOO.
KLINK
DAMMIT.
IS EVERYTHING OKAY?
YEAH...
...SURE.
STRIKE THREE...
...I WAS OUT...
....I WAS WAY OUT.
I WAS POSSIBLY THE WORLD'S BIGGEST JACKASS, RIGHT BEHIND THAT GUY WHO BACKED OUT OF A FIGHT WITH ME.
TO MAKE MATTERS WORSE, IT WAS NEARLY 3 AM AND I NEEDED TO BE UP IN FOUR HOURS.
GLUB
GLUB
GLUB
OY, WHY ME?

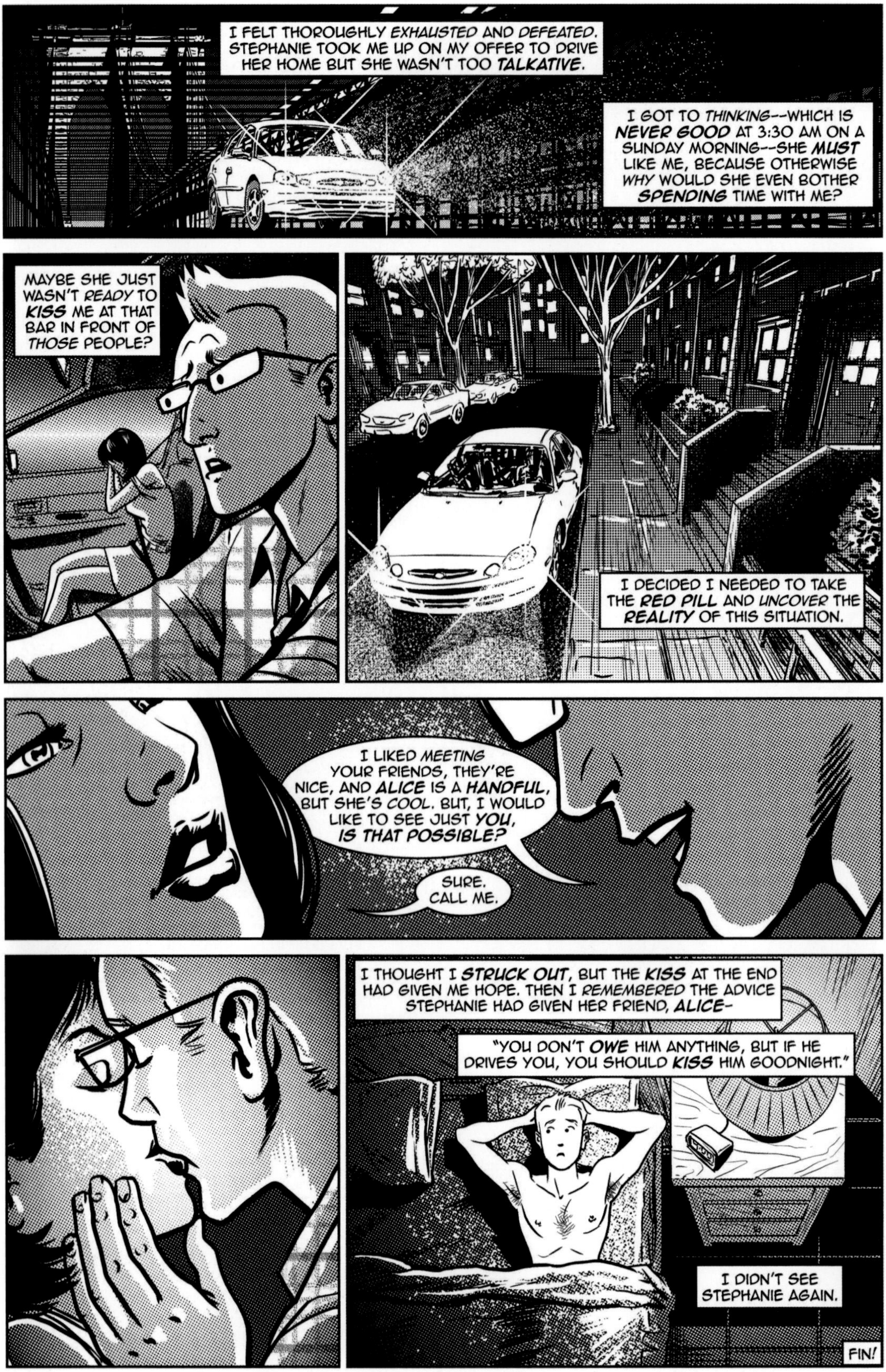

I FELT THOROUGHLY EXHAUSTED AND DEFEATED. STEPHANIE TOOK ME UP ON MY OFFER TO DRIVE HER HOME BUT SHE WASN'T TOO TALKATIVE.
I GOT TO THINKING--WHICH IS NEVER GOOD AT 3:30 AM ON A SUNDAY MORNING--SHE MUST LIKE ME, BECAUSE OTHERWISE WHY WOULD SHE EVEN BOTHER SPENDING TIME WITH ME?
MAYBE SHE JUST WASN'T READY TO KISS ME AT THAT BAR IN FRONT OF THOSE PEOPLE?
I DECIDED I NEEDED TO TAKE THE RED PILL AND UNCOVER THE REALITY OF THIS SITUATION.
I LIKED MEETING YOUR FRIENDS, THEY'RE NICE, AND ALICE IS A HANDFUL, BUT SHE'S COOL. BUT, I WOULD LIKE TO SEE JUST YOU, IS THAT POSSIBLE?
SURE. CALL ME.
I THOUGHT I STRUCK OUT, BUT THE KISS AT THE END HAD GIVEN ME HOPE. THEN I REMEMBERED THE ADVICE STEPHANIE HAD GIVEN HER FRIEND, ALICE-
"YOU DON'T OWE HIM ANYTHING, BUT IF HE DRIVES YOU, YOU SHOULD KISS HIM GOODNIGHT."
I DIDN'T SEE STEPHANIE AGAIN.
FIN!

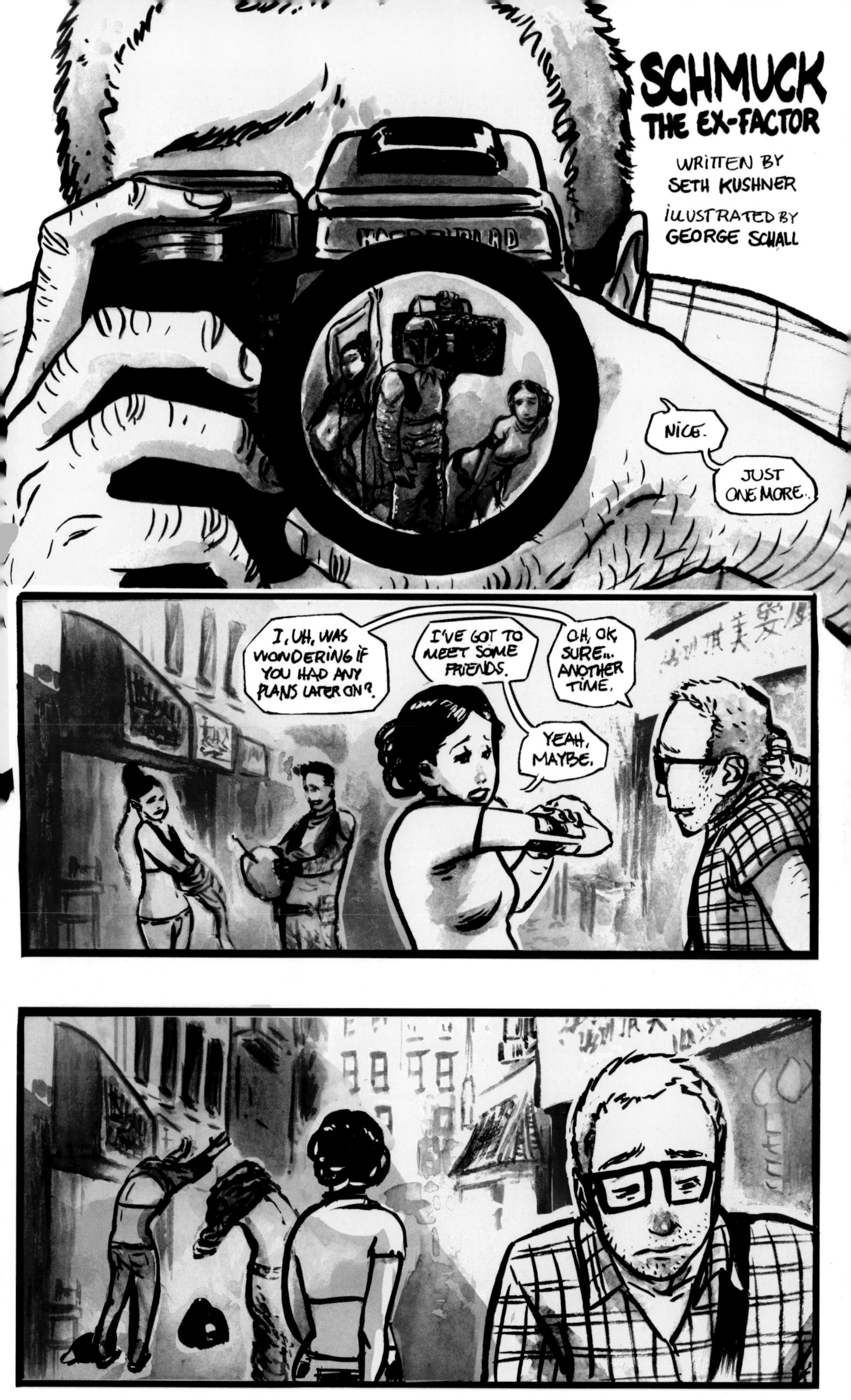
SCHMUCK
THE EX-FACTOR
WRITTEN BY
SETH KUSHNER
ILLUSTRATED BY
GEORGE SCHALL
NICE.
JUST ONE MORE..
I, UH, WAS WONDERING IF YOU HAD ANY PLANS LATER ON?
I'VE GOT TO MEET SOME FRIENDS.
OH, OK, SURE... ANOTHER TIME.
YEAH, MAYBE.

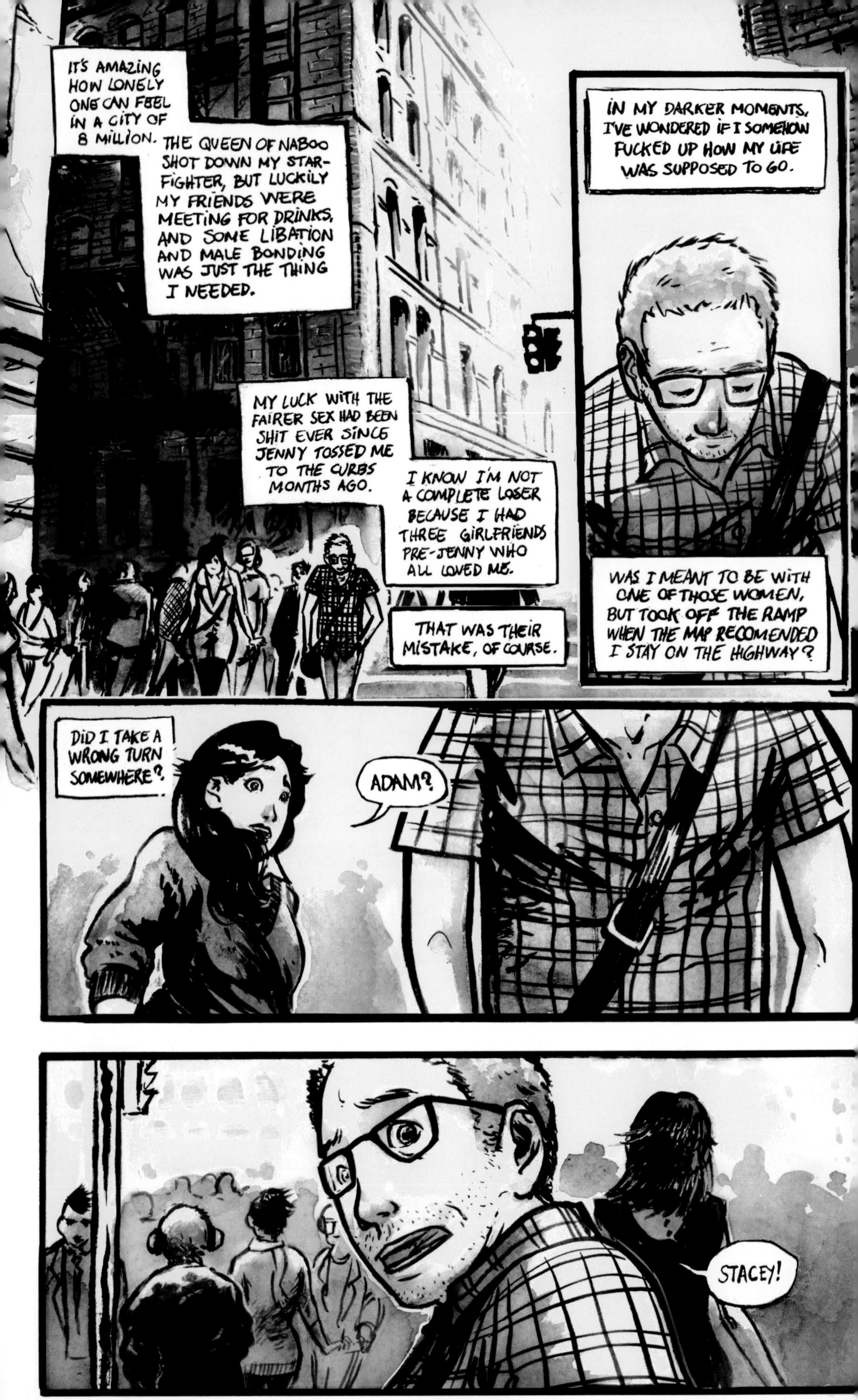

IT'S AMAZING HOW LONELY ONE CAN FEEL IN A CITY OF 8 MILLION.
THE QUEEN OF NABOO SHOT DOWN MY STAR-FIGHTER, BUT LUCKILY MY FRIENDS WERE MEETING FOR DRINKS, AND SOME LIBATION AND MALE BONDING WAS JUST THE THING I NEEDED.
MY LUCK WITH THE FAIRER SEX HAD BEEN SHIT EVER SINCE JENNY TOSSED ME TO THE CURBS MONTHS AGO.
I KNOW I'M NOT A COMPLETE LOSER BECAUSE I HAD THREE GIRLFRIENDS PRE-JENNY WHO ALL LOVED ME.
THAT WAS THEIR MISTAKE, OF COURSE.
IN MY DARKER MOMENTS, I'VE WONDERED IF I SOMEHOW FUCKED UP HOW MY LIFE WAS SUPPOSED TO GO.
WAS I MEANT TO BE WITH ONE OF THOSE WOMEN, BUT TOOK OFF THE RAMP WHEN THE MAP RECOMENDED I STAY ON THE HIGHWAY?
DID I TAKE A WRONG TURN SOMEWHERE?
ADAM?
STACEY!

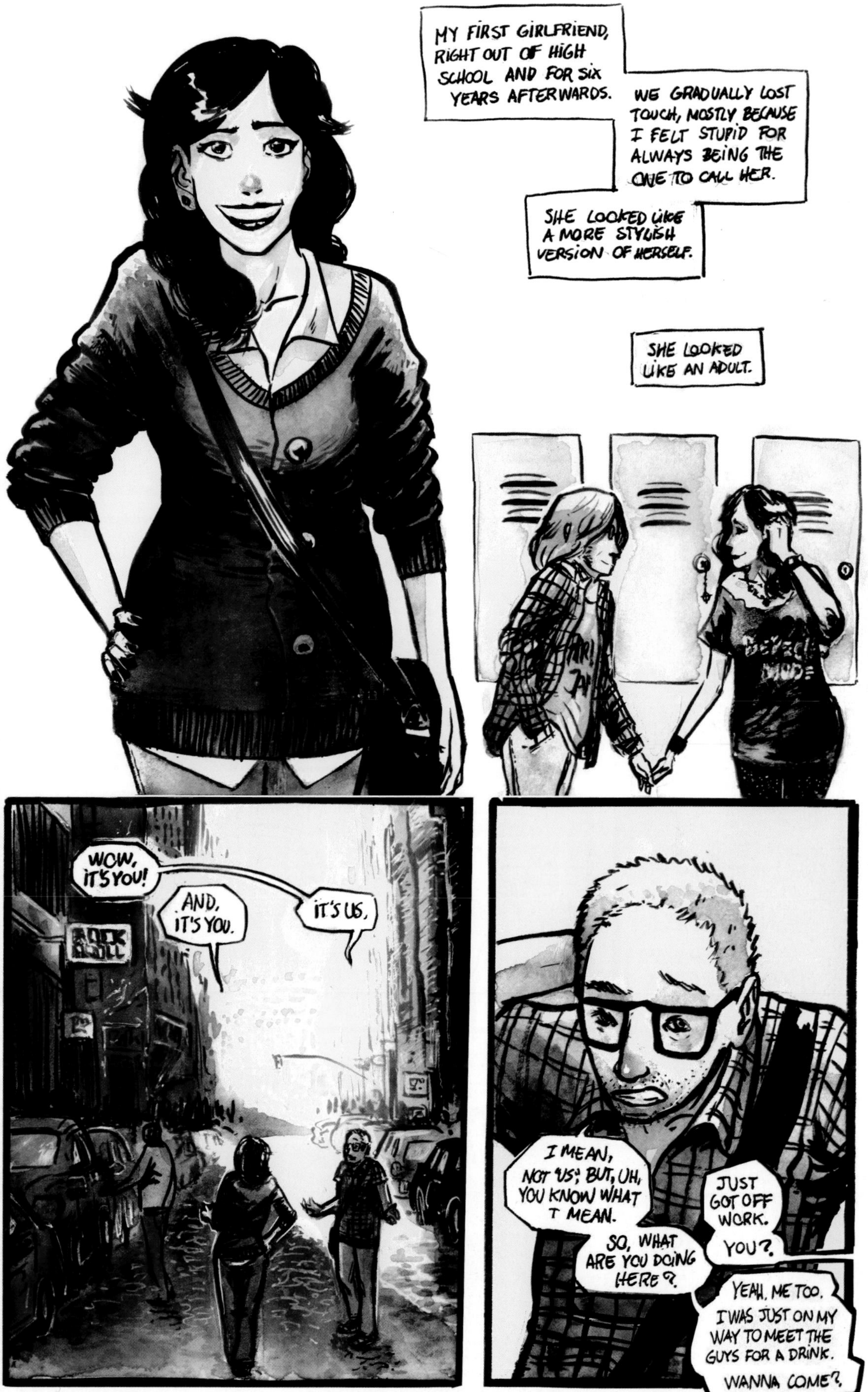
MY FIRST GIRLFRIEND, RIGHT OUT OF HIGH SCHOOL AND FOR SIX YEARS AFTERWARDS.
WE GRADUALLY LOST TOUCH, MOSTLY BECAUSE I FELT STUPID FOR ALWAYS BEING THE ONE TO CALL HER.
SHE LOOKED LIKE A MORE STYLISH VERSION OF HERSELF.
SHE LOOKED LIKE AN ADULT.
WOW, IT'S YOU!
AND, IT'S YOU.
IT'S US.
I MEAN, NOT "US," BUT, UH, YOU KNOW WHAT I MEAN.
SO, WHAT ARE YOU DOING HERE?
JUST GOT OFF WORK.
YOU?
YEAH, ME TOO.
I WAS JUST ON MY WAY TO MEET THE GUYS FOR A DRINK.
WANNA COME?

OKAY, I GUESS I CAN COME FOR ONE DRINK.

GREAT!

SO, WHAT HAVE YOU BEEN DOING?

YOU LOOK GREAT, BY THE WAY.

AS I APPROACHED MY FRIENDS, I HAD AN IDEA.

I COULD TELL THAT NONE OF THE GUYS RECOGNIZED HER.

GUYS, YOU REMEMBER STACEY... WE'RE BACK TOGETHER AGAIN.

UH, HI GUYS.

NOT FUNNY?

NO!

I HAD JUST USED MY FIRST LOVE AS A PROP FOR A STUPID JOKE.

STACEY STAYED FOR 10 MINUTES AND THEN EXCUSED HERSELF.

I HAD BROKEN UP WITH HER YEAR EARLIER, FOR AN OTHER GIRL, SO KNEW SHE OWE ME NOTHIN

SHE PROMISED SHE'D KEEP IN TOUCH, BUT I KNEW SHE WOULDN'T

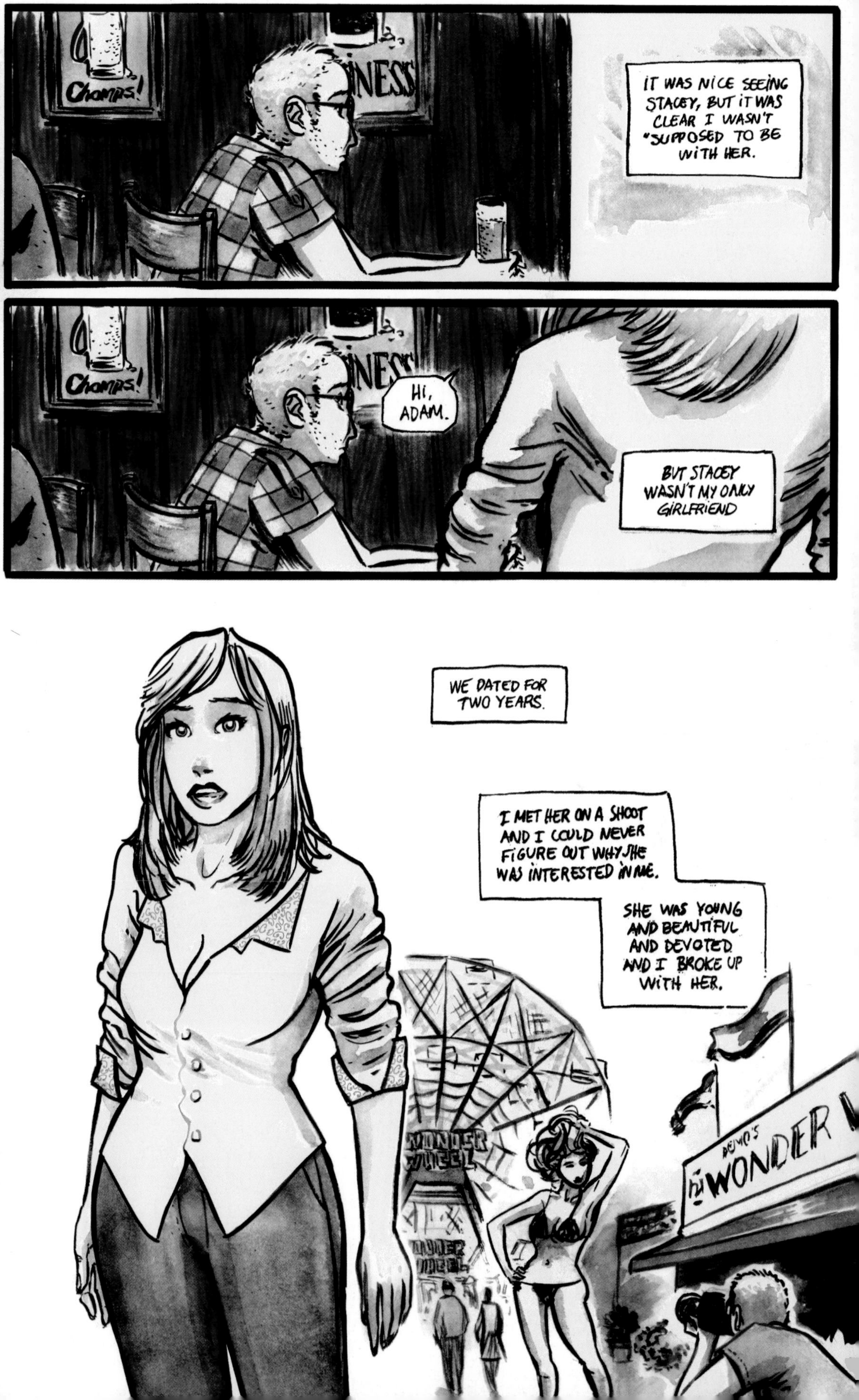

Champs!
IT WAS NICE SEEING STACEY, BUT IT WAS CLEAR I WASN'T "SUPPOSED TO BE WITH HER.
Champs!
HI, ADAM.
BUT STACEY WASN'T MY ONLY GIRLFRIEND
WE DATED FOR TWO YEARS.
I MET HER ON A SHOOT AND I COULD NEVER FIGURE OUT WHY SHE WAS INTERESTED IN ME.
SHE WAS YOUNG AND BEAUTIFUL AND DEVOTED AND I BROKE UP WITH HER.
WONDER WHEEL

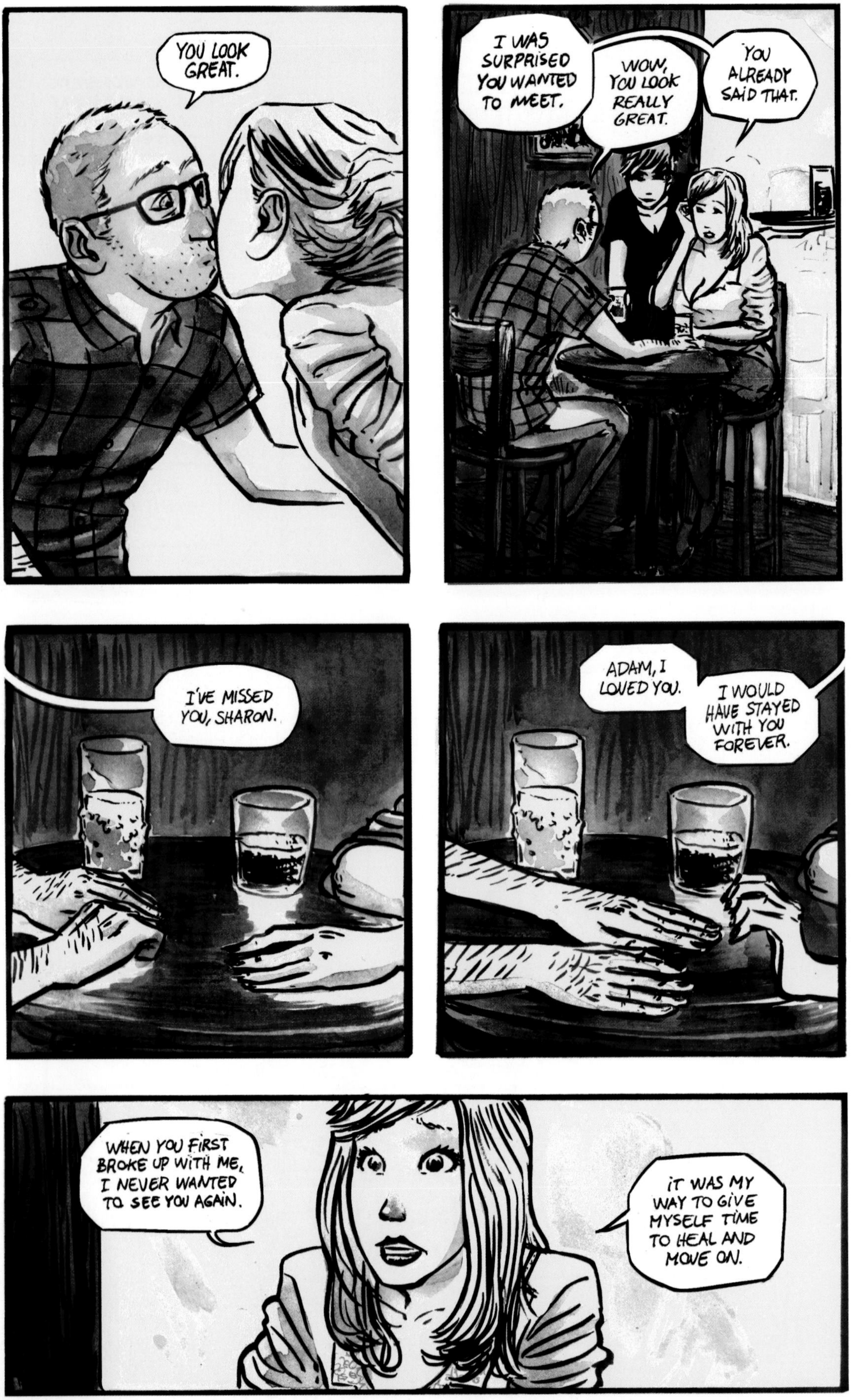
YOU LOOK GREAT.
I WAS SURPRISED YOU WANTED TO MEET.
WOW, YOU LOOK REALLY GREAT.
YOU ALREADY SAID THAT.
I'VE MISSED YOU, SHARON.
ADAM, I LOVED YOU.
I WOULD HAVE STAYED WITH YOU FOREVER.
WHEN YOU FIRST BROKE UP WITH ME, I NEVER WANTED TO SEE YOU AGAIN.
IT WAS MY WAY TO GIVE MYSELF TIME TO HEAL AND MOVE ON.

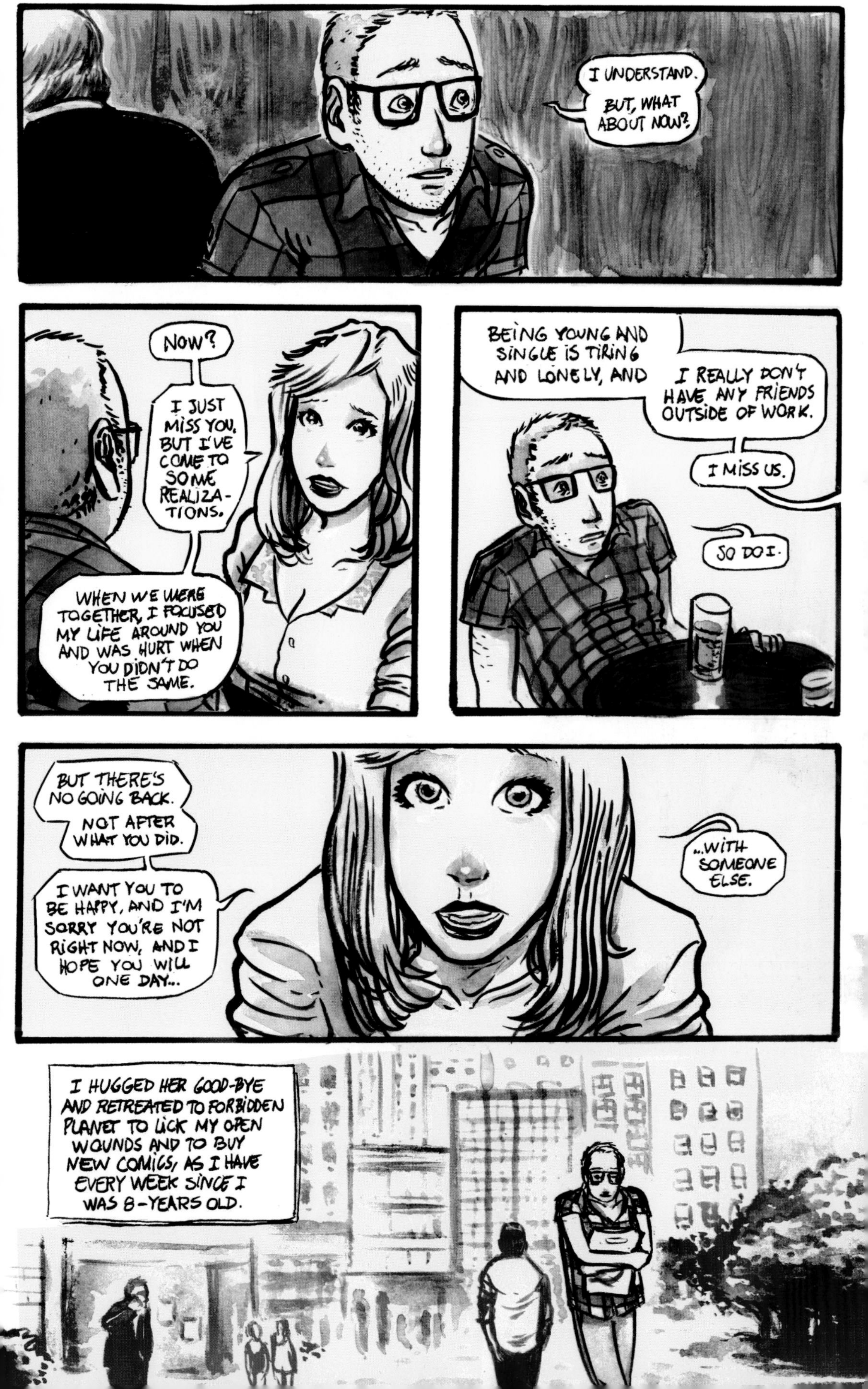
I UNDERSTAND.
BUT, WHAT ABOUT NOW?
NOW?
I JUST MISS YOU. BUT I'VE COME TO SOME REALIZA-TIONS.
WHEN WE WERE TOGETHER, I FOCUSED MY LIFE AROUND YOU AND WAS HURT WHEN YOU DIDN'T DO THE SAME.
BEING YOUNG AND SINGLE IS TIRING AND LONELY, AND
I REALLY DON'T HAVE ANY FRIENDS OUTSIDE OF WORK.
I MISS US.
SO DO I.
BUT THERE'S NO GOING BACK.
NOT AFTER WHAT YOU DID.
I WANT YOU TO BE HAPPY, AND I'M SORRY YOU'RE NOT RIGHT NOW, AND I HOPE YOU WILL ONE DAY...
...WITH SOMEONE ELSE.
I HUGGED HER GOOD-BYE AND RETREATED TO FORBIDDEN PLANET TO LICK MY OPEN WOUNDS AND TO BUY NEW COMICS, AS I HAVE EVERY WEEK SINCE I WAS 8-YEARS OLD.

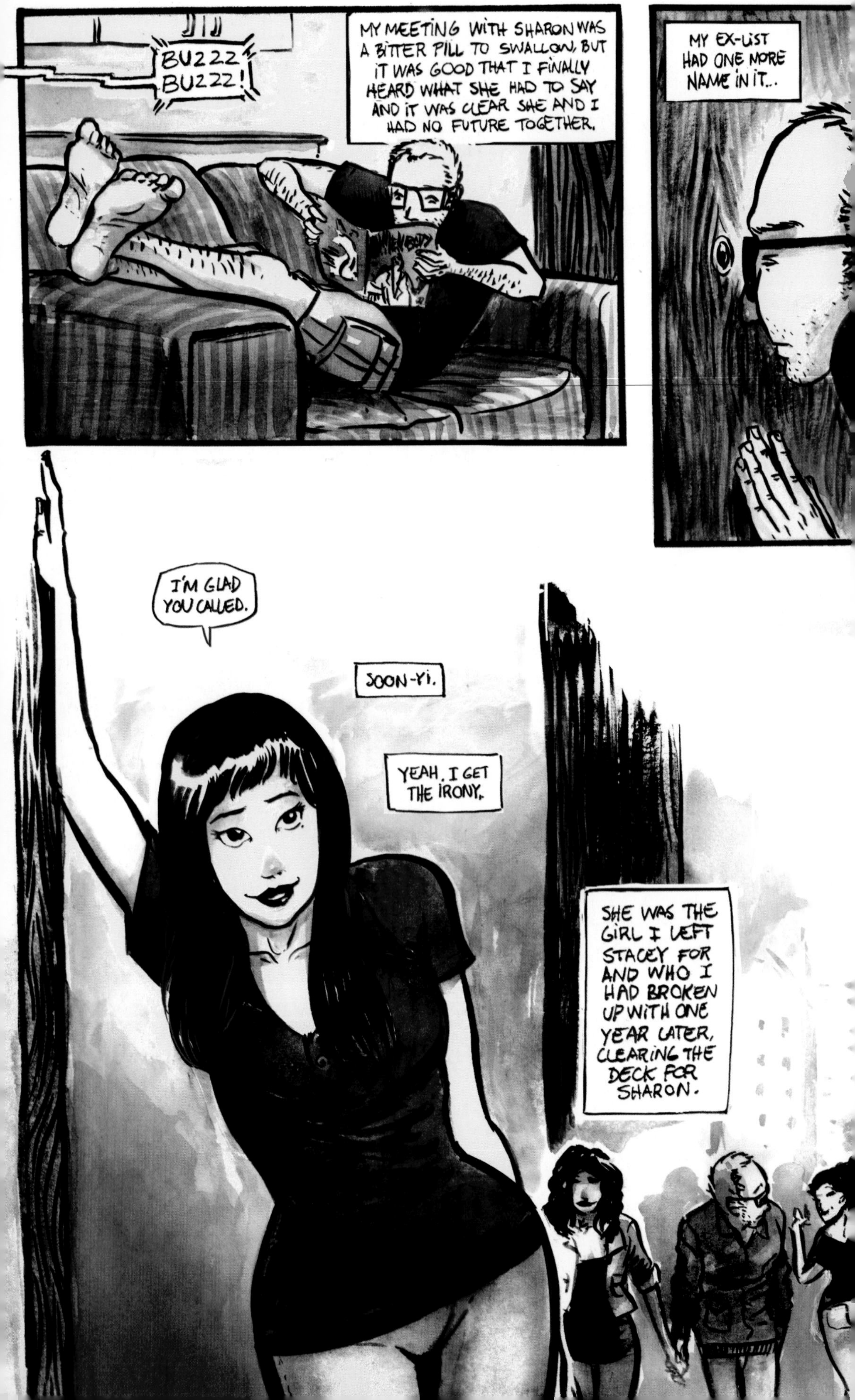
BUZZZ BUZZZ!
MY MEETING WITH SHARON WAS A BITTER PILL TO SWALLOW, BUT IT WAS GOOD THAT I FINALLY HEARD WHAT SHE HAD TO SAY AND IT WAS CLEAR SHE AND I HAD NO FUTURE TOGETHER.
MY EX-LIST HAD ONE MORE NAME IN IT...
I'M GLAD YOU CALLED.
SOON-YI.
YEAH, I GET THE IRONY.
SHE WAS THE GIRL I LEFT STACEY FOR AND WHO I HAD BROKEN UP WITH ONE YEAR LATER, CLEARING THE DECK FOR SHARON.

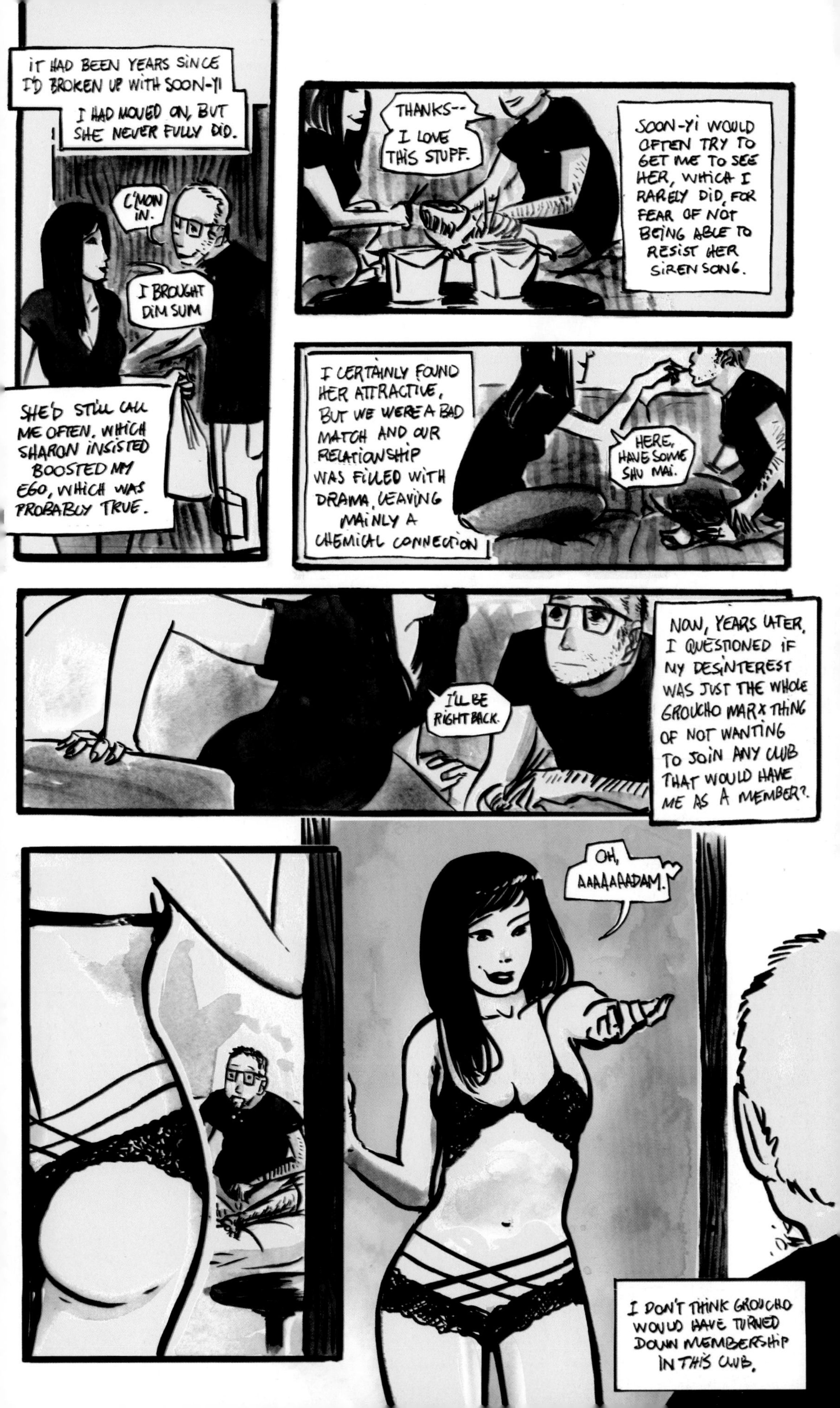
IT HAD BEEN YEARS SINCE I'D BROKEN UP WITH SOON-YI
I HAD MOVED ON, BUT SHE NEVER FULLY DID.
C'MON IN.
I BROUGHT DIM SUM
SHE'D STILL CALL ME OFTEN. WHICH SHARON INSISTED BOOSTED MY EGO, WHICH WAS PROBABLY TRUE.
THANKS-- I LOVE THIS STUFF.
SOON-YI WOULD OFTEN TRY TO GET ME TO SEE HER, WHICH I RARELY DID, FOR FEAR OF NOT BEING ABLE TO RESIST HER SIREN SONG.
I CERTAINLY FOUND HER ATTRACTIVE, BUT WE WERE A BAD MATCH AND OUR RELATIONSHIP WAS FILLED WITH DRAMA, LEAVING MAINLY A CHEMICAL CONNECTION
HERE, HAVE SOME SHU MAI.
I'LL BE RIGHT BACK.
NOW, YEARS LATER, I QUESTIONED IF MY DESINTEREST WAS JUST THE WHOLE GROUCHO MARX THING OF NOT WANTING TO JOIN ANY CLUB THAT WOULD HAVE ME AS A MEMBER?
OH, AAAAAADAM.
I DON'T THINK GROUCHO WOULD HAVE TURNED DOWN MEMBERSHIP IN THIS CLUB.

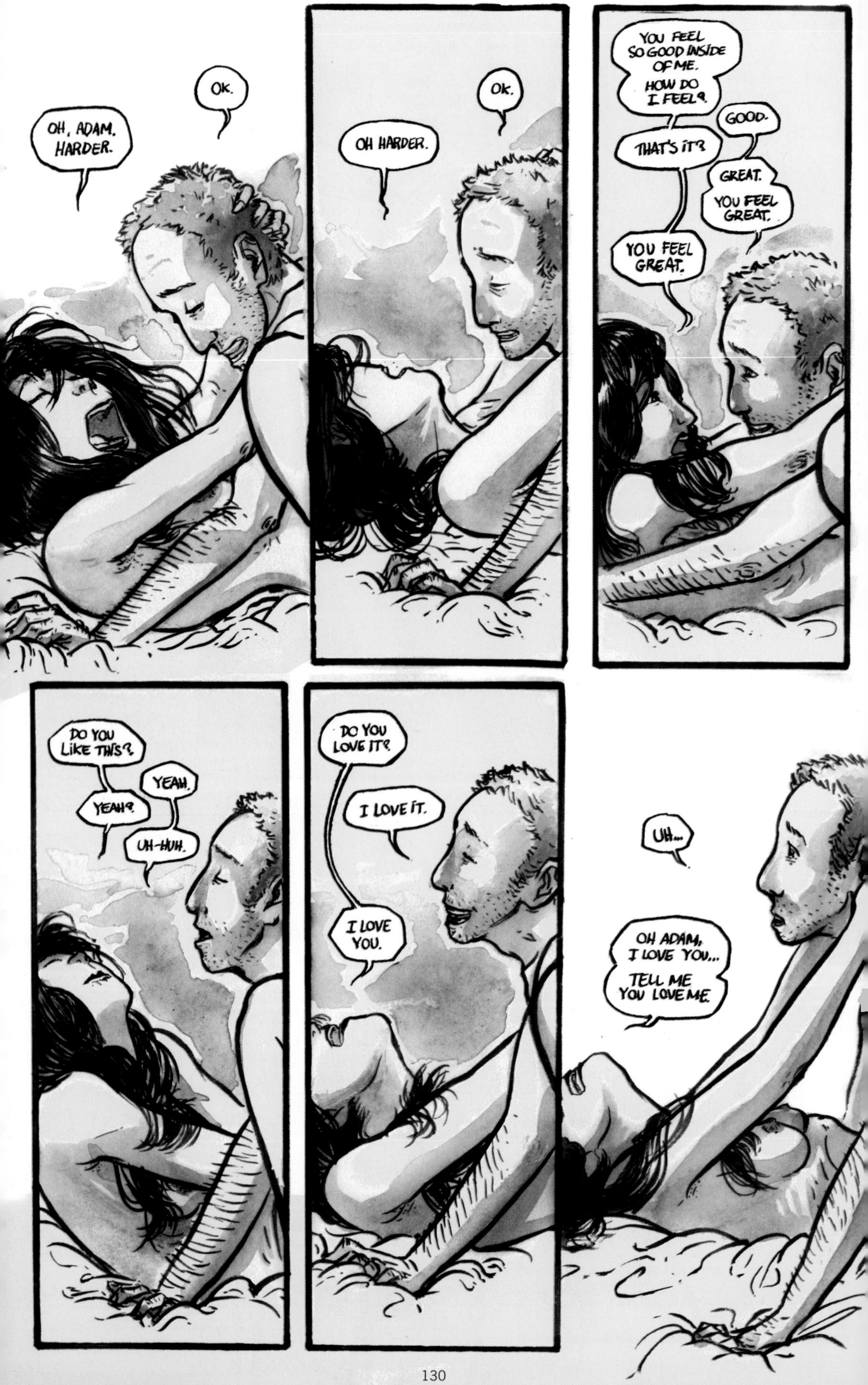
OH, ADAM. HARDER.
OK.
OH HARDER.
OK.
YOU FEEL SO GOOD INSIDE OF ME.
HOW DO I FEEL?
GOOD.
THAT'S IT?
GREAT.
YOU FEEL GREAT.
YOU FEEL GREAT.
DO YOU LIKE THIS?
YEAH.
YEAH?
UH-HUH.
DO YOU LOVE IT?
I LOVE IT.
I LOVE YOU.
UH...
OH ADAM, I LOVE YOU...
TELL ME YOU LOVE ME.

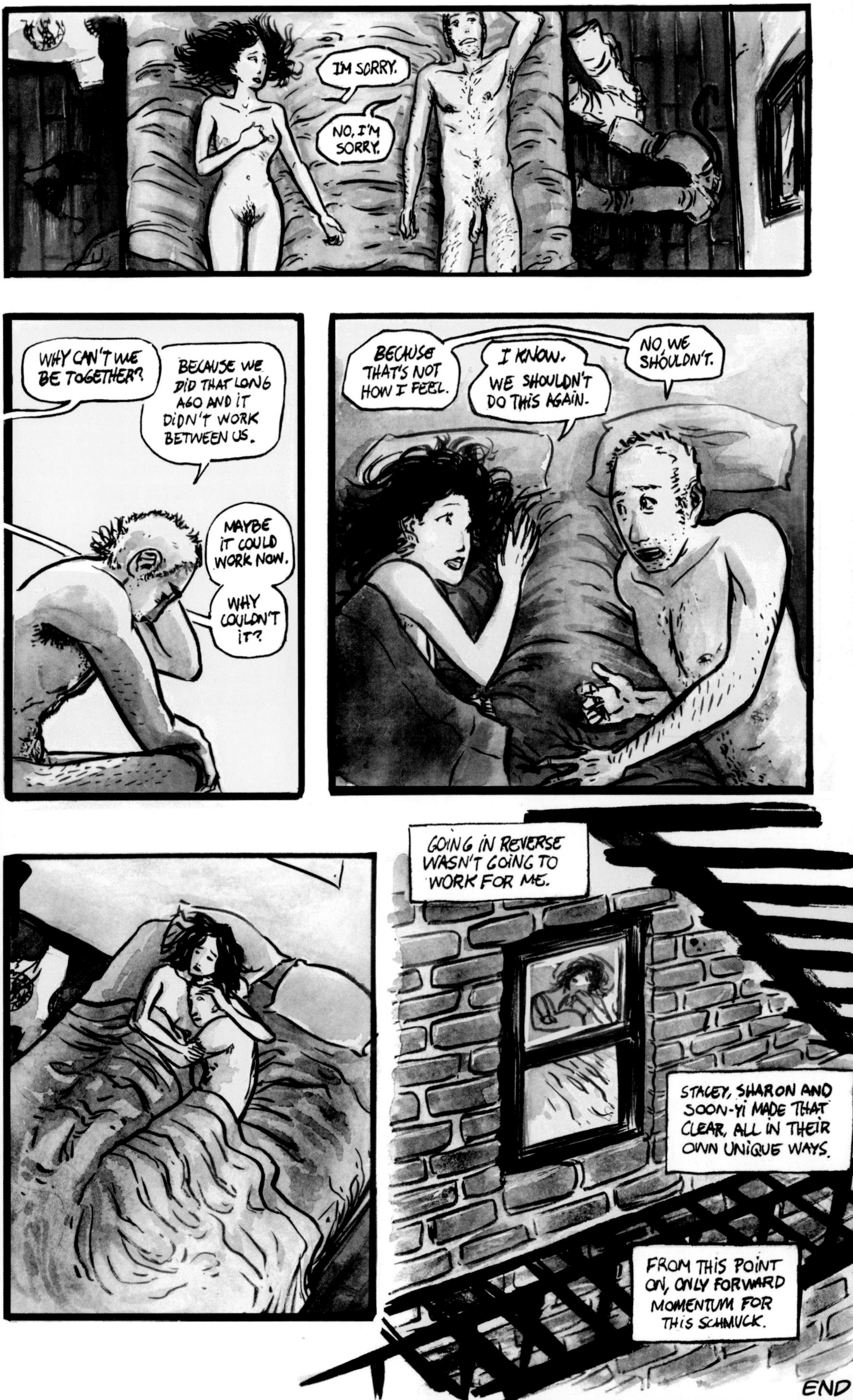
I'M SORRY.
NO, I'M SORRY.
WHY CAN'T WE BE TOGETHER?
BECAUSE WE DID THAT LONG AGO AND IT DIDN'T WORK BETWEEN US.
MAYBE IT COULD WORK NOW.
WHY COULDN'T IT?
BECAUSE THAT'S NOT HOW I FEEL.
I KNOW.
WE SHOULDN'T DO THIS AGAIN.
NO, WE SHOULDN'T.
GOING IN REVERSE WASN'T GOING TO WORK FOR ME.
STACEY, SHARON AND SOON-YI MADE THAT CLEAR, ALL IN THEIR OWN UNIQUE WAYS.
FROM THIS POINT ON, ONLY FORWARD MOMENTUM FOR THIS SCHMUCK.
END

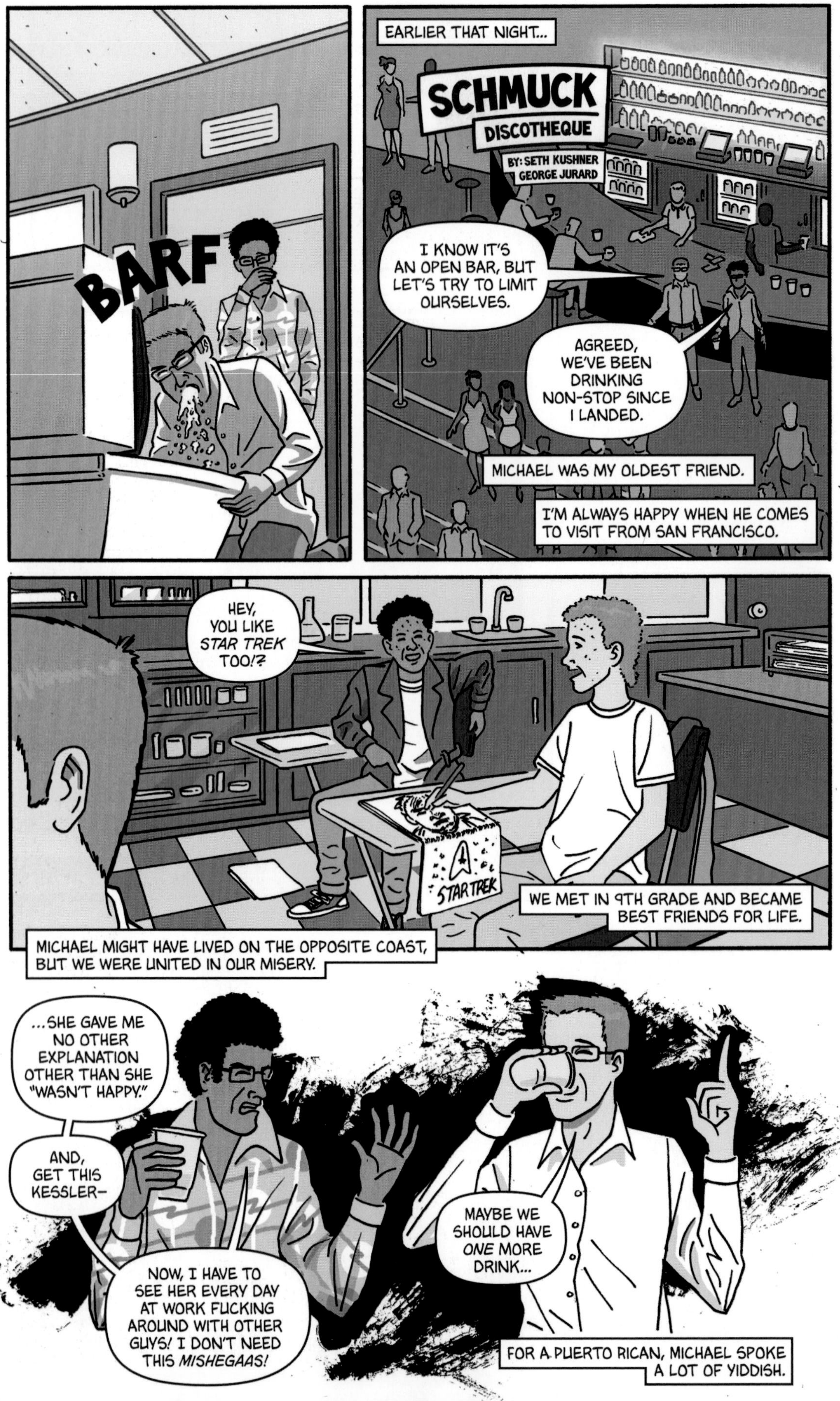
BARF
EARLIER THAT NIGHT...
SCHMUCK DISCOTHEQUE
BY: SETH KUSHNER GEORGE JURARD
I KNOW IT'S AN OPEN BAR, BUT LET'S TRY TO LIMIT OURSELVES.
AGREED, WE'VE BEEN DRINKING NON-STOP SINCE I LANDED.
MICHAEL WAS MY OLDEST FRIEND.
I'M ALWAYS HAPPY WHEN HE COMES TO VISIT FROM SAN FRANCISCO.
HEY, YOU LIKE STAR TREK TOO!?
STAR TREK
WE MET IN 9TH GRADE AND BECAME BEST FRIENDS FOR LIFE.
MICHAEL MIGHT HAVE LIVED ON THE OPPOSITE COAST, BUT WE WERE UNITED IN OUR MISERY.
...SHE GAVE ME NO OTHER EXPLANATION OTHER THAN SHE "WASN'T HAPPY."
AND, GET THIS KESSLER—
NOW, I HAVE TO SEE HER EVERY DAY AT WORK FUCKING AROUND WITH OTHER GUYS! I DON'T NEED THIS MISHEGAAS!
MAYBE WE SHOULD HAVE ONE MORE DRINK...
FOR A PUERTO RICAN, MICHAEL SPOKE A LOT OF YIDDISH.

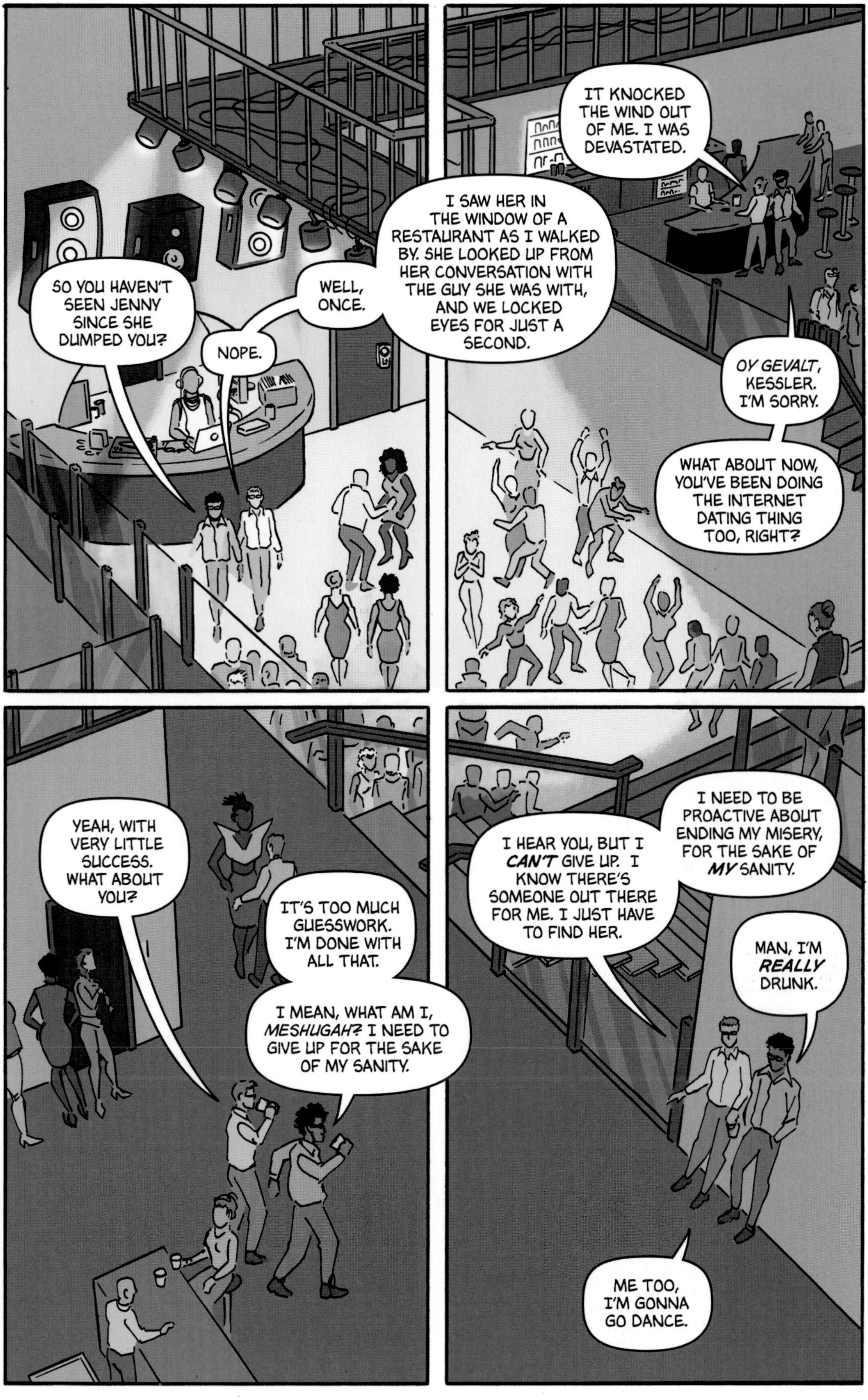
SO YOU HAVEN'T SEEN JENNY SINCE SHE DUMPED YOU?
NOPE.
WELL, ONCE.
I SAW HER IN THE WINDOW OF A RESTAURANT AS I WALKED BY. SHE LOOKED UP FROM HER CONVERSATION WITH THE GUY SHE WAS WITH, AND WE LOCKED EYES FOR JUST A SECOND.
IT KNOCKED THE WIND OUT OF ME. I WAS DEVASTATED.
OY GEVALT, KESSLER. I'M SORRY.
WHAT ABOUT NOW, YOU'VE BEEN DOING THE INTERNET DATING THING TOO, RIGHT?
YEAH, WITH VERY LITTLE SUCCESS. WHAT ABOUT YOU?
IT'S TOO MUCH GUESSWORK. I'M DONE WITH ALL THAT.
I MEAN, WHAT AM I, *MESHUGAH?* I NEED TO GIVE UP FOR THE SAKE OF MY SANITY.
I HEAR YOU, BUT I ***CAN'T*** GIVE UP. I KNOW THERE'S SOMEONE OUT THERE FOR ME. I JUST HAVE TO FIND HER.
I NEED TO BE PROACTIVE ABOUT ENDING MY MISERY, FOR THE SAKE OF ***MY*** SANITY.
MAN, I'M ***REALLY*** DRUNK.
ME TOO, I'M GONNA GO DANCE.

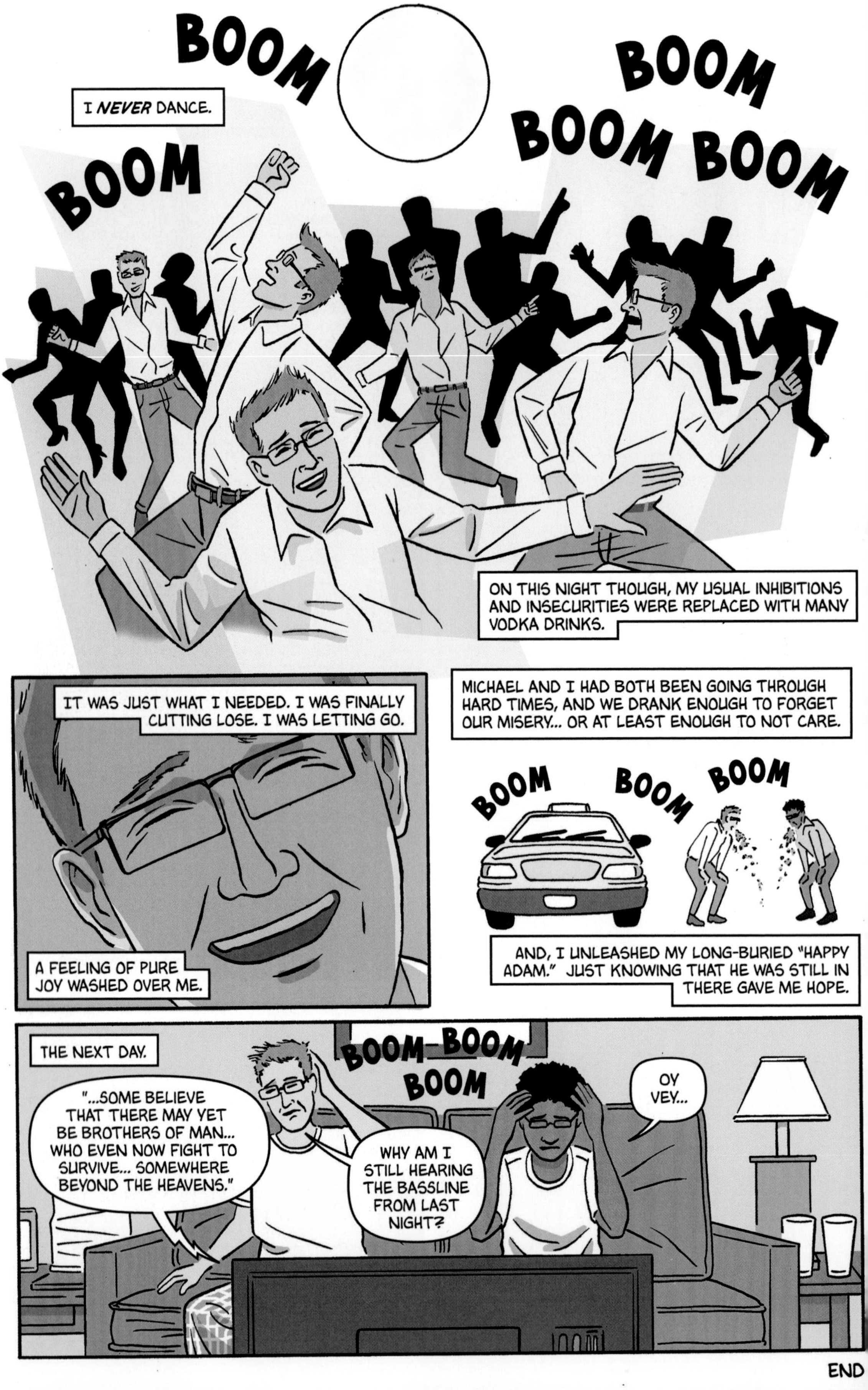
BOOM
I *NEVER* DANCE.
BOOM
BOOM
BOOM BOOM
ON THIS NIGHT THOUGH, MY USUAL INHIBITIONS AND INSECURITIES WERE REPLACED WITH MANY VODKA DRINKS.
IT WAS JUST WHAT I NEEDED. I WAS FINALLY CUTTING LOSE. I WAS LETTING GO.
A FEELING OF PURE JOY WASHED OVER ME.
MICHAEL AND I HAD BOTH BEEN GOING THROUGH HARD TIMES, AND WE DRANK ENOUGH TO FORGET OUR MISERY... OR AT LEAST ENOUGH TO NOT CARE.
BOOM
BOOM
BOOM
AND, I UNLEASHED MY LONG-BURIED "HAPPY ADAM." JUST KNOWING THAT HE WAS STILL IN THERE GAVE ME HOPE.
THE NEXT DAY.
"...SOME BELIEVE THAT THERE MAY YET BE BROTHERS OF MAN... WHO EVEN NOW FIGHT TO SURVIVE... SOMEWHERE BEYOND THE HEAVENS."
BOOM-BOOM
BOOM
WHY AM I STILL HEARING THE BASSLINE FROM LAST NIGHT?
OY VEY...
END

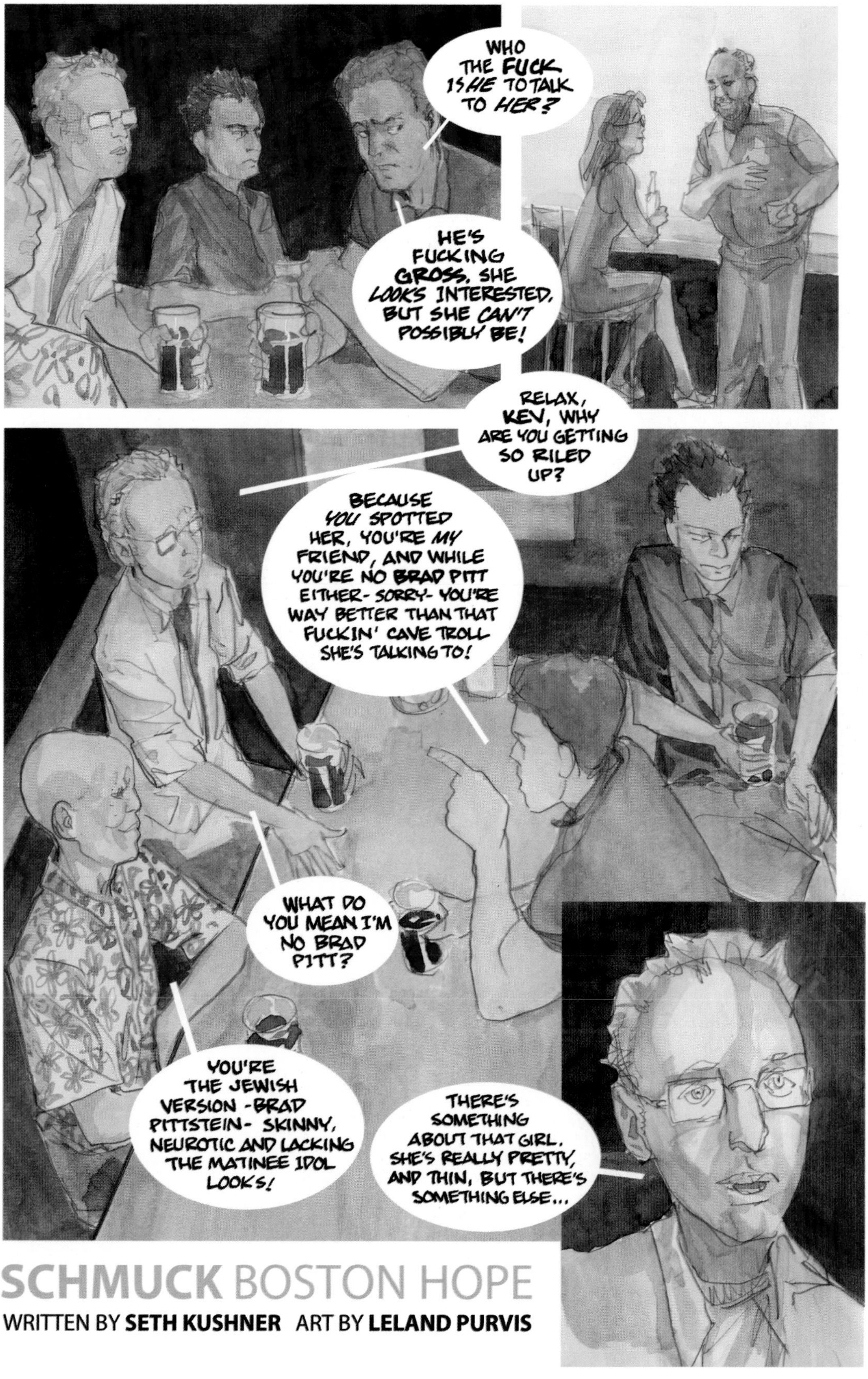
WHO THE FUCK IS HE TO TALK TO HER?
HE'S FUCKING GROSS. SHE LOOKS INTERESTED, BUT SHE CAN'T POSSIBLY BE!
RELAX, KEV, WHY ARE YOU GETTING SO RILED UP?
BECAUSE YOU SPOTTED HER, YOU'RE MY FRIEND, AND WHILE YOU'RE NO BRAD PITT EITHER- SORRY- YOU'RE WAY BETTER THAN THAT FUCKIN' CAVE TROLL SHE'S TALKING TO!
WHAT DO YOU MEAN I'M NO BRAD PITT?
YOU'RE THE JEWISH VERSION -BRAD PITTSTEIN- SKINNY, NEUROTIC AND LACKING THE MATINEE IDOL LOOKS!
THERE'S SOMETHING ABOUT THAT GIRL. SHE'S REALLY PRETTY, AND THIN, BUT THERE'S SOMETHING ELSE...

SCHMUCK BOSTON HOPE

WRITTEN BY **SETH KUSHNER** ART BY **LELAND PURVIS**

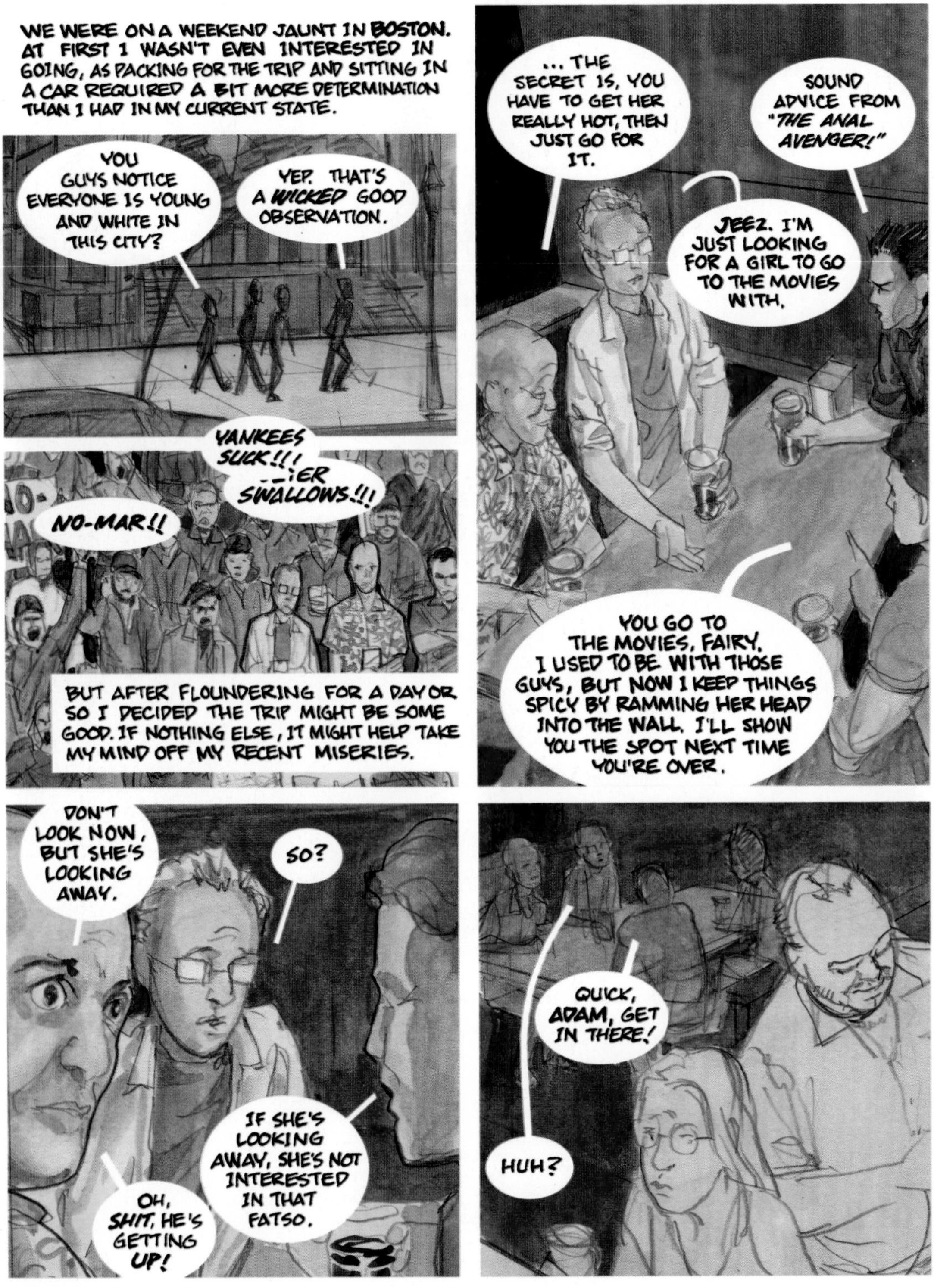
WE WERE ON A WEEKEND JAUNT IN BOSTON. AT FIRST I WASN'T EVEN INTERESTED IN GOING, AS PACKING FOR THE TRIP AND SITTING IN A CAR REQUIRED A BIT MORE DETERMINATION THAN I HAD IN MY CURRENT STATE.
YOU GUYS NOTICE EVERYONE IS YOUNG AND WHITE IN THIS CITY?
YEP. THAT'S A WICKED GOOD OBSERVATION.
YANKEES SUCK!!!
-IER SWALLOWS!!!
NO-MAR!!
BUT AFTER FLOUNDERING FOR A DAY OR SO I DECIDED THE TRIP MIGHT BE SOME GOOD. IF NOTHING ELSE, IT MIGHT HELP TAKE MY MIND OFF MY RECENT MISERIES.
... THE SECRET IS, YOU HAVE TO GET HER REALLY HOT, THEN JUST GO FOR IT.
SOUND ADVICE FROM "THE ANAL AVENGER!"
JEEZ. I'M JUST LOOKING FOR A GIRL TO GO TO THE MOVIES WITH.
YOU GO TO THE MOVIES, FAIRY. I USED TO BE WITH THOSE GUYS, BUT NOW I KEEP THINGS SPICY BY RAMMING HER HEAD INTO THE WALL. I'LL SHOW YOU THE SPOT NEXT TIME YOU'RE OVER.
DON'T LOOK NOW, BUT SHE'S LOOKING AWAY.
SO?
IF SHE'S LOOKING AWAY, SHE'S NOT INTERESTED IN THAT FATSO.
OH, SHIT, HE'S GETTING UP!
QUICK, ADAM, GET IN THERE!
HUH?

DON'T BE A PUSSY FOR ONCE!

YOU'RE ON VACATION, YOU GOT NOTHING TO LOSE!

JUST *TALK* TO HER!

I THOUGHT OF *CITIZEN KANE.* MORE SPECIFICALLY, OF A FEW WONDERFUL LINES OF DIALOG ABOUT REGRET BY THE CHARACTER BERNSTEIN, PLAYED BY EVERETT SLOAN.

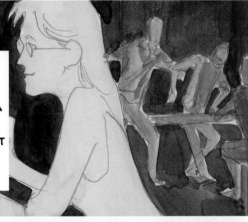

HE TOLD A STORY ABOUT A TIME MANY YEARS EARLIER WHEN HE WAS ON A FERRY AND HE SAW A GIRL ON ANOTHER PASSING BOAT. SHE NEVER SAW HIM, BUT HE'D REMEMBERED SHE WAS WEARING A WHITE DRESS...

OKAY, OKAY. I GOT THIS. I'M GOING IN.

HE NEVER SPOKE TO HER AND NEVER SAW HER AGAIN, BUT HE SAID THAT EVEN AFTER ALL THOSE YEARS, NOT A MONTH EVER WENT BY WHEN HE HADN'T THOUGHT OF HER.

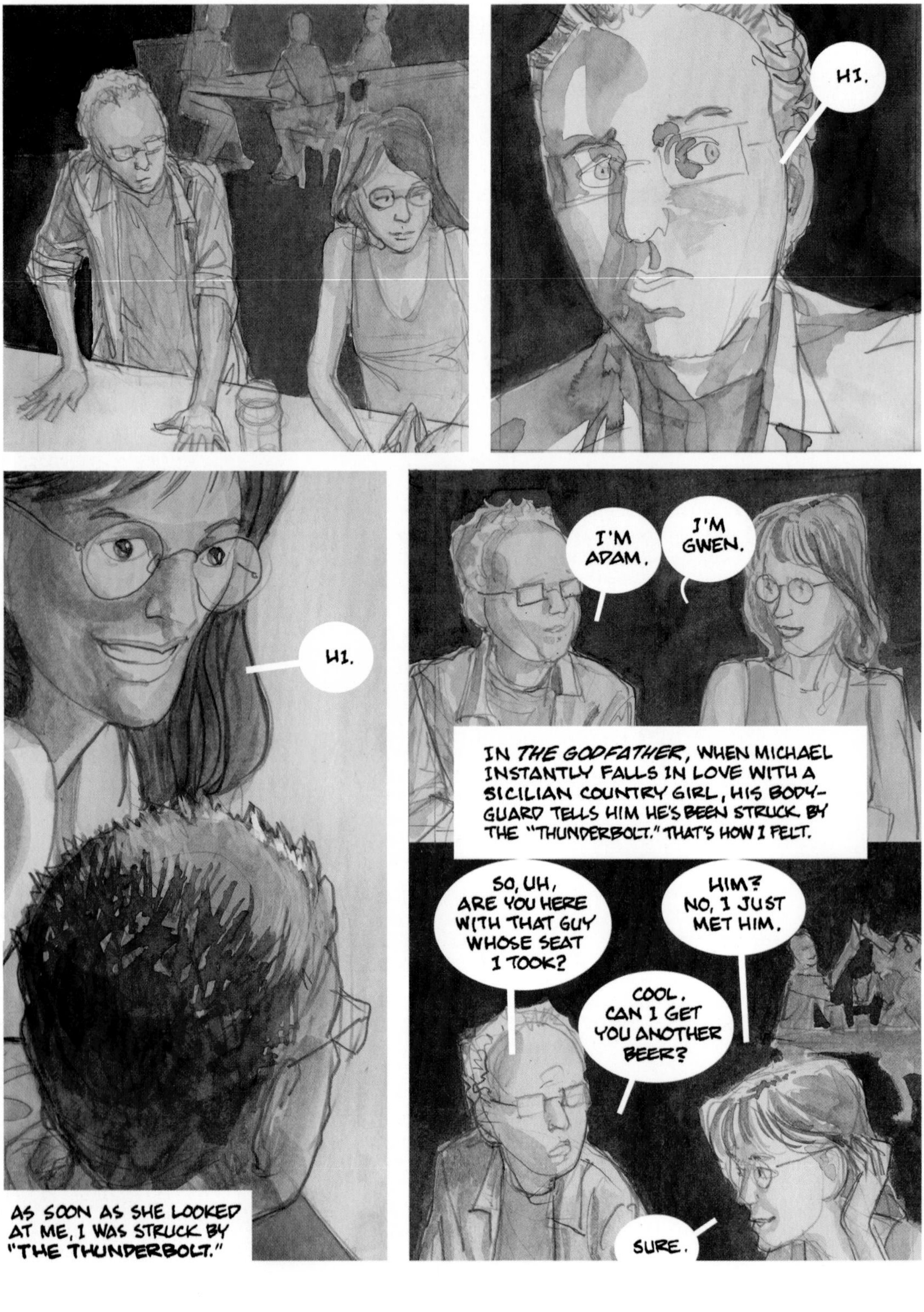
HI.
HI.
AS SOON AS SHE LOOKED AT ME, I WAS STRUCK BY "THE THUNDERBOLT."
I'M ADAM.
I'M GWEN.
IN *THE GODFATHER*, WHEN MICHAEL INSTANTLY FALLS IN LOVE WITH A SICILIAN COUNTRY GIRL, HIS BODY-GUARD TELLS HIM HE'S BEEN STRUCK BY THE "THUNDERBOLT." THAT'S HOW I FELT.
SO, UH, ARE YOU HERE WITH THAT GUY WHOSE SEAT I TOOK?
HIM? NO, I JUST MET HIM.
COOL. CAN I GET YOU ANOTHER BEER?
SURE.

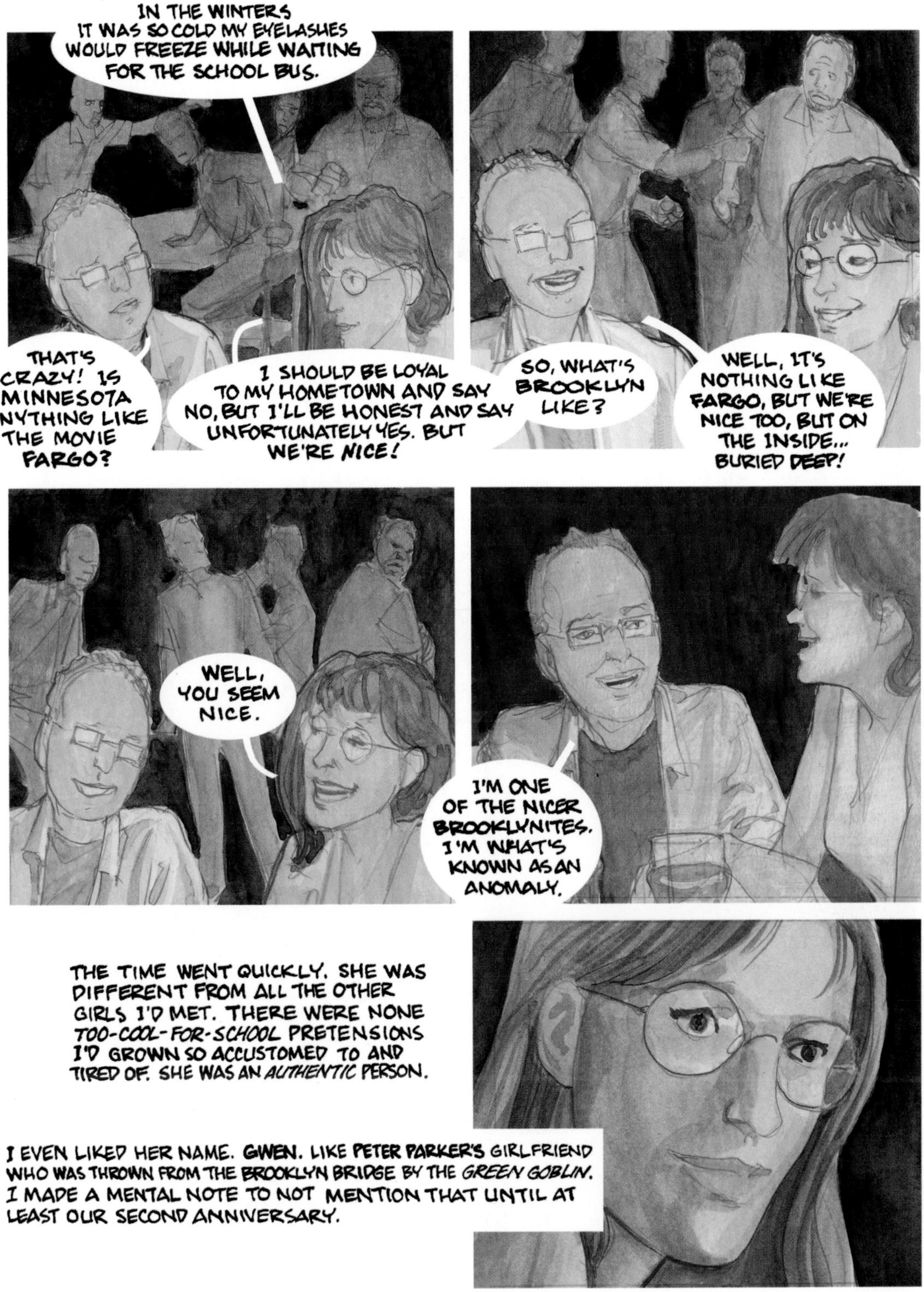
IN THE WINTERS IT WAS SO COLD MY EYELASHES WOULD FREEZE WHILE WAITING FOR THE SCHOOL BUS.
THAT'S CRAZY! IS MINNESOTA ANYTHING LIKE THE MOVIE FARGO?
I SHOULD BE LOYAL TO MY HOMETOWN AND SAY NO, BUT I'LL BE HONEST AND SAY UNFORTUNATELY YES. BUT WE'RE *NICE*!
SO, WHAT'S BROOKLYN LIKE?
WELL, IT'S NOTHING LIKE FARGO, BUT WE'RE NICE TOO, BUT ON THE INSIDE... BURIED DEEP!
WELL, YOU SEEM NICE.
I'M ONE OF THE NICER BROOKLYNITES. I'M WHAT'S KNOWN AS AN ANOMALY.
THE TIME WENT QUICKLY. SHE WAS DIFFERENT FROM ALL THE OTHER GIRLS I'D MET. THERE WERE NONE *TOO-COOL-FOR-SCHOOL* PRETENSIONS I'D GROWN SO ACCUSTOMED TO AND TIRED OF. SHE WAS AN *AUTHENTIC* PERSON.
I EVEN LIKED HER NAME. GWEN. LIKE PETER PARKER'S GIRLFRIEND WHO WAS THROWN FROM THE BROOKLYN BRIDGE BY THE *GREEN GOBLIN*. I MADE A MENTAL NOTE TO NOT MENTION THAT UNTIL AT LEAST OUR SECOND ANNIVERSARY.

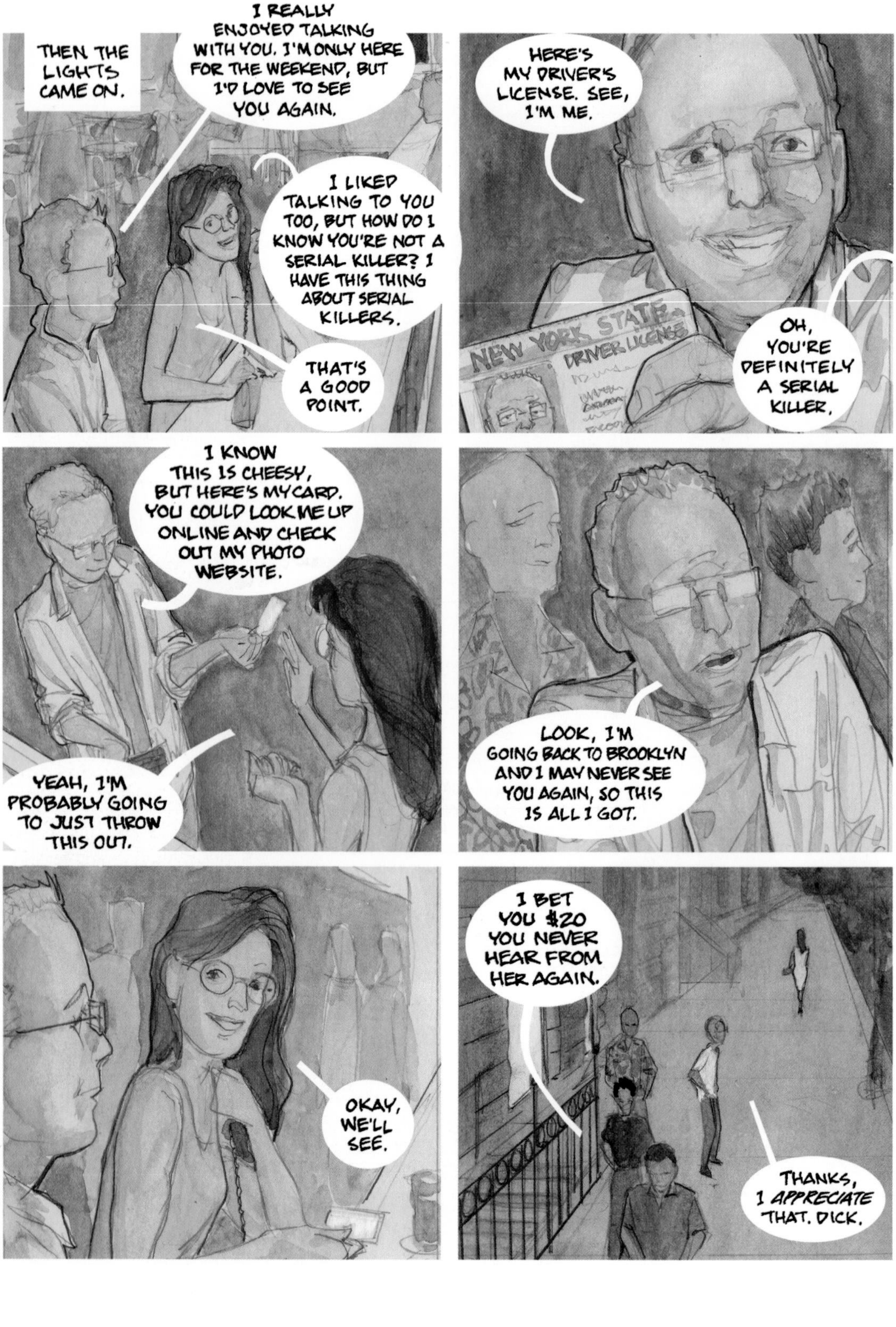
THEN THE LIGHTS CAME ON.
I REALLY ENJOYED TALKING WITH YOU. I'M ONLY HERE FOR THE WEEKEND, BUT I'D LOVE TO SEE YOU AGAIN.
I LIKED TALKING TO YOU TOO, BUT HOW DO I KNOW YOU'RE NOT A SERIAL KILLER? I HAVE THIS THING ABOUT SERIAL KILLERS.
THAT'S A GOOD POINT.
HERE'S MY DRIVER'S LICENSE. SEE, I'M ME.
NEW YORK STATE DRIVER LICENSE
OH, YOU'RE DEFINITELY A SERIAL KILLER.
I KNOW THIS IS CHEESY, BUT HERE'S MY CARD. YOU COULD LOOK ME UP ONLINE AND CHECK OUT MY PHOTO WEBSITE.
YEAH, I'M PROBABLY GOING TO JUST THROW THIS OUT.
LOOK, I'M GOING BACK TO BROOKLYN AND I MAY NEVER SEE YOU AGAIN, SO THIS IS ALL I GOT.
OKAY, WE'LL SEE.
I BET YOU $20 YOU NEVER HEAR FROM HER AGAIN.
THANKS, I *APPRECIATE* THAT. DICK.

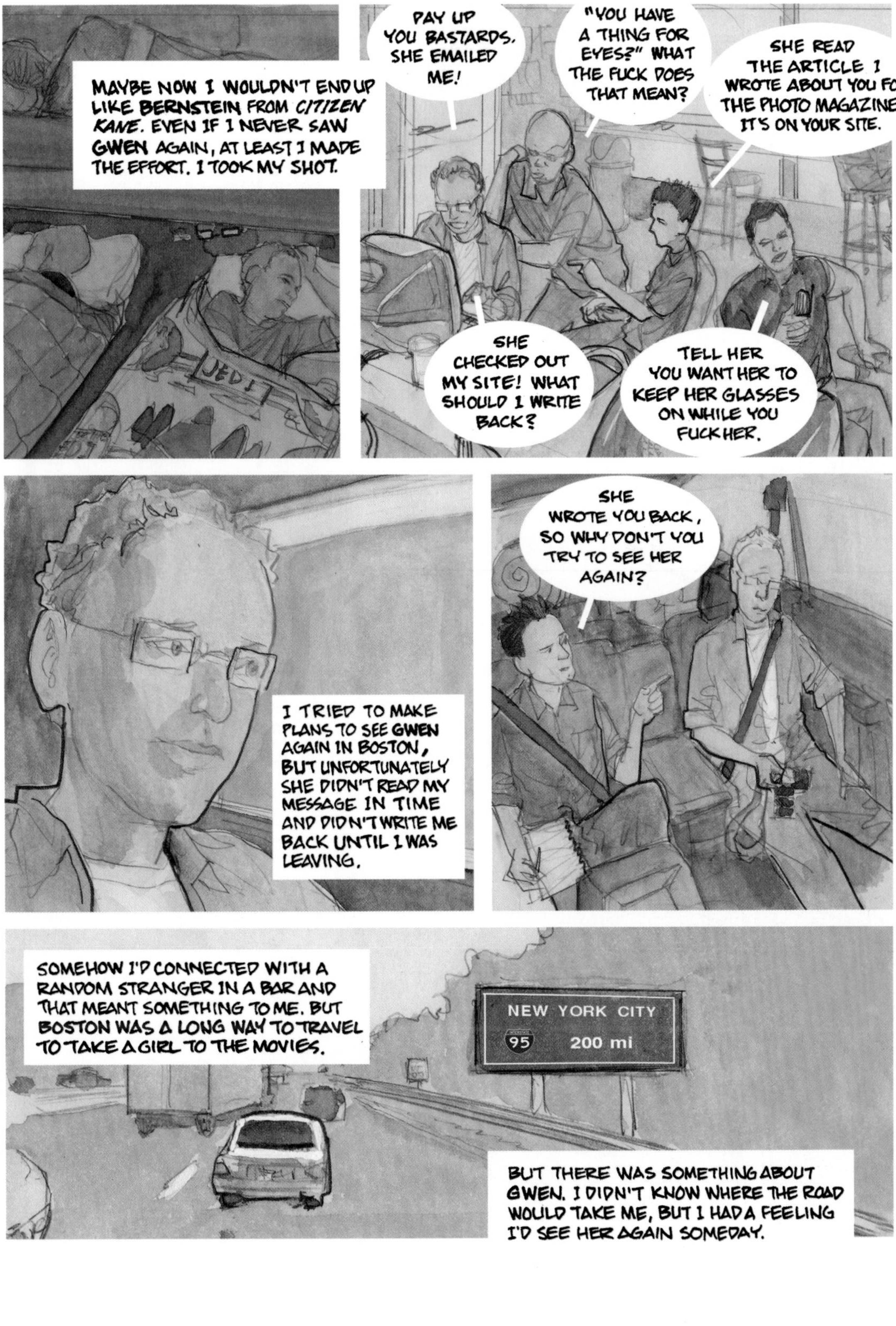
MAYBE NOW I WOULDN'T END UP LIKE BERNSTEIN FROM CITIZEN KANE. EVEN IF I NEVER SAW GWEN AGAIN, AT LEAST I MADE THE EFFORT. I TOOK MY SHOT.
JEDI
PAY UP YOU BASTARDS. SHE EMAILED ME!
"YOU HAVE A THING FOR EYES?" WHAT THE FUCK DOES THAT MEAN?
SHE READ THE ARTICLE I WROTE ABOUT YOU FOR THE PHOTO MAGAZINE... IT'S ON YOUR SITE.
SHE CHECKED OUT MY SITE! WHAT SHOULD I WRITE BACK?
TELL HER YOU WANT HER TO KEEP HER GLASSES ON WHILE YOU FUCK HER.
I TRIED TO MAKE PLANS TO SEE GWEN AGAIN IN BOSTON, BUT UNFORTUNATELY SHE DIDN'T READ MY MESSAGE IN TIME AND DIDN'T WRITE ME BACK UNTIL I WAS LEAVING.
SHE WROTE YOU BACK, SO WHY DON'T YOU TRY TO SEE HER AGAIN?
SOMEHOW I'D CONNECTED WITH A RANDOM STRANGER IN A BAR AND THAT MEANT SOMETHING TO ME. BUT BOSTON WAS A LONG WAY TO TRAVEL TO TAKE A GIRL TO THE MOVIES.
NEW YORK CITY
95
200 mi
BUT THERE WAS SOMETHING ABOUT GWEN. I DIDN'T KNOW WHERE THE ROAD WOULD TAKE ME, BUT I HAD A FEELING I'D SEE HER AGAIN SOMEDAY.

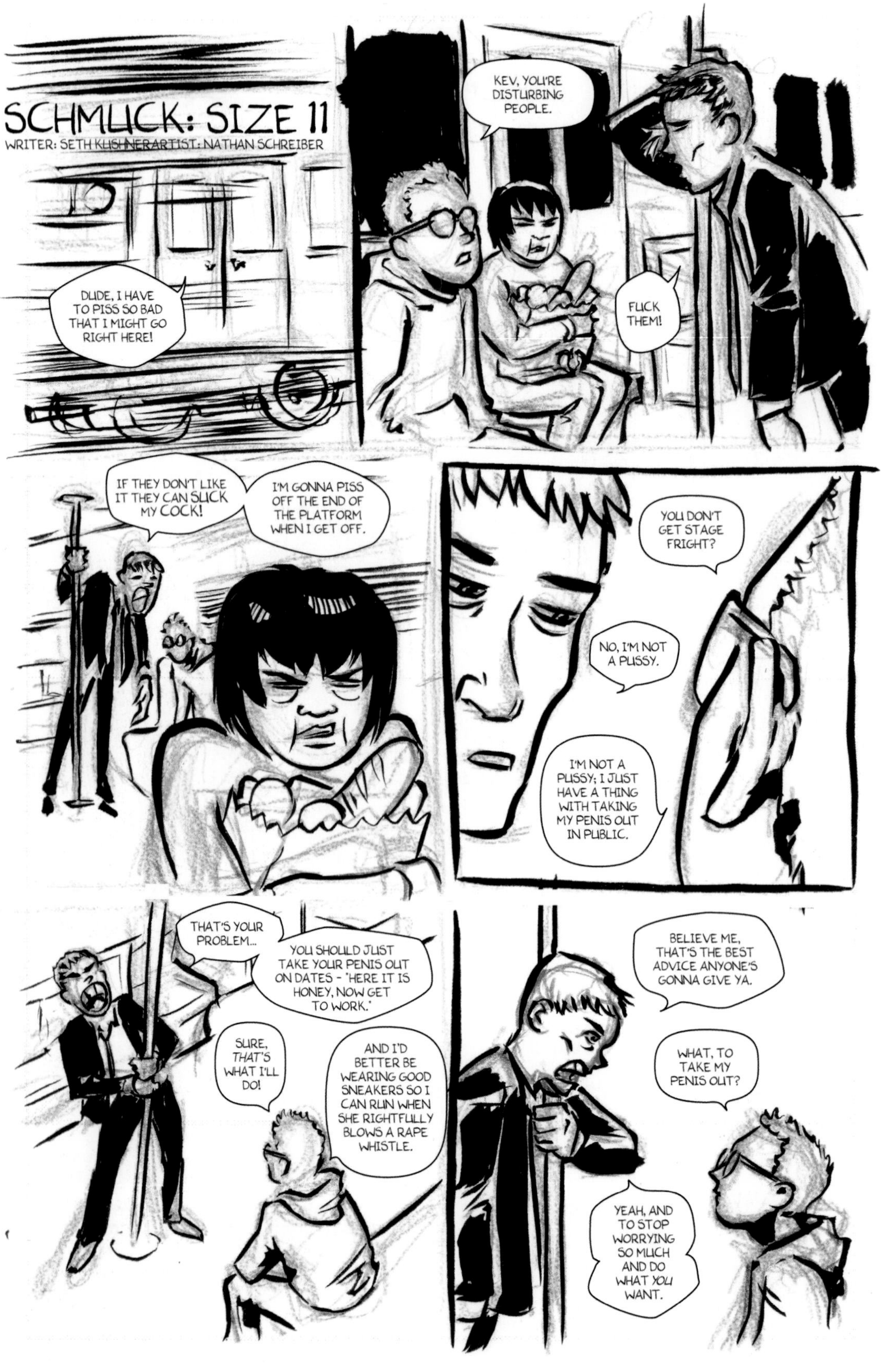
SCHMUCK: SIZE 11
WRITER: SETH KUSHNER ARTIST: NATHAN SCHREIBER
DUDE, I HAVE TO PISS SO BAD THAT I MIGHT GO RIGHT HERE!
KEV, YOU'RE DISTURBING PEOPLE.
FUCK THEM!
IF THEY DON'T LIKE IT THEY CAN SUCK MY COCK!
I'M GONNA PISS OFF THE END OF THE PLATFORM WHEN I GET OFF.
YOU DON'T GET STAGE FRIGHT?
NO, I'M NOT A PUSSY.
I'M NOT A PUSSY; I JUST HAVE A THING WITH TAKING MY PENIS OUT IN PUBLIC.
THAT'S YOUR PROBLEM...
YOU SHOULD JUST TAKE YOUR PENIS OUT ON DATES - "HERE IT IS HONEY, NOW GET TO WORK."
SURE, THAT'S WHAT I'LL DO!
AND I'D BETTER BE WEARING GOOD SNEAKERS SO I CAN RUN WHEN SHE RIGHTFULLY BLOWS A RAPE WHISTLE.
BELIEVE ME, THAT'S THE BEST ADVICE ANYONE'S GONNA GIVE YA.
WHAT, TO TAKE MY PENIS OUT?
YEAH, AND TO STOP WORRYING SO MUCH AND DO WHAT YOU WANT.

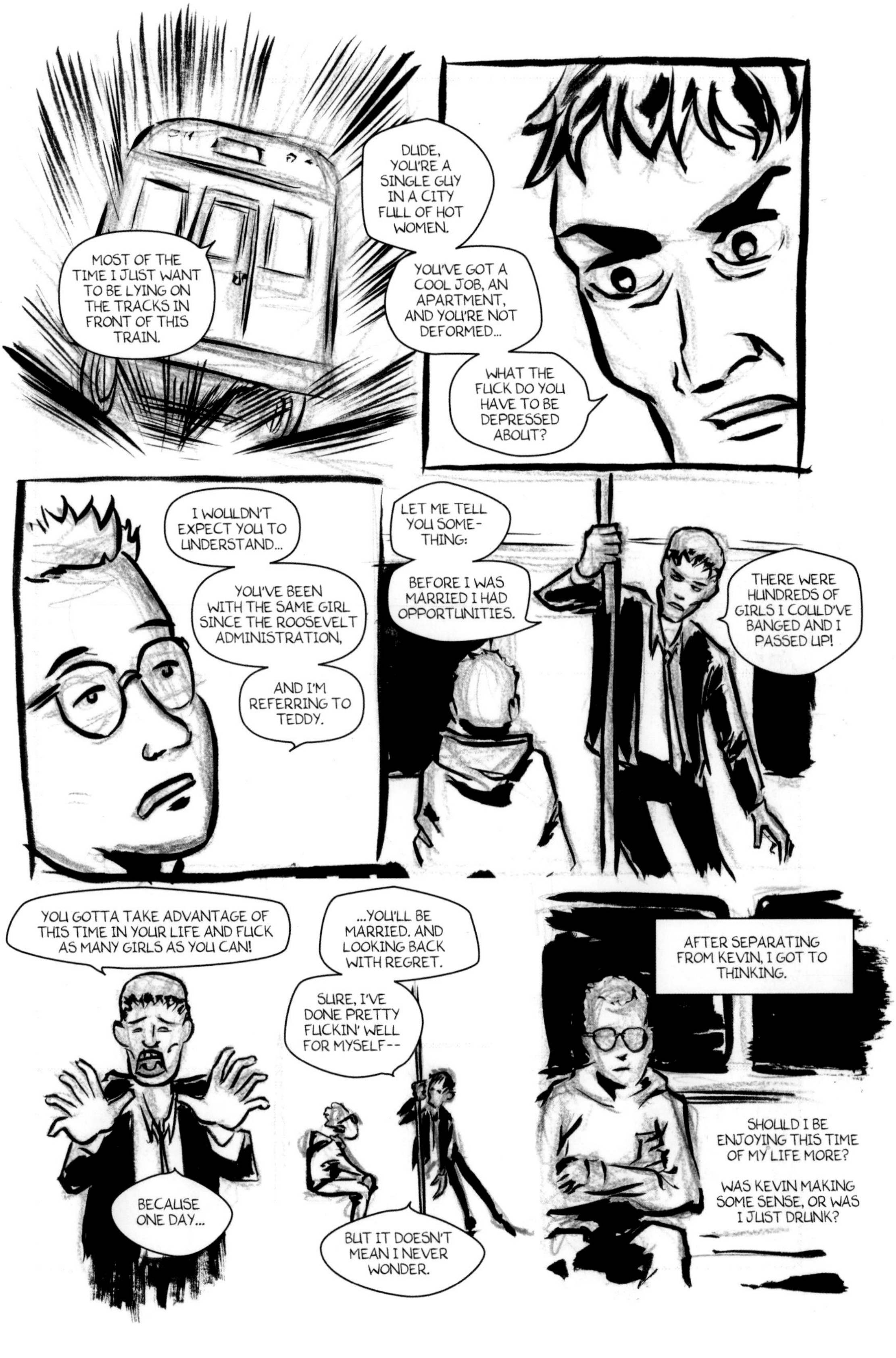
MOST OF THE TIME I JUST WANT TO BE LYING ON THE TRACKS IN FRONT OF THIS TRAIN.
DUDE, YOU'RE A SINGLE GUY IN A CITY FULL OF HOT WOMEN.
YOU'VE GOT A COOL JOB, AN APARTMENT, AND YOU'RE NOT DEFORMED...
WHAT THE FUCK DO YOU HAVE TO BE DEPRESSED ABOUT?
I WOULDN'T EXPECT YOU TO UNDERSTAND...
YOU'VE BEEN WITH THE SAME GIRL SINCE THE ROOSEVELT ADMINISTRATION,
AND I'M REFERRING TO TEDDY.
LET ME TELL YOU SOME-THING:
BEFORE I WAS MARRIED I HAD OPPORTUNITIES.
THERE WERE HUNDREDS OF GIRLS I COULD'VE BANGED AND I PASSED UP!
YOU GOTTA TAKE ADVANTAGE OF THIS TIME IN YOUR LIFE AND FUCK AS MANY GIRLS AS YOU CAN!
BECAUSE ONE DAY...
...YOU'LL BE MARRIED. AND LOOKING BACK WITH REGRET.
SURE, I'VE DONE PRETTY FUCKIN' WELL FOR MYSELF--
BUT IT DOESN'T MEAN I NEVER WONDER.
AFTER SEPARATING FROM KEVIN, I GOT TO THINKING.
SHOULD I BE ENJOYING THIS TIME OF MY LIFE MORE?
WAS KEVIN MAKING SOME SENSE, OR WAS I JUST DRUNK?

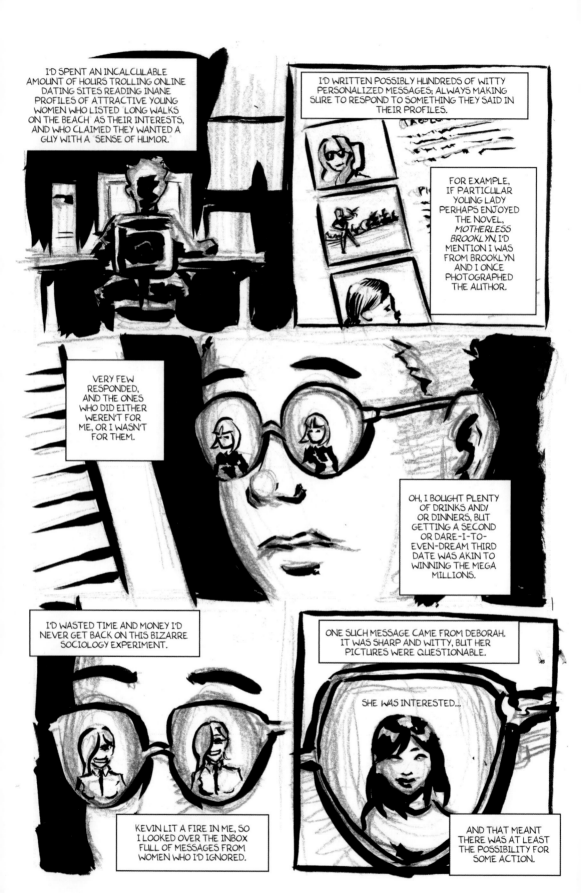

I'D SPENT AN INCALCULABLE AMOUNT OF HOURS TROLLING ONLINE DATING SITES READING INANE PROFILES OF ATTRACTIVE YOUNG WOMEN WHO LISTED LONG WALKS ON THE BEACH AS THEIR INTERESTS, AND WHO CLAIMED THEY WANTED A GUY WITH A SENSE OF HUMOR.

I'D WRITTEN POSSIBLY HUNDREDS OF WITTY PERSONALIZED MESSAGES; ALWAYS MAKING SURE TO RESPOND TO SOMETHING THEY SAID IN THEIR PROFILES.

FOR EXAMPLE, IF PARTICULAR YOUNG LADY PERHAPS ENJOYED THE NOVEL, *MOTHERLESS BROOKLYN*, I'D MENTION I WAS FROM BROOKLYN AND I ONCE PHOTOGRAPHED THE AUTHOR.

VERY FEW RESPONDED, AND THE ONES WHO DID EITHER WEREN'T FOR ME, OR I WASN'T FOR THEM.

OH, I BOUGHT PLENTY OF DRINKS AND/ OR DINNERS, BUT GETTING A SECOND OR DARE-I-TO-EVEN-DREAM THIRD DATE WAS AKIN TO WINNING THE MEGA MILLIONS.

I'D WASTED TIME AND MONEY I'D NEVER GET BACK ON THIS BIZARRE SOCIOLOGY EXPERIMENT.

ONE SUCH MESSAGE CAME FROM DEBORAH. IT WAS SHARP AND WITTY, BUT HER PICTURES WERE QUESTIONABLE.

SHE *WAS* INTERESTED...

KEVIN LIT A FIRE IN ME, SO I LOOKED OVER THE INBOX FULL OF MESSAGES FROM WOMEN WHO I'D IGNORED.

AND THAT MEANT THERE WAS AT LEAST THE POSSIBILITY FOR SOME ACTION.

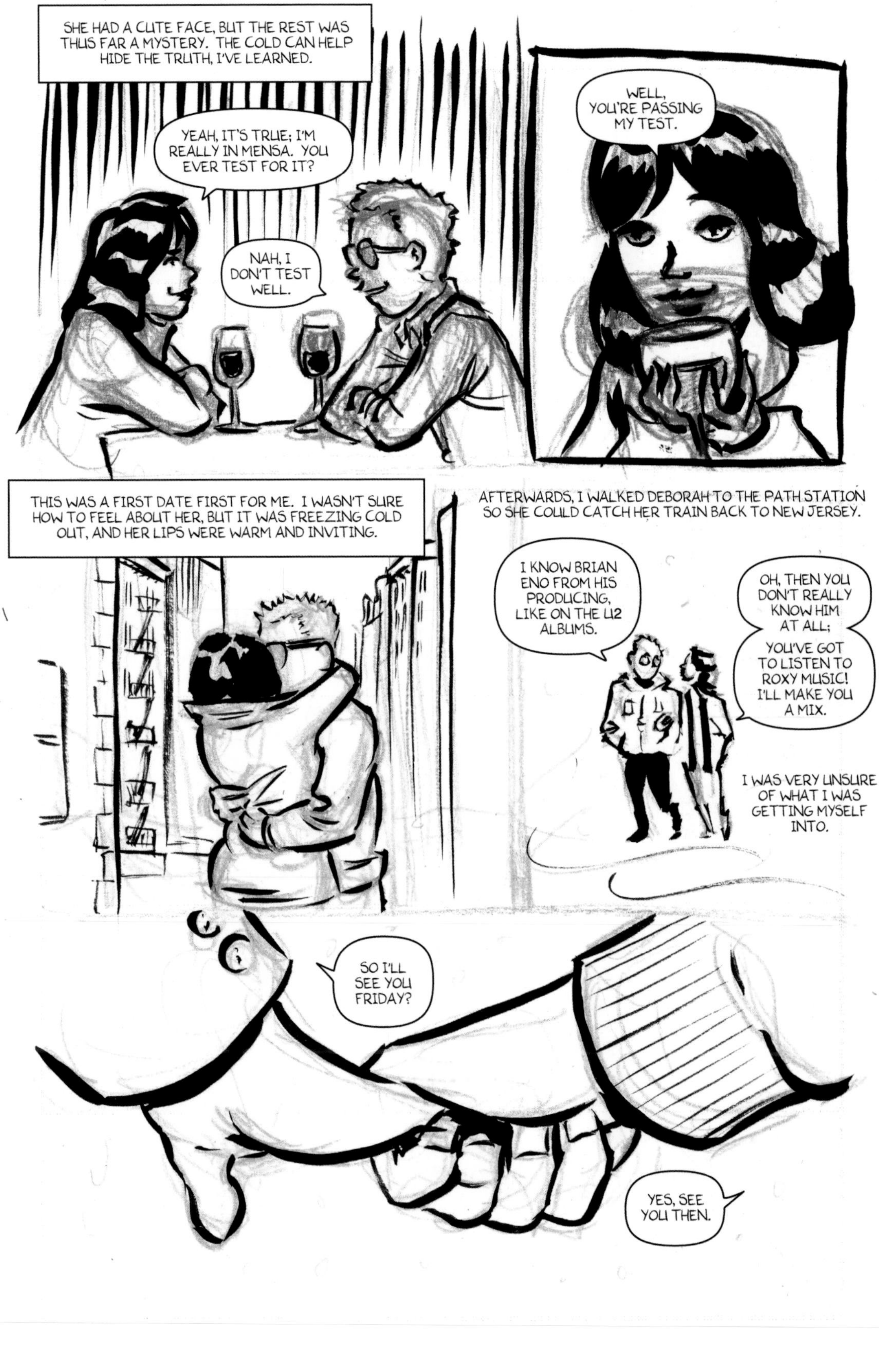

SHE HAD A CUTE FACE, BUT THE REST WAS THUS FAR A MYSTERY. THE COLD CAN HELP HIDE THE TRUTH, I'VE LEARNED.
YEAH, IT'S TRUE; I'M REALLY IN MENSA. YOU EVER TEST FOR IT?
NAH, I DON'T TEST WELL.
WELL, YOU'RE PASSING MY TEST.
THIS WAS A FIRST DATE FIRST FOR ME. I WASN'T SURE HOW TO FEEL ABOUT HER, BUT IT WAS FREEZING COLD OUT, AND HER LIPS WERE WARM AND INVITING.
AFTERWARDS, I WALKED DEBORAH TO THE PATH STATION SO SHE COULD CATCH HER TRAIN BACK TO NEW JERSEY.
I KNOW BRIAN ENO FROM HIS PRODUCING, LIKE ON THE U2 ALBUMS.
OH, THEN YOU DON'T REALLY KNOW HIM AT ALL;
YOU'VE GOT TO LISTEN TO ROXY MUSIC! I'LL MAKE YOU A MIX.
I WAS VERY UNSURE OF WHAT I WAS GETTING MYSELF INTO.
SO I'LL SEE YOU FRIDAY?
YES, SEE YOU THEN.

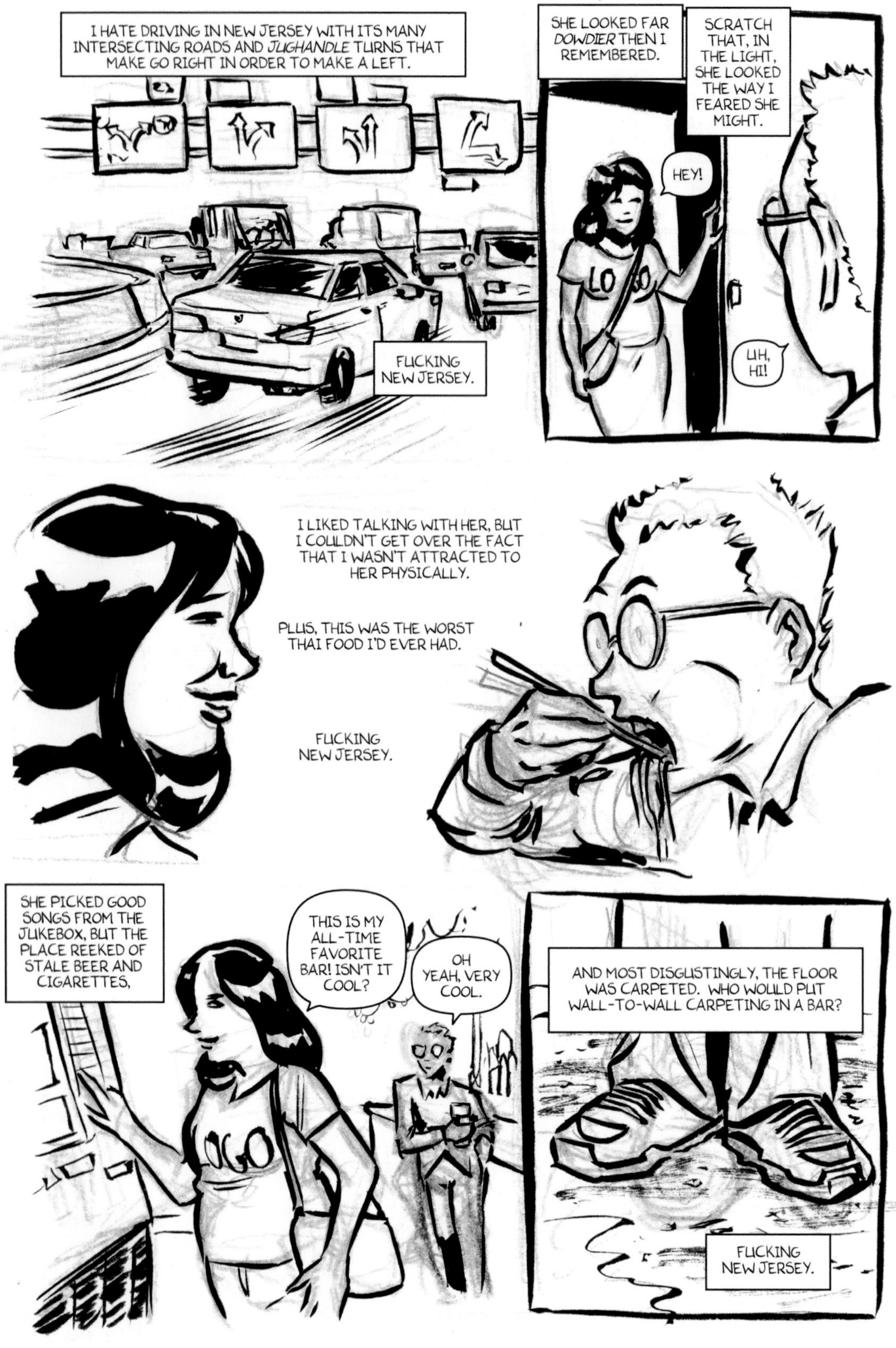
I HATE DRIVING IN NEW JERSEY WITH ITS MANY INTERSECTING ROADS AND *JUGHANDLE* TURNS THAT MAKE GO RIGHT IN ORDER TO MAKE A LEFT.
FUCKING NEW JERSEY.
SHE LOOKED FAR *DOWDIER* THEN I REMEMBERED.
SCRATCH THAT, IN THE LIGHT, SHE LOOKED THE WAY I FEARED SHE MIGHT.
HEY!
UH, HI!
I LIKED TALKING WITH HER, BUT I COULDN'T GET OVER THE FACT THAT I WASN'T ATTRACTED TO HER PHYSICALLY.
PLUS, THIS WAS THE WORST THAI FOOD I'D EVER HAD.
FUCKING NEW JERSEY.
SHE PICKED GOOD SONGS FROM THE JUKEBOX, BUT THE PLACE REEKED OF STALE BEER AND CIGARETTES,
THIS IS MY ALL-TIME FAVORITE BAR! ISN'T IT COOL?
OH YEAH, VERY COOL.
AND MOST DISGUSTINGLY, THE FLOOR WAS CARPETED. WHO WOULD PUT WALL-TO-WALL CARPETING IN A BAR?
FUCKING NEW JERSEY.

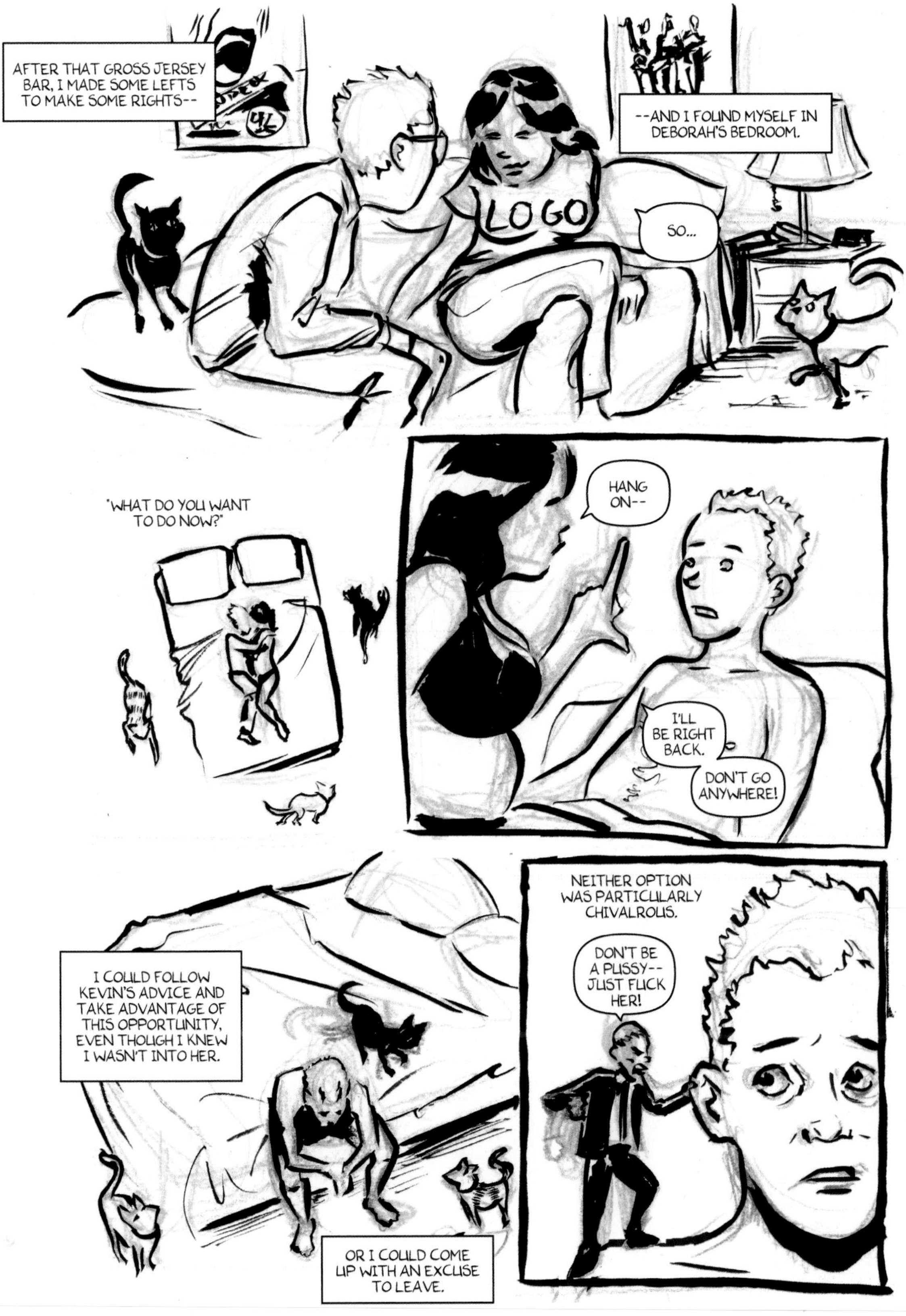
AFTER THAT GROSS JERSEY BAR, I MADE SOME LEFTS TO MAKE SOME RIGHTS--
--AND I FOUND MYSELF IN DEBORAH'S BEDROOM.
LOGO
SO...
"WHAT DO YOU WANT TO DO NOW?"
HANG ON--
I'LL BE RIGHT BACK.
DON'T GO ANYWHERE!
I COULD FOLLOW KEVIN'S ADVICE AND TAKE ADVANTAGE OF THIS OPPORTUNITY, EVEN THOUGH I KNEW I WASN'T INTO HER.
OR I COULD COME UP WITH AN EXCUSE TO LEAVE.
NEITHER OPTION WAS PARTICULARLY CHIVALROUS.
DON'T BE A PUSSY-- JUST FUCK HER!

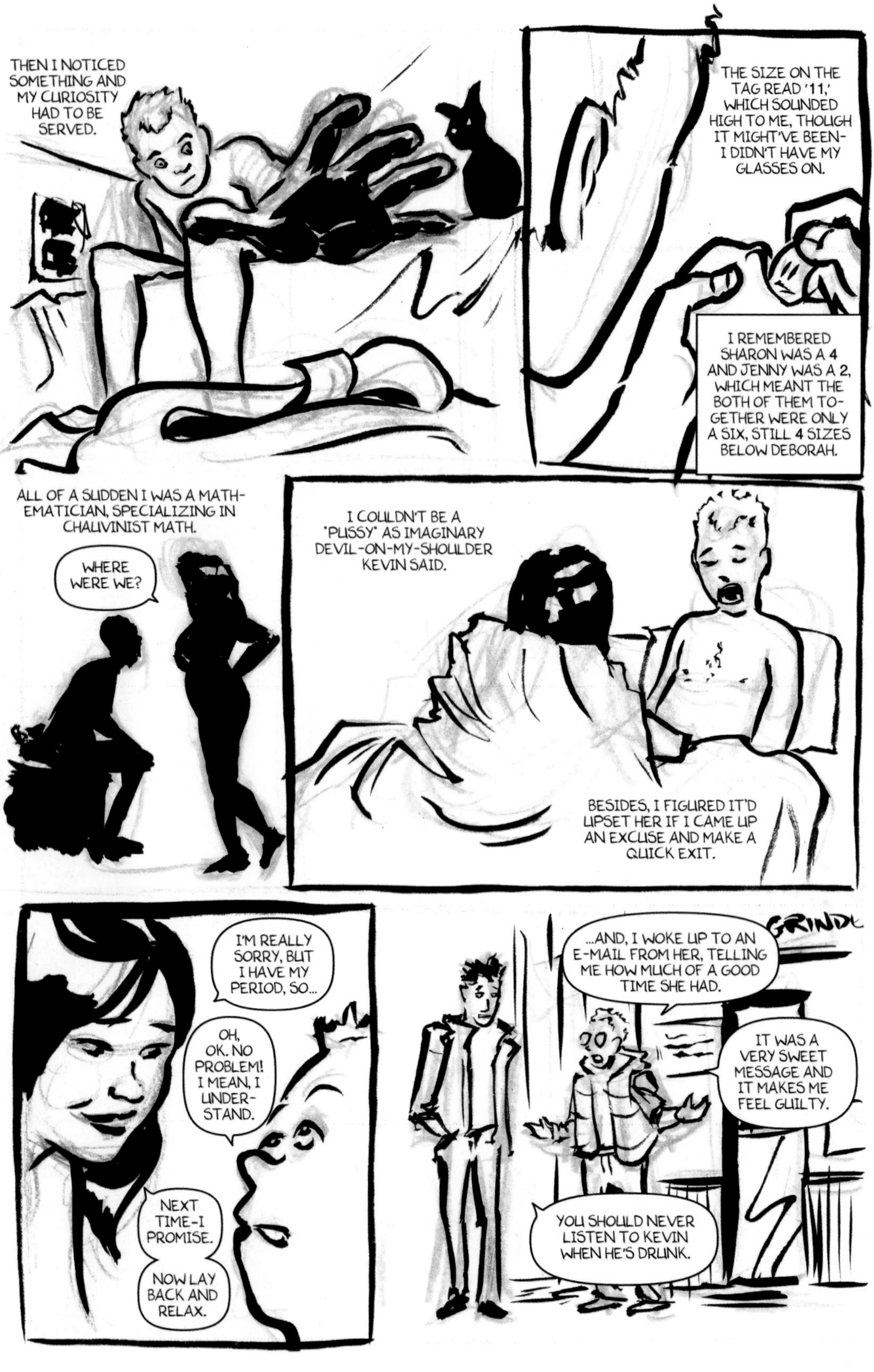
THEN I NOTICED SOMETHING AND MY CURIOSITY HAD TO BE SERVED.
THE SIZE ON THE TAG READ '11,' WHICH SOUNDED HIGH TO ME, THOUGH IT MIGHT'VE BEEN- I DIDN'T HAVE MY GLASSES ON.
I REMEMBERED SHARON WAS A 4 AND JENNY WAS A 2, WHICH MEANT THE BOTH OF THEM TOGETHER WERE ONLY A SIX, STILL 4 SIZES BELOW DEBORAH.
ALL OF A SUDDEN I WAS A MATHEMATICIAN, SPECIALIZING IN CHAUVINIST MATH.
WHERE WERE WE?
I COULDN'T BE A "PUSSY" AS IMAGINARY DEVIL-ON-MY-SHOULDER KEVIN SAID.
BESIDES, I FIGURED IT'D UPSET HER IF I CAME UP AN EXCUSE AND MAKE A QUICK EXIT.
I'M REALLY SORRY, BUT I HAVE MY PERIOD, SO...
OH, OK. NO PROBLEM! I MEAN, I UNDERSTAND.
NEXT TIME-I PROMISE.
NOW LAY BACK AND RELAX.
GRIND
...AND, I WOKE UP TO AN E-MAIL FROM HER, TELLING ME HOW MUCH OF A GOOD TIME SHE HAD.
IT WAS A VERY SWEET MESSAGE AND IT MAKES ME FEEL GUILTY.
YOU SHOULD NEVER LISTEN TO KEVIN WHEN HE'S DRUNK.

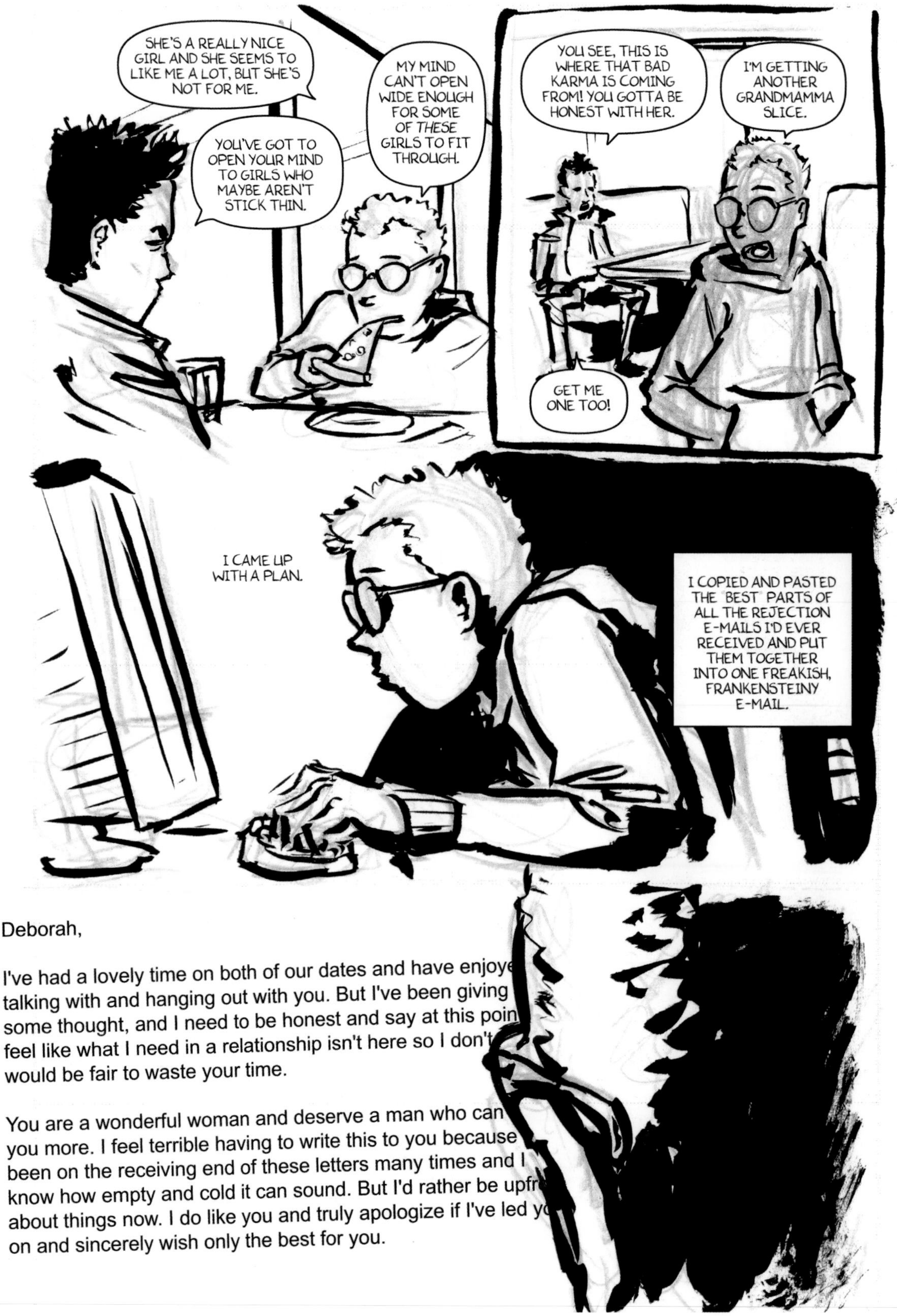
SHE'S A REALLY NICE GIRL AND SHE SEEMS TO LIKE ME A LOT, BUT SHE'S NOT FOR ME.
YOU'VE GOT TO OPEN YOUR MIND TO GIRLS WHO MAYBE AREN'T STICK THIN.
MY MIND CAN'T OPEN WIDE ENOUGH FOR SOME OF *THESE* GIRLS TO FIT THROUGH.
YOU SEE, THIS IS WHERE THAT BAD KARMA IS COMING FROM! YOU GOTTA BE HONEST WITH HER.
I'M GETTING ANOTHER GRANDMAMMA SLICE.
GET ME ONE TOO!
I CAME UP WITH A PLAN.
I COPIED AND PASTED THE "BEST" PARTS OF ALL THE REJECTION E-MAILS I'D EVER RECEIVED AND PUT THEM TOGETHER INTO ONE FREAKISH, FRANKENSTEINY E-MAIL.
Deborah,
I've had a lovely time on both of our dates and have enjoye
talking with and hanging out with you. But I've been giving
some thought, and I need to be honest and say at this poin
feel like what I need in a relationship isn't here so I don't
would be fair to waste your time.
You are a wonderful woman and deserve a man who can
you more. I feel terrible having to write this to you because
been on the receiving end of these letters many times and I
know how empty and cold it can sound. But I'd rather be upfr
about things now. I do like you and truly apologize if I've led yo
on and sincerely wish only the best for you.

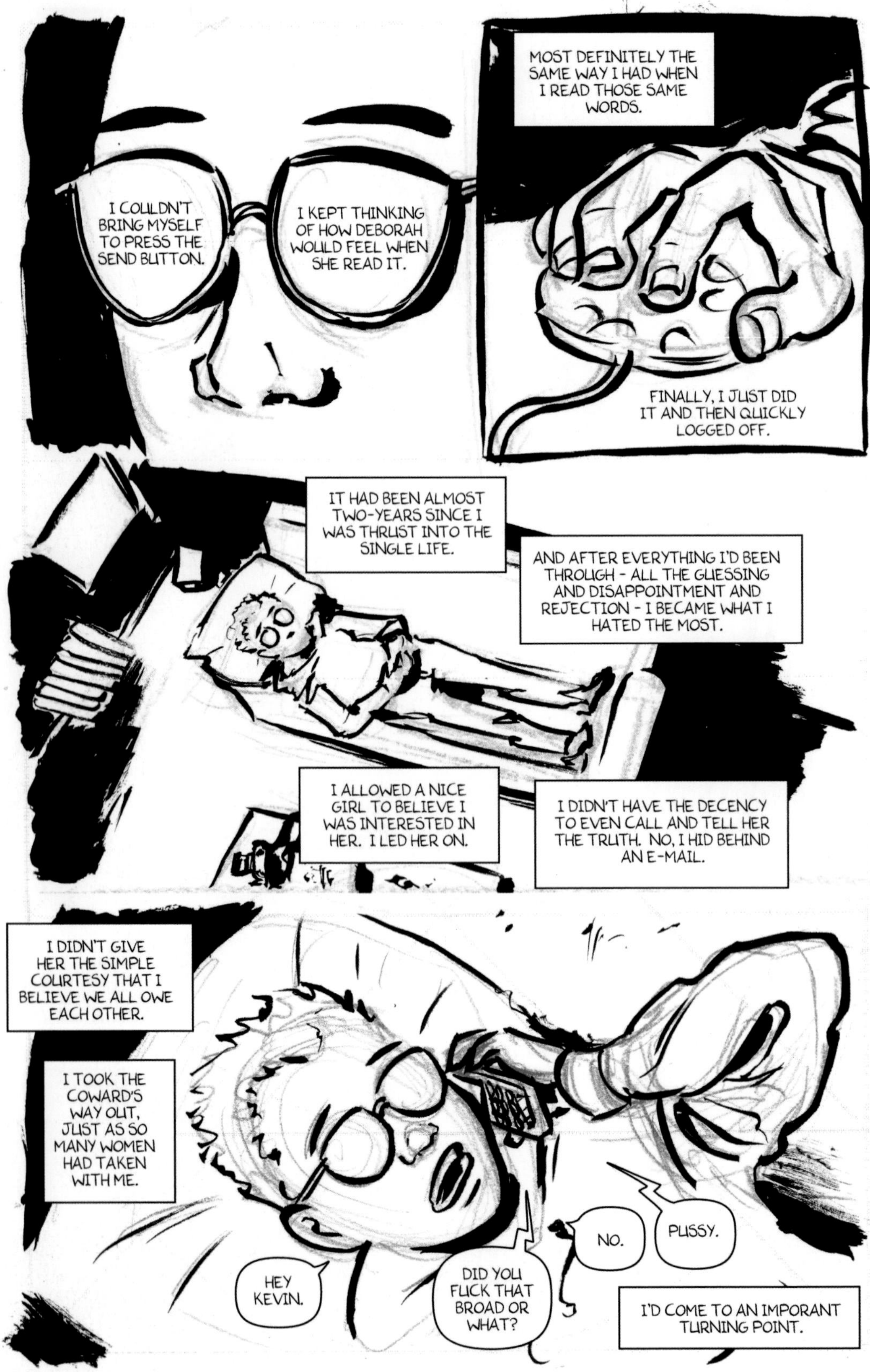
I COULDN'T BRING MYSELF TO PRESS THE SEND BUTTON.
I KEPT THINKING OF HOW DEBORAH WOULD FEEL WHEN SHE READ IT.
MOST DEFINITELY THE SAME WAY I HAD WHEN I READ THOSE SAME WORDS.
FINALLY, I JUST DID IT AND THEN QUICKLY LOGGED OFF.
IT HAD BEEN ALMOST TWO-YEARS SINCE I WAS THRUST INTO THE SINGLE LIFE.
AND AFTER EVERYTHING I'D BEEN THROUGH - ALL THE GUESSING AND DISAPPOINTMENT AND REJECTION - I BECAME WHAT I HATED THE MOST.
I ALLOWED A NICE GIRL TO BELIEVE I WAS INTERESTED IN HER. I LED HER ON.
I DIDN'T HAVE THE DECENCY TO EVEN CALL AND TELL HER THE TRUTH. NO, I HID BEHIND AN E-MAIL.
I DIDN'T GIVE HER THE SIMPLE COURTESY THAT I BELIEVE WE ALL OWE EACH OTHER.
I TOOK THE COWARD'S WAY OUT, JUST AS SO MANY WOMEN HAD TAKEN WITH ME.
HEY KEVIN.
DID YOU FUCK THAT BROAD OR WHAT?
NO.
PUSSY.
I'D COME TO AN IMPORANT TURNING POINT.

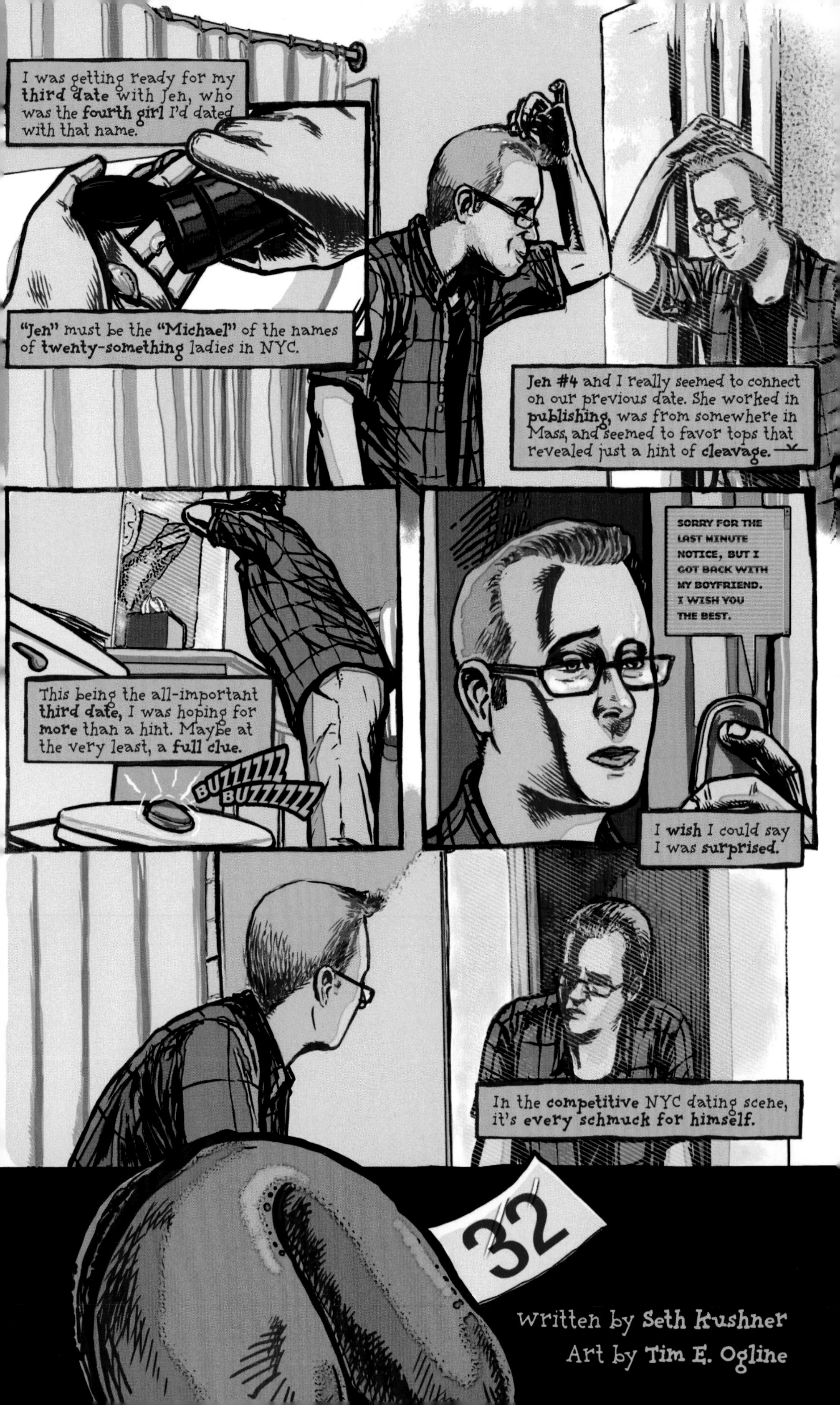
I was getting ready for my third date with Jen, who was the fourth girl I'd dated with that name.
"Jen" must be the "Michael" of the names of twenty-something ladies in NYC.
Jen #4 and I really seemed to connect on our previous date. She worked in publishing, was from somewhere in Mass, and seemed to favor tops that revealed just a hint of cleavage.
This being the all-important third date, I was hoping for more than a hint. Maybe at the very least, a full clue.
BUZZZZZZ BUZZZZZZZ
SORRY FOR THE LAST MINUTE NOTICE, BUT I GOT BACK WITH MY BOYFRIEND. I WISH YOU THE BEST.
I wish I could say I was surprised.
In the competitive NYC dating scene, it's every schmuck for himself.
32
Written by Seth Kushner
Art by Tim E. Ogline

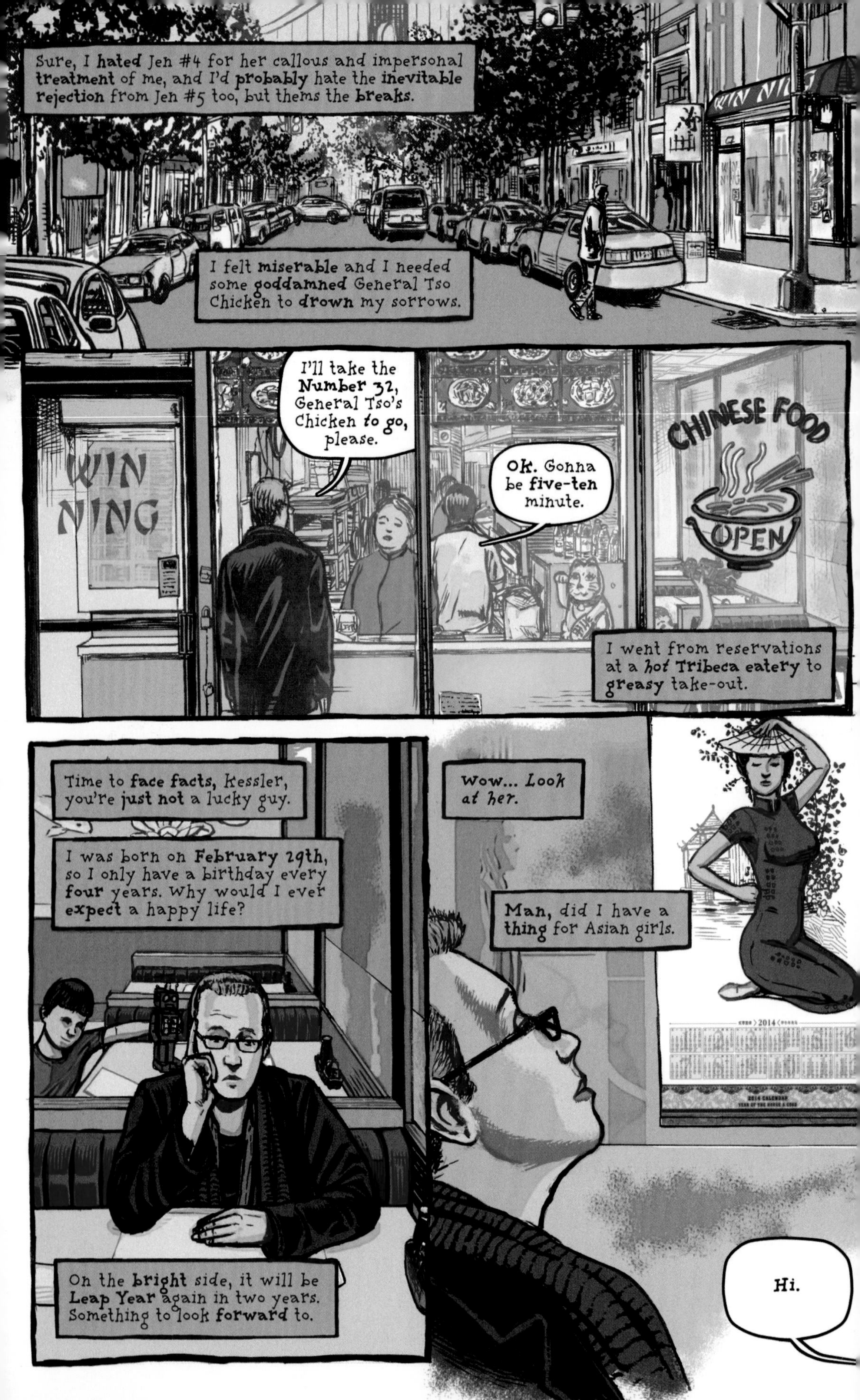

Sure, I hated Jen #4 for her callous and impersonal treatment of me, and I'd probably hate the inevitable rejection from Jen #5 too, but thems the breaks.
I felt miserable and I needed some goddamned General Tso Chicken to drown my sorrows.
WIN NING
WIN NING
I'll take the Number 32, General Tso's Chicken to go, please.
OK. Gonna be five-ten minute.
CHINESE FOOD
OPEN
I went from reservations at a hot Tribeca eatery to greasy take-out.
Time to face facts, Kessler, you're just not a lucky guy.
I was born on February 29th, so I only have a birthday every four years. Why would I ever expect a happy life?
On the bright side, it will be Leap Year again in two years. Something to look forward to.
Wow... Look at her.
Man, did I have a thing for Asian girls.
2014
2014 CALENDAR
Hi.

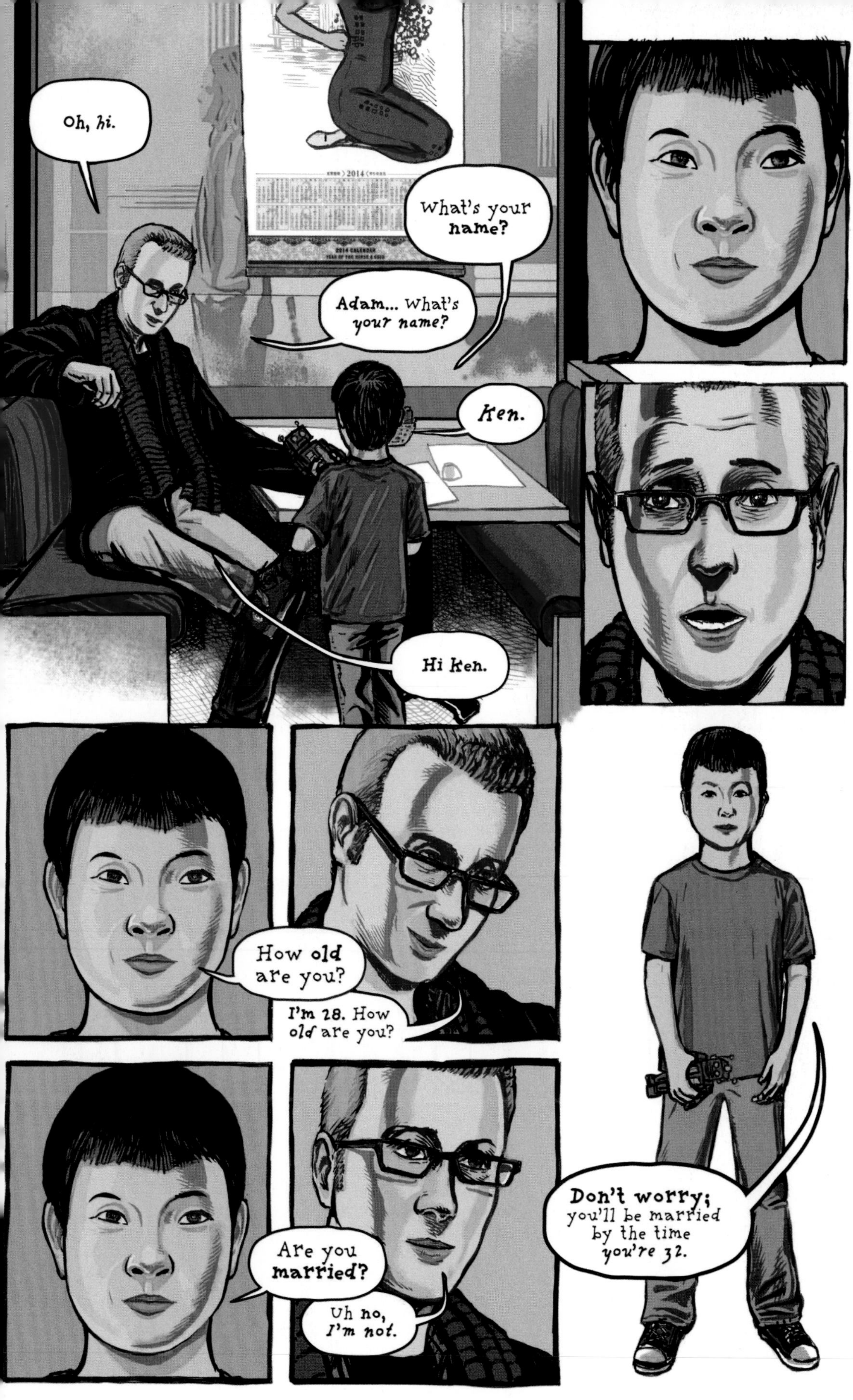
Oh, hi.
What's your name?
Adam... What's your name?
Ken.
Hi Ken.
How old are you?
I'm 28. How old are you?
Are you married?
Uh no, I'm not.
Don't worry; you'll be married by the time you're 32.

What?
What do
you mean?

How could you
know that?

I *don't*
even have a
girlfriend!

Number 32
ready.

CHINESE FOOD
OPEN

SCANDINAVIAN IMPORTE

DINNER SPECIALS
'S MADE DAI

The boy's words echoed in
my head. "Don't *worry*;
you'll be *married* by the
time you're 32."

Nothing like an MSG filled meal,
a *prophetic* boy and a fortune
cookie on a Saturday night.

No one can walk backwards
into the future.

I kept that fortune and *four*
years *later*, I showed it to my
new bride.

END

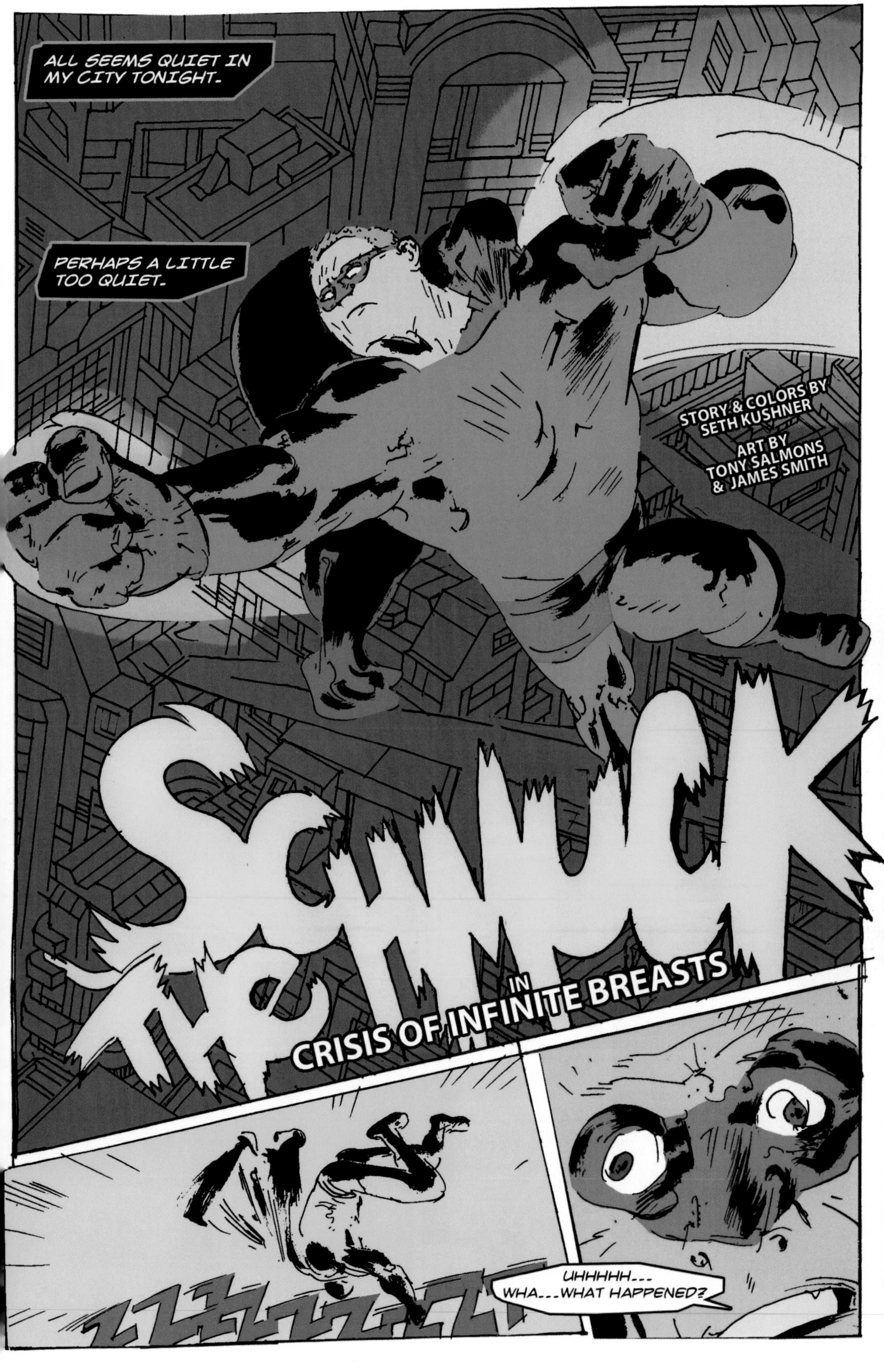
ALL SEEMS QUIET IN MY CITY TONIGHT.
PERHAPS A LITTLE TOO QUIET.
STORY & COLORS BY SETH KUSHNER
ART BY TONY SALMONS & JAMES SMITH
THE SCHMUCK
IN
CRISIS OF INFINITE BREASTS
ZZZZZZZZZZZ
UHHHHH... WHA...WHAT HAPPENED?

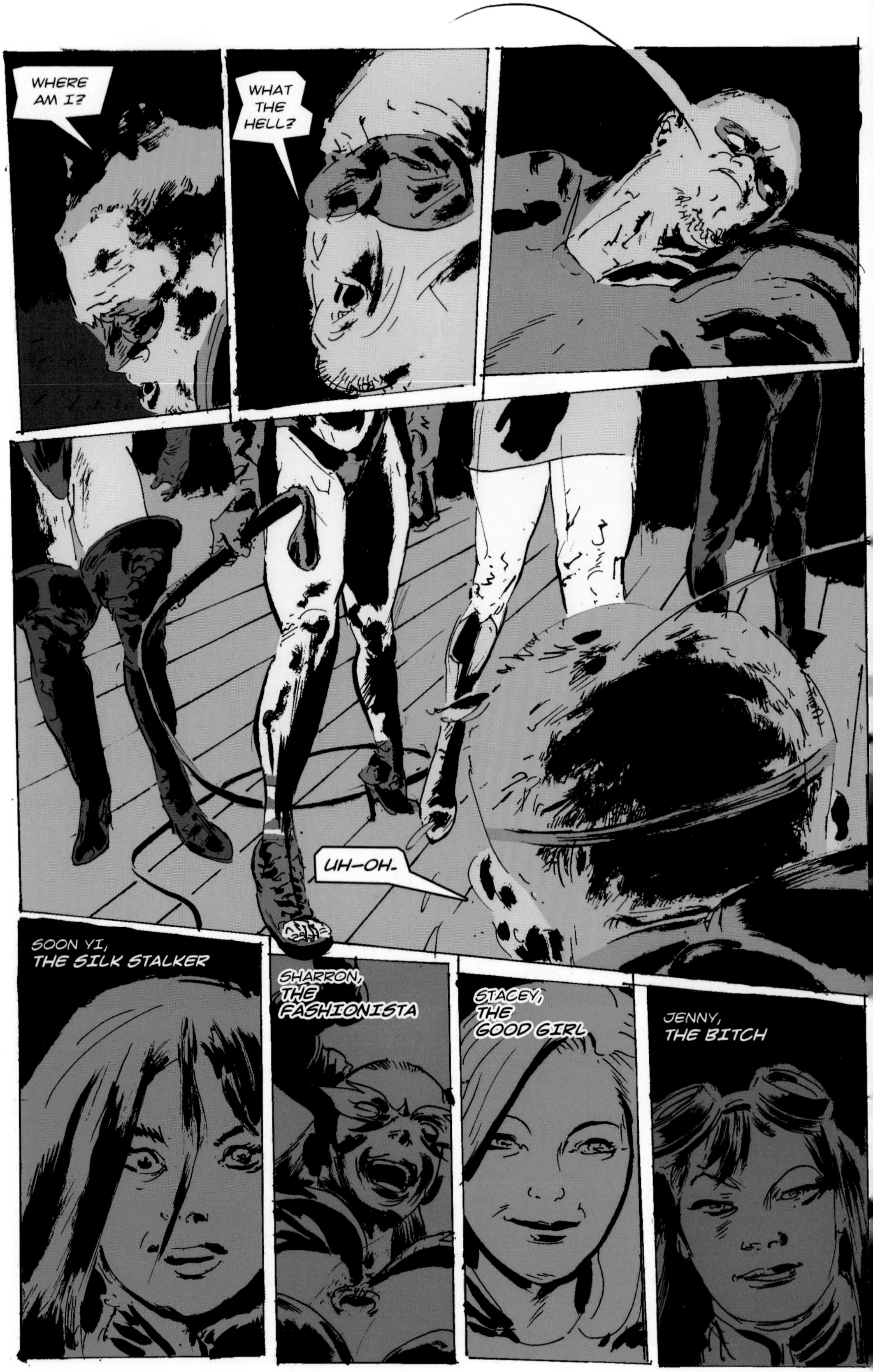
WHERE AM I?
WHAT THE HELL?
UH-OH.
SOON YI, THE SILK STALKER
SHARRON, THE FASHIONISTA
STACEY, THE GOOD GIRL
JENNY, THE BITCH

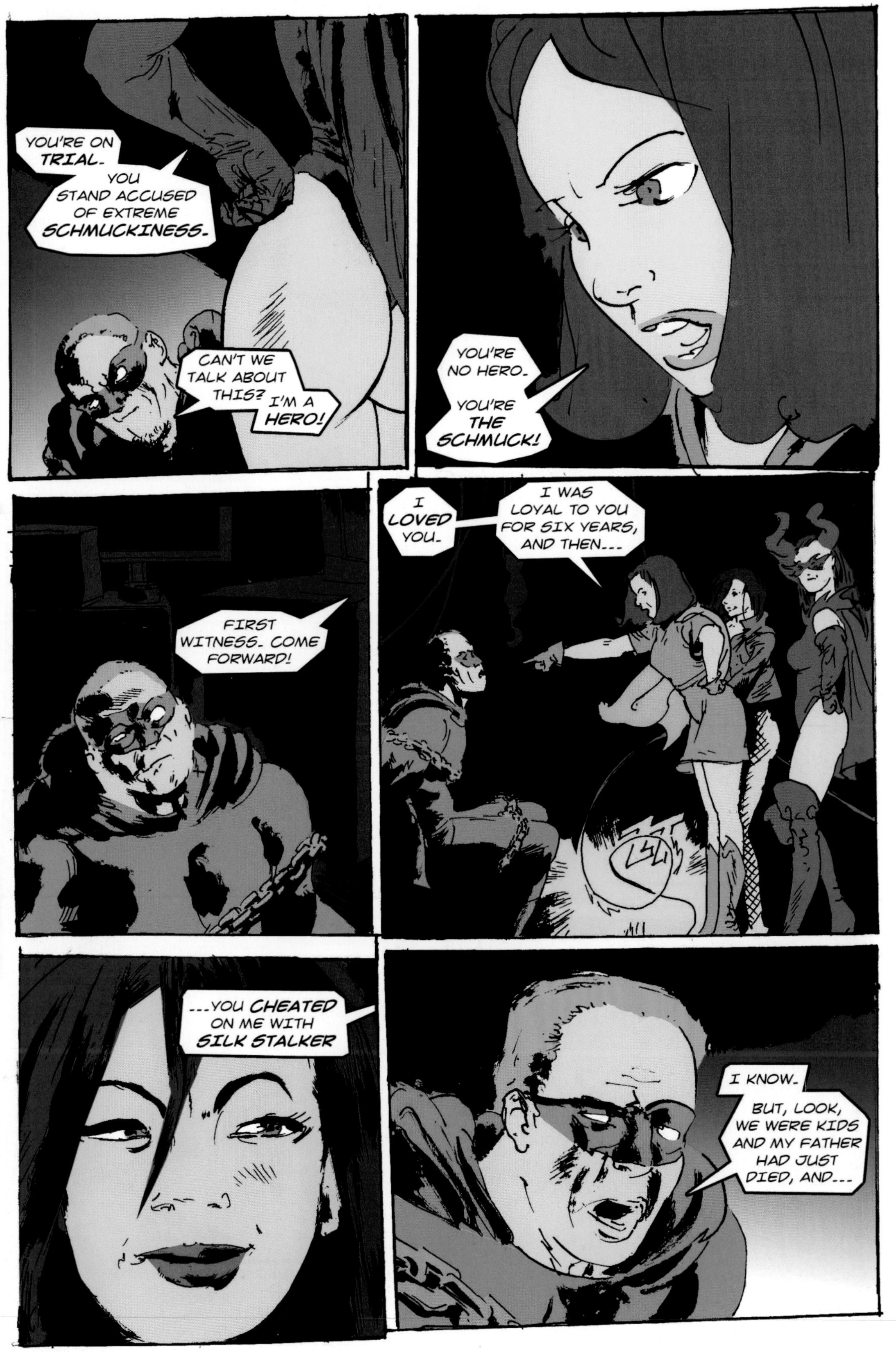
YOU'RE ON TRIAL. YOU STAND ACCUSED OF EXTREME SCHMUCKINESS.
CAN'T WE TALK ABOUT THIS? I'M A HERO!
YOU'RE NO HERO. YOU'RE THE SCHMUCK!
FIRST WITNESS. COME FORWARD!
I LOVED YOU.
I WAS LOYAL TO YOU FOR SIX YEARS, AND THEN...
...YOU CHEATED ON ME WITH SILK STALKER
I KNOW. BUT, LOOK, WE WERE KIDS AND MY FATHER HAD JUST DIED, AND...

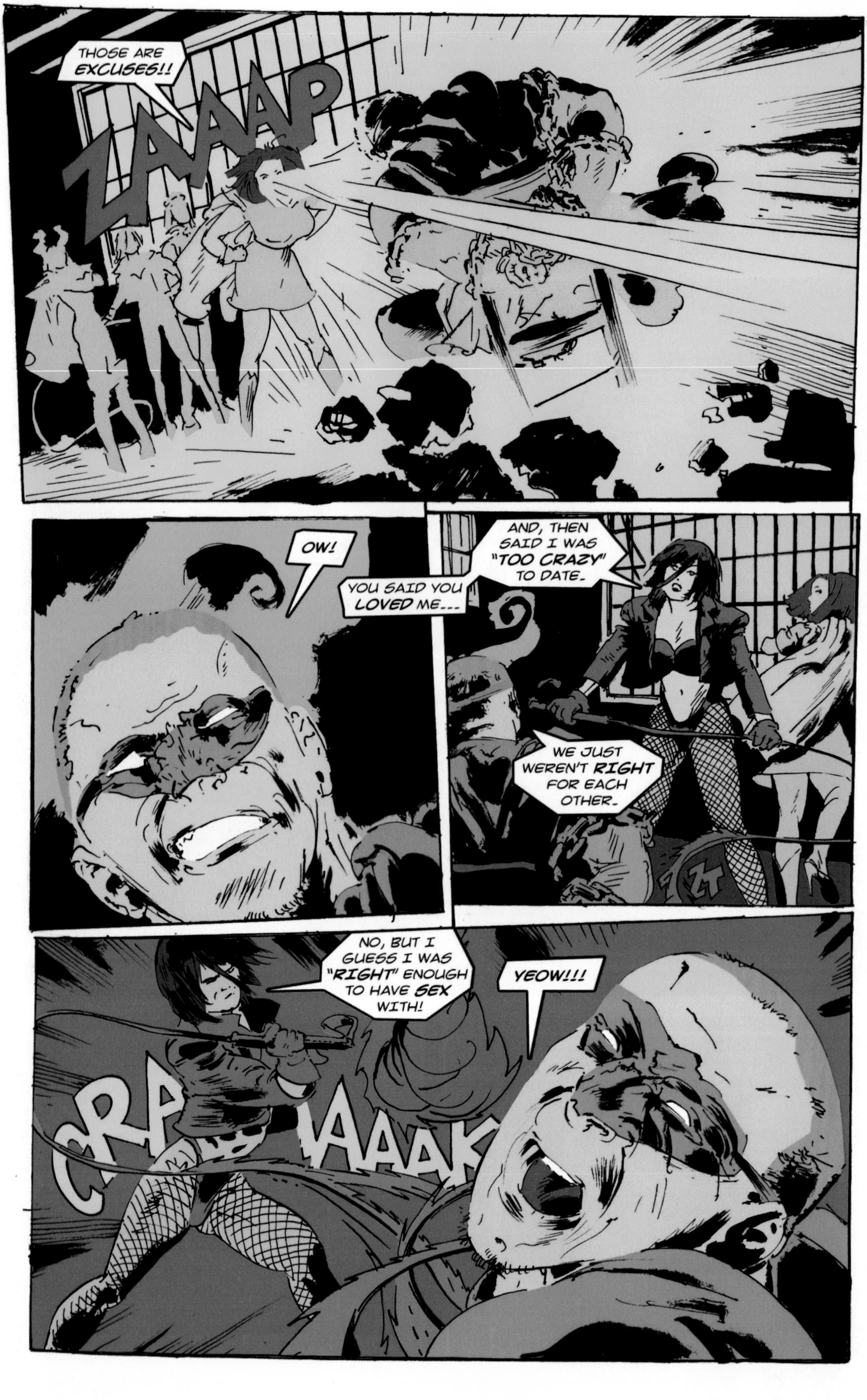
THOSE ARE EXCUSES!!
ZAAAP
OW!
YOU SAID YOU LOVED ME...
AND, THEN SAID I WAS "TOO CRAZY" TO DATE.
WE JUST WEREN'T RIGHT FOR EACH OTHER.
NO, BUT I GUESS I WAS "RIGHT" ENOUGH TO HAVE SEX WITH!
YEOW!!!

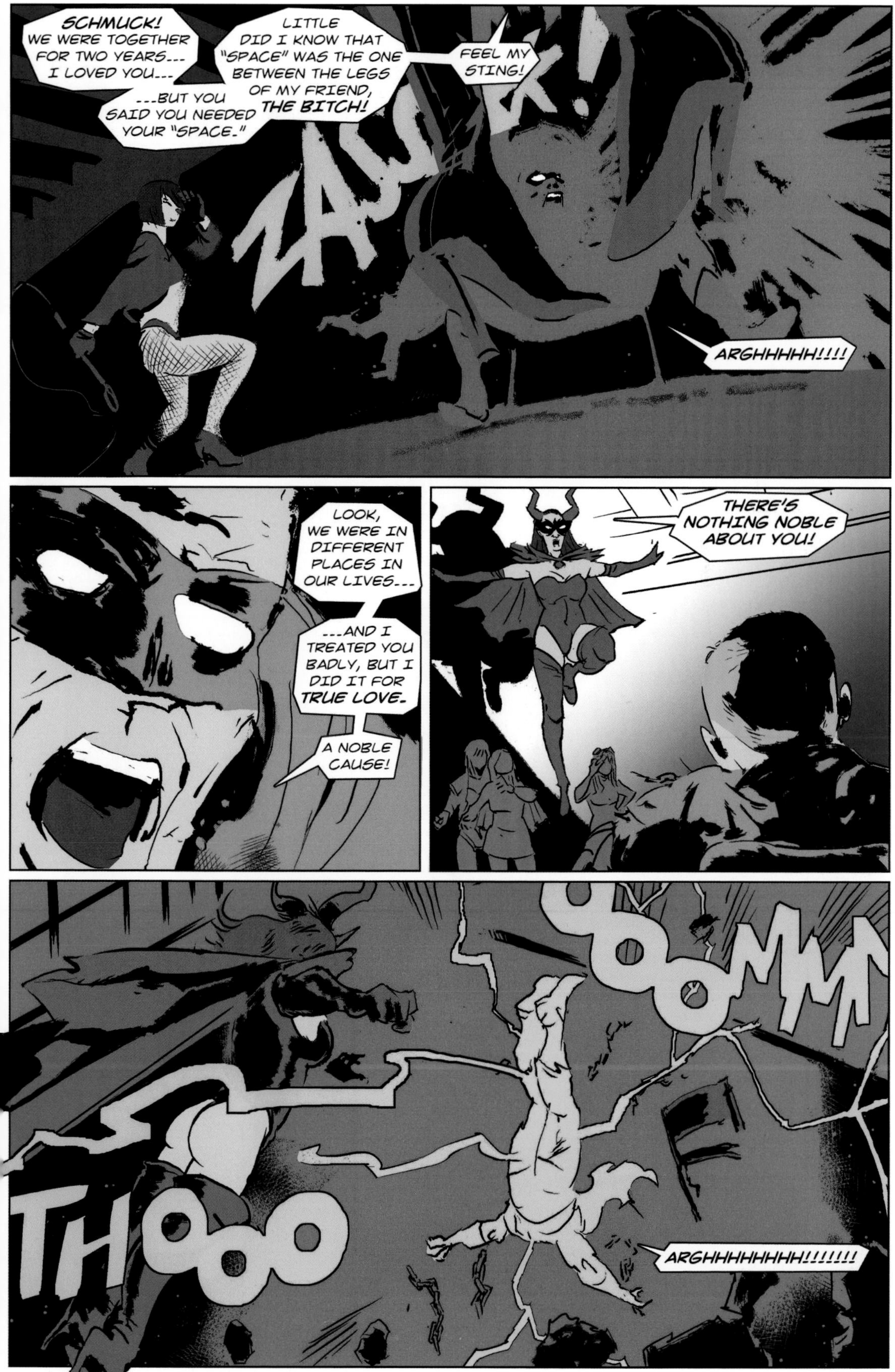
SCHMUCK! WE WERE TOGETHER FOR TWO YEARS... I LOVED YOU...
...BUT YOU SAID YOU NEEDED YOUR "SPACE."
LITTLE DID I KNOW THAT "SPACE" WAS THE ONE BETWEEN THE LEGS OF MY FRIEND, THE BITCH!
FEEL MY STING!
ARGHHHHH!!!!
LOOK, WE WERE IN DIFFERENT PLACES IN OUR LIVES...
...AND I TREATED YOU BADLY, BUT I DID IT FOR TRUE LOVE.
A NOBLE CAUSE!
THERE'S NOTHING NOBLE ABOUT YOU!
ARGHHHHHHHH!!!!!!!

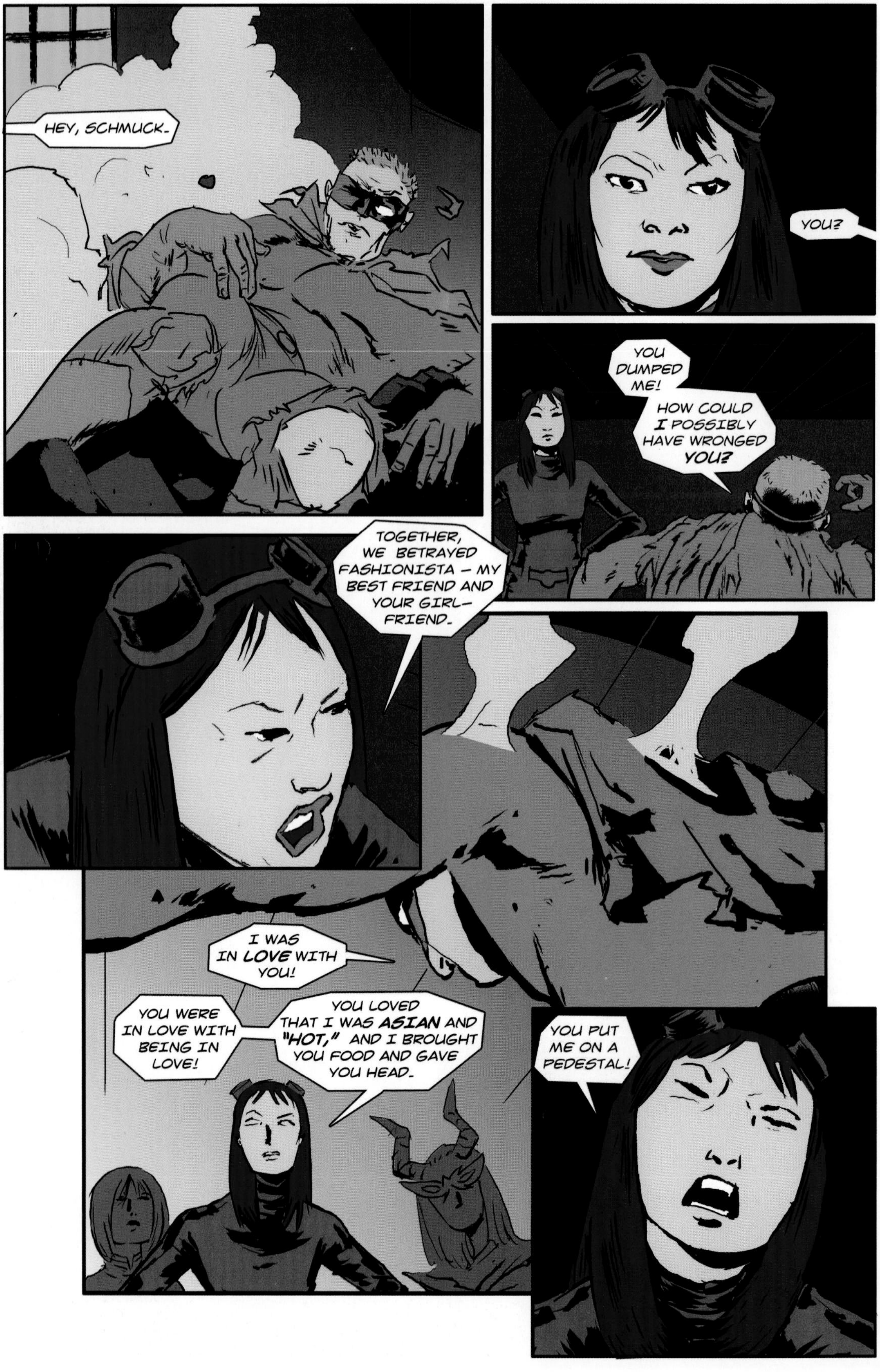
HEY, SCHMUCK.
YOU?
YOU DUMPED ME!
HOW COULD I POSSIBLY HAVE WRONGED YOU?
TOGETHER, WE BETRAYED FASHIONISTA -- MY BEST FRIEND AND YOUR GIRLFRIEND.
I WAS IN LOVE WITH YOU!
YOU WERE IN LOVE WITH BEING IN LOVE!
YOU LOVED THAT I WAS ASIAN AND "HOT," AND I BROUGHT YOU FOOD AND GAVE YOU HEAD.
YOU PUT ME ON A PEDESTAL!

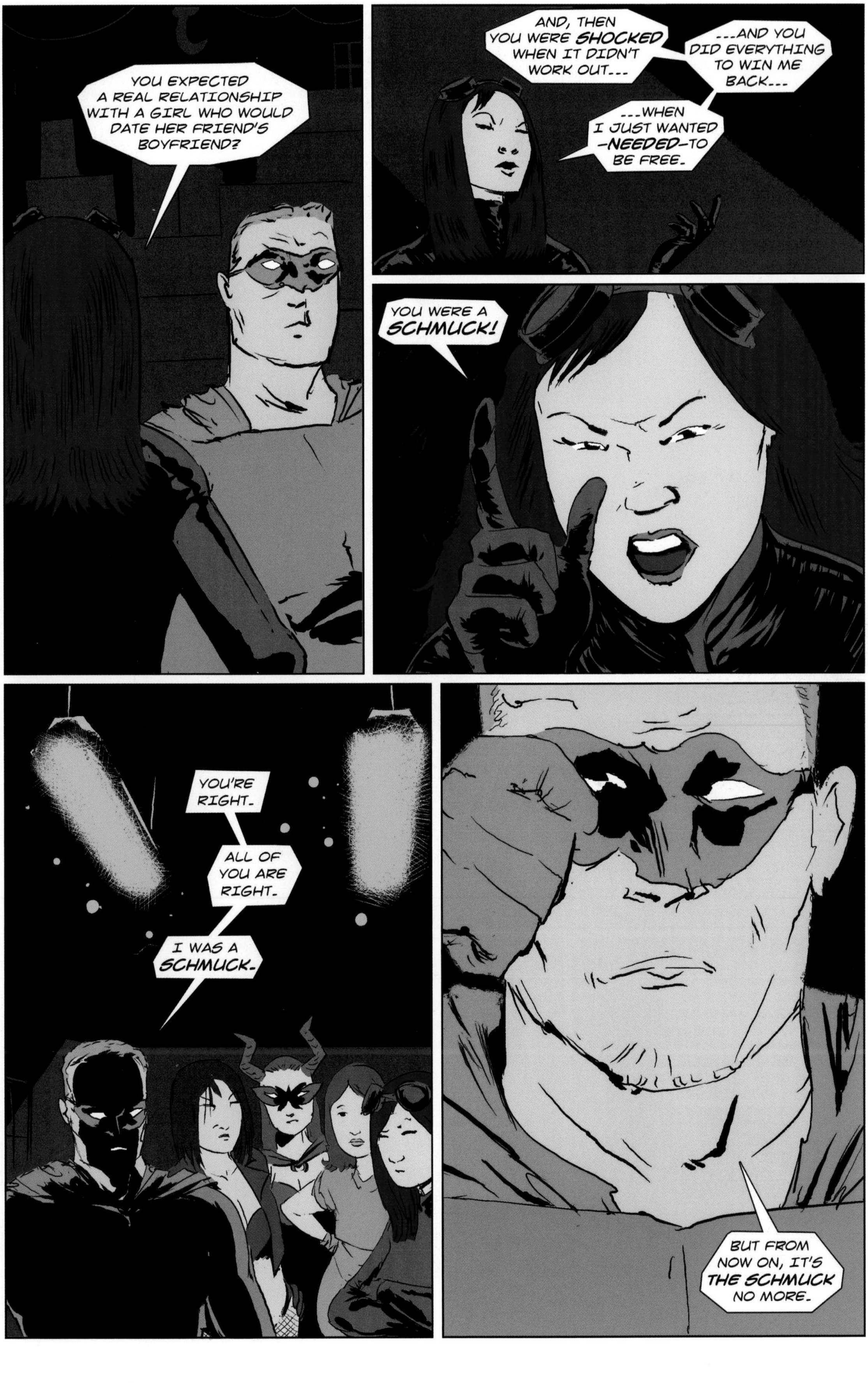

YOU EXPECTED A REAL RELATIONSHIP WITH A GIRL WHO WOULD DATE HER FRIEND'S BOYFRIEND?
AND, THEN YOU WERE SHOCKED WHEN IT DIDN'T WORK OUT...
...AND YOU DID EVERYTHING TO WIN ME BACK...
...WHEN I JUST WANTED -NEEDED- TO BE FREE.
YOU WERE A SCHMUCK!
YOU'RE RIGHT.
ALL OF YOU ARE RIGHT.
I WAS A SCHMUCK.
BUT FROM NOW ON, IT'S THE SCHMUCK NO MORE.

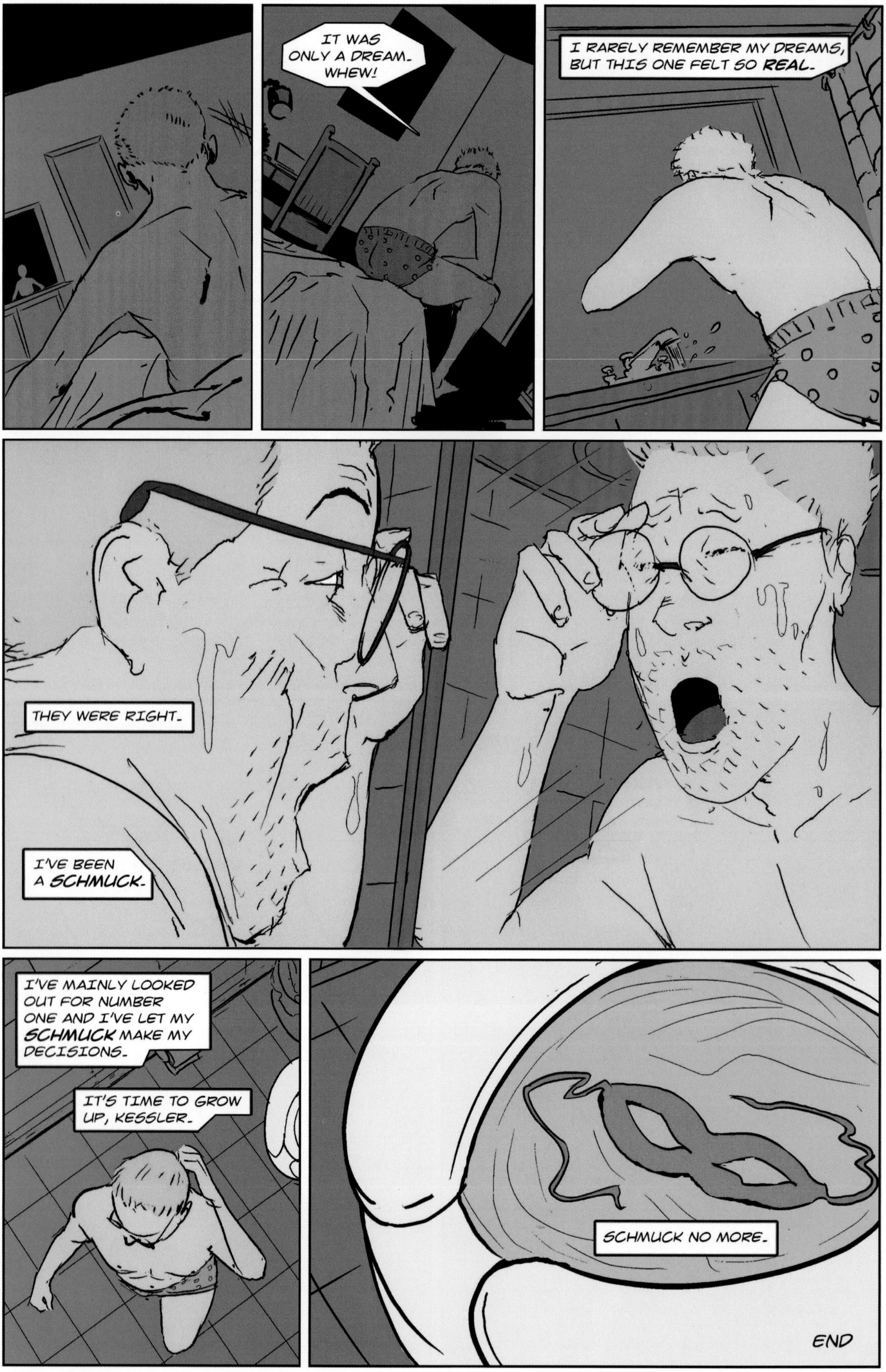
IT WAS ONLY A DREAM. WHEW!
I RARELY REMEMBER MY DREAMS, BUT THIS ONE FELT SO REAL.
THEY WERE RIGHT.
I'VE BEEN A SCHMUCK.
I'VE MAINLY LOOKED OUT FOR NUMBER ONE AND I'VE LET MY SCHMUCK MAKE MY DECISIONS.
IT'S TIME TO GROW UP, KESSLER.
SCHMUCK NO MORE.
END

SCHMUCK: JOURNEY'S END

SETH KUSHNER Story
JOSH '13 Art

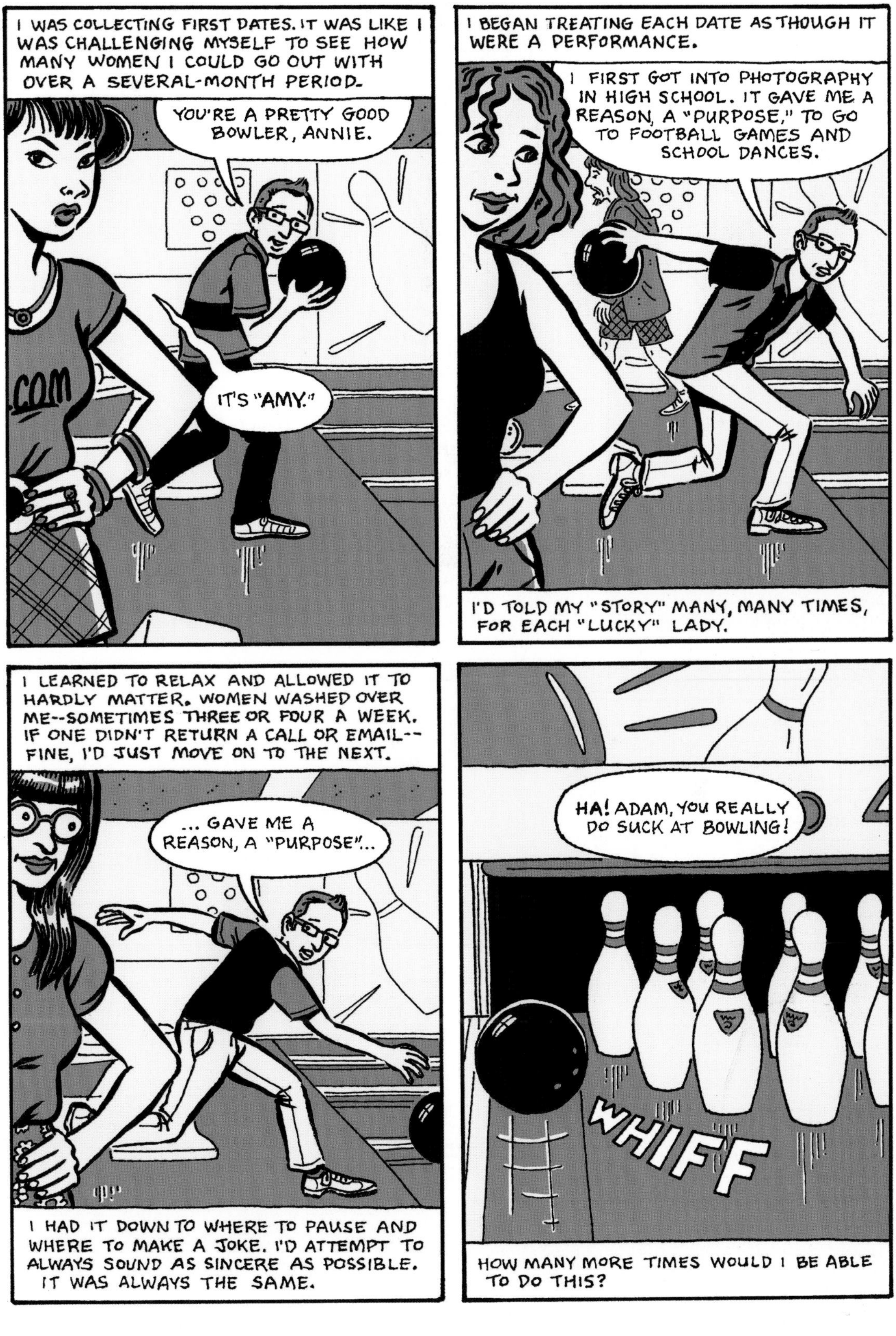
I WAS COLLECTING FIRST DATES. IT WAS LIKE I WAS CHALLENGING MYSELF TO SEE HOW MANY WOMEN I COULD GO OUT WITH OVER A SEVERAL-MONTH PERIOD.
YOU'RE A PRETTY GOOD BOWLER, ANNIE.
IT'S "AMY."
I BEGAN TREATING EACH DATE AS THOUGH IT WERE A PERFORMANCE.
I FIRST GOT INTO PHOTOGRAPHY IN HIGH SCHOOL. IT GAVE ME A REASON, A "PURPOSE," TO GO TO FOOTBALL GAMES AND SCHOOL DANCES.
I'D TOLD MY "STORY" MANY, MANY TIMES, FOR EACH "LUCKY" LADY.
I LEARNED TO RELAX AND ALLOWED IT TO HARDLY MATTER. WOMEN WASHED OVER ME--SOMETIMES THREE OR FOUR A WEEK. IF ONE DIDN'T RETURN A CALL OR EMAIL--FINE, I'D JUST MOVE ON TO THE NEXT.
... GAVE ME A REASON, A "PURPOSE"...
I HAD IT DOWN TO WHERE TO PAUSE AND WHERE TO MAKE A JOKE. I'D ATTEMPT TO ALWAYS SOUND AS SINCERE AS POSSIBLE. IT WAS ALWAYS THE SAME.
HA! ADAM, YOU REALLY DO SUCK AT BOWLING!
WHIFF
HOW MANY MORE TIMES WOULD I BE ABLE TO DO THIS?

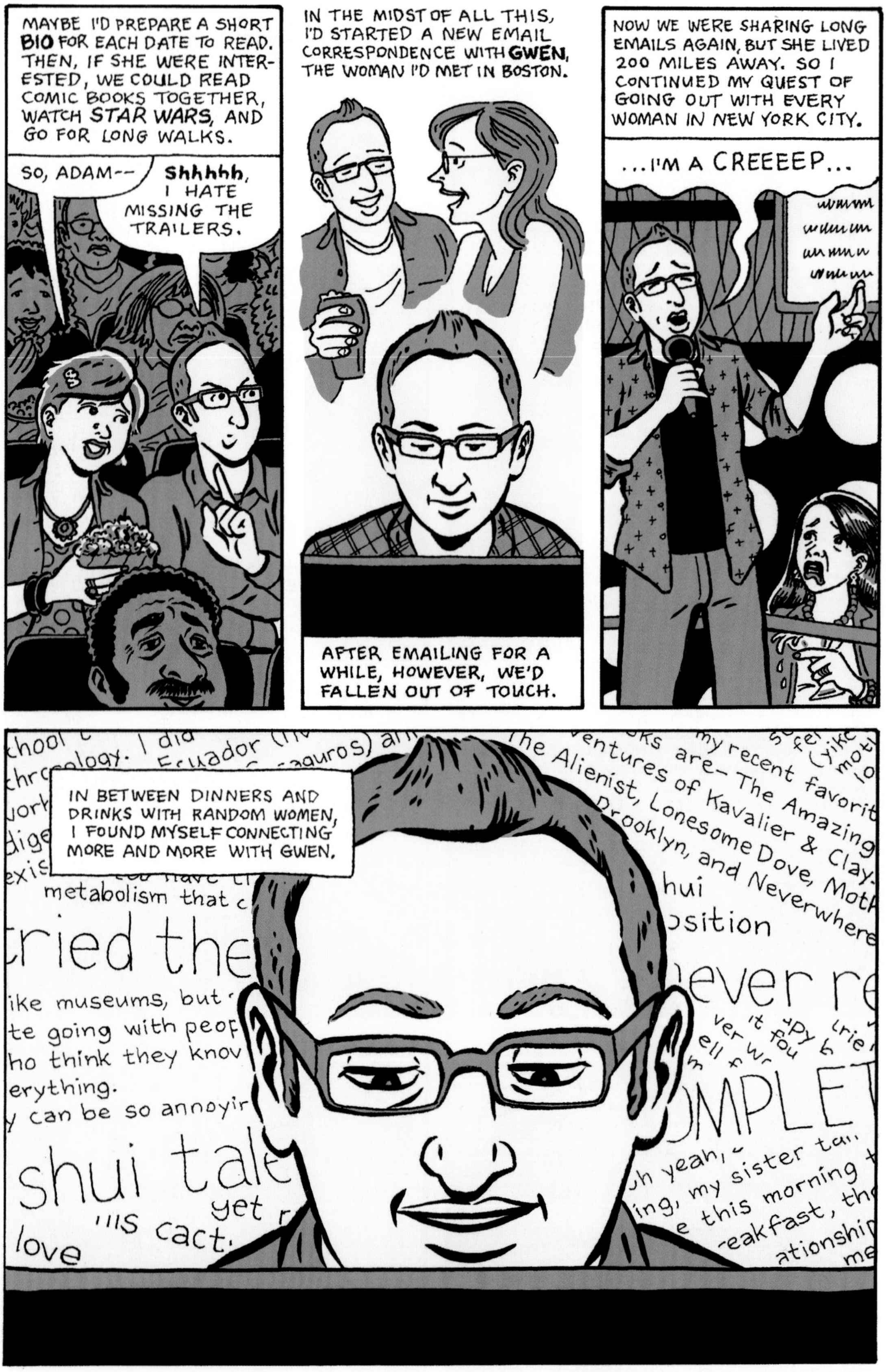
MAYBE I'D PREPARE A SHORT BIO FOR EACH DATE TO READ. THEN, IF SHE WERE INTERESTED, WE COULD READ COMIC BOOKS TOGETHER, WATCH STAR WARS, AND GO FOR LONG WALKS.
SO, ADAM--
Shhhhh, I HATE MISSING THE TRAILERS.
IN THE MIDST OF ALL THIS, I'D STARTED A NEW EMAIL CORRESPONDENCE WITH GWEN, THE WOMAN I'D MET IN BOSTON.
AFTER EMAILING FOR A WHILE, HOWEVER, WE'D FALLEN OUT OF TOUCH.
NOW WE WERE SHARING LONG EMAILS AGAIN, BUT SHE LIVED 200 MILES AWAY. SO I CONTINUED MY QUEST OF GOING OUT WITH EVERY WOMAN IN NEW YORK CITY.
...I'M A CREEEEP...
IN BETWEEN DINNERS AND DRINKS WITH RANDOM WOMEN, I FOUND MYSELF CONNECTING MORE AND MORE WITH GWEN.

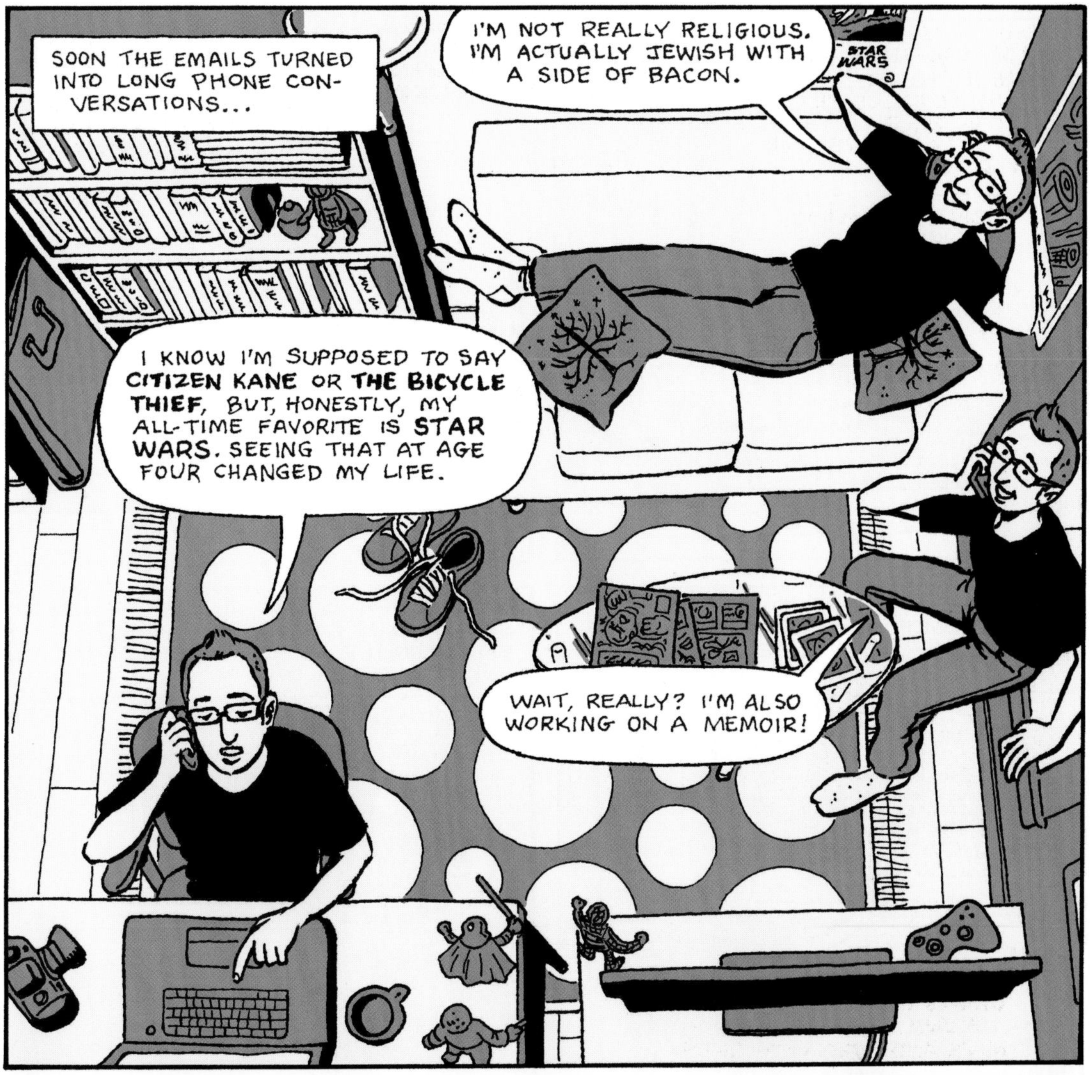
SOON THE EMAILS TURNED INTO LONG PHONE CON-VERSATIONS...
I'M NOT REALLY RELIGIOUS. I'M ACTUALLY JEWISH WITH A SIDE OF BACON.
STAR WARS
I KNOW I'M SUPPOSED TO SAY **CITIZEN KANE** OR **THE BICYCLE THIEF**, BUT, HONESTLY, MY ALL-TIME FAVORITE IS **STAR WARS**. SEEING THAT AT AGE FOUR CHANGED MY LIFE.
WAIT, REALLY? I'M ALSO WORKING ON A MEMOIR!

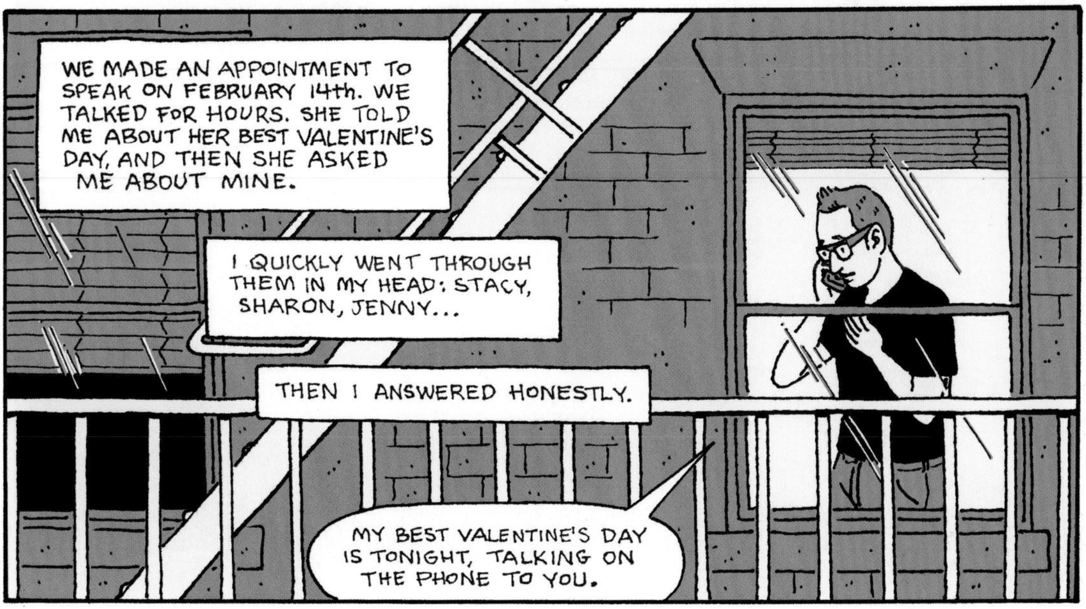
WE MADE AN APPOINTMENT TO SPEAK ON FEBRUARY 14th. WE TALKED FOR HOURS. SHE TOLD ME ABOUT HER BEST VALENTINE'S DAY, AND THEN SHE ASKED ME ABOUT MINE.
I QUICKLY WENT THROUGH THEM IN MY HEAD: STACY, SHARON, JENNY...
THEN I ANSWERED HONESTLY.
MY BEST VALENTINE'S DAY IS TONIGHT, TALKING ON THE PHONE TO YOU.

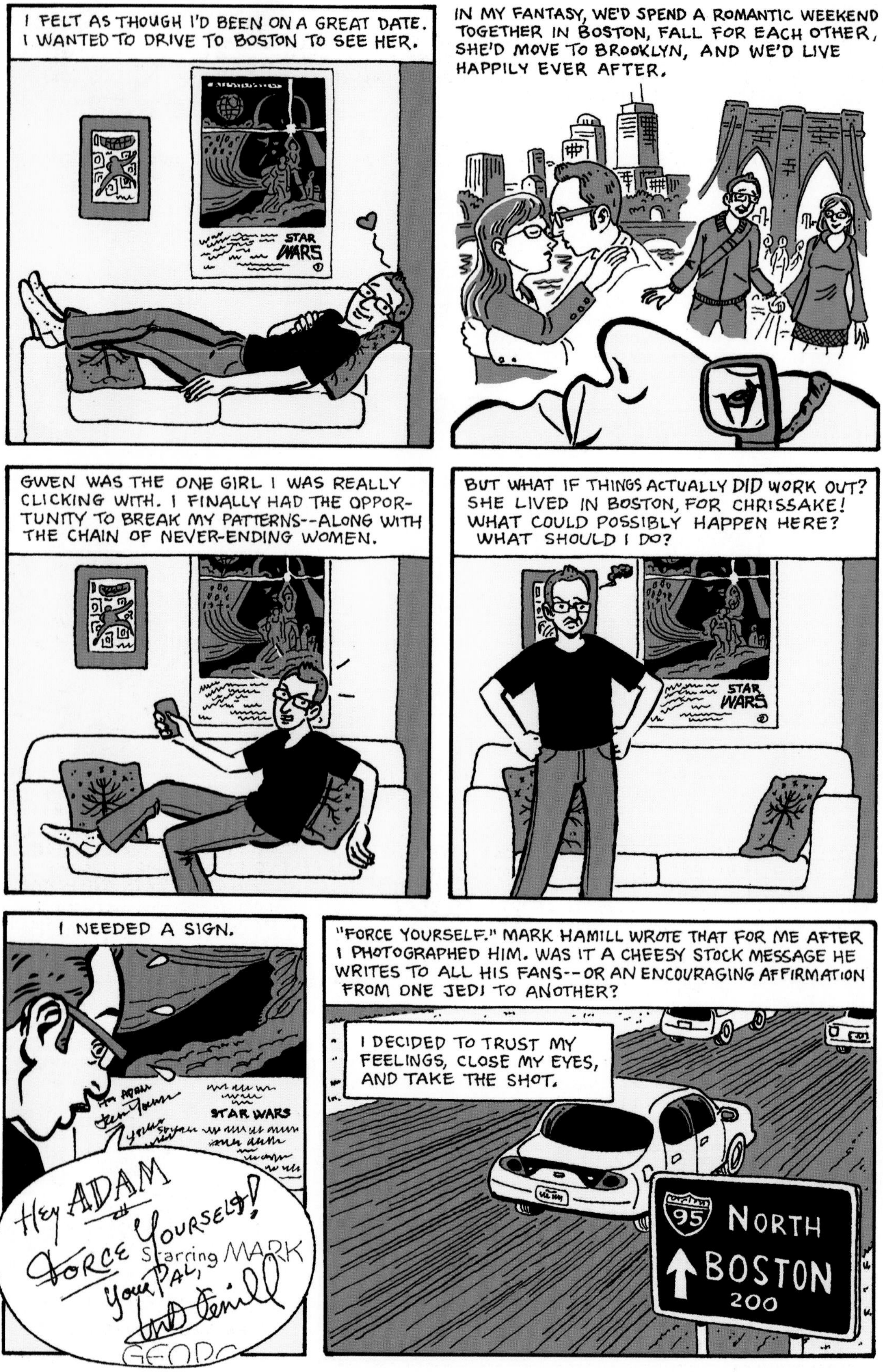
I FELT AS THOUGH I'D BEEN ON A GREAT DATE. I WANTED TO DRIVE TO BOSTON TO SEE HER.
STAR WARS
IN MY FANTASY, WE'D SPEND A ROMANTIC WEEKEND TOGETHER IN BOSTON, FALL FOR EACH OTHER, SHE'D MOVE TO BROOKLYN, AND WE'D LIVE HAPPILY EVER AFTER.
GWEN WAS THE ONE GIRL I WAS REALLY CLICKING WITH. I FINALLY HAD THE OPPORTUNITY TO BREAK MY PATTERNS--ALONG WITH THE CHAIN OF NEVER-ENDING WOMEN.
BUT WHAT IF THINGS ACTUALLY DID WORK OUT? SHE LIVED IN BOSTON, FOR CHRISSAKE! WHAT COULD POSSIBLY HAPPEN HERE? WHAT SHOULD I DO?
STAR WARS
I NEEDED A SIGN.
STAR WARS
Hey ADAM
FORCE Yourself!
Starring MARK
Your PAL,
"FORCE YOURSELF." MARK HAMILL WROTE THAT FOR ME AFTER I PHOTOGRAPHED HIM. WAS IT A CHEESY STOCK MESSAGE HE WRITES TO ALL HIS FANS--OR AN ENCOURAGING AFFIRMATION FROM ONE JEDI TO ANOTHER?
I DECIDED TO TRUST MY FEELINGS, CLOSE MY EYES, AND TAKE THE SHOT.
95
NORTH
BOSTON
200

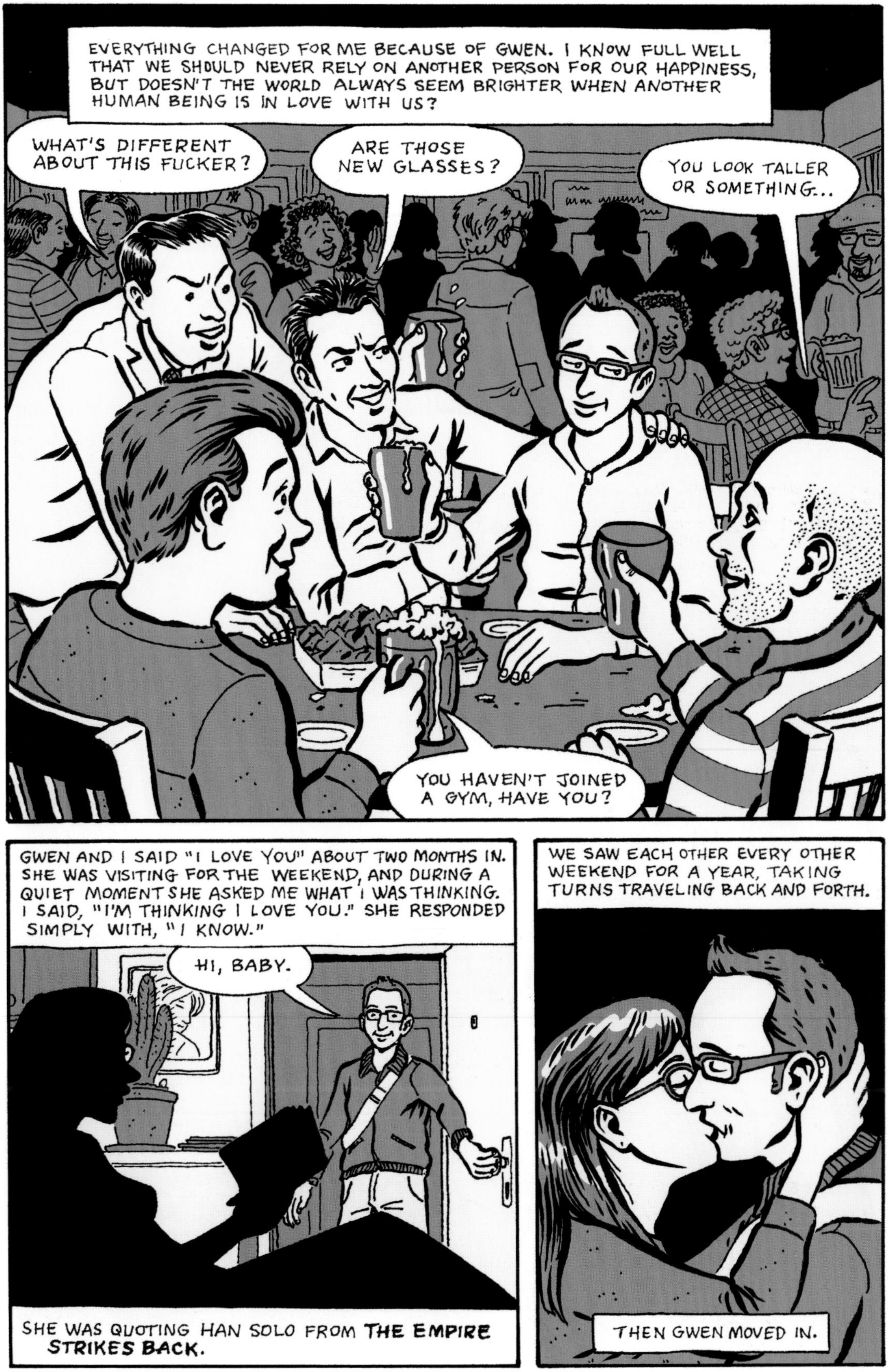
EVERYTHING CHANGED FOR ME BECAUSE OF GWEN. I KNOW FULL WELL THAT WE SHOULD NEVER RELY ON ANOTHER PERSON FOR OUR HAPPINESS, BUT DOESN'T THE WORLD ALWAYS SEEM BRIGHTER WHEN ANOTHER HUMAN BEING IS IN LOVE WITH US?
WHAT'S DIFFERENT ABOUT THIS FUCKER?
ARE THOSE NEW GLASSES?
YOU LOOK TALLER OR SOMETHING...
YOU HAVEN'T JOINED A GYM, HAVE YOU?
GWEN AND I SAID "I LOVE YOU" ABOUT TWO MONTHS IN. SHE WAS VISITING FOR THE WEEKEND, AND DURING A QUIET MOMENT SHE ASKED ME WHAT I WAS THINKING. I SAID, "I'M THINKING I LOVE YOU." SHE RESPONDED SIMPLY WITH, "I KNOW."
HI, BABY.
SHE WAS QUOTING HAN SOLO FROM THE EMPIRE STRIKES BACK.
WE SAW EACH OTHER EVERY OTHER WEEKEND FOR A YEAR, TAKING TURNS TRAVELING BACK AND FORTH.
THEN GWEN MOVED IN.

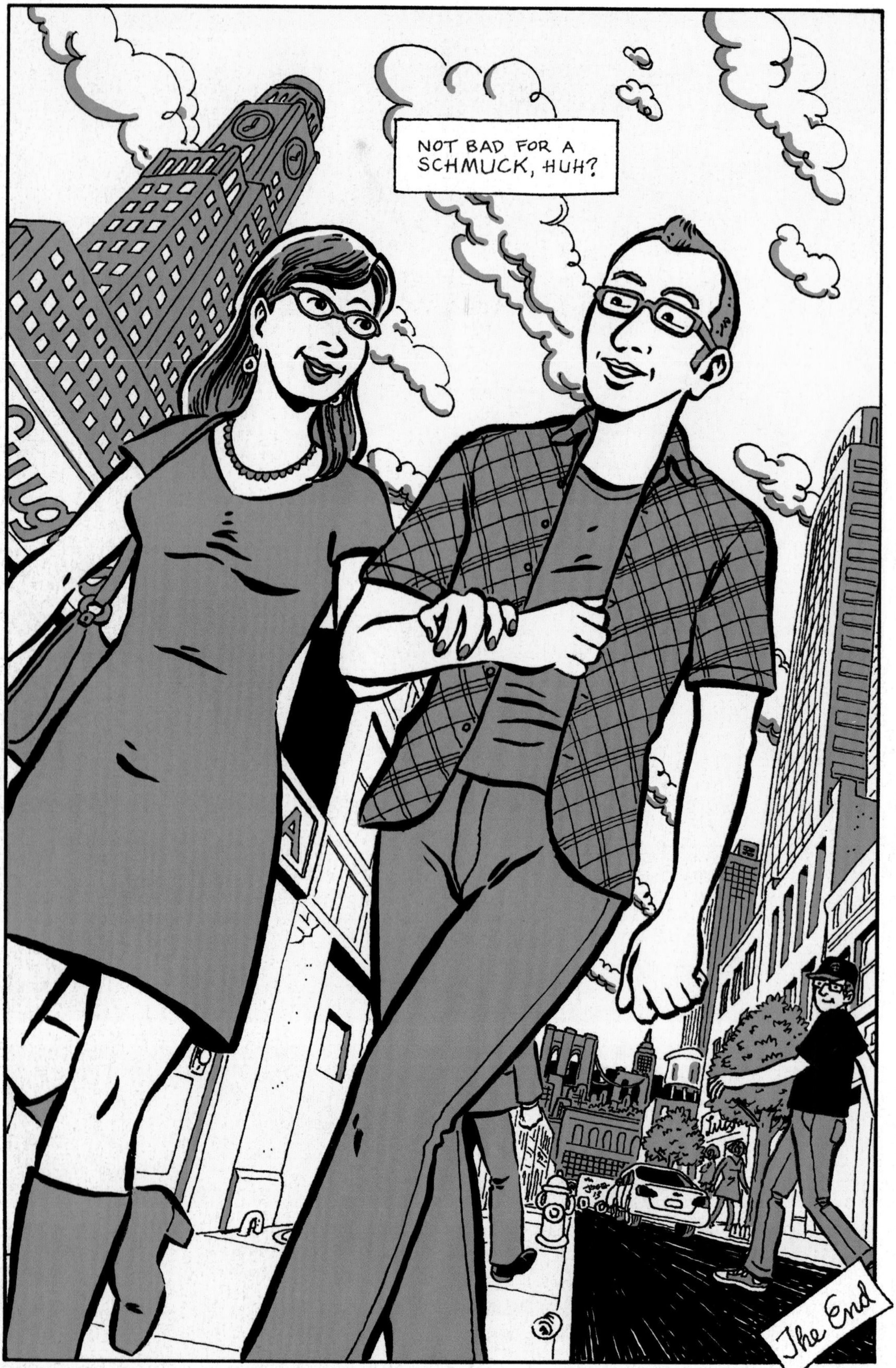
NOT BAD FOR A
SCHMUCK, HUH?
The End

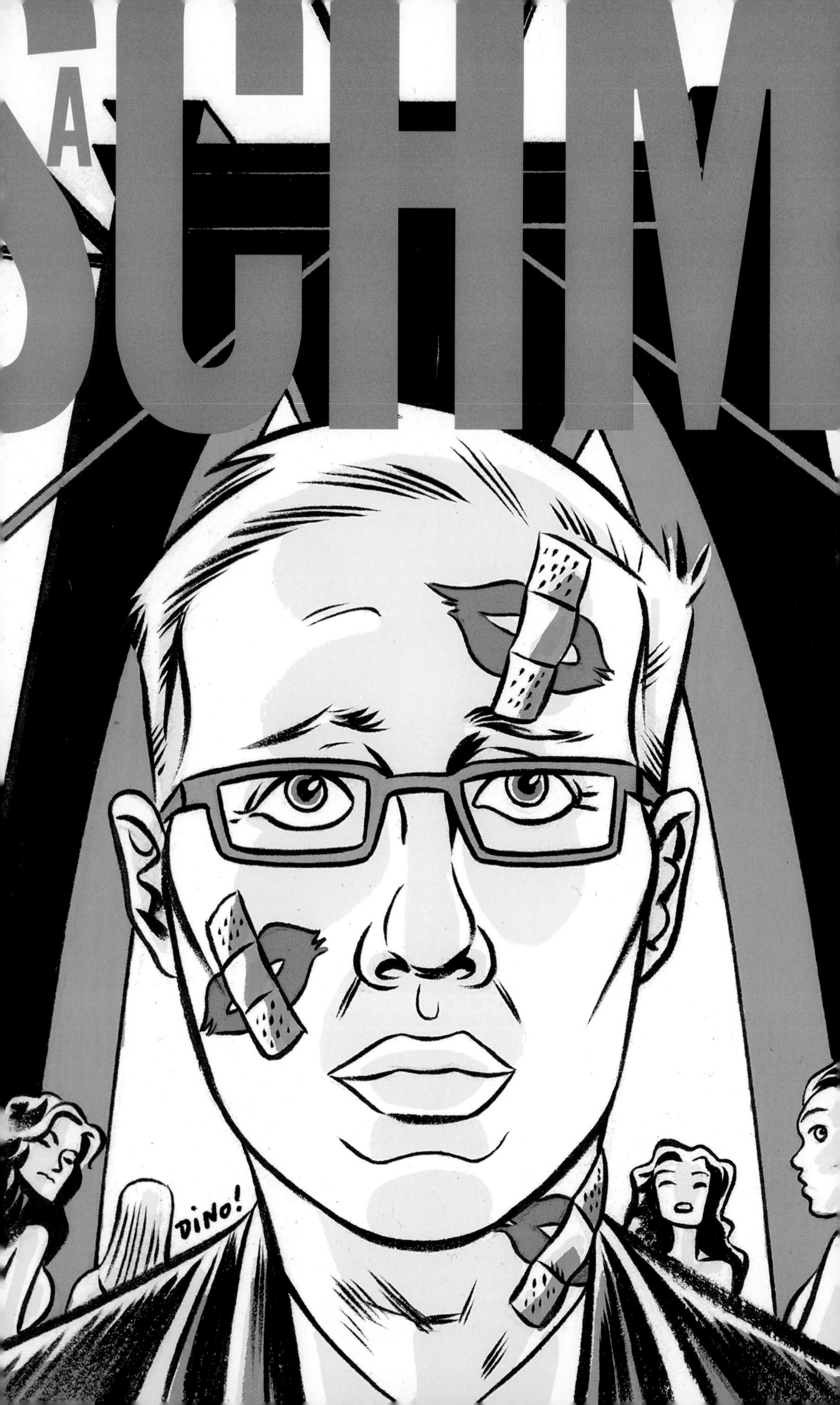

A
SCHIM
DINO!

LUCKY HISTORY

BY SETH KUSHNER

Illustration by Dean Haspiel

WHEN I WAS GROWING UP my mother often called me a "Schmuck." It was part insult and part term of endearment. For the uninitiated, "Schmuck" is a Yiddish insult, an obscene term for penis, usually referring to someone who did a stupid thing. It was the first title that sprang to mind for the prose novel I started writing in 2003.

The idea to write a book came partly from inspiration and partly from need for self-analysis. Back in 2003 I was single and miserable. My post-high school to late 20s string of long-term relationships

had come to an end when I was callously dumped by my dream girl and I was alone for the first time in my adult life. I found myself unprepared for meeting women and jumped between fix-ups, Internet dating and random hooks-ups, and I was failing at them all. But, as depressed as I was, I found myself collecting stories. I was experiencing life outside of my comfort zone, and I was sharing these stories with my friends. A close female friend found my tales of woe particularly entertaining and encouraged me to write them.

When I started writing, I was simply recording the events, mostly as they happened. I found it therapeutic. After a while, I began shaping the stories into a narrative and making chapters out of experiences that shared a common theme, like a collection of fix-ups by my mom with "nice Jewish girls." Soon, I had the beginnings of a book. I didn't have an ending, because I knew it had to end with my finding true love, but I kept writing. Eventually I had my ending (spoiler alert if you're reading this before reading the book!) and after five years, and seven drafts, I had a 392-page manuscript. At the time, I thought I had the great American novel and I was going to be the next Nick Hornby. Looking at it now, I find it rough and too angry and sarcastic, having written it while it was happening.

I sent it to a few publishers, but they weren't interested, so I sat on it, and it wasn't until 2008 when I began working with and befriending the amazing comic book creators on the project which would become my book, *Leaping Tall Buildings: The Origins of American Comics* (with Christopher Irving, powerhouse Books, 2012), that I had the notion of turning my story into a comic, which honestly made sense because comics were my first love since my dad introduced me to them when I was four years old.

In 2006 I got my first taste of seeing my words translated into comics form when my wife and I decided we wanted our wedding invitation to be comics oriented. Okay, maybe it's what I wanted, but she liked the idea too. We had the notion of turning the story of how we met into a short comic and we commissioned cartoonist Michel Fiffe (*Copra, All-New Ultimates*) to draw it. I sent Fiffe the chunk of my manuscript that covered the parts of the tale we wanted to tell and he adapted it into a 4-panel strip, which we then reformatted into our hand-made invites. I remember feeling a certain thrill from seeing my first "comics collaboration."

Back to 2008. I began working at adapting my manuscript to comics format, but I had no idea how to write a comic. Using Brian Michael Bendis' *Powers* Script Book, and a Neil Gaiman *Sandman* script found in the back of one of the collections, I learned the basics of how to form a comic script.

Over a week's time I eked out 17 pages of comics script from my prologue. It was challenging but a real learning experience. I felt pleased reading it over, but my lack of experience left me wondering if it was actually any good. I sent an email to my good friend, cartoonist extraordinaire Dean Haspiel (*Billy Dogma, Beef With Tomato*) and asked if he'd mind taking a look at what I had. Dean—God bless him—came back with great, constructive feedback.

With Dean's advice, I took another crack at it, and with my freshly polished script, it was time to find an artist. I had no idea how to do that, so I went back to Dean. He thought about it for a moment and said, "Why not bug Colden?" He was referring to Kevin Colden, whose work I'd admired from his Xeric award-winning comic on ACTIVATEcomix.com, *Fishtown*, since released as an Eisner-award nominated graphic novel from IDW. I was nervous to approach Kevin, since he was an accomplished artist and wouldn't need to work with me, I thought. But, having come so far, I was determined, so I sent him an email explaining the project and attached my script. The next day Kevin said *Schmuck* was just the type of project that interested him. We agreed we'd make a proposal and pitch it to publishers as a 200-page graphic novel.

A few weeks later I received the first four pages from Kevin, fully inked! It was an unbelievable feeling to gaze upon Kevin's visual translation of my words. I loved Kevin's depiction of the main character and avatar, Adam Kessler. Kevin drew Adam in a way that didn't exactly look like me, but instead felt like me. I loved the way Kevin drew the city and how he paced the panels. Kevin found creative ways of making talking heads look interesting. and he took moments of humor I had written and sold the jokes with the characters' expressions. Kevin's sensibility and ability to tell a story made him the ideal collaborator for me. The whole thing came alive, and finally felt real.

A few weeks later I received 14 pages, all inked and lettered, which would act as our proposal and be shopped around by our agent. We were ready to get the thing sold and get working on the rest of the planned 200 pages, but first, we decided to serialize the first chapter of *Schmuck* (Kevin's pages plus six pages of fumetti photo pages I created) on the ACTIVATEcomix.com over six weeks, in an attempt to build a bit of buzz.

The proposal was shopped around to publishers but didn't sell. We tweaked it, and our agent re-shopped it the following year, but again, it was a no go.

I moved on to other projects, including *CulturePOP Photocomix*, (utilizing and evolving a fumetti style) and wrote some more scripts, but SCHMUCK never left my thoughts.

In November 2011, I helped launch

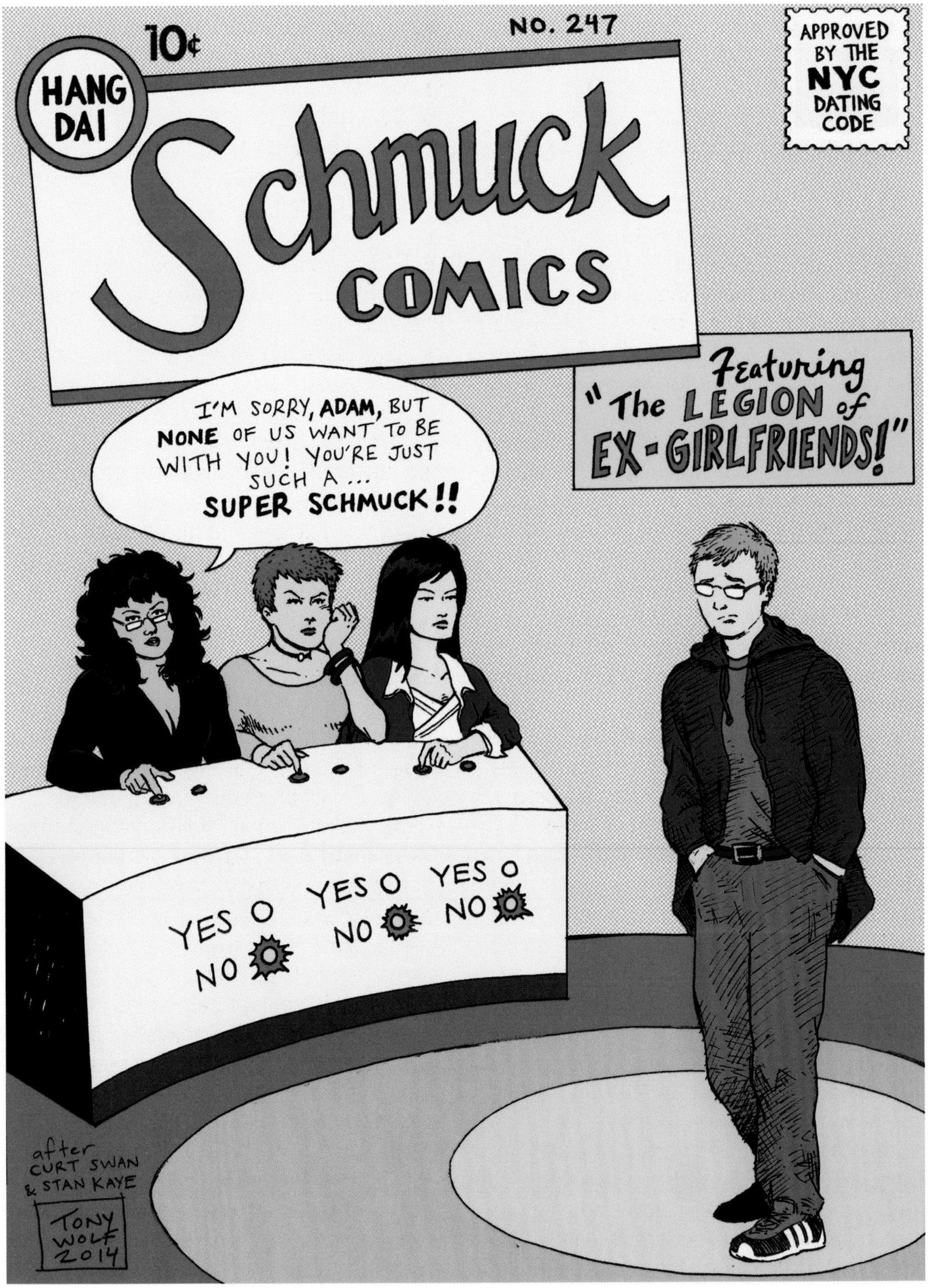

10¢
NO. 247
HANG DAI
Schmuck COMICS
APPROVED BY THE NYC DATING CODE
Featuring "The LEGION of EX-GIRLFRIENDS!"
I'M SORRY, ADAM, BUT NONE OF US WANT TO BE WITH YOU! YOU'RE JUST SUCH A ... SUPER SCHMUCK!!
YES O NO
YES O NO
YES O NO
after CURT SWAN & STAN KAYE
TONY WOLF 2014

Promotional illustration by Tony Wolf

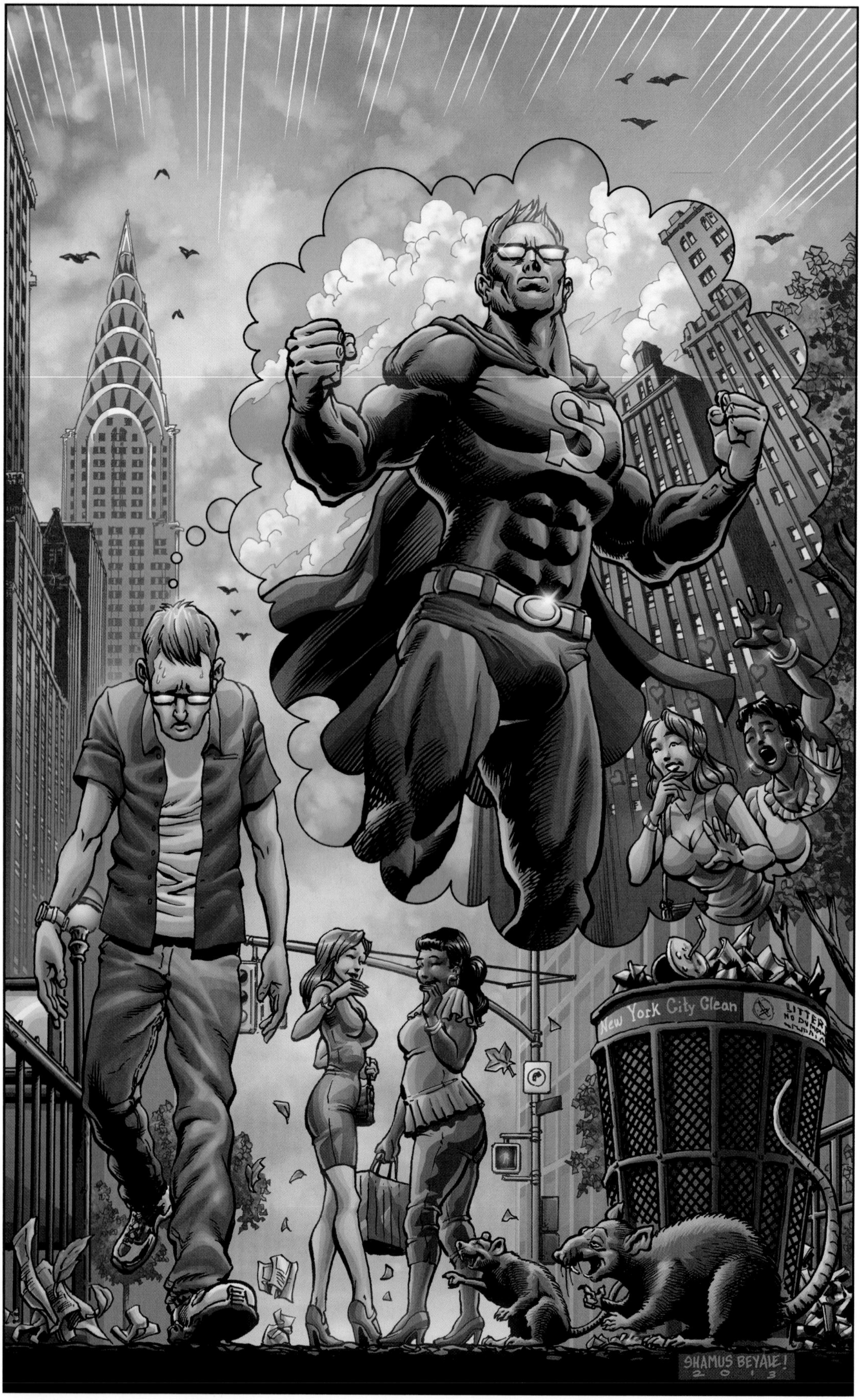
New York City Clean
LITTER
SHAMUS BEYALE!
2013

Promotional illustration by Shamus Beyale

TripCity.net, a venue for a select group of creator/content makers to showcase their signature works. I began by continuing my *CulturePOP Photocomix* series and writing a series of personal/pop-culture essays, but it wasn't long before my *Schmuck* started itching.

One thing I'd learned about the comics industry (and publishing in general) is how increasingly difficult it's become for an independent creator to find a publisher who will pay him for his "new" creation. So, many creators decide to self-publish or post online in order to get their signature work seen. That's what I decided to do.

I formulated a new plan: *Schmuck* would be an anthology series with different artists illustrating short "schmucky stories," which when collected would tell my complete narrative. I excitedly began writing scripts, 12 at first (eventually 22), eight to twelve pages each, mostly adaptations of my favorite stories from my manuscript. In most cases I used my prose as a guide for the comics, as retrospect and newly developed skills allowed me to rework, re-master and expand my stories.

One thing I thought about a lot while writing both the original prose version and the comics was how I would portray myself. Long ago I decided Seth Kushner would be called Adam Kessler, not because I wanted to hide behind a pseudonym, but because I thought it would allow me to divorce myself at least a bit from me and write myself as a "character." The same applied to all the other characters in the story. While I still consider my writings to be "memoir", when I allowed myself the distance from reality, the stories became much stronger. The truth is important, but sometimes it needs to be stretched for the purposes for dramatic or comedic impact. As for "Adam," I wanted to be honest in my portrayal. I never wanted him to be too "cool." I wanted him to be human, with foibles and insecurities. He would be superficial and petty at times and he would often be a schmuck, as the title suggests. There are many parts of my story which I could (or should) find embarrassing, but the act of laying myself bare is therapeutic and it's

to these aspects that I believe readers will relate the most. There are parts where you might hate Adam, or feel ashamed for him, but I think you'll understand him. If I did my job well, you'll find him overall likable.

My initial digital publishing plan was to post one installment per month on TripCity. net until the end of the series, and then I'd figure out a way to collect in print form.

Managing this massive project became a part-time (and sometimes a full-time) job. There were many delays along the way, including artists dropping out, having to find new artists, those artists getting paid gigs and needing extra time, etc. My "monthly" series became sporadic and took over two years to complete. Along the way, I made a stapled B&W minicomic and the color floppy, *Schmuck Comix #1* to sell at cons and in local comic stores, mainly to help get the "*Schmuck*" name out there.

Working with such an array of artistic talent, from super-talented newcomers such as Shamus Beyale to acclaimed seasoned pros such as Nick Bertozzi has been an amazing experience and I learned from every one of them. Writing *Schmuck* has been comic book school for me, and has prepared me to graduate to other projects.

Schmuck has been a labor of love and the project I had to make. It's my personal story, which I think is also a universal story. Because it is so near and dear to my heart, I decided I wouldn't pitch to publishers to make the print collection. Instead, I would do it on my own. Last fall, my studio-mates, Dean and Gregory Benton and I launched the independent publishing imprint, Hang Dai Editions, as a venue to publish our signature works. We were soon joined by Josh Neufeld. We each self-published a floppy comic through the imprint and as well as the anthology, *Hang Dai Studios Comix*. But, our ultimate goal is to make books. I planned for *Schmuck* to be the first book released under the imprint.

I turned to Kickstarter to help fund the printing of my dream project. My campaign was an ambitious one, because I was asking potential backers not just to fund the book, but to help launch HANG DAI Editions into the book world. I planned to print the book for backers, of course, but I also planned to print a quantity to get into stores, Amazon, etc., through a distribution deal I'd made with Alternative Comics.

My reasoning to crowd-fund was a simple one. I did my first two books with a traditional publisher, (*The Brooklynites,* 2007 and *Leaping Tall Buildings: The Origins of American Comics,* 2012). Unless you're J.K. Rowling or Stephen King, the system is not set up for the author to make any real money. Publishing a nice book is expensive and the graphic novel and art book markets are relatively small, so everything works the way it does so the publisher doesn't lose money. By funding the printing, Kickstarter allowed me to retain complete control over my creation. Having done the math, I won't make a fortune on *Schmuck*, but at least I won't have to share profits with a publisher. Also, *Schmuck* is MY story, so it's appropriate to take this opportunity to experiment with independent publishing.

This book version of *Schmuck* is a very different reading experience for those who read the online version. All the individual comics have been re-mastered, in many cases colored (often by me and in two cases by Shiraj Ganguly), since most of the series ran in black and while online, and they've been re-ordered into a complete and sequential narrative, since the online version was really meant to be read individually in bite-sized bits, while the book represents a complete story. This collection, with design by Eisner award-winning designer Eric Skillman and cover illustration by Joseph Remnant (*Harvey Pekar's Cleveland*) on the general release version, and Dean Haspiel on the Kickstarter version, represents the ultimate, schmuckiest version of my story.

My mother always called me a "schmuck." Hopefully, now it's paying off.

—SETH KUSHNER,
APRIL 2014

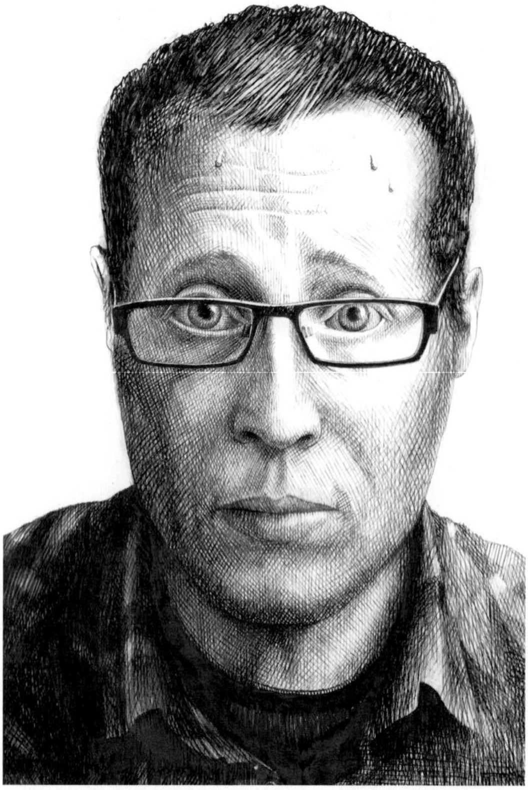

"Adam Kessler" by Joseph Remnant

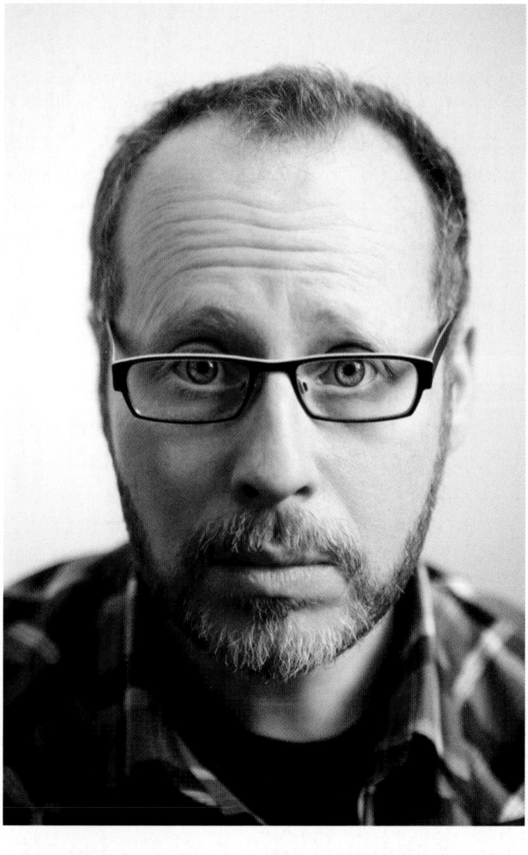

Seth Kushner, 2014, by Carlos Molina

SPECIAL THANKS TO:

Special thanks to: my wife, Terra, who saw something in this schmuck and made me far less schmucky. My son, Jackson, who I know will never be as schmucky as his dad. My Mom for giving me my title and for her continued support. My Dad for buying me my first comics and for encouraging me to follow my dreams. Dean Haspiel for mentoring me on how to make comics and for being my go-to editor. Jonathan Ames for writing a glorious intro. My favorite designer Eric Skillman for coming up with the schmuckiest and coolest cover design ever and for just being his clever self. All the amazing artists who lent their talents to this book. My HANG DAI studio-mates who encouraged me; Gregory Benton, Chris Miskiewicz, Amy Finkel, Krista Dragomer, Nick Bertozzi, Christa Cassano, Jon Allen, Jess Ruliffson and Shiraj Ganguly. My friends who shared in my schmucky adventures; Carlos Molina (who also took my author photo and shot my Kickstarter video), Martin Cuevas, Jason Smollar (and for legal advice), Anthony LaSala, Lloyd Sabin (and for writing advice), Ron Scalzo, Gene Kogan and Frank Tuccillo. Miana Jun for the initial encouragement to write. Publicist extraordinaire David Hyde for going above and beyond. Special thanks to Jimmy Palmiotti, Jeff Newelt and Marc Arsenault. The Wallachs, for always being there. Shamus Beyale and Tony Wolf for providing additional art for the book.

Supercool members of the press; Hannah Means-Shannon and Rich Johnston / Bleeding Cool, Heidi McDonald / Comics Beat, Megan Sass / Heeb, Dan Greenfield / 13th Dimension, Tim O'Shea / Robot 6, Mat 'Inferiorego' Elfring / Comic Vine, Rich Barrett / Mental Floss, Tyler Chin-Tanner / Broken Frontier, Tom Spurgeon / Comics Reporter, Brendan McGinley / CBS Man Cave, Keith Silva / Comics Bulletin, Oscar Russell / We The Nerdy, Russ Burlingame / Comic book.com, Cory Doctorow / Boing Boing, Whitney Matheson / USA TODAY Pop Candy, Gary Makries / Geeks of Doom, Dan Casey / Nerdist, Beth Scorzato and Justin Fah / Spandexless, Brett Schenker / Graphic Policy.

Thanks to Natalie Portman and all the women who are part of my story who have no idea a version of them appear in this book.

Finally, thanks so much to all my generous Kickstarter backers;

Adam Garcia
Adam goldberg
Adam McGovern
Aditya Bidikar
Adrian Gines
Alex P
Allison Schwartz
Amy Chu
Amy Finkel
andra passen
Andres Vera Martinez
Andrew Gebbia
Andrew Jackson
annmarie avila
arlen schumer
Avri Klemer
Ben Mehne
Beth Scorzato
Betty K Delgado
Bizhan Khodabandeh
Bradford Tree
Brandon Lieu
Brian
Calum Johnston /
    Strange Adventures
Carlos Molina
Carlos Padilla
Carol Holsinger
Cassidy James
charles fetherolf
Chip Mosher
Chris Anderson
Chris Call
Chris Haynes
Chris Miskiewicz
Chris Robinson
Christa Cassano
Christopher Irving
Ciaran Downey
Colleen Bradley
Crystal Mank
Dan Casey
Dan Goldman
Dan Hill
Dan Rivera
Daniel Ahrendt
daniel silverman
Daniel Stedman
dannyhellman
Dare2Draw
Dave Dellecese
Dave Kelly
Dave Ryan

David Gershon
David Golbitz
David Marcus
David Peter
dennis l. dragomer
Devin Michaels
dezmo
dgehen
Dominic Quach
Dominic Umile
Doug Bunton
Doug Latino
Douglas O'Neill
Dylan Avery
E K
eggogallego
Elad
Elena Scripps
Ellen Abramowitz
Emre Ozdamarlar
Eóin P. Galvin
Eric Damon Walters
Eric Skillman
Erik Aucoin
Ethan Young
Eugene Kogan
Evil Twin Comics
Ford Thomas
Frank Tuccillo
Fred
Fred Van Lente
Frederik Hautain
Gabe Carras
Gary Dunaier
Gary Makries
gene bresler
Genevieve Cipes
George Michail
gerard folz
Gerard Folz
Glynnis Fawkes
Gordi
gregory benton
Guy Thomas
Hadar Susskind
Hector Fernandez
Henry Matthew Leinen
Here ticked
Howard Wallach
Hyeondo Park
Ian McAllister
igor glushkin
Ingrid Rios

Jack Sherman
Jackie McCabe
Jaimie Friedland
Jake Betancourt-La-
    verde
Jamie S. Rich
Jamie Tanner
Jane Brokaw Eve
Jason A. Quest
Jason Doctor
Jason Smollar
Jason Stumer
Jay Lofstead
Jay Perry
Jayme Lim
Jeanine Ramirez
Jeff Barbanell
Jeff Berg
Jeff Levinson
jeff newelt
Jeffrey C. Burandt
Jeffrey Grzybowski
Jen Ferguson
jennie fiske
Jennifer Hayden
Jenny Lee
Jeremy Donahue
Jess Ruliffson
Jesse Mazer
Jesse W. [w5748]
Jessica Abel
Jessica O'Ma-
    honey-Schwartz
Jesus Delgado
JiHAE
Jim Dougan
Jimmy Hooker
JIMMY PALMIOTTI
Joe Bettis
Joe Dallacqua
Joe Infurnari
Joe Tasillo
Johannes Braun
John and Jana
John Biggs
John Fitter
John Muller
John Paul Bergner
Jon Allen
Jonathan MacFarlane
Jonathan Murray
Joseph Rodriguez
Josh Gorfain

Joshua Fialkov
Joshua Leto
JR Rothenberg
Justin Collins
Justin Gray
Karen Green
Kathleen Ching
keith silva
Kevin Babineau
Kevin Dorr
Kevin Kainula
Kevin McClean
Kevin Volo and
    Max Volo
Kickstarter
Kristen Curtis
KS Wlodyga
Kurt Hoss
Kyle Rose
Landon Reagan
Lars Ingebrigtsen
Last Night On Earth
Laura Johnson
Laura Lee Gulledge
Laura Nichols
Laurie Harrison
Lawrence 'D' Denes
Lawrence J Miller
Levanah and Stan
    Tenen
Linda Bovich
linda kushner
Lloyd Sabin
Loni Berman
Lorin Wiener
Malka schwartz
Marc C.
Marc Ewert
Mari
Mario Candelaria &
    Karl Slominski
Mark Simons
Martin Cuevas
Mat Elfring
Mat Heagerty
Mathieu Doublet
Matt Hatfield
Matthew Bencivenga
Matthew Berkowitz
Matthew Kolberg
Matthew Sherman
Mazouza Elayan-
    Abdelfattah

Meg Lemke
Megan Sass
Michael Farah
Michael Furth
Michael Regnier
Michael Ulrich
Mike Lee
Mike Meltzer
Mike Rende
Mike Scigliano
Mindy Indy
Murat Cem Menguç
Nadine Drucker
    Antopol
Nate Whelan
Nathan Bond
Nathan Schreiber
Nick Bertozzi
Nick Hines
Ofelia Carrara Segura
Olga Karmansky
omar angulo
Pang Peow Yeong
patrick awesome
Patrick Wedge
Paul Connolly
Paul Engelberg
Paul Hoppe
Paula Dimango
Pier Brito Ureta
Rafael Mejia
Rama Murali
Ramsey
Randy Gentile
Rebecca Levi
Richard Bruning
Richard Kronenberg
Richard Meehan
Rick Nelson
Rick Parker
Rick Symonds &
    Landon Reagan
Robbie Busch
Robert Earl Sutter III
Robin Anderson
Rommel Martinez
Ron Scalzo
royblumenthal
Russell Willis
Ryan Luft
Ryan Oakes
Samuel Satin
Sandra Beasley

Sanne Muurling
Sarah Simon
Scott victor
Sean
serena dv
Shane W Smith
Shannon Tierney
Shasti O'Leary
    Soudant
Shawn Dean
Shayna Kulik
Shean Mohammed
Simon Fraser
Sonam Kushner
spongefile
Stefan Blitz
Stephen Harrick
Stergios Botzakis
Steve Altes
Steve Meyer
Steve Sanders
Steven Bergson
Steven Goldman
Steven Kushnir
Steven Pennella
Steven T. Seagle
Tamisha
Tara Hill Solomon
thatraja
TheWildRose
Thomas Adam Lundy
Thomas Mets
Thomi Richards
Threemoons
TISHON
Tony Eng
Tracey Mashhadi
Trent Thompson
Ty Hudson
Tyler & Wendy
    Chin-Tanner
valeria ott
Vera Greentea
Victor Von Zoom
Vito Delsante
Waller Hastings
Wayne Beamer
William Cusick
William Morland
yowicymama
Zach Kalatsky

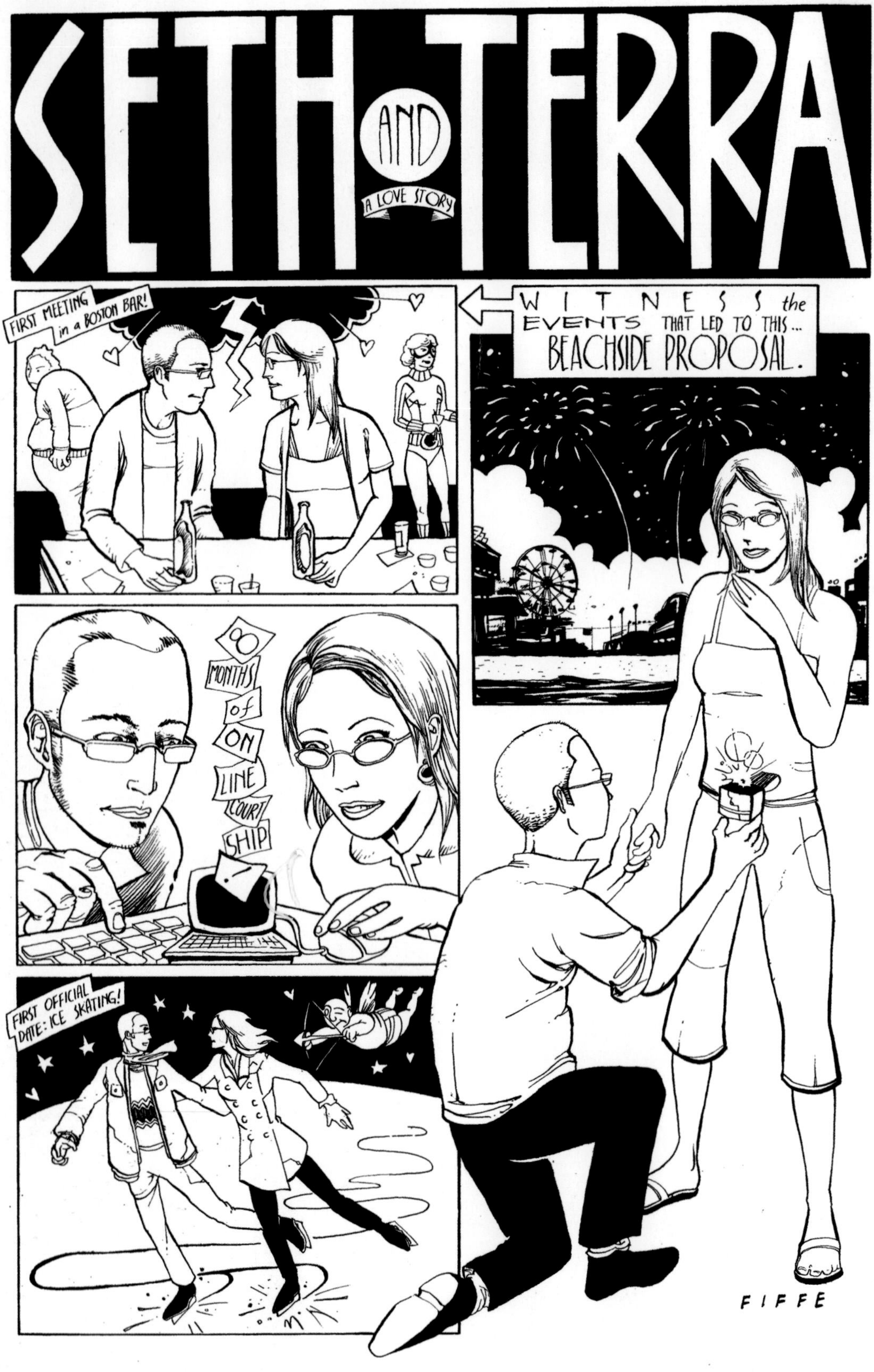
SETH AND TERRA
A LOVE STORY
FIRST MEETING in a BOSTON BAR!
WITNESS the EVENTS THAT LED TO THIS... BEACHSIDE PROPOSAL.
8 MONTHS of ON LINE COURT SHIP
FIRST OFFICIAL DATE: ICE SKATING!
FIFFE

Above: Seth's wedding invitation, by Michel Fiffe
Opposite: Schmuck Comics #1 cover by Gregory Benton

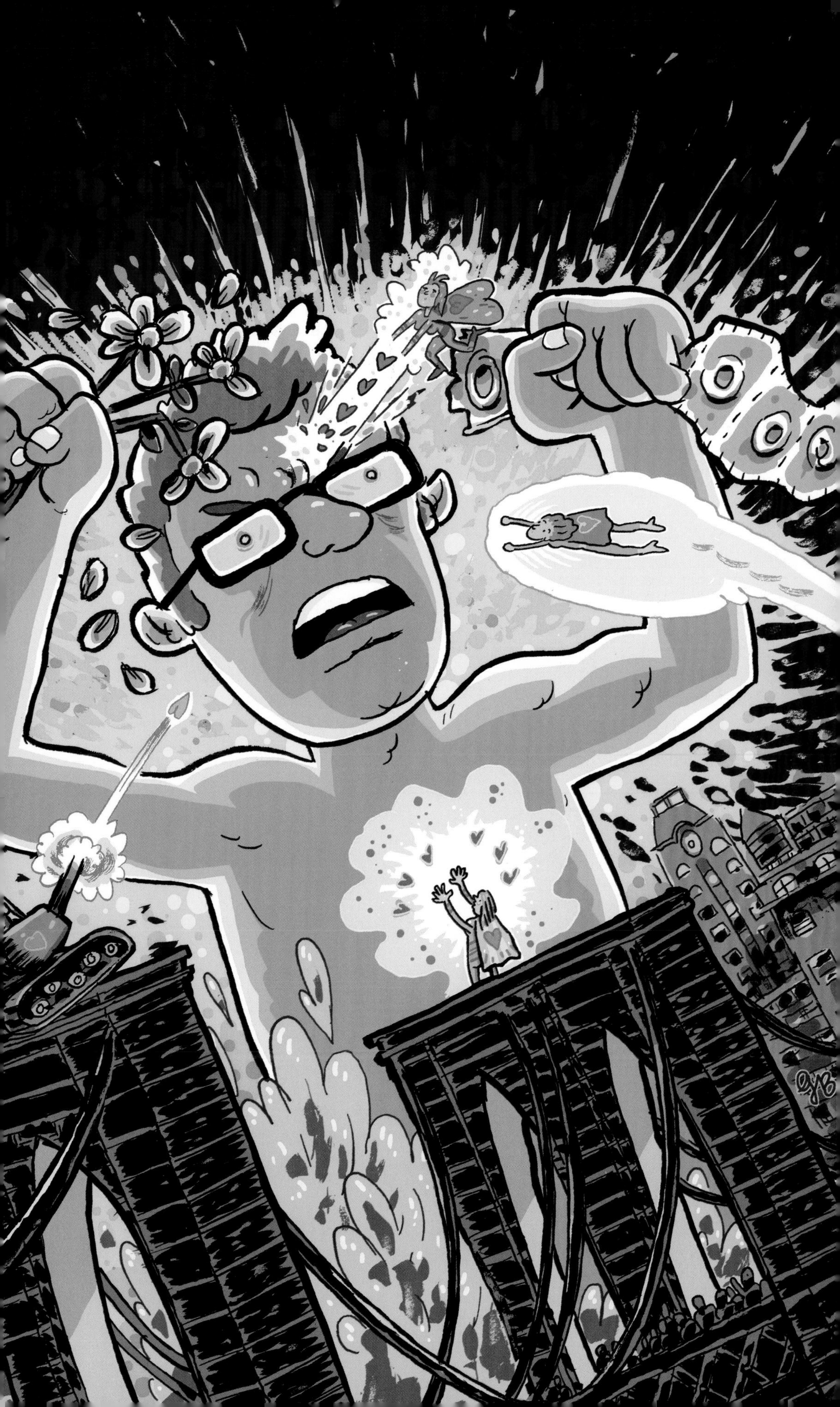

BIOGRAPHIES

SETH KUSHNER grew up reading comics and wanting to be an artist. He graduated from the School of Visual Arts in 1995 and began a career as a photographer. His photography has appeared in *The New York Times Magazine, Time, Newsweek, L'Uomo Vogue, Sports Illustrated, The New Yorker* and others. Seth's published books include, *The Brooklynites,* (powerHouse Books, 2007), *Leaping Tall Buildings: The Origins of American Comics* (powerhouse Books, 2012). Seth is a co-founder of TripCity.net, the Brooklyn based digital arts salon, which was the original home to his photocomix profile series, *CulturePOP* and the web-comic version of *Schmuck*. In 2013, Seth co-founded Hang Dai Editions, an independent publishing imprint.

JON ALLEN is a web developer by day and a cartoonist the rest of the time. He recently finished a graphic novel, *Vacationland,* and is currently serializing his comic *Ohio Is For Sale* in print and on the web. His work can be found at jon-allen.us.

OMAR ANGULO is an illustrator, designer and noise maker documentarian. His art is a graphic combination of mark making, music, comics, film and design. Since the 1990s, he has collaborated with artists, labels, and promoters to create album art, custom packaging for punk rock and experimental music labels, and limited edition collectible art and merchandise. Omar is perhaps best known for his punk rock album covers and his poster art for bands across the musical spectrum ranging from artists such as Against All Authority and the Misfits to Odd Future, John Waters and many others. His previous comics include:

"Hurricane Wilma, (or How I Stopped Hating and Learned to Love my Neighbor)" and "Primates Everywhere" on Activatecomix. com. He can be found drawing, making comics, posters or putting out music with his label Audio Electric. omarangulo.net

GREGORY BENTON has been making comix since 1993. He is a founding member of Hang Dai Editions. Gregory's Hang Dai Editions titles include *Force of Nature, STAKE!,* and the Pocket Book sketchbook series. In April of 2013, his book *B+F* was awarded the Museum of Comic and Cartoon Art's inaugural Award of Excellence at MoCCAFest. An expanded version of *B+F* was published in the autumn of 2013 through Adhouse Books (USA) and Editions çà et là (France). In 2014, *B+F* was selected by The Society of Illustrators for its first Comics and Cartoon Art Annual exhibition. gregorybenton.com

NICK BERTOZZI is the Harvey Award-winning author of *Lewis & Clark, Persimmon Cup, The Salon,* and the *New York Times* bestselling *Shackleton: Antarctic Odyssey.* He has collaborated with Jason Lutes on *Houdini: The Handcuff King,* and with Boaz Yakin on *Jerusalem: A Family Portrait.* He managed a comic shop, worked at DC Comics, and has taught cartooning at NYC's School of Visual Arts for a decade. He lives in NYC with his wife and daughters.

SHAMUS BEYALE grew up in the Navajo Nation in New Mexico and received a Gates Millennium Scholarship to School of Visual Arts in NY. Shamus has worked on art direction for the DC Universe Online game, published works with Zenescope

Entertainment, drew the creator-owned comic, *Man Cop,* and has done storyboards for Discovery Channel shows and various commercials. He lives in Brooklyn, NY with his wife. shamusbeyale.blogspot.com

CHRISTA CASSANO has exhibited work in
galleries and museums across the country and in Italy, where she won the Espoarte 2000 Award of Excellence in contemporary art. She studied at Cooper Union and was the recipient of two Lloyd Sherwood Grants. In 2012 Cassano attended a graphic novel residency at The Atlantic Center for the Arts which began a career in writing and drawing comics. She has recently self-published *The Giant Effect,* and is currently adapting John Leguizamo's one man show, *Ghetto Klown,* into a graphic novel for Abrams.

KEVIN COLDEN writes and draws, among
other things. His past work includes *The Crow,* several Robert Bloch adaptations and the Eisner Award-nominated *Fishtown* for IDW, *Strange Adventures* and *I Rule the Night* for DC and the colors for Dynamite's *Miss Fury* and *GRIMM: Portland,* Wu digital comics. He is currently working on his serial graphic novel *Antioch.*

STEPHEN DESTEFANO began his career as
a professional cartoonist at the age of 15. He's drawn the comic book adventures of SpongeBob and Mickey Mouse, has been the chief licensing artist on Popeye the Sailor for 25 years, and served as a storyboard artist, voice artist and designer in television animation on the *Ren and Stimpy* Show, *Superman,* and *Batman.* He is currently a character designer for Disney TV and Sony Animation Features, and is working on the second volume of his graphic novel for Fantagraphics Books, *Lucky in Love.* Stephen lives in Hoboken, New Jersey with his four cats, Mia, Mona, Ole and Lila.

PIERCE HARGAN is a freelance artist and
writer from Los Angeles. He has directed his first video in 2014 and is working on his first "big" project. He has been fortunate to work for *Time Magazine* and the once most famous art store Pearl Paint. He currently lives in a room without windows somewhere in Brooklyn. Don't forget to follow him on tumblr: pierehargan.tumblr.com, facebook: facebook.com/juxboxtoposition, and twitter: @pjhargan

DEAN HASPIEL, Emmy award winner
and Eisner and Harvey Award nominee, created Billy Dogma, illustrated for HBO's "Bored To Death," was a Master Artist at the Atlantic Center for the Arts, is a Yaddo fellow, a playwright, and is a co-founder of Hang Dai Editions. Dino has written and drawn many comix including *The Fox, The Fantastic Four, Spider-Man, X-men, Deadpool, Batman, Godzilla, Mars Attacks,* and semi-autobio collaborations with Harvey Pekar, Jonathan Ames, Inverna Lockpez, Stan Lee, and Jonathan Lethem. Keep track at DeanHaspiel.com

GEORGE JURARD doesn't really understand
the concept of "thinking realistically", hence his pursuit of cartooning as a career. He first realized this at the age of 12 during a baseball game, when he attempted to tap into his non-existent mutant abilities and alter the trajectory of the ball the pitcher had just thrown, guaranteeing a strike. When this little endeavor resulted in an unforced error, George couldn't figure out whether he was on the verge of tears because he let his team down, or because he finally realized that he'd never be able to join the X-Men. He enjoys pinch harmonics, muted color, L-O-N-G walks, Hennessy, finding embalming fluid humorous, deep breathing, green tea, and Demi Moore. He takes himself very seriously.

SKUDS MCKINLEY is a professional comic
book artist and illustrator based in Doylestown, PA. His first self published comic work, *I'll Take You To The Moon & Leave You There Vol.1,* was met with fantastic reviews and quickly sold out of print. In 2013, Mckinley also released *Book Face* (with illustrator Dan Elisii) and *Rumble Moon Vol. 1.* His comic series *Plunder* (with writer Swifty Lang) was released by BOOM! Studios in 2015. He has also designed merch and album covers for heavy metal

and punk bands alike and works with some of the influential hip hop artists in his mind. http://skudsink.com

JOSH NEUFELD is the writer/artist of the bestselling nonfiction graphic novel *A.D.: New Orleans After the Deluge* (Pantheon), about Hurricane Katrina. In addition, he is the illustrator of the bestseller *The Influencing Machine: Brooke Gladstone on the Media* (W.W. Norton). He was a 2013 Knight-Wallace fellow in journalism at the University of Michigan. Neufeld is a Xeric Award winner for his comics travelogue *A Few Perfect Hours (and Other Stories of Southeast Asia & Central Europe)*. His series *The Vagabonds* is being published by Hang Dai Editions. Neufeld lives in Brooklyn, New York, with his wife, the writer Sari Wilson, and their daughter. To learn more, visit www.JoshComix.com.

TIM E. OGLINE is the author/illustrator of *Ben Franklin For Beginners* (published by For Beginners), which has been called "beguiling" by Pulitzer Prize winner Joseph J. Ellis and "nothing short of totally brilliant" by Geekadelphia.com. Tim is also the owner/operator of Ogline Design and has served a clientele that has included Pennsylvania Governor (and former Philadelphia Mayor) Ed Rendell, Historic Philadelphia, the University of Pennsylvania, the White House, the National Governors Association, Big Brothers Big Sisters Southeastern Pennsylvania, and many more. Tim is also an instructor at the Tyler School of Art and Moore College of Art & Design. Ogline's award-winning and concept-driven illustration work has been commissioned for a number of publications including *The Philadelphia Inquirer, The Wall Street Journal, Institutional Investor, the Utne Reader, Outdoor Life, This Old House Magazine, Philadelphia Style, Loyola Lawyer,* and *Mensa Bulletin* among others.

SEAN PRYOR is an artist hailing from Freehold, NJ. He has contributed art and comics to such fine publications as *Engadget Distro, Revolver Magazine, Royal Flush Magazine,* and the Pekar Project, while currently working on his bio/autobiographical comic *Idiot Uprising* along with his science fiction comic *The Pack*. Besides making art, Sean plays drums in the punk band Executors and teaches comics to children and adults at Colorest Art Supplies in Red Bank NJ.

LELAND PURVIS is an artist and craftsman currently working in graphite and pigments on paper, using pictures to tell stories. His major works in recent years have been graphic novels, historical fiction, largely aimed at younger readers. He prefers baseball, single malt highland scotch, the speed of sailboats and the smell of horses. And he secretly believes the national anthem should be changed to Copland's Fanfare for the Common Man, and that many science fiction movies are in fact documentaries. Purvis is a sixth-generation resident of Portland, Oregon where he lives with his wife and best friend who are conveniently the same person. http://lelandpurvis.blogspot.com

JOSEPH REMNANT is a Los Angeles-based artist/cartoonist whose comics and illustrations have appeared in *Arthur Magazine, Juxtapoz* and *The New York Times.* He's the creator of the comic book series *Blindspot* and was a frequent collaborator with the late, great comics writer, Harvey Pekar. Remnant began illustrating short stories with Pekar for *Smith Magazine's* Pekar Project which led to his being asked to illustrate the full length graphic novel, *Harvey Pekar's Cleveland.* It was released April 2012 by Zip Comics and Top Shelf Productions. He's currently working on the graphic novel *Cartoon Clouds.* Early chapters can be found on The Expositor, a shared destination with fellow cartoonist Noah Van Sciver. josephremnant.com

TONY SALMONS was born in Rolla, Missouri, and grew up in Casa Grande, Arizona, with stops in New York City and San Francisco. His art has appeared most notably in *Vigilante: City Lights, Prairie Justice, Captain America: Red, White & Blue, Dakota North, Savage Sword of Conan* and *Marvel Fanfare.* http://www.tonysalmons.net

GEORGE SCHALL is a comic book author whose works can be seen in *Dark Horse Presents,* brazilian Mauricio de Souza's "Monica's Gang" *MSP 50* and the graphic novels *Sabor Brasilis , Moschitto , Hitomi* and *Grizzly.* He lives in São Paulo, Brasil, and his mustache is made of solid gold. georgeschall.com

NATHAN SCHREIBER left the fashion industry in 2008 to focus on comics full time. His comic Power Out won a 2009 Xeric award and has been nominated for an Eisner and multiple Harvey awards. In 2012 he illustrated the *New York Times* bestseller *Health Care Reform: What It Is, Why It's Necessary, and How It Works* and wrote and illustrated the science fiction comic 4090 for independent publisher Retrofit. His comics have appeared in *L'Uomo Vogue, Overflow, Smith Magazine,* and ACT-IVATE.com. He's completed two residencies in Angoulême, France, at the Maison des Auteurs. He is currently living in Brooklyn working on *Science Ninjas,* an action-comedy-romance packed comic designed to provide a comprehensive elementary science education. www.nathanschreiber.com

JAMES O. SMITH is an editor and illustrator. He is the creator of the online graphic novel *Gang of Fools,* artist of the children's book *Ancient Lands,* a contributor to *I Saw You, Ray Bradbury's Martian Chronicles* and several other anthologies you haven't read. He lives in Brooklyn with his girlfriend and two horrible animals. Find him online at jamesmith.org

RYAN ALEXANDER-TANNER is a Portland-based cartoonist and educator. He was awarded a Xeric grant in 2007 to self-publish his one-man anthology comic, *Television,* and went on to co-author and illustrate *To Teach: the Journey, in Comics,* a collaboration with activist and educator Bill Ayers, for Teachers College Press. www.ohyesverynice.com

BOBBY TIMONY, New Jersey born artist, has been writing and illustrating comics and drawing storyboards for over a decade. Bobby's career in professional art started with some of America's top advertising agencies—including Bates Advertising, JWT, and BBDO, where he drafted storyboards for M&M, Campbell's Soup, and Gillette. In 2007, Bobby, along with his collaborator and twin brother Peter, debuted his paranormal detective webseries *The Night Owls* with DC Comics. In 2009, *The Night Owls* was nominated for multiple Harvey Awards for Best New Series and Best Online Series, and earned Bobby a nomination as the Best New Talent. When the print edition of *The Night Owls* debuted in 2010, the book received a Lulu nomination for Best Female Character and a Cybil Award nomination for best Young Adult Graphic Novel. His work has been featured on MTV, *Comic News Insider,* and *Publishers' Weekly.* Most recently Bobby has been hard at work on his own comics such as *Goblin Hood* on Comixology and *Detectobot* at Monkeybrain. He's also been busy working on some storyboards and concept art at Disney. Bobby counts Carl Barks, Jack Cole, and E.C. Segar among his influences and is compelled to capture a bit of that unapologetic fun in his own work. He is an active member of the National Cartoonist's Society, is a bona fide "No Prize" recipient, and lives in California with his wife and bunny.

NOAH VAN SCIVER first came to readers' attention with his comic book series *Blammo,* which has earned him 3 Ignatz award nominations. His work has appeared in the Alternative weekly newspaper *Westword, Mad* magazine and multiple graphic anthologies. He has four graphic novels: *The Hypo: The Melancholic Young Lincoln, Youth Is Wasted, Saint Cole* and *Fante Bukowski: Struggling Writer.* noahvansciver.tumblr.com

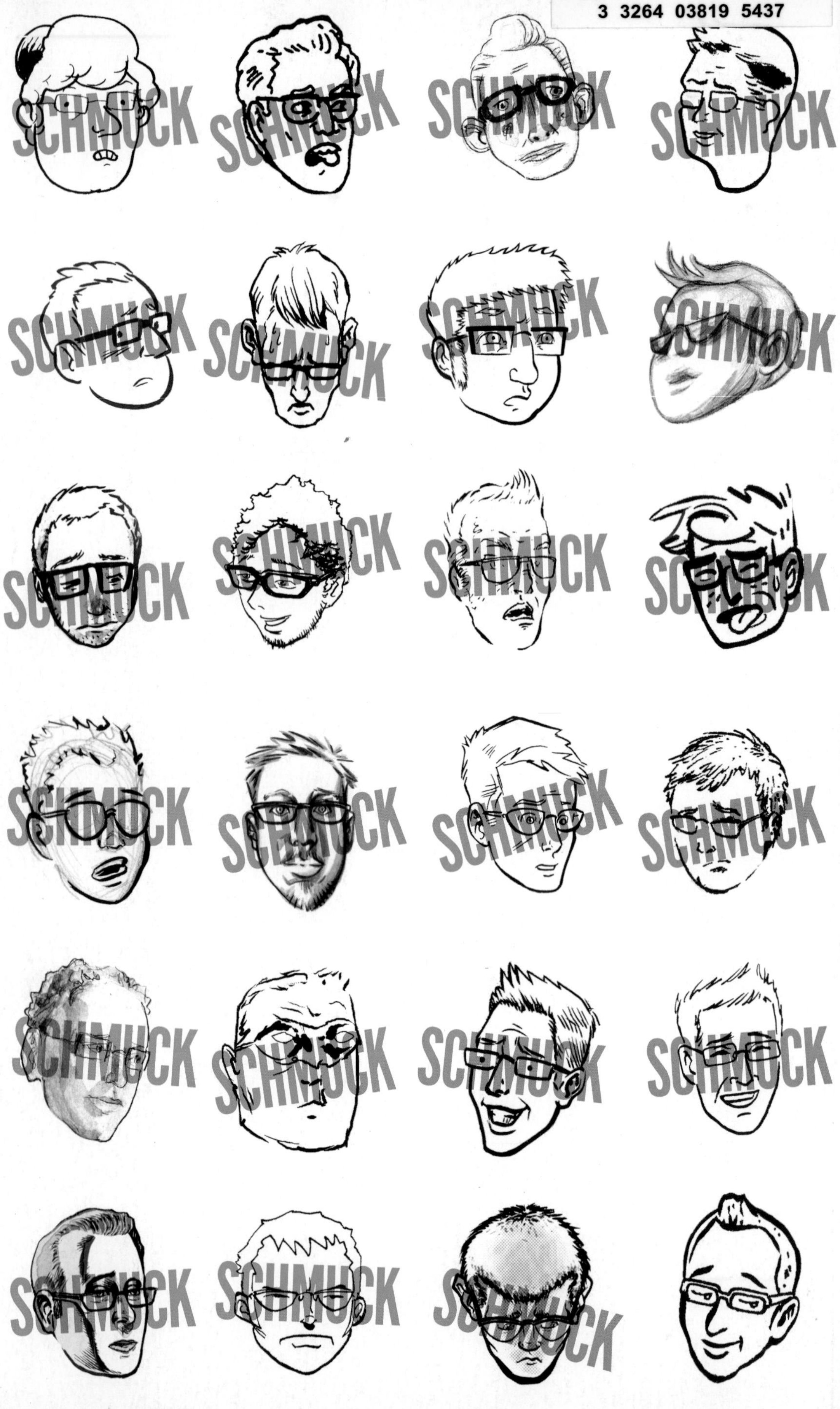